in and out of
BOSTON
with (or without)
children

BICENTENNIAL EDITION

in and out of
BOSTON
with (or without)
children

by BERNICE CHESLER

Illustrations by JOAN DRESCHER

BARRE PUBLISHING
Barre, Massachusetts
Distributed by Crown Publishers, Inc.
New York

Inquiries should be addressed to Clarkson N. Potter, Inc.,
419 Park Avenue South, New York, N.Y. 10016.

Printed in the United States of America
Published simultaneously in Canada by General Publishing Company
Limited

Library of Congress Cataloging in Publication Data

Chesler, Bernice.
    In and out of Boston with (or without) children.

    Published in 1966 and 1969 under title: In and
out of Boston with children.
        1. Boston—Description—1951–   —Guide-books.
2.   Boston region, Mass.—Description and travel—
Guide-books. I.   Title.
F73.18.C5   1975   917.44'61'044   75-19417
ISBN 0-517-52184-9

All information, including prices, hours, and programs, is subject
to change.

Maps on pp. 69, 73, 78, 82, 85, 88, 92, 96, and 99 redrawn by Laurie Zuckerman

To Mark, Lisa, Stan

CONTENTS

An Introduction to the Area 21

INFORMATION CENTERS: Boston Visitors and Information Center; Boston and Massachusetts Information Desk; Bicentennial Bonus; Rest Rooms; Events Information: Recorded Information, Listings; Useful Numbers: 24-hour Pharmacy, Recorded Information, Live and Helpful; Mailing Lists.

TRAVEL: Getting Around the City; Massachusetts Bay Transportation Authority; Getting In and Out of Boston: Air, Boat, Bus, Train; Massachusetts Turnpike; Northeast Travelers' Information.

FOOD: Coops, 24-hour Supermarkets, Ice Cream, Yogurt Cones. Restaurants: All Over; Back Bay; Beacon Hill; Government Center; Market District (City Hall Area); Chinatown; Downtown; Kenmore Square; North End; Prudential Center; South End; Waterfront; Cambridge: Central Square; MIT Area; Harvard Square; Outside Harvard Square.

Animals 37

Animal Rescue League of Boston; Aquarium (Woods Hole); Atlantic Aquarium; Benson Animal Farm; Boston Zoological Society; The Buddy Dog Humane Society, Inc.; Capron Park Zoo; Cats: Ellen M. Gifford Sheltering Home; Drumlin Farm; Duck Feeding; Fish: National Hatcheries, State Hatcheries, Fish Ladders; Franklin Park Zoo: Children's Zoo, A Bird's World, Range Area; Horseback Riding, Hay and Sleigh Rides; Massachusetts Society for the Prevention of Cruelty to Animals; New England Aquarium; Southwick's Wild Animal Farm; Walter D. Stone Memorial Zoo; Weston Dog Ranch and Weston Dog Training Club; Willow Brook Farm and the Country Store.

The Arts 47

LIVE PERFORMANCES: Adventures in Music, Inc.; Associate Artists Opera Company; Boston Ballet; Boston Children's Theatre; Boston Conservatory of Music; Boston Philharmonia Orchestra; Boston Symphony Orchestra; Brookline Youth Concerts; The Cambridge Ensemble; Caravan Theater; Gilbert and Sullivan presentations; The Greater Boston Youth Symphony Orchestras; National Theatre for Children; New England Conservatory of Music; Opera Company of Boston; Peabody-Mason Music Foundation; Plays for Children; Pocket Mime Theater; The Proposition; Puppet Show Place; Shakespeare & Co.; Theater Workshop of Boston; Toy Cupboard Theatre and Museums; Young Audiences of Massachusetts, Inc.; Youth Concerts at Symphony Hall.

FILM: Loans and Rentals; Film Showings.

RADIO AND TELEVISION: Public Radio and Television; Massachusetts Educational Television; The Spider's Web; Television Participatory Possibilities; Action for Children's Television.

RESOURCES AND ORGANIZATIONS: Advisory for Open Education; Boston Center for the Arts; Cambridge School of Ballet, Inc.; Children's Neighborhood Art Center; Chinese Cultural Center; The Community Music Center of Boston; Cooperative Artists Institute; Educational Arts Association; Folksong Society of Greater Boston; The Joy of Movement Center; The Learning Guild; Massachusetts Association of Craftsmen; Massachusetts Council on the Arts and Humanities; Metropolitan Cultural Alliance; The National Center of Afro-American Artists; New England Theatre Conference; Office of Cultural Affairs; Pinebank Art Center in the Park; Poets Who Teach; Old Schwamb Mill; Society of Arts and Crafts; Wheelock College; Youth Pro Musica.

Day Trips   65

ORGANIZATIONS that organize trips.

PLACES: Cape Cod National Seashore; Concord; East Bridgewater; Edaville Railroad; Fall River; Gloucester; Lexington; Marblehead; Mystic Seaport; Newport; Old Sturbridge Village; Plymouth; Rockport; Salem; Sandwich; Strawbery Banke, Inc.; Sudbury.

Historic Sites and Exhibits   107

BOSTON NATIONAL HISTORICAL PARK.

THE FREEDOM TRAIL: Suggestions, General Information
    Loop One (Downtown): Faneuil Hall; Quincy Market; Boston Massacre Site; Old State House; Birthplace of Benjamin Franklin; Old South Meeting House; Old Corner Book Store; Statue of Benjamin Franklin; Site of the First Public School; Granary Burying Ground; Park Street Church; Boston Common; State House; King's Chapel.
    Loop Two (North End): Paul Revere House; Paul Revere Mall; Old North Church; Copp's Hill Burying Ground.

BLACK HERITAGE TRAIL: The African Meeting House; Smith Court Residences; The Smith School; Colonel George Middleton House; John J. Smith House; Lewis Hayden House; George Grant House; The Charles Street Meeting House; State House; 54th Regiment Monument; Boston Massacre Monument; Old Granary Burying Ground; Old South Meeting House; Boston Massacre Site; Copp's Hill; The Emancipation Group.

OTHER PLACES OF HISTORIC INTEREST IN BOSTON: Beacon Hill Mansions; Boston Tea Party Ship; Bunker Hill Monument; Gibson House; Massachusetts General Hospital; New England Life Insurance Building; New England Telephone Headquarters Building; Nichols House Museum; Harrison Gray Otis House; U.S.S. Constitution.

SOME HISTORIC SITES IN NEARBY COMMUNITIES: Arlington, Bedford, Beverly, Braintree, Brookline, Cambridge, Danvers, Dedham, Haverhill, Hingham, Lynn, Medford, Newton, Quincy, Saugus, Scituate, Waltham, Watertown, Wenham.

Looking at the City 135

VIEWPOINTS: Custom House Observation Tower; John Hancock Tower Observatory; Locks and Drawbridge; Logan International Airport; The Skywalk.

BUS TOURS

WALKING: Suggestions. Areas: Back Bay; Beacon Hill; Cambridge; Chinatown; Faneuil Hall Area (Government Center); North End; Waterfront.

Museums 157

Addison Gallery of American Art, R.S. Peabody Foundation for Archaeology; Blue Hills Trailside Museum; Boston Tea Party Ship; Brockton Art Center; Busch-Reisinger Museum; Children's Museum; DeCordova and Dana Museum and Park; Fogg Art Museum; Fruitlands Museums; Isabella Stewart Gardner Museum; Hammond Museum; Francis Russell Hart Nautical Museum; John Woodman Higgins Armory, Inc.; Institute of Contemporary Art; London Wax Museum; Merrimack Valley Textile Museum; Museum of Afro American History; Museum of the American China Trade; Museum of Fine Arts; Museum of Science; Museum of Transportation; Rose Art Museum; Seashore Trolley Museum; Semitic Museum; The Slater Mill Historic Site; Cardinal Spellman Philatelic Museum; University Museum (Harvard): Museum of Comparative Zoology (Agassiz Museum), Botanical Museum, Mineralogical Museum, Peabody Museum; Whaling Museum; Worcester Art Museum; Worcester Science Center.

Open Space 183

ISLANDS: Bumpkin; Grape; Gallops; Brewster; George's Island, Peddocks.

PLACES IN OR VERY NEAR BOSTON: The Arnold Arboretum; Beaver Brook Reservation; Boston Common; Castle Island; Charles River Reservation; Fenway; Franklin Park; Fresh Pond Park; Jamaica Pond; Larz Anderson Park; Mount Auburn Cemetery; Stony Brook Reservation.

PLACES NORTH OF BOSTON: Breakheart Reservation; Halibut Point; Ipswich River; Lynn Woods; Middlesex Fells Reservation; Harold Parker State Forest; Bradley W. Palmer State Park; Parker River National Wildlife Refuge.

PLACES WEST OF BOSTON: Ashland State Park; Broadmoor Sanctuary; Carlisle State Park; Case Estates of Arnold Arboretum; Cochituate State Park; Cutler Park; Drumlin Farm Nature Center; Garden in the Woods; Great Meadows National Wildlife Refuge; Hammond Pond; Harvard Forest; Hemlock Gorge; Laughing Brook Education Center and Wildlife Sanctuary; Menotomy Rocks Park; Prospect Hill Park; Quabbin Reservoir; Walden Pond State Reservation.

PLACES SOUTH OF BOSTON: Ashumet Holly Reservation; Blue Hills Reservation; Borderland State Park; Cape Cod National Seashore; Moose Hill Sanctuary; Myles Standish State Forest; Rocky Woods; Stony Brook Nature Center; Wompatuck State Park; World's End.

ORGANIZATIONS: American Youth Hostels, Inc.; Appalachian Mountain Club; The Charles River Watershed Association, Inc.; The Elbanobscot Foundation, Inc.; Robert Sever Hale Reservation; Massachusetts Audubon Society; Massachusetts 4–H Center; Massachusetts State Parks and Forests; Metropolitan District Commission; Middlesex Canal Association; National Parks Service; Outward Bound, Inc.; Sierra Club; Trustees of Reservations.

Recreation   205

Amusement Parks; Ballooning; Beaches; Bicycling; Boat Launching Areas; Boat Rentals; Boat Rides in Boston; Boating Education; Boat Trips That Leave from Boston's Waterfront; Boat Trips to Block Island; Boat Trips to Martha's Vineyard and Nantucket; Boat Trips to Star Island; Bowling; Camping; Canoeing; Clam Digging; Farm Vacations; Fishing; Folk Dancing; Golf; Hang Gliding; Horses; Ice Skating; Mountain Climbing; Orienteering; Parachuting; Playgrounds; Roller Skating; Sailing; Skiing: Downhill, Cross Country; Snowmobiling; Spectator Sports (Professional); Square Dancing; Swimming; Tennis; Tobogganing and Sledding.

ORGANIZATIONS: Information; American Youth Hostels, Inc.; Appalachian Mountain Club; The Boston YWCA; Cambridge Sports Union; Ponkapoag Outdoor Center; Sierra Club.

Tours and Visits   247

LOCAL SUGGESTIONS

PLACES: Ashway Farm; Boston City Hall; Boston Edison Company; Boston Globe; Boston Public Library; Boston Stock Exchange; Brattle Book Shop; Brigham's Candy Plant; Brigham's Ice Cream; Christian Science Center; John Donnelly & Sons; Fisher Junior College; General Motors Assembly Division; H. E. Harris & Co.; Harvard University; Logan International Airport; Lowell Canal Tours; Massachusetts Institute of Technology; MIT Boathouse; Morgan Memorial Goodwill Industries; Ocean Liners; Old Schwamb Mill; Pairpoint Glass Works; Parker Brothers; Phillips Candy House; Priscilla of Boston; Putnam Pantry Candies; Quabbin Reservoir; Sherburne Lumber Co.; Star Market Co.; Stop & Shop, Inc.; Trinity Church; U.S. Postal Service—South Postal Annex; Wilson Farms, Inc.; WLVI-TV; WNAC-TV.

The World Around Us   263

VIEWING SITES: Babson World Globe; Boston University Observatory; Harvard College Observatory; Mapparium.

PEOPLE: Boston Council for International Visitors; English Speaking Union; International Friendship League, Inc.; International Institute of Boston, Inc.; Pan American Society; UNICEF; U.S. Servas, Inc.; Other Local Host Possibilities: Colleges, American Field Service, The Experiment in International Living; Volunteering: General Information, Organizations.

ENVIRONMENT: Environmental Protection Agency Library; Margaret C. Ferguson Greenhouses; Habitat Institute for the Environment; County Extension Offices; Massachusetts Department of Agriculture; Massachusetts Horticultural Society; Massachusetts Junior Conservation Camp; University of Massachusetts Suburban Experiment Station; Urban Awareness and Environmental Understanding Program.

LIBRARIES: Boston Public Library; Kirstein Business Branch of the Boston Public Library; French Library; Goethe Institute; John F. Kennedy Library.

ORGANIZATIONS AND AGENCIES: Boston Association for the Education of Young Children; Child Care Resource Center; The Child Study Association of Massachusetts, Inc.; Children in Hospitals, Inc.; Explorers Councils; La Leche League of Massachusetts; Massachusetts Children's Lobby; MIT High School Studies Program; Massachusetts Mothers of Twins Clubs; Office for Children; Student Service Center; Vocations for Social Change.

DO-IT-YOURSELF: Advisory for Open Education; Jim Bottomley, New England Craftsmanship Center, Workshop for Learning Things, Inc.; Frameworks; Mudflat; The Big Picture.

FOR CHILDREN WITH SPECIAL NEEDS: Child Advocacy Project of the Easter Seal Society; W. E. Fernald State School Media Resource Center; Medford Public Library Instructional Materials Center; National Braille Press; *The Exceptional Parent.*

SCROUNGE: Where?; What?; How to Use.

MAPS

PREFACE

It may be reasonable to say that the growth of this book parallels the growth of the author's family.

Having toddlers reinforced the need to have detailed information:
... How can I check to see if the Swan Boats are running?
... Where can we look through a telescope?
... How much time does it take to go through Paul Revere's House—or the Constitution—or the Old State House ...?

The book was first written with about 500 suggestions; not all were necessarily youth-oriented, but the information allowed readers to make their own decisions—and perhaps become acquainted with hitherto unknown opportunities. The second edition, more comprehensive than the first, was twice the size.

Always the intent has been to pull together more than the what-where-when-how much. Those details we think of during or after a trip have been duly recorded. The resource information is offered to eliminate hours of telephoning.

Many of you have suggested that "with children" be dropped from the title. One ten-year-old suggested that it be "without parents!"

The offspring are now teen-agers. We are finally listening. The new title is a compromise.

During the six years since In and Out was last published, the requests have continued:

... Where can you go into a building when you walk around Back Bay?
... What else can be seen without a car?
... What is available for older citizens?
... Why not include more combinations of short-visit suggestions?
... Who stresses participation with exhibits?
... What new outdoor facilities or recreational possibilities exist?
... Find other companies that will offer a tour through their facilities.

Ten years of research have included hundreds of conversations and visits and, just as important, dozens of workshops. Librarians, parents, teachers, college students, organizations, group workers—thank you all for your comments. Staffs of each institution have been most gracious; neighbors, friends—and their children—have contributed. The Easter Seal Society helped with information for the handicapped.

And still something may be missing. My apologies to the mother who asked for places where one might nurse a baby. (She offered a very practical suggestion of a particular department store.)

Metropolitan Boston is an exciting and stimulating area with special appeal for all ages. The changing look of this compact and diverse region involves culture, history, and recreation. The book uses the City of Boston as a core, and surrounding areas for day trips.

If the reader is inspired to explore other possibilities, or is reminded of similar activities, one can only feel that the project is all the more worthwhile.

BERNICE CHESLER

KEEP IN MIND . . .

ADDRESSES: They are in Boston unless designated otherwise. All communities are in Massachusetts unless designated otherwise.

DISTANCES AND DIRECTIONS: They are calculated from Boston.

ADMISSIONS: They may change. Reduced rates may be available for groups, students, senior citizens, and servicemen. Sometimes an I.D. is required. Inquire!

HOURS: They sometimes change. It is safer to check before you leave. It is a challenge (to creative thinking) to arrive and find that there is a special reason for closed doors on a particular day.

FOOD: It is possible to picnic in and out of Boston. There are many advantages to bringing your own food. Restaurants tend to be crowded from 12 to 1:15; eat earlier or later.

GROUPS: Suggestions for field trips.
   . . . Reservations are neither necessary or preferred.
   . . . Whenever possible, leaders should make the trip in advance.
   . . . Transportation involves expense, insurance, and parental permission slips. Allow enough time to plan these details.
   . . . Schools may wish to think about fall or winter trips. Spring bookings are filled early in the school year.
   . . . Rainy summer days bring a deluge of requests to the larger institutions; use the book to think of the less obvious!
   . . . Inquire about available advance materials. Orientation helps the interest level. Follow-up is follow-through. (Those with young children sometimes role play before the big excursion.)
   . . . Supervision: 1 adult for every 10 children is a recommended ratio: 1 for every 6 is better. If possible, separate and meet the other groups at a specified time.

BOSTON'S BICENTENNIAL

A bonus! The Bicentennial is designed to make Boston more enjoyable for visitors and residents. Boston has not had an abundance of signs (directional or informational); plans call for many that will remain long after the Bicentennial years.

Other advantages:

... kiosks about town that tell you "where you can go from here."

... a rearranged, more manageable Freedom Trail (p. 110).

... an oral history project that allows neighborhoods to have recorded recollections of residents who lived in the area since 1900. Taped conversations are transcribed into booklets.

... 285 historical markers permanently installed throughout the city.

... acceptance of the decal system that indicates facilities for the handicapped, rest rooms, foreign language interpreters.

... restoration projects for many sites in the city.

... burying grounds (King's Chapel, Granary, Copp's Hill) now have permanent visual displays with a map, biographies of people buried there, and descriptions of gravestone carvings, symbols, epitaphs, and letters—and discussion of their cultural significance.

... 8 major neighborhood trails highlight contemporary and historically significant sites. Each is adjacent to an MBTA station. Locations: Downtown, North End, Charlestown, Waterfront, Beacon Hill, Back Bay, South End, Cambridge.

Current Events

Telephone information: "Where It All Begins," Tel. 338–1975
   Daily information on main events, performances, and Bicentennial activities.
"Operation Central," Tel. 338-1976 Live, helpful service, 9 A.M.–7 P.M. seven days a week.
Boston News-Letter, a biweekly, 4-page newspaper and calendar, is free at all Boston 200 information centers.

Information Desks

Major centers, open year round:
   Boston Common
   Lobby of new John Hancock Building
   Boston City Hall (accessible inside and out)

All centers hace comprehensive information and trained personnel. Included is the new brochure Access to Boston in '76, a guide to all historical and cultural sites and those support services that are accessible to our handicapped and elderly populations. In addition to containing information about hotels, restaurants, department stores, pharmacies, and transportation facilities, the guide includes resources for equipment loan and repair, trailer space, a "hot line" for the elderly and the availability of emergency medical services.

Visitor Hospitality Center

Located on the fourth level of Boston City Hall, May-October. Services include rest rooms, baby-changing facilities, drinking fountains, seating, public telephones, food, tables with umbrellas, a free children's playground (for ages 7–10) where accompanying adults are expected to provide supervision for their youngsters, a child drop-in center (fees charged) for children 3–6, and a women's information kiosk.

Major Exhibits
Multimedia Presentations

18th Century: The Revolution: Where It All Began
Planned for Quincy Market Building, adjacent to Faneuil Hall.
Length: 20 minutes–2 hours, depending on your interest.
Admission: Adults, $1.50; children 6–12, 75¢; under 6, free.

19th Century: The Grand Exposition of Progress and Invention
Located in the Stuart Street Armory in the Back Bay.
Length: 20 minutes–2 hours, depending upon your interest.
Admission: Adults, $1.50; children 6–12, 75¢; under 6, free.

20th Century: Where's Boston: Visions of the City
Located at the Prudential Center in a structure built over the skating rink.
Length: 45 minutes.
Admission: Adults, $2; senior citizens, half price; children 6–12, $1; under 6, free.

Author's Note: All of the above was the latest information at press time. Please call 338-1975 or 338-1976 for current details.

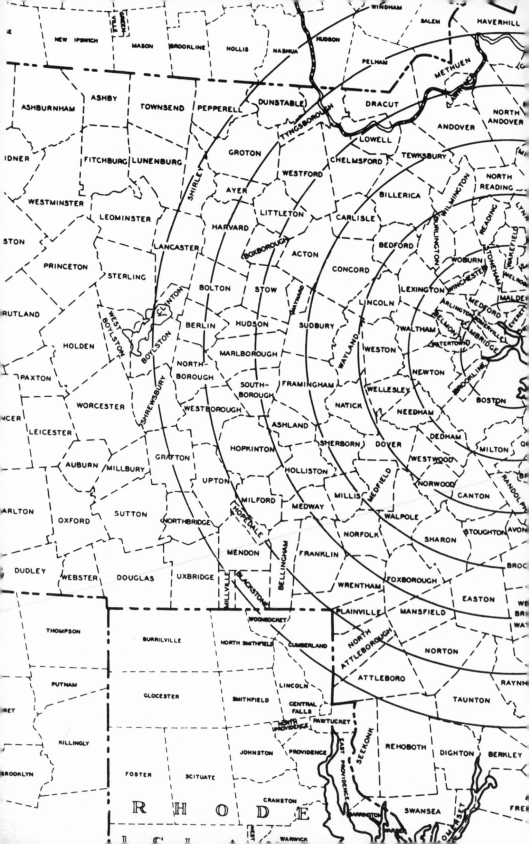

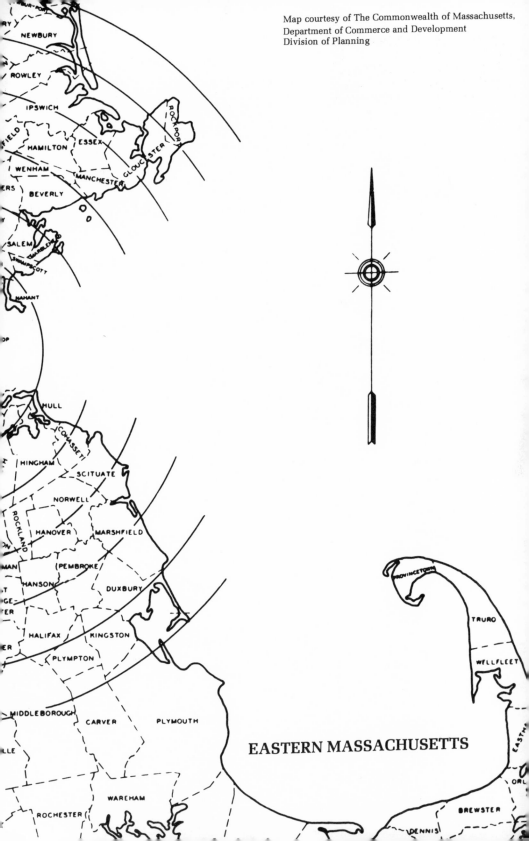

EASTERN MASSACHUSETTS

DOWNTOWN BOSTON

Legend

City Routes ....

One Way Streets ....

U. S. and State Routes ....

Scale of Miles

0   1/8   1/4   1/2

POINTS OF INTEREST

1. Boston Massacre Site
2. Boston Tea Party
3. Museum of Science
4. City Hall
5. Copp's Hill Burying Ground
6. Court House
7. Custom House
8. Faneuil Hall
9. Franklin's Birthplace
10. Hatch Mem. Shell
11. King's Chapel
12. Mass. Dept. of Public Works
13. New Eng. Medical Ctr.
14. Old Corner Book Store
15. Old Granary Burying Ground
16. Old North Church
17. Old State House
18. Old South Meeting House
19. Paul Revere's House
20. Paul Revere Statue
21. Post Office
22. Public Library
23. State House
24. Sen. Saltonstall State Bldg.

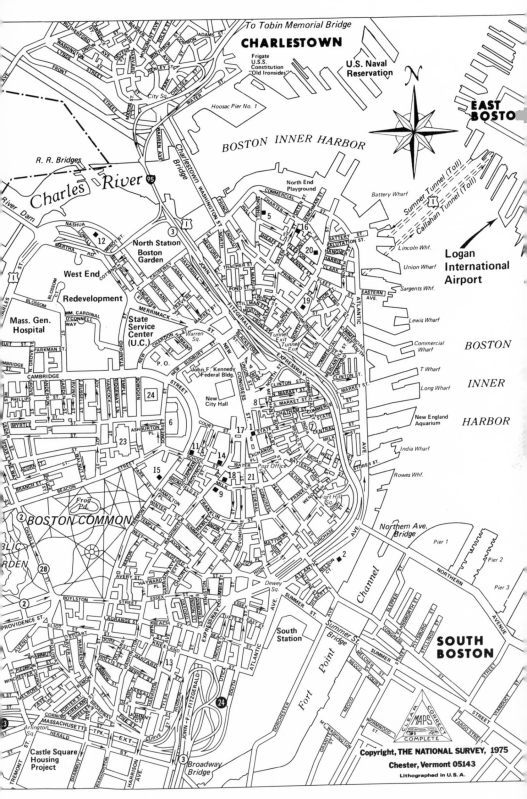

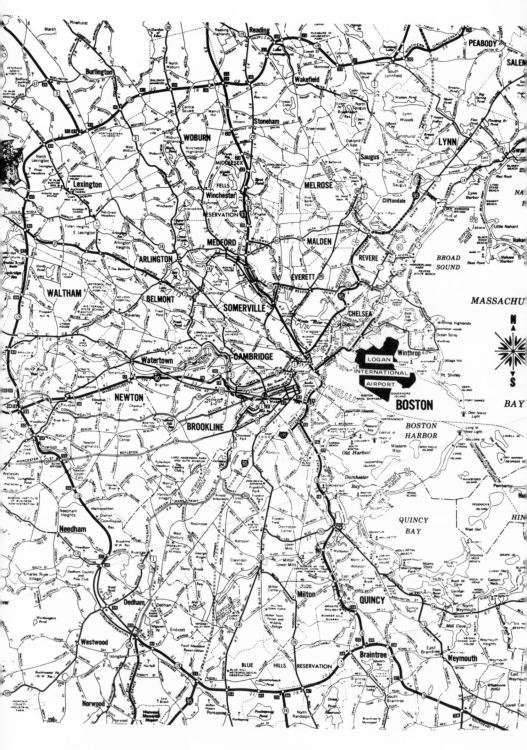

ROAD MAP

AN INTRODUCTION TO THE AREA

Information Centers

BOSTON VISITORS AND INFORMATION CENTER   Boston Common
(Tremont Street at West Street)   Tel. 426–4948
Open: 7 days a week. Closed Thanksgiving, Christmas, and New Year's Day.

BOSTON AND MASSACHUSETTS INFORMATION DESK (See p. 30 for each New England state tourist office address.)   At the State House on Beacon Street, the Desk is just inside the door of the East Wing, the section to the right of the main entrance. During the winter months the Desk is just inside the main entrance in Doric Hall.
Open: Monday-Friday 10–4 year round, 7 days a week during summer months. Volunteers from the Civic Center and Clearing House, Inc., provide answers to specific questions. Printed material on places throughout Massachusetts is available here. Brochures are issued on their own Blue Line Walking Tour, which takes you from the State House to the Prudential Center.

BICENTENNIAL BONUS   It is possible that the need for more—and more complete—information centers will be filled with the Bicentennial. Several organizations are working on the situation and we may reap the benefits.

Rest Rooms

TOILET FACILITIES. *Boston Common—*Ladies' Room (Tremont and West streets); Men's Room (toward the ball field near tennis courts). Facilities are open June 15-September 15 and Thanksgiving-January 6, 7 days a week, 9–5. September 15-Thanksgiving and January 6–June 15, Monday-Friday 9–5. *Boston Public Garden—*That little green house to the left of the bridge (as you walk away from the bridge toward the Charles Street center entrance) is a Ladies' Rest Room that is open year round, 9–5 on most days. *Boston City Hall* —Fourth floor, enter from the plaza. *Others:* Department stores always seem to have their facilities on one of the upper floors; the trip of necessity becomes an excursion. Hotels and restaurants usually have facilities on the first or second floors.

Events Information

Recorded Information:
> Arts Line (cultural events), 261–1660
> RKO Concert Information, 931–1505
> Boston Garden (upcoming events), 227–3200
> Children's Museum, 522–5454
> Gardner Museum, 734–1359
> Museum of Fine Arts, 267–9377
> Museum of Science, 742–6088
> New England Aquarium, 742–8870
> Zoo information, 442–0991

Extensive listings are in many publications:
Daily newspapers:
> *The Boston Globe:* All Thursday editions have *Calendar,* a supplement.
> *The Herald-American* has *Show Guide* in the Sunday edition.
> *The Christian Science Monitor* has calendars of events in the Thursday issue of the New England edition.

Two weeklies that are on the newsstands on Sunday:
> *The Boston Phoenix* (35¢) and *The Real Paper* (25¢)

Monthly:
> *Boston Magazine* (75¢)

Useful Numbers

The only 24-hour pharmacy for miles around:
PHILLIPS DRUG   155 Charles Street, Boston   Tel. 523–1028
It is located at the Charles Street Circle opposite Massachusetts General Hospital.

Recorded Information:
> Weather, 936–1212
> Time, 637–1234
> Marine weather (spring-fall), 569–3700
> Voice of Audubon (what birds have been seen where), 259–8805
> Smithsonian Observatory (earth and space reports), 491–1497
> MBTA delays and special information, 722–5050

Live and Helpful:
BOSTON EMERGENCY PHYSICIAN SERVICE   Tel. 482–5252
Locates doctors for house calls for extreme emergencies.

BOSTON POISON INFORMATION CENTER   300 Longwood Avenue Tel. 232–2120
A 24-hour information service. Calls are taken in rotation by representatives of four teaching pediatric services (Children's Hospital Medical Center, Boston City Hospital, Massachusetts General Hospital, and Boston Floating Hospital). Other Massachusetts centers are in Fall River, New Bedford, Springfield, and Worcester.

CALL FOR ACTION   Tel. 787–2300   Monday-Friday 11–1
Information and referral service—a-y: addiction-youth—that provides telephone follow-up on the assistance given to callers.

CITIZEN INFORMATION SERVICE   Office of the Secretary of the Commonwealth   State House   Boston   Tel. 727–7030 (Boston), 1–800–392–6090 (outside Boston). Monday–Friday 9–5.

This new public information service is designed to eliminate some red tape by answering questions related to any state agency.

COMMUNITY SEX INFORMATION   Tel. 232–2335

It is a telephone counseling service, which is free, anonymous, and nonjudgmental on all matters concerning human sexuality. Business address: Box 47, Waban 02168, Tel. 738–0430.

FEDERAL INFORMATION CENTER   John F. Kennedy Federal Building
Government Center   Boston 02203   Tel. 223–7121
Open: Monday-Friday 8–4:50.
This office answers questions about government programs and services: Where to get a passport, who is eligible for food stamps, what surplus government property is for sale, etc.

HELP FOR CHILDREN   727–8997

A service through the Office for Children (p. 276), which provides information on where to go for services, referral to an appropriate agency providing the service, and follow-up to assure that the service was satisfactory. Regional offices are listed on p. 276.

SENIOR HOT LINE   Tel. 722–4646   Monday-Friday 9–5

An information and referral service that deals with the full spectrum of situations of older people, including personal problems, dealing with agencies, loneliness, and emergencies.

U.S. CONSUMER PRODUCT SAFETY COMMISSION   408 Atlantic Avenue
Boston 02210, Tel. 223–5576, takes complaints and checks them out. Pamphlets sent on request. An extensive one, recently published, is on hundreds of banned products. Speakers provided for adult programs. The toll-free consumer product safety phone is 1–800–638–2666.

VOTER INFORMATION PROGRAM   357–5880; outside metropolitan Boston area, toll free, 1–800–882–1649

Monday-Friday 10–2. Volunteers from the League of Women Voters of Massachusetts answer questions on government, elections, registration, and voting.

Mailing Lists

(See also The Arts, pp. 47–63.)

BOSTON UNIVERSITY   Public Information   232 Bay State Road
Boston 02215   Tel. 353–3665   Weekly calendar of events.

HARVARD GAZETTE   1350 Massachusetts Avenue   Cambridge

A weekly list of events open to the public. Subscription: $5 academic year, $3 one term. Available free at Harvard's Information Center at Holyoke Center.

LOEB DRAMA CENTER (Harvard)   64 Brattle Street   Cambridge 02138

No charge for place on mailing list of series and special events. Written requests, please.

MASSACHUSETTS INSTITUTE OF TECHNOLOGY   Public Relations Department   77 Massachusetts Avenue   Cambridge
Calendar of events: $6 academic year, $3 one semester. Published weekly.

MUSEUM OF FINE ARTS   Ancient Instrument Room (p. 170) publishes a monthly calendar of all Boston music events with historic instruments.

TUFTS UNIVERSITY THEATER   Medford 02155   Tel. 623–3880
Prologue published quarterly; sent free upon request. Articles and editorials, as well as a complete list of theatrical events including late afternoon student performances.

WELLESLEY COLLEGE   Coordinator of Special Events   Wellesley 02181
Weekly bulletin. Academic year $1.

Getting Around the City

FRIDAY AFTERNOON deserves special mention. After 3 or 3:30 P.M. traffic is particularly heavy.

COMMUTING   Rush hours are 7:30–9:30 A.M. and 4–6 P.M. If you don't mind heavy traffic, most of the highways serving communities close to Boston have moving cars at these hours; the exception is the Southeast Expressway. For driving directions call the local police department in the community of your destination.

PARKING   If you must drive into the city, plan to pay for parking facilities. (Sundays present an exception to this in some areas.) Some garages are often full; much depends upon what is going on in town.

Boston Common Underground Garage: Tel. 523–7395   Entrance: Charles Street near Beacon.
   All pedestrian exits bring you onto the Boston Common. From 8 A.M. to 6 P.M. it is 50¢ for each of first 3 hours, $2 for the day. 6 P.M.–midnight: 50¢ hour, maximum $1. 24-hour period: $2.50. Free bus service every 10 minutes Monday–Saturday. Buses run 8 A.M.-midnight and go around the block—up Beacon, along Tremont, and back along Boylston.
Handicapped: Elevator brings you to Beacon and Charles streets. Use outside (street) sidewalk rather than Common paths.

Government Center Garage: New Sudbury Street
   Madness! Easy to be unsure of yourself when looking for the next level up. Coming down is comparable to a tightly wound carnival slide for all 8 floors. 50¢ first hour; 25¢ each hour thereafter; $2 up to 6 hours.

Prudential Center Garage: 75¢ first hour; 75¢ each additional hour; $3 for 10 hours.

TRAVELING WITHIN BOSTON   The most practical way to travel in downtown Boston is by the underground facilities of the ⓣ —away from the traffic that is harrowing for the best of the natives. The uninitiated driver will surely be frustrated by the crowded narrow streets. One-way streets are often undesignated as such on maps. And if there is the slightest precipitation, add the greatest of patience.
   There could be complaints about rush hour on the ⓣ —try to travel at just about any other time with or without children—or lack of service to some suburbs, but Boston's public transportation system is relatively simple to learn and it is recommended to visitors. If the children (or you) are not foot-weary, inquire before entering a station, as it may even be easier to walk to some destinations.

MBTA (Massachusetts Bay Transportation Authority) Ⓣ
The nation's oldest subway had its first run from Park to Boylston in 1897. Changes and major improvements are still being made and others are under consideration.

Telephone numbers (*Note:* Telephone information numbers are almost always busy):
> 722–5000 (6 A.M.–11 P.M. daily) connects all numbers
> 722–5700 (8:15 A.M.–4:30 P.M. Monday-Friday) Customer Service for mailing of schedules and maps
> 722–5657 Park Street Information Center (schedule information) Monday-Saturday 7:15 A.M.–10:45 P.M., Sundays 8:15 A.M.–11:45 P.M.
> 722–5050 Recorded transit conditions 7 A.M.–5:30 P.M. Monday-Friday

Color Code:
> Orange Line is Wellington Circle (Medford) to Forest Hills.
> Red Line is Harvard to Ashmont, Quincy.
> Blue Line is Bowdoin-Wonderland (connects with Orange Line at State and with Green Line at Government Center).
> Green Line is Lechmere-Park-Riverside, Arborway, Boston College, Cleveland Circle.

(*Note:* Copley lacks a pedestrian walkway joining inbound and outbound areas. Necessary transfer can be made at Arlington.)

Rapid Transit Service: Depends upon the line. First trains leave for Boston about 5:15 A.M. Last trains leave Boston about 12:30 A.M.

Fare Structure:
> *Rapid transit lines'* basic fare is 25¢.
> (Quincy and Riverside require an additional 25¢ when you get off on the surface.)
>
> *Dime Time* is in operation year round 10 A.M.–2 P.M. Monday-Friday and all day Sunday on all rapid transit lines with the exception of the Green Line's surface routes and the Red Line Quincy extension. (Half fare applies on the Quincy extension during those hours.)
>
> *Surface fare:* 20¢ within the city is charged by most bus routes, including the bus from Airport Station to all airport terminals. It is also charged by Green Line's Huntington, Beacon, and Commonwealth lines once they emerge from subway.
>
> *Express bus routes* that operate into downtown Boston from some suburbs have a different basis for their fare.
>
> *Children 5–11 inclusive:* 10¢ with free transfer privileges.
>
> *Pupil fares:* 10¢ with badge acquired from school.
>
> *Senior Citizens:* Half fare to lowest nickel on all rides with card obtained at Government Center Station. (Person must be legal resident of Ⓣ district and have reached 65th birthday.)

Maps:
> Distributed by Park Street Information Center (located inside turnstile underground) and Customer Service, 722–5700.
> Available in several forms:
> Wallet-sized cards have rapid transit lines.
> Large foldout map has subway, bus, and rail information.
> Tactile Route Map distributed by National Braille Press, Inc., 88 St. Stephen Street, Boston 02115.

Getting In and Out of Boston

AIR TRAVEL. *Logan International Airport.* (Call 411 for number of desired airline.)
> Ⓣ **Stop:** Blue Line to Airport Station. Three minute ride (20¢ more) to all terminals.

BOAT. For short trips—most leave from piers near Aquarium Ⓣ Station. The ocean liners leave from Commonwealth Pier.

BUS. If in doubt as to who services what community, Call Greyhound but plan to wait your turn for an answer.

In the Park Square Area:
> Greyhound terminal, Tel. 423–5810, Ⓣ : Arlington on Green Line.
> Trailways terminal, Tel. 482–6620, Ⓣ : Boylston on Green Line.
> (*Note:* Almeida Bus in Trailways terminal provides connections to Martha's Vineyard and Nantucket.)

Going to New York:
> TRAILWAYS leaves from Park Square and from their terminal on Speen Street between Rt. 9 and Rt. 30 (Exit 13 on the turnpike). Reservations for those who leave from Natick are recommended; make them by phone: Wellesley 235–5445, Natick 653–5660.
> GREYHOUND leaves from Park Square and stops at Riverside Ⓣ Station. (Parking available.) Space reservations for those who leave from Riverside are suggested; make them by phone: 969–8660 (Newton).

TRAIN. THE BACK BAY STATION, 5 minutes from South Station, is a short walk from the Copley Ⓣ Station. There is no public transportation, but a large free parking area is at the RT. 128 STATION in Dedham. *North Station,* Tel. 227–5070, Ⓣ Stop: North Station on the Green or Orange Line.

Off-peak Fares: A bargain! The Boston and Maine offers these special rates that are *not* valid on trains scheduled to arrive in Boston between 6 A.M. and 9:45 A.M. or on trains scheduled to depart from Boston between 3:30 P.M. and 7:05 P.M. on weekdays. They *are* valid on all other trains, including all trains on Saturdays, Sundays, and holidays. Off-peak fares are about half price. For schedules and rates, call North Station 227–5070 or 227–6000.

Cyclists: Sorry, bicycles not allowed, unless you're a large group that has made advance arrangements (and then there is an extra charge).

South Station, Tel. 1–800–523–5720, Ⓣ Stop: South Station on Red Line. Penn Central Information: 482–4400

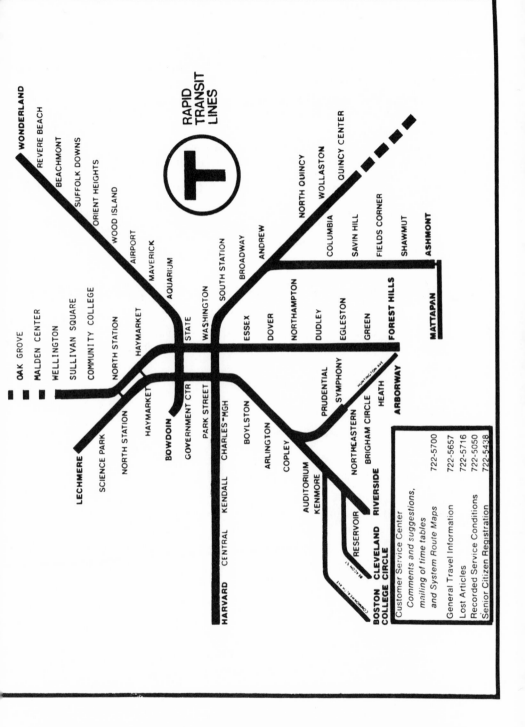

RAPID TRANSIT LINES

MASSACHUSETTS BAY TRANSPORTATION AUTHORITY

Customer Service Center	
Comments and suggestions,	
mailing of time tables	
and System Route Maps	722-5700
General Travel Information	722-5657
Lost Articles	722-5716
Recorded Service Conditions	722-5050
Senior Citizen Registration	722-5438

MASSACHUSETTS TURNPIKE

During winter months, weather and road condition advisory service available 24 hours a day, Tel. 237–3250

To get OUT of the city, entrances going west on the pike:
Allston at Cambridge Street

From in town:
Massachusetts Avenue near Newbury Street
Huntington Avenue–Copley Square at intersection of Huntington and Dartmouth streets
Another Copley Square on ramp at Clarendon Street (take Stuart to Clarendon)
Arlington Street near Tremont
From Congress Street, High Street, or Cross Street to Southeast Expressway to Massachusetts Pike west

Northeast Travelers' Information

CANADIAN Government Office of Tourism. Currently at Tel. 536–1730. The office is about to move. Check with operator for new telephone number.

Division of Tourism Promotion Services
CONNECTICUT Department of Commerce
210 Washington Street
Hartford, Connecticut 06106

MAINE Department of Commerce and Industry
State House
Augusta, Maine 04330
It may have a toll-free information number in the summer.

MASSACHUSETTS has 13 vacation areas. For addresses contact the Massachusetts Department of Commerce, Division of Tourism, 100 Cambridge Street, Boston 02202, Tel. 727–3201

NANTUCKET accommodations, Tel. 228–9559. This office acts as a clearinghouse for overnight accommodations, and will save you from making a series of telephone calls to learn of openings.

NEW HAMPSHIRE Office of Vacation Travel
Division of Economic Development
Box 856
Concord, New Hampshire
Toll-free taped information, Tel. 1–800–258–1140
Regional associations:
Dartmouth-Lake Sunapee Region, Box 246, Lebanon 03766
Lake Region, Box 300, Wolfeboro 03894
Merrimack Valley, Box 634, Manchester 03105
Monadnock Region, Box 269, Peterborough 03458
Seacoast Regional Association, 33 Winnacunnet Road, Hampton 03842
White Mountains, P.O. Box A, Lancaster 03584

NOVA SCOTIA (toll free) Tel. 1–800–341–6709. Open spring through early fall 7:30 A.M.–8:30 P.M. 7 days a week. October-March, Monday-Friday 9–5.

RHODE ISLAND Department of Economic Development
Tourist Department
1 Weybosset Hill
Providence, Rhode Island 02903
Toll free: 1–800–556–3884 Monday-Friday

VERMONT Agency of Development and Community Affairs
61 Elm Street
Montpelier, Vermont 05602

Food

COOPS

If you want to form or join a food cooperative, you may get helpful information from the New England Food Cooperative Organization (NEFCO). The directory coordinator changes from time to time, and at the moment there is no office. Call the Boston Food Coop, 12 Babbit Street, Boston, Tel. 267–9090, for the current NEFCO coordinator's number.

24-HOUR SUPERMARKETS

STORE 24 has several locations.
STAR MARKET has one in the Prudential Center, Porter Square (Cambridge), and at Kilmarnock Street. STOP & SHOP has one in the area of the Christian Science Center on Westland Avenue near Massachusetts and Huntington avenues.

ICE CREAM

First it was "jimmies," then the exotic flavors or toppings, and now it is the "make our own" place that holds the attention of ice-cream lovers. Whatever, Bostonians do have definite opinions. BAILEY'S is considered to have the chocolatiest chocolate. BRIGHAM'S still gives free jimmies. The one and only CABOT'S at 743 Washington Street, Newton (between Newton Corner and Newtonville), serves combinations that are almost unheard of. FRED'S at 962 Massachusetts Avenue, Cambridge, corner of Bay Street near the Orson Welles Cinema, FRED'S at 47 Charles Street in Boston, and KELLY'S at 156 Cambridge Street, Boston (near Massachusetts General Hospital), make their own right before your eyes. But the one that is worth making a special trip for is STEVE'S ICE CREAM parlor at 191 Elm Street, Somerville. Not only is the fantastic ice cream churned in the one small bucket that is strategically placed in the window, but Steve has created an atmosphere that all ages should experience at least once. Even standing in line is fun as you read the posted reviews of the place. Hand-lettered signs give you all the answers: what flavors, how the ice-cream machine works, what combinations are possible for what price. Should you mix in candy, have hot fudge sauce, real whipped cream, or eat it plain? Such decisions! Put a dime in the player piano, sit in a purple chair at a yellow table—and enjoy. Open 7 days a week 2–11:30 P.M. Tel. 623–9449.

YOGURT CONES

There is more than one place where they are sold. In Boston: Chock Full O'Nuts on Winter Street near the Boston Common and the Sheraton Boston Hotel, p. 138, in the Prudential Center. In Cambridge: The Spa, p. 146, and Elsie's, p. 35.

Restaurants

Not intended as a gourmet guide, most are
suggestions of places where you may feel
comfortable with young people.

Prices: At the moment they seem to be changing daily. $2–$3 would be considered inexpensive, $4–$5 moderately priced. Many of the more elegant—and expensive—restaurants have, but do not feature, children's plates; often you have to ask.

Hours: They too may change. Call to check before you travel any distance. Most Italian and Chinese restaurants are open 7 days a week.

If you want to catch either the latest "in" or newest place, pick up a copy of *CHOMP*, a monthly newspaper distributed here and there around Boston, or get a subscription for $2.50 a year from 161 Elm Street, Somerville 02144.

ALL OVER

Brigham's. Varying hours. Clean, quick, and takeout service. Hamburgers, hot dogs. Milk shake served in two large glasses.

Friendly's. Another ice-cream place that is in the business of sandwiches, hamburgers, and hot dogs.

Howard Johnson's offers full dinners for children for 79¢ on Sundays; Monday-Friday it offers some feature with seconds on the house ($2.50–$3).

National fast-food places are now in the city as well as on the road.

BACK BAY

The English Room, 29 Newbury Street (near the Boston Public Garden), Tel. 262–5566, is open 11 A.M.–9 P.M. 7 days a week. Closed some holidays. Quick service. Homecooked meals with delicious salads and rolls. Lunch prices ($2–$3) include one vegetable, salad, and rolls. Dinner ($3.50–$4.50) includes two vegetables, rolls, salad, appetizer, dessert, and beverage. Close sitting. Quick turnover. Menus change about 4 P.M.

Hai Hai, 423 Boylston Street (near Berkeley Street), Tel. 536–8474. A fast-food Japanese restaurant that is restful! The soup is something even most kids will like. Japanese shish kebab is good too. The chefs may share recipes. Open: 12–2:30, 5–9, Sundays evenings only. Moderately priced.

BEACON HILL

21 Charles Street serves char-broiled hamburger, baked potato with sour cream for 99¢. Salad too. Special available Monday-Saturday 11–3. Cafeteria style. General hours: 11 A.M.–10 P.M. 7 days a week.

Havah Nagila, 280 Cambridge Street (across from Massachusetts General Hospital), Tel. 523–9838. Open: Noon-midnight 7 days a week. Inexpensive Israeli-Middle Eastern food. Pita (pocket) bread stuffed with anything or everything or full meals. (There is another one at 1653 Beacon Street, Brookline, Tel. 277–3433.) Have your dessert at Kelly's Ice Cream (p. 31).

GOVERNMENT CENTER

The JFK Federal Building cafeteria, complete with view of Government Center plaza, is open to the public. Open: Monday-Friday 7–4. Lunch is served

11–2. The grill (with hot dogs and hamburgers) is open until 3:30. They have swirl takeout ice-cream cones too. Food is simple and reasonable.

MARKET DISTRICT
(City Hall Area)

Al Capone's in the middle of the vendors et al. right on Blackstone Street. Hardly room to stand. No place to sit. Thick crisp crusted pizza with dripping cheese. You can watch them form the crust and see the finished product coming out of the ovens. Enormous pieces for 30¢; with something (beans, onions, mushrooms) 35¢. Open 6 days a week.

Durgin Park at 30 Market Street, Tel. 227–2038, is open 11:30–9. Closed Sundays and holidays. Good traditional cooking; heaping helpings. Checkered tablecloths at long or round tables. Noisy enough so that children needn't be hushed. Dinner prices go into effect promptly at 2:30. Only way to avoid at least a half-hour wait is to buy a drink at the Gaslight Pub and be ushered up a private stairway for almost immediate seating. Everything is à la carte. Several meat and potato dishes for $1.50 at lunch. Dinner main dishes start at $4.50. Indian pudding (special) 75¢.

The Union Oyster House, 41 Union Street, Tel. 227–2750, features seafood, has the oyster bar (first floor at the window) where clams and oysters are shucked before your eyes; it is picturesque, but these are not necessarily children's favorites. The restaurant has a children's special of hamburger, French fries, cole slaw, beverage, and dessert for $1.50. Open: Sunday-Thursday 1–9, Friday 11–9:30, Saturday 1–10. Air-conditioned.

CHINATOWN

Ho Yuen Bakery, p. 147, 54 Beach Street, offers exotic baked goods daily 9–9.

There is a wide choice of reasonably priced restaurants. Most are modest in decor—and one flight up or down. Some suggestions:

Bo Shek Coffee House, 63 Beach Street, Tel. 482–4441, is informal, inexpensive, and good. It has a counter and some tables. The curry beef buns (35¢) will outdo a hamburger any day. The pastry takeout service is particularly busy.

Shanghai, 21 Hudson Street, Tel. 482–4797. Particularly known for its Chinese pastry menu, which is offered Saturdays and Sundays 11:30–2:30. (Go early for a picturesque array in the center of the dining room.) It is a fun, tasty—and filling—experience. Steamed bun with pork and vegetables is better than you expect; the thousand layer cake is not what you expect.

Yee Hong Guey, 34 Oxford Street, Tel. 426–6738. Open until 8:30. Best buy is lunch.

Moon Villa, 23 Edinborough Street (facing the Expressway), Tel. 423–2061, has simple decor, dishes that aren't overloaded with sauce; it is good and inexpensive. Open 9 A.M.–2 A.M. daily.

DOWNTOWN

Bailey's, 74 Franklin Street (near Filene's), Tel. 482–7266. Meals served 10:30–3 Monday-Saturday, sandwiches 11–5:30 Monday-Saturday. Crowded at noon. Known for its apple pie.

Mr. C's Thin Place, 154 State Street (opposite Custom House), Tel. 723–9380. Calories of each dish given on menu. Informal place. Eggplant parmigiana, egg salad, tuna supreme, beef dishes. $1–$2. Open Monday-Friday 7–3.

KENMORE SQUARE

Aegean Fare, 539 Commonwealth Avenue, Tel. 267–2202. (Also located in Cleveland Circle, Brookline.) Open: 7 days a week until 1 A.M. Lunch minimum of 50¢ would buy bagel, cream cheese, and jelly; dinner minimum of 75¢ would buy a small Greek salad. Good shish kebab, hamburger, moussaka. Inexpensive-moderate. Informal. Quick service.

NORTH END

A restaurant that appeals to families—and can accommodate large groups—

European, 218 Hanover Street, Tel. 523–5694. All kinds of Italian dishes. Pizza too. Children's spaghetti plate for $1.25. Open: 11 A.M.–12:45 A.M. 7 days a week.

Just for pizza—

Pizzeria Regina, 11½ Thatcher Street (between Prince and No. Washington), long considered "the best" by many.

Umberto Galleria, 28 Parmenter Street, is not a sit-down place. It serves square, thick, slightly soft crust with spiced tomato and cheese sauce.

PRUDENTIAL CENTER

Bird Cage Restaurant, Lord and Taylor, 750 Boylston Street, Tel. 262–6000. $2.63 flat rate for lunch; sandwich, beverage, and dessert for children $1.58. Fathers may be allowed to have an extra dessert. Open: 11–2:30 Monday-Saturday and Wednesdays 5–7.

Peter's Restaurant, 242 Newbury Street, Tel. 262–2074. Shish kebab, hamburgers. Very informal. Open: 8–8 6 days a week. Closed Sundays.

Top of the Hub (expensive) has a view and a popular Sunday brunch served 11–2. $4.75 adults, $2.75 children. At the top of the Prudential Tower. Tel. 536–1775.

SOUTH END

Nadia's Eastern Star, 280 Shawmut Avenue (not far from Boston Center for the Arts), Tel. 338–8091. Near Hanson Street. Lebanese. A popular family-run restaurant. Open: 5 P.M.–2 A.M. 7 days a week. Dinners are around $4.

WATERFRONT

Chart House, 60 Long Wharf, Tel. 227–1576, has a child's beef patty plate for $1.50; regular prices are $4.65–$8.95. Salad served family style. Open: 5–11 P.M. Monday-Thursday, until 12 on Fridays and Saturdays, Sundays 4–10. Lunch Monday-Saturday 11:30–2:30. Average $3.

Dom's, 236 Commercial Street (near Aquarium), Tel. 523–8838. Expensive. Children may have meatballs, spaghetti, and beverage as guests of the house. Hanging plants, brick walls, and windows.

No Name, 15½ Fish Pier, Tel. 338–7539. No sign, no number, but it is there in the middle of the pier. (Turn left onto the pier just before entering Jimmy's Harborside parking lot.) The little back room has a view of the fishing boats. It is a small, almost dinerish setting, which is popular with more than the local fishermen. There is usually a line on summer evenings and Friday nights. A bowl of seafood chowder (95¢) has 14 ounces of fish in it. Nick Contos will give you the recipe, but he claims that yours won't taste the same because he uses fresh fish. Homemade bread and pies served. The seafood platter is really big enough for two. Open: 8 A.M.–9 P.M. Fish plates $2.50–$3.50. Clam roll $1.75. Pie 50¢.

Winery, Lewis Wharf, Tel. 523–3994. All-you-can-eat salad bar. Dinners start at $4.95. Open: Monday-Friday 11:30–4, 5–11; Saturdays 5–11; Sundays 3:30–11. Brick walls, good food, lots of plants.

CAMBRIDGE:

CENTRAL SQUARE

Middle East, 4 Brookline Street, Tel. 354–8238 (right near Massachusetts Avenue). Family run, good food, quick service, Formica tables, skewered meat and rice, inexpensive. Open: Monday-Saturday 11:30–2, 5–10 P.M., Sundays 5–9 P.M.

Brookline Lunch, 9 Brookline Street, Tel. 354–9473. Almost the last of its kind. Wide variety of patrons. As is—not redecorated: old equipment, sturdy chinaware, few booths, counters with stools. Home-cooked specialties: New England boiled dinner (corned beef and cabbage) on Thursdays, fish on Fridays. All food is home-cooked with fresh ingredients. Open: Monday-Friday 7 A.M.–8 P.M., Saturdays 7–6.

Hunan Restaurant, 700 Massachusetts Avenue, Tel. 876–7000. A new Mandarin/Szechuan place that has been well received. Open: noon–10 P.M. 7 days a week. Luncheon specials $2 and up. Regular menu about $3.50 up. The interesting mild or hot spices may be new to you; specify your taste when ordering.

MIT AREA

Try the student grill in the MIT Student Center across from Massachusetts Avenue. Almost always open. Deli sandwiches.

Colleen's Chinese Cuisine, 792–794 Main Street (off Massachusetts Avenue), Tel. 661–1660. Mandarin and Szechuan food, moderately priced. Lunch served noon–2 P.M., dinner 5:30–10. Closed Tuesdays. Weekends dinner only. The hot pot (fondue) has to be ordered in advance.

HARVARD SQUARE (all informal places)

Cardell's-Buddy's Sirloin Pit, 39 Brattle Street, Tel. 864–4470. Welsh rarebit for 70¢. Cafeteria-style food from Cardell's. In front: char-broiled hamburger, potato with sour cream, salad, French bread with butter as a special for $1.50. Open: Monday-Saturday 11:30–9.

Elsie's, 71 Mt. Auburn Street, Tel. 354–8362. Stools or stand-up arrangements. Good for takeouts. Try the special (roast beef at $1.10), take it back to the Holyoke Center to watch the action in the Square—or down to the riverside.

Grendel's Den, 89 Winthrop Street, Tel. 491–1757. Open 7 days a week. Lunch Monday-Saturday 11:30–2:30. Sunday-Thursday 5–midnight, Fridays and Saturdays 5:30–1 A.M. It is dark and atmospheric inside. Service outside on patio in good weather. All-you-can-eat salad bar every day except Fridays and Saturdays—$1.95 for lunch, $2.25 for dinner.

Mr. Bartley's Burger Cottage, 1246 Massachusetts Avenue, Tel. 354–9830. Open: Monday-Saturday 9–6. Thick juicy hamburgers start at 99¢. Twenty-eight specialties with everything from blue cheese to pineapple.

The Underdog (opposite The Bicycle Exchange), 6 Bow Street, Tel. 661–0388. Open 7 days a week. They do all sorts of things to the Hebrew National hot dog (grilled cheddar, bacon, tomato . . .) 60¢–$1, depending on what is done to it.

OUTSIDE HARVARD SQUARE

Lucky Garden, 282 Concord Avenue, Tel. 354–9514. Unpretentious. Mandarin and Szechuan food. Open 11:45 A.M.–10 P.M. 6 days a week, Mondays 4–10 P.M. Chinese pastries served Saturdays and Sundays noon–2. Moderately priced.

Newtowne Grille (Porter Square), 1945 Massachusetts Avenue, Tel. 868–3845. Red tablecloths, pizza and pasta, veal, chicken, steak (try eggplant parmigiana). Relaxing atmosphere. Inexpensive-moderately priced.

La Pinata, Davis Square (Somerville), Tel. 623–9762. Open: 11:30–9. Closed Sunday. Mild or hot Mexican food. A "hole in the wall" discovered by students. Often a wait. Inexpensive. Good. Try tacos for kids. (Have your dessert at Steve's Ice Cream, p. 31.)

ANIMALS

ANIMAL RESCUE LEAGUE OF BOSTON   10 Chandler Street (corner Arlington and Tremont streets)   Tel. 426–9170

Ⓣ **Stop:** Arlington, Green Line (8-minute walk, cross over Turnpike via bridge).

Pets for Adoption Kennel: Monday-Friday 10–4, Saturdays 9–11:30 Parking lot available.
In addition to dogs and cats, birds and small cage pets may be acquired through adoption. If you can possibly arrive about 10 A.M., you have the best selection. The donation for a male or a spayed female is $5.

Tours: Fall through late spring: Monday-Friday 10–4 by appointment. Maximum number: 75. Length of tour: 30–45 minutes. Minimum age: 6 years, first grade. Visitors see the Pets for Adoption Kennel, the "lost animal kennels," with hundreds of waiting dogs and cats in cages, and areas for feeding and exercising. You see the veterinary clinic and a pet-care movie. It is a noisy, educational visit.

Pet Patrol: If you have lost or found a pet, announcements are made daily by WCOP radio (11:50 A.M.).

Dog Obedience Group Training Classes: Wednesday evenings. $10 for a 6-week course. All ages, breeds, and breed mixtures. Preregistration required. Visitors welcome fall through late spring. Pet-care pamphlets available free of charge.

AQUARIUM   National Marine Fisheries Service   Albatross Street Woods Hole   Tel. 548–7684
Woods Hole is an embarkation point for boats to Martha's Vineyard and Nantucket (p. 220).

Open: Mid-June–mid-September 10–4:30.

Admission: Free.

Two harbor seals are in an outdoor pool. Inside there are about 35 species of local fish and invertebrates displayed in tanks. Pictures, models, and samples of instruments used in fisheries research and the study of the oceanic environment are on display. Among the labeled exhibits are the shells of New England, the American lobster—showing eggs, young and adult stages—and the life history of the haddock.

ATLANTIC AQUARIUM   One State Park Road   Nantasket Beach Hull   Tel. 925–3474

Directions: Rt. 3 to Rt. 228 to Nantasket Beach (p. 211) and Paragon Park (p. 206).

Open: Year round. Closed Mondays. Summer 10–8, winter Tuesday-Friday 10–4, weekends 10–6.

Parking: Free in winter; 50¢ (MDC area) in summer.

Admission: Adults, $2.25; children under 12, $1; senior citizens, $1; students 13–17, $1.75.

Three dolphins provide the highlight of the visit as they perform for about a half hour; the presentation is given several times a day. Exhibits include Edward Rowe Snow artifacts of Boston Harbor, a tidal pool simulation where you may handle starfish, anemones, and crabs, and eye-level tank displays with eels, giant turtles, an octopus—and native New England and tropical fish.

BENSON ANIMAL FARM   Hudson, New Hampshire (3 miles from Nashua, 45 miles northwest of Boston)   Tel. 882–2481

Directions: Rt. 128 north to Rt. 3 to Rt. 3A, take right over Merrimac River Bridge in Tyngsboro to Hudson, right on Rt. 111 to Benson's.

Open: Mid-April–November 1, 10–5 daily. The closing hours vary depending on the season. In April the closing hour Monday-Friday is 4, Saturdays 5, and Sundays 6 or 7 P.M. With more daylight hours the farm remains open later.

Admission: Adults, $1.40; children 3–11, 70¢. Group rates available if you write for reservations. Amusement rides: Adults, 25¢; children, 15¢.

Picnic area and snack bar available. Grills allowed. Bring your own stroller.

Animal training programs—complete with whip-cracking trainers, ball-spinning seals, tigers, elephants, and chimpanzees—are given daily, weather permitting, starting at 1:30 A.M., with about 45 minutes between each act. There are likely to be fewer programs on Monday, but that is hardly a handicap when there are barns to walk in; a small garden maze to get lost in; a monkey house with moustache monkeys, pigtail monkeys, colorful baboons; attractive outside areas with flamingos, macaws, and cockatoos; sheep from Sardinia on rocky terrain; dozens of young spotted deer; and white and colored proud peacocks who may spread their feathers several times a day. The farm is continually expanding.

As you walk (aplenty) around some of the more than 100 acres, you will find manicured lawns, flowers, blossoms on century-old apple trees in the spring, and many picturesque spots to rest. The amusement area, hidden by tall yews, is across the willow-tree-bordered lake with a fountain in the middle.

Some visitors have commented on crowds (particularly on Sundays and holidays), small cages for large animals, and dustiness in hot weather—and the wish to avoid the amusement area. (Even though it is off in the distance, you can hear it.) Whatever, it is a very popular and colorful place.

BOSTON ZOOLOGICAL SOCIETY   Franklin Park   Dorchester   Tel. 442–2002

This is the organization that is working to have Greater Boston zoos as recreational, educational, and research facilities. It provides zoo tours, educational programs on endangered species, birds, animals that eat animals or plants, and teacher-aid study materials. Film series offered.

Memberships: Individual, $5; family, $10. Benefits include free admission to the Children's Zoo, Franklin Park, and Stone Memorial Zoo, a newsletter, and "our undying gratitude."

Zoomobile: A large and colorful vehicle that transports about 15 small exotic animals to schools, fairs, day camps. Habits of the animals are discussed during the demonstrations given by trained personnel, and in many cases "touching" is encouraged. Available for nonprofit and commercial organizations. Two hour minimum.

THE BUDDY DOG HUMANE SOCIETY, INC.   1014 Pearl Street   Brockton   Tel. 1–583–8555

This nonprofit, independent organization, founded in 1961, shelters abandoned, homeless, or stray dogs until good homes can be found. Because quarters are limited, it is necessary to check the space situation before you bring a dog to them. There is a set scale of fees, starting at $15 for puppies, for those who bring a dog to the shelter. If you feel that you have the right place to keep a dog and wish to adopt one, you may visit and see about a "match." Donations start at $15 for a crossbreed; a purebred with registered papers is $35. If you have a desire for a particular breed, write or call and the society will contact you when such a dog arrives.

Group Visits: Please call in advance.

CAPRON PARK ZOO   Rt. 123   County Street   Attleboro   Tel. 223–3047
> This could be combined with a trip to the North Attleboro Hatchery (p. 41) about 4 miles away.

Open: 8 A.M. to dark. No admission charge.

The main feature in this small well-kept zoo is the rain forest (in a building) that has a section where birds fly freely among tropical plants. The only divider between you and the birds is the thin mist of water that the birds do not cross. The rest of the zoo has 14 large felines, a monkey house, bears, and hoofed animals.

Picnicking: Special area with tables and grills. Children's playground equipment nearby.

CATS   ELLEN M. GIFFORD SHELTERING HOME   30 Undine Road   Brighton   Tel. 254–2962

Contact: Mrs. John Slight

Directions: Coming from Boston along Commonwealth Avenue, turn right on Lake Street at Boston College, first left onto Undine.

Open: Monday-Saturday 9–5.

This amazing, immaculate home for cats has been in existence since 1889. If you have an "extra" kitten or cat (in good health), you may leave it here. Adult visitors may adopt one of the 150 felines that they accommodate. Those that are adoptable are the small kittens, females that have been spayed, and males that are neutered.

As there is an endowment that takes care of the finances, no charge is made for services, but donations are accepted. Just to see the fenced-in yard with this aggregate of cats is an experience!

DRUMLIN FARM (p. 191).

DUCK FEEDING   (MDC area on Norumbega Road along the Charles River in Newton, near Commonwealth Avenue—Rt. 30—and Rt. 128)
> Could be combined with Canoeing, p. 217.

Directions: Going west on Commonwealth Avenue, pass Marriott Hotel, and then the MDC Police Station, take first right, then the next right down the ramp, and follow "Duck Feeding" sign.

Hundreds of ducks always hungry. They may greet you in the parking area in the winter. (Fewer ducks—just as hungry—are in the Boston Public Garden, p. 141, Beaver Brook, p. 185, and Larz Anderson Park, p. 187.)

It is about a half-mile ride (or uphill cycle) along Norumbega Road to Norumbega Tower where there is a small park with a few fireplaces and picnic tables. For an open air observation point overlooking the Charles River, climb the narrow circular stone steps of the tower.

FISH   NATIONAL HATCHERIES are open daily 8–4 and have troughlike structures with different sized fish (some are "this big"), which are used by the U.S. Department of the Interior Bureau of Sport Fisheries and Wildlife Service to stock public fishing waters. Fish are kept until they are of "catchable" size. You may come to look anytime, but if a group can make advance arrangements, managers would give a guided tour that would help visitors understand fish culture.

The two locations nearest Boston are:

> **Nashua, New Hampshire,** 151 Broad Street.
> This trout fishery is on Rt. 130 going from Nashua toward
> Hollis. Take Exit 6 North off the Everett Turnpike in
> Nashua. *Note:* No picnic or rest room facilities available.

By appointment groups can see the spawning process with eggs being taken from adult fish in October and early November; egg development can be noted most in November and December. The greatest variety of fish can be seen in April and May. This is one of the oldest fisheries in the country, but it has been modernized several times.

> **North   Attleboro,   Massachusetts.**   (You   could   combine   this
> with Capron Park Zoo, p. 40.) Located on Bunday Road off Rt. 152
> near Rt. 95. From 95, take North Attleboro exit, go north on 152.

Here they raise Atlantic salmon, brook, brown, and rainbow trout, large- and smallmouth bass, and bluegill sunfish. Group tours could be 30 minutes to 2 hours. Arrangements should be made 1 week in advance. Pets must be on leashes.

Nature Trail: Open year round. It is a particularly good trail that allows you to see mud duck houses, turtles, snakes during a 45-minute walk around the swampy pond that is part of the water supply for the hatchery. Pick up a leaflet (free), which explains the views and vegetation at 20 numbered observation points. There are benches at several of these locations, but children may be too busy looking for woodchuck burrows to sit down. If group leaders would like to plan advance meetings around the nature-to-be-seen, write to the hatchery for a copy of the trail leaflet.

FISH   STATE HATCHERIES are open every day of the year from 9 to 4. They grow trout to stock Massachusetts streams, ponds, and lakes for recreational fishing purposes. If groups would like a conducted tour, write to the culturist for an appointment. The chief culturist may be able to provide special arrangements; he can be contacted at the McLaughlin Trout Hatchery, Belchertown, Massachusetts 01007.

Locations:
Sunderland on Rt. 16. (Combine with maple-sugaring, p. 284.)
Montague on Turners Fall Road. (Combine with maple-sugaring, p. 284.)
Sandwich, Rt. 6 A. (See p. 102 for other Sandwich attractions.)
Belchertown, East Street (near Quabbin Reservoir, p. 195).

FISH LADDERS (p. 286).

FRANKLIN PARK ZOO   Franklin Park   Dorchester   Tel. 442–2005
Recorded information: 442–0991

At this writing there are three up-to-date areas that are worth visiting: The Children's Zoo, A Bird's World, and the Range Area. They are about a 10-minute walk from each other.

Ⓣ **Stop:** Orange Line to Egleston Station, then a Blue Hill Avenue bus to zoo.

Directions: Follow Jamaicaway to Arborway to Howard Johnson's rotary, and turn into the zoo and follow signs. Or take Exit 17 off the Southeast Expressway and follow Columbia Road for about 4 miles to the zoo.

Admission: Right now the Children's Zoo is the only area with a charge. Call 442–0991 to see if this has been changed. When the entire zoo is re-vitalized, there will be a single admission charge for all exhibits.

Safari Train: Leaves from the gate of Children's Zoo and gives an open-air ride through the zoo. Adults, 50¢; children, 35¢.

CHILDREN'S ZOO

At Seaver Street and Blue Hill Avenue   Tel. 442–2216

Open: Late April-October 31, Monday-Saturday 10–5, Sundays and holidays 10–6. (Sunday mornings are the exception to a busy weekend operation.)

Admission: Adults, 75¢; children, 25¢; senior citizens, 40¢. Group rates available. *Note:* As zoo plans become a reality, there may be changes in admission policy. Call recorded zoo information, 442–0991, to check.

Pet Ring Shows: Every hour on the half hour. The natural history of one individual animal is presented, with children allowed to touch the animal.

Animal Feeding by Children: Bottle feeding the baby goats and sheep at 11, 2, and 4.

Eating: Picnic area provided. Refreshments sold.

You can cover the whole area in about an hour even with small children, but it is quite possible to spend more time in this fun place. The spider monkeys and gibbons manage to steal the show, but everyone will find lots more to see: an African elephant, raccoons, porcupines, camels, snakes, turtles, lizards, parrots, and barnyard animals. The cow is milked twice daily.

Some well-placed play equipment is in the zoo. (Can you find your monkey?) Mingling with the goats and sheep seems to be popular; not everyone is able to feed the goats, but it is worth being there at that time.

Stop by the window of the kitchen to see food being prepared. And the animal nursery has a feeding schedule posted. As the zoo opens every spring with some newborns, you may see a lion cub or leopard being bottle-fed.

A BIRD'S WORLD

Inside open 10–4 year round, **outside open** all the time.

Inside and out there is something special and spectacular—a feeling of grace and beauty. When you step onto the elevated outdoor walkway, you are in a flight cage with storks and toucans and hornbills and doves. The plantings, the brook that flows into a marsh area, and the movement of the birds will fascinate everyone. Between the Bird House and Flight Cage is a beautiful flamingo pool—and there they stand on one leg or two. The picturesque water-fowl ponds have many varieties of ducks, geese, and swans.

As you open the doors of each environment in the Bird House, you quickly become aware of temperature changes, sounds or the lack of them, and vegetation differences and smells. Birds are everywhere—in a swamp, the rain forest, desert, and mountainside. These areas are reproduced with the aid of fiber glass, rocks, real trees, plants, and water. The Bird House is ramped except for the educational exhibit, one of the best in town. It is participatory and is inviting for all ages: Compare a bird's heartbeat with your own, become aware of how beaks are used as tools, and learn about the survival hazards of a robin.

If this is a sample of Boston's new zoo, we anxiously look forward to the target date of 1977. When the total plan is completed, visitors will be immersed in an extensively developed series of environments designed to encourage looking: a tropical forest, bush forest, desert, and veld.

RANGE AREA

It is about a half-mile walk around the range where eight moated exhibits give an unobstructed view of llamas, deer, camels, antelope, yak, and the tarpan, a once extinct species of wild horse that has been reconstructed. Free admission.

HORSEBACK RIDING, HAY AND SLEIGH RIDES (p. 228).

MASSACHUSETTS SOCIETY FOR THE PREVENTION OF CRUELTY TO ANIMALS   180 Longwood Avenue   Tel. 731–2000

Angell Memorial Hospital Clinic Hours: Monday-Friday 8:30–6, Saturday 8–4. Emergency cases that require treatment will be received at any hour of the day or night including Sundays and holidays.

Ⓣ**Stop:** Longwood on Green Arborway Line.

Adoption Ward Hours: Monday-Saturday 10:30–3:30.

Tours: 20 minutes by appointment only.   **Minimum Age:** 8.

NEW ENGLAND AQUARIUM   Central Wharf (foot of State Street, off Atlantic Avenue)   Tel. Recorded information, 742–8870; administrative offices, 742–8830

Ⓣ**Stop:** Aquarium station on Blue Line (that 42-foot-long escalator is an adventure). Two-minute walk.

Directions: Along Central artery going north take Atlantic Avenue, Northern Avenue exit; going south take Dock Square exit to Atlantic Avenue.

Open: Monday-Thursday 9–5, Fridays until 9, Saturdays, Sundays, and holidays 10–6. Closed Thanksgiving, Christmas, and New Year's Day.

Parking: Adjacent parking garage—75¢ first hour, 50¢ each hour after.

Aquarium Admission: Adults, $2.50; children 6–15, $1.25; under 6, free; senior citizens and military personnel with IDs, $1.25.

Discovery Admission: Adults, $2; children 6–15, senior citizens and military personnel with IDs, $1; under 6, free.

Combination Admission for main AQUARIUM exhibits and DISCOVERY: Adults, $4; children 6–15, $2; senior citizens, military personnel, and college students with IDs, $2.

Average Visit: 1½ hours in Aquarium. Discovery offers a 45-minute program.

Groups: Spring groups should book before Thanksgiving. Special rates for Discovery.

School Groups: Special programs for K-college. Request school programs brochure. Wide variety of possibilities, including teacher orientation workshops, independent study programs, and touch-and-see for K-1.

Handicapped: Because the exhibit areas are designed with ramps, everything is easily accessible.

Courses: Contact Education Department for current offerings, which may include field trips.

Speakers for Groups: Minimum age for audience—elementary school. Two weeks' advance notice. No fee. Areas covered: ecology, sea, fish, aquatic animals.

Volunteer Program: Minimum age: 16.

DISCOVERY

The new dolphin exhibit, now permanently docked by the Aquarium, introduces visitors to the amazing learning and physical capabilities of dolphins and sea lions—in a unique vessel that houses a 1,000-seat observation stadium and three pools with a total of ¼ million gallons of water. Programs are designed to be informative as well as fun, and are accompanied by audio-visual presentations showing the animals in their natural environments.

MAIN AQUARIUM

After you have watched (no charge) the seals cavorting in their outdoor pool, you will enter the main building that emphasizes the world of water and the creatures that live in it. Lights in the many tanks (the only light in the Aquarium) and the thousands of colorful inhabitants provide an unusual visual experience. The "open architecture" of the structure allows for dramatic views of the four-story central tank and the first level tray from just about every surrounding gallery. This openness also means that the din of crowds is part of busy times; generally Sunday mornings are relatively quiet.

Displays are intended for education as well as entertainment. As most exhibits are live, the appeal is widespread. At peak times traffic is allowed in one direction only, and during capacity attendance visitors may have a wait before entering the building.

Some Highlights: The TRAY on the first floor level almost completely surrounds the giant ocean tank. It may take careful looking to spot some of the inhabitants in their retreat places. GALLERY TANKS along the ramp, which takes you up and around the walls of the building, may be heated or cooled, salt- or freshwater.

Black-footed penguins may occasionally make a braying sound, otters may be sliding on their rocks, and there are sea horses and an octopus as well as an electric eel, which is discharged regularly. Each of the gallery tanks (there are more than 70) has been arranged to resemble the occupants' native area so that visitors have the opportunity to see unusual plant life. (Have you ever been able to observe the underside of a floating lily?) The graphics on nearby descriptive and colorful panels help identify the animals, and an informative text is arranged so that simplest concepts are in largest type.

The HARBORVIEW ROOM (third level south): You can hear ships' underwater sounds with the harbor monitoring (participatory) exhibit. This is the only area with outside windows for visitors, a place to rest, the all-important bubbler, and an impressive sweep of the harbor. The CHILDREN'S AQUARIUM on the third level has tropical fish, turtles, frogs, salamanders, and snakes, but the unique tide pool where the ebb and flow is simulated every 20 minutes may be most remembered by youngsters. Visitors sit around the pool on a rug and are allowed to handle starfish, hermit crabs, sea urchins, and clams as an attendant explains and answers questions.

What Some Consider the Best of All:

THE GIANT OCEAN TANK (40 feet in diameter): The ramp that takes you to the top of the Aquarium leads to the life-size shark-paneled wall (illuminated with ultraviolet tubes) and the open top of the 200,000-gallon tank. From this point divers enter for cleaning and feeding (5 times a day for 45-minute periods). It is possible that a communications system will be arranged for divers to talk to viewers. Sharks are among the 300 animals swimming through the tunnels and caves of the central island reef. The varying sizes and the different eating habits can easily be seen through wide glass panels. Although the tank is lighted, you can notice the darkening water as you travel downward toward the coral-sanded floor where the bottom vertical glass panels are 4 inches thick.

In addition to the tanks, there is a model of Perry's submarine, a suspended skeleton of a North Atlantic right whale (the one with most oil when first discovered), and a huge globe that depicts the terrain of land under ocean. It may take several visits to "see all."

Films: Monday-Friday at 2:30. Also presented Friday evenings and weekends.
Eating: Small concession outside in good weather. Public walkway surrounding Aquarium has benches and an ocean view.

SOUTHWICK'S WILD ANIMAL FARM   Mendon   Tel. 883–9182
Directions: Massachusetts Pike west to Rt. 495 south. Take Milford exit, Rt. 16 west to Mendon. Follow sign at Gulf Station in Mendon.

Open: May-October, 10–6 daily.

Admission: Adults, $2; under 12, $1; 3 and under, free.
Charges (25¢ and 35¢) for some kiddie rides.
Group Rates: 75¢ each including leaders Monday-Saturday.

This is the temporary home for 1,000 birds and animals from all over the world as the farm supplies zoos all over the United States. Giraffes, zebras, kangaroos, mountain lions, monkeys, cockatoos, rare and endangered species—there is a large assortment to be seen. Many baby animals (e.g., camels, leopards) are born here.

For young children there is a playground and a walk-in kiddie zoo where you can pet and feed tame deer and goats.

When you look at the cages, keep in mind that Southwick's was, until about 10 years ago, a supplier—not open to visitors. Rather than being established as a model zoo, it happened upon the tourist aspect. Picnic grove provided.

WALTER D. STONE MEMORIAL ZOO   Pond Street   South Stoneham
Tel. 438–3662

Directions: Rt. 93 North to the Stoneham-Melrose exit, first right, short drive to zoo. Or from Rt. 128 take Rt. 93 south to second exit, turn right for about a mile to zoo.

Open: Every day of the year 10–4:30 winter, 10–5 in summer (late May-Labor Day).

Admission: Free. (This may change soon. Check with recorded zoo information, 442–0991.)

The highlight is the four-story aviary where more than 100 tropical birds are actually flying—or perched—around you. The simulated natural environment, complete with pools, plantings, and a waterfall, has some birds that blend with the foliage while others have vivid coloring. A panel of photographs provides the key to identification.

The comparatively small zoo has a circular layout, allowing for a see-all visit. Swans, ducks, and geese are in the attractive central pond, and the surrounding areas have one or two of each species in the houses for giraffes, elephants, penguins, seals, baboons, and polar bears.

The Boston Zoological Society hopes to be able to make this zoo less building-oriented.

WESTON DOG RANCH AND WESTON DOG TRAINING CLUB   248 North Avenue   Rt. 117   Weston   Tel. 894–1684

Observers are welcome at the outdoor classes (May-October, weather permitting) held under floodlights. Classes in obedience training are given Tuesday evenings, 7–11, year round. Minimum age for dogs: 5–6 months. Minimum age for handlers: 12.

WILLOW BROOK FARM AND THE COUNTRY STORE   118 Framingham Road   Southboro   Tel. 485–1680
Could be combined with Ashland State Park or on the way to or from the Higgins Museum, p. 167.

Directions: Farm is on Framingham to Marlboro Road. Take Rt. 9 through Framingham Center, travel in left lane to take overpass to Marlboro.

Open: Tuesday-Saturday 9–6, Sundays and holidays 10–6. Closed Mondays except holidays. No fees.

Buffalo are a rare sight and people come from miles around to see the 10 bison, 3 Appaloosa horses, and 9 Texas longhorn cattle at this Willow Brook (1680) Farm. It is a commercial enterprise that is trying to re-create the "Old West image." Groups may ask permission to get closer to the pens for picture-taking. The store itself has the right touch for the atmosphere intended.

ZOO INFORMATION (RECORDED): Tel. 442–0991.

THE ARTS

. . . Arts in Boston have considerable recognition. But support is another thing. A few groups included here are new and burgeoning. Others are well established.

. . . Children's theatre differs from season to season and almost from month to month. Reasons include funding—and sometimes critics!

. . . Arts centers are everywhere. Local communities are establishing their own cultural centers with exhibits, classes, and performances.

. . . Classes: There are zillions. If you are looking for a center—or an individual teacher—check the resources and organizations section in the latter part of this chapter.

. . . Local symphonies may have children's concerts. Some have open rehearsal policies.

. . . Touring performances and guest artists: Often the chemistry of the receiving group (orientation and mood) and the guest individual(s) varies from one location to another. It is an interesting phenomenon.

. . . Colleges. Many have touring music ensembles and dance groups. Arrangements vary from year to year.

. . . Field trips may be a walk to a local artist's studio.

. . . Programs for artists-in-residence for a day or more—in a school or public place—allow for accessibility and exposure.

Live Performances

Note recorded events telephone numbers, p. 22.

In fairness to performers—and to members
of the audience—it is suggested that groups
of children be adequately supervised (one
adult for every ten children).

ADVENTURES IN MUSIC, INC.   P.O. Box 71   Lincoln 01773
Inexpensive, professional performances expressly designed for children aged 5
to 12 are provided by this nonprofit, educational corporation of parent volunteers from seventeen participating towns. Each year four programs are given
at various locations on weekends. All are open to the public. (In addition, AIM
has in-school presentations.) Tickets $2 each, series $7.

Presentations include visual, dramatic, and/or verbal elements. Often the
audience is invited to participate in some way—all in keeping with Music
Director Newton Wayland's goal of exposing children to professional performances of a large musical repertoire—orchestral, operatic, ballet, classical, folk,
and popular.

ASSOCIATE ARTISTS OPERA COMPANY   National Theater   Boston
Center for the Arts   551 Tremont Street   Tel. 542–0308
Three presentations are given by this professional company. Series tickets
sold; individual tickets available final week before performance. Annual Christmas presentation (p. 300). Dress rehearsal preview series for grade-school
through high-school students. $1.50 per student; no charge for teachers. Sea-
son: November-February.

BOSTON BALLET   19 Clarendon Street (corner Warren Avenue)   Boston
02116   Tel. 542–3945
A repertoire of more than 60 modern and classical ballets is now part of the
company that was established in 1965 through a Ford Foundation grant. Programs include world premieres of new works by distinguished choreographers.
Tickets: Call for current information. Sunday matinees are geared toward family audience.

Nutcracker: Annual presentation (p. 300).

Lecture-demonstrations: By staff members and professional dancers, planned
according to the age of audience. Possible programs: Comprehensive history of dance and excerpts from well-known ballets. Fees arranged.

Classes: Offered for preschoolers through adults.

BOSTON CHILDREN'S THEATRE   Performances in New England Life
Hall, 225 Clarendon Street. For dates and reservations: 263 Commonwealth
Avenue, Tel. 536–3324

Box Office Telephone (after 10 A.M. day of performance): 266–7262.

Ⓣ **Stop:** Copley (1 block walk).

Admission: Tickets range from $1.50 to $2.50 and reservations are strongly
recommended. Series subscriptions and group rates available.

Four plays are given during the school year on Saturday mornings and after-noons, some Sundays, and on weekdays during school vacations. Casts are selected from youngsters of the Boston Children's Theatre School. Productions vary in age appeal; call for information and for a place on the mailing list. As it is a medium-sized theatre, many young children prefer the close center section seats.

Touring Company: During the school year it is available on weekends for neighboring areas. A sponsor usually books the group as a fund-raising activity.

Stagemobile (p. 293): Summer project.

Classes: Registration includes an interview and takes place the week before each of the three 10-week sessions ($25 each), which start in September, December, and March. Weekly drama classes are scheduled Monday-Friday after school and on Saturdays for boys and girls 8–16. No previous training necessary. Some scholarships available.

BOSTON CONSERVATORY OF MUSIC   8 The Fenway   Boston   Tel. 536-6340

Ⓣ**Stop:** Auditorium or Prudential, 5-minute walk.

Many student performances (operas, plays, musicals, and recitals) are given during the year. You may call and request a place on the mailing list of the drama, music, and/or dance departments. Few of the concerts have an admission charge. Student-choreographed works are given about once a month; there is no charge, but a tambourine is passed for the benefit of the scholarship fund.

Classes: Modern dance and ballet offered for age 6 and up.

Lecture-demonstrations: May be arranged November-May. Faculty and/or students will travel to a group. Fee charged.

BOSTON PHILHARMONIA ORCHESTRA   6-concert season, October-May, National Theater, Boston Center for the Arts. For schedule and booking information, contact Boston Philharmonia, 551 Tremont Street, Boston 02116, Tel. 426–2387

A professional chamber orchestra, the Philharmonia was founded in 1967 by Boston musicians convinced that New England needed an orchestra that would play music that larger ensembles often neglect. Its programs and conductor must be approved by the musicians themselves. The orchestra has premiered many new works and has brought to Boston for the first time such conductors as Alexander Schneider, Michael Tilson Thomas, and Leon Fleisher. Student tickets are $2.

BOSTON SYMPHONY ORCHESTRA   Symphony Hall   Boston   Tel. 266–1492

Ⓣ**Stop:** Symphony (at the door).

Box Office: Opens at 10. (When other performances are scheduled in Symphony Hall it opens at 1 P.M. on Sundays.) Write for the regular schedule of concerts (September-April).

There are several series, and new subscribers should inquire about tickets the previous late winter or early spring. Individual seats are available for:

Open Rehearsals: Wednesdays at 7:30. After first rehearsal, individual seats are sold to other concerts.

Friday Afternoon Concerts: Rush seats for any of the 22 concerts in this series are sold. The line forms about 9 A.M. (the general box office opens at 10); the concert starts at 2 P.M.

BROOKLINE YOUTH CONCERTS   Brookline High School Auditorium
Tappan Street   Brookline

ⓣ **Stop:** Brookline Hills on Green (Riverside) Line.

Presented: Three Saturday afternoons during the school year.

Admission: Single tickets: Adults, $1.50; children, $1.25. Series: Adults, $3; children, $2.50. All seats unreserved.

Classical, contemporary, or folk music may be combined with ballet, puppets, or slides during these programs intended for kindergarten through grade 8. Recent groups that have appeared are the Harvard-Radcliffe Orchestra, the New York Pickwick Puppet Theatre, and the Boston Ballet Company.

Tickets are sold through the Brookline schools or can be ordered by mail. For the name of the present ticket chairman, call William Seymour, Supervisor of Music, 734–1111.

THE CAMBRIDGE ENSEMBLE   1151 Massachusetts Avenue   Cambridge
Tel. 876–2544

The Cambridge Ensemble is a professional acting company that offers several major productions during the winter season. One children's play is presented every year; the latest was based on children's poetry written by Boston-area youngsters. Ticket price range for children's productions: $1.75. Group rates available.

The company also offers workshops for junior high school age and up in improvisation, body awareness, and theatre skills.

CARAVAN THEATER   Harvard-Epworth Methodist Church   1555 Massachusetts Avenue   Cambridge   Tel. 868–8520

This resident experimental theatre group offers a touring group and occasional children's performances. Adult plays are presented October-June.

GILBERT AND SULLIVAN operas are performed each year by students at Harvard and Radcliffe at the Agassiz Theater (particularly good sight lines in a semicircular intimate audience arrangement) and by the Boston University Savoyards, 855 Commonwealth Avenue, Tel. 353–3341.

THE GREATER BOSTON YOUTH SYMPHONY ORCHESTRAS   855 Commonwealth Avenue   Boston   Tel. 353–3348

Rehearsals: September-May every weekend, are open to the public. Fall rehearsals Sundays 1:15–4:30 P.M., after Thanksgiving, Saturdays 8:45 A.M.–12:30 P.M.
GROUPS: Minimum age—upper elementary—should call the office in advance. Family groups may arrive unannounced. There is no charge for attending these working sessions, and you may stay for any part or all of a morning.

GBYSO is a nonprofit, self-supporting organization under the sponsorship of Boston University. It is composed of three orchestras: the Greater Boston Youth Symphony Orchestra, the GBYSO Repertoire Orchestra, and the GBYSO Wind Orchestra, which offer professional orchestral training to talented junior- and senior-high-school instrumentalists. The more than 300 student members come from Massachusetts, Rhode Island, New Hampshire, and Connecticut. Members are first recommended by their music directors and then selected by audition in the spring of each year. Concerts are given January-June in the Greater Boston area. When concerts are sponsored, there is an admission charge; other concerts are free.

NATIONAL THEATRE FOR CHILDREN   90 Sherman Street   Cambridge Tel. 661–0830

Performances: Year round at the Charles Playhouse, 76 Warrenton Street, Boston. Every Saturday.

Participatory theatre, semiprofessional company. Available for touring.

NEW ENGLAND CONSERVATORY OF MUSIC   290 Huntington Avenue Boston   Tel. 262–1120

Branch School: 169 Grove Street, Wellesley, Tel. 235–4156

If you wish notices of student recitals, vocal and instrumental programs, orchestral and operatic performances, request a place on the mailing list. Most concerts are free. Auditions for the New England Conservatory Youth Orchestra, Singers, Afro-American Youth Ensemble, and Massachusetts Youth Wind Ensemble are held in May and September. Teen-age musicians are eligible. Rehearsals are held Saturday afternoons throughout the school year.

Preparatory School: The minimum age for enrollment is 5. Classes in eurythmics, ensemble, and musicianship, private lessons for classical piano, voice, and orchestral instruments. There are fixed charges for the lessons, which are offered September-May.

Community Services: Offers a music education to those who are not in a position to afford lessons. It serves ages 6–60 and offers music education in ensemble playing, theory, private and class instrumental instruction.

OPERA COMPANY OF BOSTON   Administrative offices: 172 Newbury Street   Tel. 267–8050

Under the artistic direction of Sarah Caldwell, the company has received international recognition. Plans for young people vary from season to season and may include some performances during the day for children, in-school programs, dress rehearsals, a New England tour, or some special vacation production.

Regular subscriptions $12–$72 for 4 operas scheduled January-June. Student and group discounts available. Single tickets sold 2 weeks before performances.

PEABODY-MASON MUSIC FOUNDATION   P.O. Box 153, Back Bay Annex Boston   Tel. 262–4848

Admission: All tickets are free for the 6 or 7 concerts scheduled with performers from all over the world November-April. Most take place in Sanders Theater, Cambridge. The concerts begin at 8:30. Children under 10 are not admitted.

If you wish to receive this year's brochure (ready in September), send a letter with a self-addressed stamped envelope. (Announcements are also made in newspapers.) Then enclose a similar envelope with ticket requests, which should be postmarked no sooner than 1 month before a concert. Applications for each concert should be made separately and requests for more than 2 tickets must be made individually.

Non-ticket-holders may obtain some of the few tickets distributed at 7:45 the night of each concert or wait until 8:25 when any empty seats are available.

PLAYS FOR CHILDREN   (See New England Theatre Conference, p. 62.)

POCKET MIME THEATER   Performances in the Church of the Covenant 67 Newbury Street   Tel. 266–1770

Season: September-June.

Tickets: Reasonable (probably $2–$4).

Boston's resident mime company performs Thursday-Saturday nights for a young adult and adult audience. It is available for workshops, lecture demonstrations, and touring performances. Because its experience has shown that few mimes are necessarily child-oriented, a children's company will be formed to give regularly scheduled weekend performances this year. The theatre acts as a *clearinghouse* for mime information.

THE PROPOSITION   202 Hampshire Street   Cambridge   Tel. 661–1776   (theatre is at 241 Hampshire Street)

This improvised review with music has a 4-member cast that works from audience suggestions, and a pianist helps to create the mood for a series of skits. The performances for children are the Proposition Circus, using the same general framework. Call for the current location of the Circus.

Both shows are available for bookings. Workshops, lecture-demonstrations, and teacher-training workshops are offered periodically.

PUPPET SHOW PLACE   30 Station Street   Brookline Village   Tel.
731–6400

Ⓣ **Stop:** Brookline Village on Riverside Green Line and you are there!

Performances: Every weekend year round at 2 and 4 P.M. Some weekday programs given. Special bookings possible.

Tickets: $1 per person. Group rates available.

Length of Performances: 45 minutes.

At last! A central home for the world of puppets. It holds about 120 people
and most puppeteers spend some time with the audience after a performance.

The Puppet Show Place, as a center for the New England Guild of Puppetry, has visiting puppeteers, rents films, recommends lecturers, maintains a
news file, and has a display of books on puppetry. Handmade puppets and
books are for sale.

If you are looking for a puppet company to travel to your location, call.
If you are wondering about workshops at the Show Place or elsewhere, inquire.

SHAKESPEARE & CO.   539 Tremont Street (Boston Center for the Arts)
Tels. 426–5000, 542–0365

A touring company of four actors brings selections from Shakespeare and other
classical—and contemporary—drama to schools and community groups.
Classes are offered at the center for junior and senior high school students.

THEATER WORKSHOP OF BOSTON   551 Tremont Street (Boston Center
for the Arts)   Tel. 482–4778

As a center for environmental theatre production, this group offers plays for
adults and some participatory theatre for youngsters between the ages of 4
and 10. Call for this season's schedule.

In addition to performances: Workshops for children and entire families,
lecture-demonstrations for groups, and an acting growth program for all ages.

TOY CUPBOARD THEATRE AND MUSEUMS   57 East George Hill Road
South Lancaster 01561   Tel. 365–9519. (You are in apple and maple-
sugaring country, pp. 284, 297.)

Directions: Rt. 495 to 117 west to 110, then 1 mile south to South Lancaster.
Fork at five corners, Bolton Road to East George Hill Road.

Shows: July and August—Wednesdays and Thursdays at 2 and 3:30 P.M.; the
1st Saturday of the month September-June at 10:45 A.M. Puppets and
marionettes alternate each month year round. Shadow plays may also be
included on some puppet days. Send for folder.

Admission to Puppet Shows: 75¢ per person.

Museum Hours: Open on puppet show days, 1–6 P.M.

Museum Admission: Adults, 75¢; children under 12, 25¢.

Groups: Traveling programs, birthday parties with favors, and special presentations at the theatre can be arranged. Appointments should be made well
in advance for guided tours (minimum age: 6 or 7). Special group rate
(minimum: 30) is 75¢ per person for show and museum.

Picnicking (simple, please): Allowed on the grounds.

Step through one of the three archways of the little theatre (seats about 75), take your place on a pine bench, and view an adaptation of a children's classic performed from a puppet stage with a deep red curtain and footlights. Since 1941 presentations—geared for ages 3–10—have been given in the theatre, which was designed from a woodshed 200 years old, with pine-sheathed walls and pegged beams. After the 45-minute program you are invited backstage for a closer look at the puppets, which are constructed in such a manner that children can make and operate them themselves. Punch and cookies are served to everyone, and there are lollypops and balloons—all "on the house."

The Museums have delightful collections that are not really overwhelming for children. You may spend 30 minutes to an hour looking at cutouts (representing theatrical and movie personalities), which were once given as souvenirs, and some very old children's books. There are also toy and model theatres, puppets and marionettes from many countries, dollhouses, and toys. If you are enchanted by the paper dolls published before 1850, reissues with several elaborate costumes and headdresses are sold, uncolored, for $2.

The area is still a "typical New England village with colonial atmosphere." The charm seems to increase with each additional display facility. The Museums are RACKETTY-PACKETTY HOUSE—Mr. Hosmer's home—erected with parts of the house built on this site in 1690—with some history that provides a ghost story for today's visitors; THE LITTLE BOOK HOUSE (c. 1790), moved from the center of Lancaster in 1965 and restored in the form of an eighteenth-century dollhouse, and the Chicken Little Bookshop, now housing a growing collection of early juvenile books, originally one story high, and believed to have been the building of Carter and Andrews, publishers known for their wood engravings; part of the PUPPET THEATRE; and a proposed pavilion that will be an exact duplicate of the exterior of the theatre. The buildings face a small sunken garden, with stone figures of cherubs representing the seasons and a fountain of a boy riding a dolphin.

YOUNG AUDIENCES OF MASSACHUSETTS, INC.   74 Joy Street   Tel. 742–8520

The Massachusetts chapter of this national nonprofit organization provides vocal and instrumental performances of fine music and dance programs. Classroom workshops are scheduled either before or after the small professional ensembles give the youth-oriented presentations that are a combination of demonstrations, explanations, short selections, and question and answer periods. Although most concerts are given in schools, arrangements may be made by other groups who wish to support a particular concert.

YOUTH CONCERTS AT SYMPHONY HALL   251 Huntington Avenue Boston 02115 (corner of Massachusetts Avenue)   Tels. 266–1492, 267–0656

Held: Saturdays and some weekdays in November, January, March.

Admission: $7 per series of 3 concerts. Advance tickets for the annual sold-out series may be purchased through schools, or send a stamped self-addressed envelope to Anita Kurland, Symphony Hall, Boston. Some single tickets available the morning of the concerts at $3 each at the Symphony Hall Box Office.

Ages: Grades 5–9.

Harry Ellis Dickson, music director, conducts members of the Boston Symphony Orchestra in works of classical and contemporary composers in 1-hour concerts especially prepared for young people. Each concert has a specific theme and often includes dance, opera, narration, or other art media, in addition to the orchestra. Auditions for qualified high-school instrumental soloists are held periodically and the winners are invited to perform with the orchestra at a concert.

Ancient Instruments Room: Lectures and demonstrations on the ancient instruments before and after the concerts. (10–11 and 12–1 on Saturdays; 9–10 on weekdays.) Laning Humphrey discusses the evolution of the present-day instruments from the ancestors in the collection. Groups need reservations.

Film: Loans and Rentals

. . . Free loans and rentals are listed under "Motion Picture Film Libraries" in Yellow Pages.

Additional Film Resources:

ANTI-DEFAMATION LEAGUE OF B'NAI B'RITH   72 Franklin Street Boston 02110   Tel. 542–4977

The annotated catalog (free) includes age levels. Films range from about 8 minutes to full length, and rates are $3.50 to about $15. (There is an extensive publications library.)
    The purpose of ADL is to fight prejudice and discrimination as it relates to all groups in American life, to strengthen American democracy through the development of healthy intercultural attitudes, and to promote intergroup understanding. The films may be used as a springboard for discussion groups.

BOSTON PUBLIC LIBRARY   Copley Square   Boston   Tel. 536–5400

Films from the audio-visual department may be borrowed by registered organizations only. The catalog, which lists over 1,600 films and filmstrips, is revised every 2 years; two supplements are published in between. Use the catalog at the library or send a check for $5 for a copy. Bookings accepted Monday-Friday 9–5. Loan period is 3 days; 4 days over weekends.

CANADIAN CONSULATE GENERAL   500 Boylston Street   Boston 02116   Tel. 262–3760   Attention: John Doorneweerd

The catalog and supplement cover a wide range of interests and related subjects (ecology, history, folklore). Films in English and French. Heavily booked, particularly for school year. Early arrangements necessary. Records available in English, French, and Spanish. No charge. Bookings should be made at least 10 days in advance.

CONSUMER PRODUCT SAFETY COMMISSION   Boston Area Office 408 Atlantic Avenue   Boston 02110   Tel. 223–5576 (see p. 24).

Films that may be borrowed without charge concern fire hazards, toy safety, household poisons, and labeling. Speakers available for groups.

EDUCATIONAL DEVELOPMENT CENTER   Film Department   39 Chapel Street   Newton   Tel. 969–7100
Catalog available. Rentals $10–$45 for a 4-day period. All films relate to a specific area of education. Publications for sale.

ESPOUSAL CENTER   554 Lexington Street   Waltham   Tel. 893–3465
Catalog $1. Films pertain to education, religion, and entertainment. Rentals $2–$75.

The center offers workshops and programs for members of the helping professions, business people, and families interested in improving personal relations. It also offers retreats, trips, and film showings for various age and interest groups.

THE ABRAHAM KRASKER MEMORIAL FILM LIBRARY   Boston University.   School of Education   765 Commonwealth Avenue   Boston 02215   Tels. 353–3272, 353–3278
Annotated catalog of 8,000 educational 16mm films. Available to anyone, but rented (nominal rates) mostly by schools. The films are from many sources including National Educational Television.

MASSACHUSETTS AUDUBON SOCIETY   Great South Road   Lincoln 01773   Tel. 259–9500
Annotated list of films available. Rates: $7.50–$10 (one is free).

WESTON WOODS   Weston, Connecticut 06880, has its own films of outstanding children's books. Rental fees vary.

YELLOW BALL WORKSHOP   62 Tarbell Avenue   Lexington 02173   Tel. 862–4283
Descriptions of the short (4–20-minute) prize-winning 16mm color, sound, animated films by children—and rates—are included in a brochure with photographs. Write for a copy.

Film Showings

. . . Several commercial theatres are beginning to try to fill the void in good children's film programming. The newspapers carry their ads.

. . . Some of the better film programs (not necessarily youth-oriented) are at colleges and universities. Showings are sometimes free or under $1. Consult *The Boston Phoenix* or *The Real Paper.*

. . . Special film centers try to present a series of quality films. THE MAGIC LANTERN offers weekday showings for schools and possibly a Saturday series for the public. Call the Center Screen Film Society, 253–7612, to learn what is going on.

. . . Several commercial theatres offer group rates for regular performances and may arrange a special showing if the size of the group warrants it.

. . . The Boston Public Library, some of its branches, and some suburban community libraries regularly schedule children's films.

Radio and Television

PUBLIC RADIO AND TELEVISION
WGBH   125 Western Avenue   Boston 02134   Tel. 868–3800

Prime Time is the monthly calendar of programs for WGBH–TV, Channel 2, WGBX–TV, Channel 44, and WGBH Radio 89.7 FM. A 1-year subscription is sent to those who contribute $15 or more.

MASSACHUSETTS EDUCATIONAL TELEVISION   54   Rindge   Avenue
Cambridge 02140   Tel. 876–9800

Aired during in-school hours on Channel 2. These presentations—music, art, science, and more—are aired late September-early June (vacation periods excepted). The precocious young one, the sick school-aged child, and interested adults may well enjoy these programs at home or in the hospital.

> Because visual presentations are now woven into the fabric of daily living, there are few opportunities to listen and imagine.

A radio series of special note:

THE SPIDER'S WEB, WGBH–FM, 89.7, Monday-Friday at 12:30 and 6:30 P.M., a half-hour radio storybook presented by readers with extensive acting experience. Fantasy and folktales, biographies, stories of different lifestyles, and scripts from local authors are enhanced by carefully researched suitable music. Intended for ages 6–12. (Listeners often send in drawings of storybook characters.)

TELEVISION PARTICIPATORY POSSIBILITIES for youngsters differ from season to season. Call stations for current programming and audition arrangements. Age range could be from about 4 through high school.

Boston Television Stations:

Channel 2 WGBH and Channel 44 WGBX 125 Western Avenue, Allston, Tel. 868–3800

Channel 4 WBZ   1170 Soldiers Field Road, Brighton, Tel. 254–5670

Channel 5 WCVB   5 TV Place, Needham, Tel. 449–0400

Channel 7 WNAC   RKO General Building, Government Center, Tel. 742– 9000

Channel 38 WSBK   83 Leo Birmingham Parkway, Brighton, Tel. 783–3838

Channel 56 WLVI   75 Wm. T. Morrissey Blvd., Dorchester, Tel. 288–3200

Organization:

ACTION FOR CHILDREN'S TELEVISION   46 Austin Street   Newtonville   Tel. 527–7870

A small group of well-intentioned parents has grown to a highly respected national organization that is dedicated to child-oriented quality television without commercialism. In four years their efforts have resulted in reducing the number of commercial minutes per hour on children's television by 40 percent, the advertising of vitamins to children has been eliminated, and the practice of host-selling to children has been discontinued. ACT has also petitioned the Federal Trade Commission to issue a regulation banning all advertising for food, toys, and vitamins from children's television. It is an action-oriented, very human group.

Media Resource Library: Open to the public without charge. Used extensively by students, parents, educators, and adults working with children. It is a model collection of up-to-date materials including film catalogs, research studies, transcripts and speeches from congressional hearings, educational journals, newspaper clippings, and magazine articles. Here you may document answers to very practical questions.

Publications: Latest information with a newsletter ($1), Nutrition Survival Kit (50¢), *The Family Guide to Children's Television* ($2.95), and SWITCH!, an educational game for children about TV viewing ($1.50). Stay tuned. More to come, including publications about specialized topics relating to children's television. Membership $15. Subscription to quarterly $5.

Film: ". . . *but first, this message.*" Reactions from children and comments from professionals who work with children are included in this 15-minute film, which is often used as a springboard for discussion. Rental fee.

Resources and Organizations

. . . Not intended as a survey. Many of the following are clearinghouses for various art forms.

ADVISORY FOR OPEN EDUCATION   90 Sherman Street   Cambridge Tel. 661–0830

". . . a nonprofit trust, provides consultant services to public and independent schools, Headstart programs, day-care centers, colleges and universities . . . offers a cross-institutional setting where teachers, students, educational associations, and parents have a place, materials, and time to continue to learn and to integrate that learning into their lives." Marvelous facilities (p. 277).

Teachers' Book Shop: Open 9–9 Monday-Saturday. Most of the 3,000 titles are unavailable in the Boston area. For sale are books, published here and abroad, focusing on the arts for the classroom, environments, and special education.

BOSTON CENTER FOR THE ARTS   539 Tremont Street   Boston   Tel. 426–5000

Ⓣ **Stop:** Arlington on Green Line, 10-minute walk.

This is the home of various arts organizations, schools (opera, music, dance, theatre, architecture, photography), and artists' studios—all in a complex of eight buildings, including the National Theater. Exhibits, art galleries, and special events are scheduled throughout the year. Many of the groups have their own offices; the center acts as a clearinghouse of information for all of them.

It is an interesting complex. A garter factory space has been converted to a dance studio. The Cyclorama was originally built to house a 400-foot circular painting of the Battle of Gettysburg and since has seen varied uses, e.g., as a bicycle riding academy and most recently as a wholesale florists' market. Mae West, Bob Hope, and Gene Autry were among the vaudeville acts that once played in the enormous National Theatre.

CAMBRIDGE SCHOOL OF BALLET, INC.   15 J. R. Sellers Street   Cambridge 02139   Tel. 864–1557

A nonprofit educational organization offering graded classes in pre-ballet, elementary through advanced techniques, and pointe. The Cambridge Ballet Theatre, the performing student dance repertory company, is available for bookings.

Emphasis is placed upon preparatory professional training in classical ballet. Limited scholarships available.

CHILDREN'S NEIGHBORHOOD ART CENTER   515 Tremont Street   Tel. 262–6638

An outgrowth of a local seven-year-old program, this new location has plans to be a center for the metropolitan area. There will be an extensive afterschool program including everything from filmmaking to pottery on a registration basis, a summer program, a children's art gallery, which may eventually have an international exchange program, a drop-in visitors' area, a full program integrated with the public schools, and an artmobile available to Greater Boston communities. Much is dependent upon funding.

CHINESE CULTURAL CENTER   651 Beacon Street (Kenmore Square)   Tel. 266–3754

Open: Monday-Friday 3–9 P.M., Saturdays and Sundays 1–5.

Rotating exhibits open to the public without charge. Courses and workshops offered in several areas, including cooking, painting, and kung-fu; call for fees and schedules. Demonstrations (e.g., calligraphy and brush painting) may be arranged periodically.

THE COMMUNITY MUSIC CENTER OF BOSTON   48 Warren Avenue   Tel. 482–7494

This is a private, nonprofit organization that offers individual and group instruction in all areas of music for ages 3 and up. Fees are based on a sliding scale.

CREATIVE MUSIC THEATRE FOR CHILDREN is a performing workshop in improvisation, theatre games, dramatic music, and other theatre-related skills open to persons aged 9–14 by audition. Participants put on an original musical as an outgrowth of workshops.

COOPERATIVE ARTISTS INSTITUTE   6 Marmion Street   Jamaica Plain   Tel. 521–0560

CAI is a resource center and consulting firm for schools, community and arts groups, and cultural organizations. Its approach to integrating arts with everyday life has been applied to both short- and long-term and year-long arts programs. Programs and workshops are designed for all ages, preschool through adult, and are readily adaptable to a special education context.

EDUCATIONAL ARTS ASSOCIATION   90 Sherman Street   Cambridge   Tel. 661–0830

This is an international organization of educators, arts specialists, and community leaders who have a collective commitment to the concept that the arts must be an integral and accustomed part of the general education of all children at the preschool, elementary, and secondary levels.

Locally it offers workshops for teachers in ways to use the arts in the classroom.

Publication: *New · ways.* A most informative newsletter with articles, suggestions, and resources published jointly by EAA and the Advisory for Open Education (p. 59). One year $6.

FOLKSONG SOCIETY OF GREATER BOSTON   P.O. Box 137   Cambridge 02138   Tel. 965–2696

People who are actively interested and involved in traditional folk music have formed this marvelous organization. The involvement varies from just listening to performing. There are monthly evening concerts with a special guest, periodic workshops, singing parties, and family picnics, as well as fall and spring getaway weekends. An extensive newsletter is published monthly September-June; it includes a complete calendar of upcoming folk events for children and adults.

Membership: $3 includes newsletter and reduced admission at FSS concerts.

If you are interested in professional children's performers, this organization can help. Inquire. Tels. 965–2696, 244–0144.

THE JOY OF MOVEMENT CENTER   536 Massachusetts Avenue   Cambridge   Tel. 492-4680

Offers courses year round in about 50 different forms of dance, including calypso, flamenco, Chinese classical, tap, ballet, folk, and belly dancing. It is all for the joy of the experience. (Fees charged; series of classes scheduled seasonally.)

The staff is interested in promoting sessions for the elderly, the blind, preschoolers, and special children, as well as family sessions.

THE LEARNING GUILD   551 Tremont Street   Tel. 426–0101

This ever-expanding group represents people interested and involved in the performing arts, theatre, music, dance, arts and crafts, education, literature and language, and personal, spiritual, and body development. The guild gives workshops and will custom-tailor a program or series.

MASSACHUSETTS ASSOCIATION OF CRAFTSMEN

If you are interested in demonstrations and/or lectures, the association can refer you to specific members. This is a professional organization representing all the crafts (e.g., batik, woodworking, enamel, jewelry, pottery, weaving). Contact: Cyrus Lipsitt, President, 9 Glen Avenue, Arlington, Tel. 646–6161.

MASSACHUSETTS COUNCIL ON THE ARTS AND HUMANITIES   14 Beacon Street   Boston 02108   Tel. 727–3668

As the state agency that reflects the Commonwealth's concern for the arts, artists, and audiences, it "encourages development of talent, supports excellence in programs and services, makes the arts and hmanities widely available to everyone in Massachusetts, preserves cultural heritage, and strengthens our cultural organizations." Just how much the council accomplishes often depends on the budget. Call or write for information about current grants and activities. The council is in a position to answer all questions. It has the answer or at least can start you on the right track.

Publication: A newsletter on council activities and news in the field is published occasionally and is issued without charge. If you would like a place on the mailing list, send a written request to the council.

METROPOLITAN CULTURAL ALLIANCE   37 Newbury Street   Tel. 247–1460

This is a service organization to nonprofit cultural institutions in Greater Boston. It was established to increase communications among the organizations, strengthen their management abilities, and support collaborative efforts. Individuals may join.

Two useful publications are the monthly calendar ($5 annually to nonmembers), which covers events of member organizations, and *Culture Cracks the Blackboard* ($1.50), a book that details the facilities and offerings (particularly to schools) of the 95 participating members.

THE NATIONAL CENTER OF AFRO-AMERICAN ARTISTS
Within the Center: **Elma Lewis School of Fine Arts**   122 Elm Hill Avenue
(at Seaver Street across from Franklin Park)   Roxbury   Tel. 442–8820

Elma Lewis knows the community and its potential. She has established the center as an important place with year-round programs and classes.

... More than 400 classes are given weekly in all art disciplines, including costuming, dance, theatre, music, and crafts.
... Professional and student groups are available for touring.
... Prison inmates receive instruction in all the arts.
... The museum has changing exhibits with works by black American, West Indian, and African artists.

Mobile Museum: Varying exhibits of several cultures (African, Afro-Caribbean, and Afro-American) with touchable objects, including sculpture, masks, traditional headdresses, musical instruments, dance costumes, religious artifacts, and utilitarian objects. Audio-visual aids show how the materials were originally used. Call for travel schedule and arrangements.

Annual Events: *Celebration,* a June extravaganza by black performers, free entertainment nightly over a 3-month summer period in Franklin Park, and *Black Nativity* tours in December.

NEW ENGLAND THEATRE CONFERENCE   Executive Secretary: Marie L. Philips   50 Exchange Street   Waltham 02154   Tel. 893–3120 (after 5:30 P.M.)

This is a nonprofit association of individuals and theatre-producing groups in New England, who, either professionally or as an avocation, are actively engaged in or have a particular interest in theatre: children's, secondary school, college, and university, as well as community or professional.

Memberships: Start at $7.50 for individuals, $3.50 for students. Mailings include bimonthly newsletter of events and productions throughout New England.

Programming: Workshops and conferences are open to the public, usually at a guest fee of $1–$3. Interested young people are welcome at these gatherings, which are usually organized around a production (or several) and its evaluation, at discussions and demonstrations of technical aspects of a production, and at sessions with a notable speaker. Annual children's theatre program.

Services: If you are interested in scheduling a performance locally for children, Miss Philips has the most complete list of all theatre-producing groups, including children's, in New England. You then write directly to the group for booking information.

OFFICE OF CULTURAL AFFAIRS   Boston City Hall   Boston 02201
Tel. 722–4100, ext. 497, organizes *Summerthing*, Boston's Neighborhood Festival, which presents thousands of performances and workshops each summer. Members of various Boston communities work closely with OCA. It is also responsible for ARTSLINE (p. 22), June Art in the Park (p. 290), the City Hall Galleries, and multicultural festivals.

OLD SCHWAMB MILL (p. 123).

PINEBANK ART CENTER IN THE PARK   The Jamaicaway   Boston
Tel. 522–2503 (keep trying). It is located on Jamaica Pond next to the Park and Recreation Boat House. Boston residents are eligible for the free instruction offered year round in all the visual and performing arts. Minimum age: 8. Evening sessions for adults.

POETS WHO TEACH   11 Loring Street   Newton Centre   Tel. 332–3760
In recent years thousands of children and adults have had the opportunity (in small groups) to work with poets through a Massachusetts Council on Arts and Humanities program and independent arrangements. Recently formed, Poets Who Teach is a nonprofit organization that provides single workshops or a series to schools (all levels) and community institutions.

SOCIETY OF ARTS AND CRAFTS   69 Newbury Street   Tel. 266–1810
Open: Tuesday-Saturday 10–5. No admission charge.

Professional contemporary crafts are exhibited in a small second-floor area. Everything is for sale, or a sample can be special ordered. Touching sometimes allowed. Children should be accompanied by an adult. Call if you wish to bring a group. The intimacy provides a marvelous atmosphere for looking at beautiful creations.

Note: The society is accumulating a library of books, periodicals, and films to be made available to the public.

WHEELOCK COLLEGE   200 The Riverway   Tel. 734–5200
The students have a touring company in schools in December and the spring. Other presentations (story theatre, traditional theatre, musicals, and new material) are given at Wheelock in January and February.

YOUTH PRO MUSICA   7 Eisenhower Avenue   Natick 01760   Tel. 653–1092

This is a community chorus, an affiliate of Chorus Pro Musica of Boston, and is open to 60 boys and girls (unchanged voices) between 9 and 15. Its repertoire extends from pre-baroque to contemporary literature. Admission is by audition. Rehearsals are held Wednesdays in West Newton. For specific information about membership or performances, contact Roberta Humez.

DAY TRIPS

. . . Picnic lunches may save time, money, and nerves.

. . . There is always more to see than time allows. Start early.

. . . Some readers are very energetic and go far afield for day trips. Others find that confinement has its limitations. Some *survival suggestions* (there is no magic formula): Pack snacks, books, or wrapped surprises for children. Start a story and let others finish it. Count categories of things you see en route. Find signs that begin with every letter of the alphabet. Stop at a playground along the way.

. . . See p. 13 for field-trip suggestions.

Day Trip Organizations

MYSTIC VALLEY RAILWAY SOCIETY, INC.   P.O. Box 32   Mattapan

The main thrust of this organization is to make people aware of the field of transportation through trips. It annually conducts 6 public railroad tours throughout New England. Other trips range from 1 to 3 days and may go as far as Pennsylvania Dutch country. Membership is not necessary for participation in trips. Families are welcome.

Mailings: First 3 arrive free, after that only sent to members.

Membership: $2, families $3.

Other organizations that have day trips open to individuals and families are:
SIERRA CLUB, p. 204.
APPALACHIAN MOUNTAIN CLUB, p. 200.
AMERICAN YOUTH HOSTELS, p. 213.
The opportunities with all these organizations vary and usually include some active participation: hiking, cycling, mountain climbing, exploration of a particular site, or cross-country skiing.

Places

CAPE COD NATIONAL SEASHORE (p. 197)

CONCORD

20 miles northwest of Boston

Train: From North Station, Tel. 227–5070. Note off-peak fare information, p. 28.

When you have had enough of sight-seeing, try Walden Pond (crowded around beach) or Great Meadows Wildlife Refuge (not usually crowded anywhere). Or paddle a canoe (p. 215).

Eating: Picnic at Fiske Hill (see below) or Walden Pond, p. 195. Brigham's (on Main Street) and Friendly's (on Sudbury Road).

Suggestions: THE COUNTRY STORE at 15 Monument Street has penny (2¢) candy; open Monday-Saturday 8:30–5:30. ANDERSON'S on Main Street has fresh fruit in street stalls. If youngsters are the HOUSE TOUR type, you may wish to select the Antiquarian Museum from the many possibilities. BICYCLES are for rent behind Kussins, 79 Main Street, in the center of town. The train is having a comeback of sorts in Concord. And there within the CONCORD DEPOT is a palatable mini-mall. At the moment it is open 6 days a week; it may be 7 someday. Even if you are not the shopping or browsing type, go in. There are several shops, yes, but maybe best of all is the penny scale or old gumball machine (with a mirror—remember?)—and they really work for 1¢. Railroad memorabilia include bells that you can ring, a locomotive headlight, all sorts of signs (one directs you to a parlor car). The depot offers local maps, guides, tourist and bus information. It publishes its own Boston and Maine railroad schedules. A big find: PUBLIC REST ROOMS.

There is a lot to see and do in this very peaceful town. Here are some of the places grouped by proximity:

. . . Wright Tavern near the Information Booth in Concord Center
. . . Railroad Station, Thoreau Lyceum
. . . Emerson House, Antiquarian Museum
. . . Orchard House, The Wayside, Original Concord Grapevine—and a few miles down the road, Fiske Hill
. . . Sleepy Hollow Cemetery, Great Meadows National Wildlife Refuge
. . . Old North Bridge, Old Manse

THE CONCORD ANTIQUARIAN MUSEUM   (Box 146)   200 Lexington Road   Tel. 369–9609
Open: Mid-March–October, Monday-Saturday 10–4:30; Sundays 2–4:30. Closed Easter.

Admission: Adults, $1.50; children under 15, 75¢. Group rates available.

Handicapped: Turnstile and 3 steps in front. Once inside everything accessible.

One of the two lanterns that hung in the Old North Church on the night of Paul Revere's famous ride is here. There is a Thoreau room with the bed he slept in at Walden, his flute, and surveying instruments. There is a replica of Ralph Waldo Emerson's study with its original furnishings. Outside the house you will find an herb garden and flowers from the nearby gardens of Emerson, Hawthorne, and Alcott. It takes about 45 minutes for the guided tour through 17 rooms with furnishings of the seventeenth–nineteenth centuries. Visitors will see the changing life-styles over 200 years.
  "We welcome young people, although those under the age of second grade may be restless."

GRAPEVINE COTTAGE   491 Lexington Road
The original Concord grapevine bears grapes in September. People are welcome to read the plaque on Lexington Road and come into the yard to view the vine.
  Ephraim Wales Bull never received the proper remuneration for his cultivation of the Concord grape. He hybridized several more that may have been superior to the Concord, but he would not market them because he felt he had been cheated. He died a poor embittered old man on the Concord "Poor Farm."
  Grapevine Cottage is one of the oldest Concord houses. It was owned by various blacksmiths until 1790.

THE OLD MANSE   Monument Street   Tel. 369–3909
Open: April 19-June 1 and October 15-November 11 weekends only. June 1-October 15 daily, Monday-Saturday 10–4:30, Sundays 1–4:30.

Admission: Adults, $1; children 14 and under, 35¢. Educational group rates available.

Guided Tours: For students of at least junior-high age who are studying American literature. One half hour.

The home that Ralph Waldo Emerson's grandfather, the Reverend William

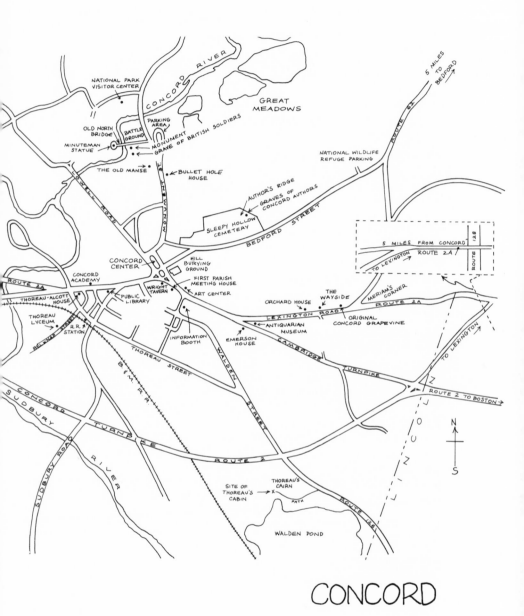

CONCORD

Emerson, occupied during the Revolution later became the home of Nathaniel Hawthorne, and has essentially seen no changes since it was built. You can see diamond writing on the windowpanes done by the Hawthornes, and original wallpaper and furnishings dating back to 1769.

"Very young children are apt to be a bit bored. They are welcome, however, if they are well-behaved."

R. W. EMERSON HOUSE   28 Cambridge Turnpike   Tel. 369–2236

Open: April 1-November 1, Monday–Saturday 10–5, Sundays 2–5. Last tour leaves at 4:30.

Admission: Adults, $1; children under 12, 25¢; students, 50¢.

A 30-minute tour is provided through the house, which is just as Mr. Emerson left it—except for a few modern conveniences such as lights.

ORCHARD HOUSE OF THE LOUISA MAY ALCOTT MEMORIAL ASSOCIATION   399 Lexington Road (Rt. 2A)   Tel. 369–4118

Open: Mid-April–mid-November, Monday-Saturday 10–4:30 and Sundays 1–4:30. Closed Easter.

Handicapped: First floor accessible to wheelchairs.

Admission: Adults, $1; children under 16, 50¢. Group rates available on weekdays only. (Not recommended for under second grade.)

A half-hour tour is given through the house of Louisa May Alcott, the author of *Little Women* and *Little Men*. "Quiet children are welcome."

Note: Educational preparatory packets are free to groups. Theatrical packets on the Alcotts' interest in dramatics can be purchased by children's groups for $1.25. A Victorian game packet can be rented ($3) by appointment.

SLEEPY HOLLOW CEMETERY

Directions: Turn on Bedford Street off Monument Street near Concord Center.

The second entrance leads you to Author's Ridge, with the graves of Emerson, Thoreau, the Alcotts, Nathaniel Hawthorne, and Margaret Sidney. If you are thinking twice about whether to go to this site or not—go. The setting is quite beautiful. It is a place that out-of-towners see and many Boston-area residents miss.

Handicapped: Some areas are very hilly.

THE THOREAU LYCEUM   156 Belknap Street   Tel. 369–5912

Directions: From Old North Bridge go through Concord Center on Main Street, pass library, turn left on Thoreau, and take first right.

Open: Year round, every day Monday-Saturday 10–5, Sundays 2–5. Closed Christmas, New Year's Day, April 19, July 4, Memorial Day, and Labor Day.

Admission: Adults, 50¢; children, 25¢; students, 35¢.

Minimum Age for Groups: 1st grade. Tour can be adapted to age group.

Handicapped: Door too narrow for wheelchair.

The Thoreau Lyceum is dedicated to preserving the image and ideals of the Concord naturalist writer-philosopher. It has a library, natural history room, and changing exhibitions based on the world of nature through photographs and paintings as well as Concord history and literature. Memorabilia on display includes survey maps, letters, pictures, and possessions of Thoreau and his family. A replica of the Walden House has been built behind the Lyceum.

"The whole set up is so different from the usual 'historic' house. We are very loosely structured so that we can provide the visitor with the kind of information he needs. Since Thoreau had so many interests and talents, there is something for everybody which is why we really have no age limits."

MINUTE MAN NATIONAL HISTORICAL PARK
Tel. 369–6993

Directions: Massachusetts Turnpike and Rt. 128 North to 2A.

Open: 8 A.M. until sunset year round.

Admission: Free. No parking fee.

Parts of Lincoln, Lexington, and Concord are being developed into the Minute Man National Historical Park. It will include up to 750 acres and embrace many homes of 1775 vintage and the foundation remains of others. By removal of modern buildings and restoration of the landscape and historic houses, the park scene will gradually be returned to the appearance of April 19, 1775, the opening day of the Revolutionary war.

Special Services: Available for organized groups if advance arrangements are made. Write: Superintendent, Minute Man National Historical Park, P.O. Box 160, Concord, Massachusetts 01742, or telephone. Available: Short historical talks at the North Bridge area. Orientation visits (self-guided) to sites where archaeological work has been or is in progress (summers only). Off-site talks for local groups within a 25-mile radius of the park. As personnel are available, speakers will be provided upon reasonable advance notice to present illustrated talks about the events of April 19, park development, or the National Park System. No fees are charged for this service.

NORTH BRIDGE VISITOR CENTER

Directions: Follow signs from Concord Center out Lowell Road to Liberty Street, or a 10-minute walk from the North Bridge.

Open: Daily 8–5, summer hours 8–6. Parking area near building. Rest rooms provided.

Handicapped: Ramp available.

Presentations: 12-minute audio-visual program every half hour. Special living history programs presented by costumed volunteers and staff include musket-firing drills, eighteenth-century town meetings, craft demonstrations, and eighteenth-century children's games at various times during the summer. Most programs take place Saturday and Sunday afternoons.

Exhibits and informational services are provided at the center, which is located in the former Buttrick Mansion built in 1911. The building, which was on the property when the land was acquired, has beautifully landscaped grounds.

OLD NORTH BRIDGE

Parking: Parking areas at Visitor Center or on Monument Street.

Note: You can enter Great Meadows Wildlife Refuge near parking area across the street from Old North Bridge.

Talks (20 minutes): Given by ranger historians near the bridge, on the hour, 9–5 June-September, on weekends in the spring and fall, and by request at other times.

Here, on the morning of April 19, 1775, advancing Americans drove off a detachment of British regulars in a brief but noted clash. The bridge, the fourth reproduction built at the scene of "the shot heard round the world," is pleasant at dusk, during the summer heat, after a snowfall, with spring blossoms or fall foliage. Daniel Chester French's statue of the Minuteman is located nearby. If you walk (5–10 minutes, hot in the summer) the road between the Visitor Center and the bridge, you will tread on about 200 feet of the restored road along which the Patriots marched in 1775. The location was uncovered by archaeologists who had studied a rare map of 1792.

THE WAYSIDE
Lexington Road (1 mile east of Concord Square on Rt. 2A)

Open: April 1-June and September 1-October 31 10–5:30; closed Tuesdays and Wednesdays. Summer: Daily 10–5:30.

Admission: Adults, 75¢; under 16, free.

This was the home of Samuel Whitney, Muster Master of the Concord Minutemen on April 19, 1775. Nathaniel Hawthorne, the Alcotts, and Margaret Sidney, author of *The Five Little Peppers* books, also lived here. The house is decorated as it was when Margaret Sidney lived there from 1883 to 1924. Tours average 45 minutes, are limited to 6 people per tour. No reservations accepted.

FISKE HILL INFORMATION STATION
Near intersection of Rts. 2A and 128 in Lexington

Open: 8 A.M. to sunset. Closed during winter months.

Picnic Area: Located in a wooded glen. No fires.

Parking Area: No charge.

Handicapped: All accessible. Level ground.

A shelter with exhibits and a recorded message provides visitor information. Park personnel on duty during summer months. A 1-mile self-guided historical trail with markers leads across old fields and over the wooded height of Fiske Hill to the foundation remains of the eighteenth-century Fiske farmhouse.

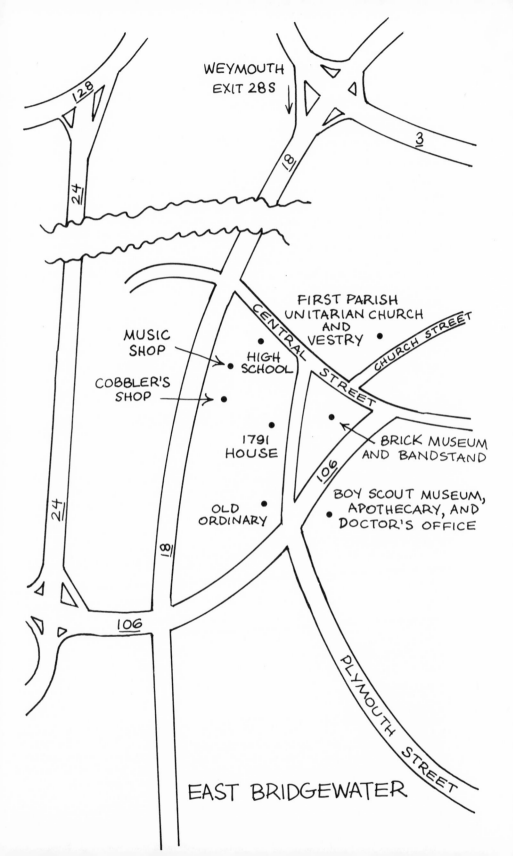

WEYMOUTH
EXIT 28S

128

24

18

3

FIRST PARISH
UNITARIAN CHURCH
AND
VESTRY

CENTRAL STREET

CHURCH STREET

MUSIC
SHOP

HIGH
SCHOOL

COBBLER'S
SHOP

BRICK MUSEUM
AND BANDSTAND

1791
HOUSE

106

BOY SCOUT MUSEUM,
APOTHECARY, AND
DOCTOR'S OFFICE

OLD
ORDINARY

24

18

106

PLYMOUTH STREET

EAST BRIDGEWATER

EAST BRIDGEWATER

35 miles from Boston off Rts. 106 and 18

Directions: Rt. 128 south, Rt. 24, Rt. 106 east, Rt. 18N to East Bridgewater Center, sharp right onto Central Street

Cycling: Contact AYH, p. 213, for a detailed map (15¢). Generally Rt. 3 to Rt. 18.

West Bridgewater is still another town. But it is East Bridgewater that Reverend Paul John Rich has changed. He has been the minister at the Unitarian Church for about 15 years—and is responsible for the museums and dozens of programs that are open to the public—as well as many more with and for the community. Please note that he says that "we prefer opportunities to get to know people rather than tourists."

Four additions have been built onto the 1723 church, an aluminum spire has replaced one damaged by a hurricane, and the box pews have been rearranged. Services are at 11 A.M. Sunday mornings in what Reverend Rich calls "the largest liberal church on the South Shore." You may never have heard a sermon such as his.

The town Common, property of the church, has the Ames House with a mannequin watching color television 24 hours a day; its message is carried through by having the house face the new bandstand "where people do things."

One way to spend some time here is through membership in American Youth Hostels, p. 213, because the Canadian Pacific Railway sleeper *Rosemere* is parked next to the church and used as a hostel. It is heated and open year round.

The choice of activities is immense:

Nature Trails: Marked through woods and fields.

Eating: Picnicking allowed in town forest on Bridge Street near Central. The Joppa Grill is in the center of town. Saturday night church suppers ($1.50) are at 6 P.M. and open to the public. Pick-your-own blueberry farm (p. 291).

THE STANDISH MUSEUMS, restored old buildings, are constantly increasing. They are minutes from each other, are subject-oriented, and not overwhelming in size. It is possible to sustain the interest of non-museum-going youngsters in these exhibits.

Open: Year round, Monday-Saturday 10–5, Sundays 1–5.

Admission: For the major houses it is $1; smaller museums usually included in major house fee. Art gallery and church exhibits are free.

THE BRICK MUSEUM has tools, machines, molds, and photos relating to the craft of the brickmaker. It is located under the bandstand on the beautifully landscaped town Common. WASHINGTON'S APRON includes a rare collection of books, manuscripts, and Revolutionary War currency in the Old Ordinary. THE SCOUTING MUSEUM is rivaled only by the collections at national Boy Scout headquarters in New Jersey and has posters, founder Lord Baden Powell books, pictures, merit badges. APOTHECARY SHOP AND DOCTOR'S OFFICE has a fantastic collection of bottles and tools once common in the medical world. Phonographs, sheet music, a piano, and paintings are in the MUSIC HOUSE. There is a MODEL RAILROAD building and a COBBLER'S

SHOP. By the time you arrive, other plans may have come to fruition: a blacksmith shop, Greek and Egyptian Revival Museum, windmill and waterwheel, fountains, large herb gardens, even tunnels between properties.

Reverend Rich recently designed a GRAVESTONE WALK: "Go through playground, by anchor and swings, past rear of church with Revere Bell, straight to circle (Millet, famous artist and war reporter, buried near circle), keep left around back of Catholic Church, sharp left until oldest section comes in view. Old part has many interesting carvings—graves of ministers and colonial leaders, odd inscriptions. Return by main road." (Gravestone rubbing allowed in old burying ground right behind the Unitarian Church.)

THE SATUCKET CYCLE CENTER, open daily, has pollution-free transportation at hourly rates.

Open: Monday-Thursday 2:30–8, Fridays 2:30–6, Saturdays 8–8, Sundays 1–6.

. . . People-powered vehicles (three-wheelers that seat two and can be used on a special course), $1

. . . The Satucket River (no swimming) can be used for paddle boats ($2.50) or canoeing ($2.50)

. . . Tandem bicycles are $2.50 per hour, three- and ten-speed bicycles $1.50

SATUCKET BIKE TRAIL, a 7½-mile (moderate) bike route, takes you through the town on quiet streets.

EDAVILLE RAILROAD

South Carver   Tel. 866–4526

40 miles south of Boston, off Rt. 58 (follow signs)

Directions: Southeast Expressway, Rt. 3 to 44 to 58, or Rt. 3 to 18 to 58, or Rt. 128 to 24 to 25 to 58, follow signs.

Open: Spring: Sundays in April, May, and early June, plus Memorial Day 12–5. Summer: Mid-June–Labor Day, daily 10–5:30, Sundays 12–5:30. Fall: Labor Day–mid-October Monday-Friday 10:30–3 (diesel engine); Saturdays, Sundays, and holidays 12–5 (steam engine).

Admission: Combination ticket (train and museum); Adults, $2.40; children, $1.20. Admission to grounds and train ride: Adults, $2; children under 12, $1. Group rates available for minimum of 15. A few extras (optional): Rides such as a Model T for 35¢.

Where to Eat: Snack bar on grounds. Barbecued chicken dinner—Adults, $2.50; children, $1.90. Served last weekend in May, every Sunday in June, daily late June through Labor Day, fall Sundays. Picnic tables provided in a grove.

The half-hour ride on the old-fashioned steam train, built in 1907, on 5½ miles of narrow gauge railroad through woods and Cape Cod cranberry bogs, is the real "draw" for coming. If you go during late summer or fall, there is the opportunity to see the bogs being "wet" or "dry" picked, as the train slows down in the appropriate area. But there are other attractions: Plenty of "touch" possibilities for curious youngsters. The Bridgton and Saco car has a wooden interior and seats that "go either way." Climb on steamrollers or into the cab of a train. Walk among displays of flowers and lawns. Surprises include the charming carousel that was built in 1858 in Amsterdam, Holland.

The Edaville Museum (no touching here) is quite extensive and provides something of interest for everyone. Look in the windows of the re-created nineteenth-century village; while you are noticing the scene in the drugstore, barbershop, or clothier's, youngsters may be reading the fine print on the toothache gum label. Elsewhere in the museum are large displays of antique autos, horse-drawn fire equipment, the largest collection of toy trains in America, a collection of Kentucky rifles, and all sorts of railroad memorabilia.

It is an active, sometimes noisy place that has a touch of an amusement park-mixed-in-with nostalgia kind of atmosphere about it.

FALL RIVER

45 miles southeast of Boston

Directions: Rt. 128 south to Rt. 24 to Rt. 195 West, Exit 11. You park in one place and walk to all the attractions.

Know your interests—and those of your youngsters. To some this is a thrilling experience. Others may view much of it as something they would rather avoid.

Combined Admission (includes admission to all three ships and the Marine Museum): Adults, $3; children 6–13, $1.25; children 2–5, 50¢.

Open: Year round daily except Thanksgiving and Christmas. May-October, 9–5, November-April, 9–4:30.

Average Length of Visit: 2 hours on the ships.

The Ships:

U.S.S. LIONFISH   Tour this first. It is a quick down-and-out tour through the submarine, which may actually be rather frightening to very young children.

U.S.S. MASSACHUSETTS   State Pier   Tel. 678–1100

The entire main deck area (twice the size of a football field) is open and there is plenty of up-down-back-and-forth in order to see the forecastle, the stern, the ward room (snack bar open here daily in summer and weekends during other seasons), the open bridge, the conning tower, and galleys where meals were prepared for over 2,300 officers and men. There are knobs and wheels to turn, guns to aim, and turrets to climb. Taped information and sound effects at each of 48 stations give an idea of what life on board was like.

THE U.S.S. JOSEPH P. KENNEDY, JR.   The destroyer launched just after World War II saw service during the Korean and Vietnam conflicts. Only the outer deck is open. A memorial room to men and women who died in Korea and Vietnam is expected to open soon.

It is possible that other ships will be added to the grouping.

The other major attraction at Battleship Cove:

MARINE MUSEUM   Battleship Cove   Tel. 674–3533

Open: Year round, Monday-Friday 9–5, weekends and holidays 12–5. Closed Thanksgiving, Christmas, and New Year's Day.

Admission: Adults, $1.25; children under 12, 75¢. Group rates available.

Membership Fees: From $10.

Parking: Free.

Groups: Guided tours (1–2 hours) provided. One week advance notice required. Minimum age: 1st grade. Minimum number: 15.

Viewing level of children has been taken into consideration for the ship models from the Seamen's Church Institute of New York. The smallest model is ½ inch and the most spectacular is the 14-foot builder's model of the Fall River Line steamer, *Puritan.* Many varieties of crafts are represented, but steamships dominate.

Slide Presentations: One on modern whaling and one on the history of the Fall River Line, which terminated its 90-year service in 1937.

Arts and Crafts Corner: Someone is at work some of the time—perhaps a scrimshaw artist, a wood-carver, or a modelmaker.

Note

Fall River and New Bedford (p. 179) have many manufacturers who have factory outlets. Pick up brochure, *Bargain Hunter's Paradise,* at information booth for directions to: Raincoat Outlet, 1637 Main Street (men's and women's outercoats and raincoats), open Monday-Saturday; Fall River Knitting Mills, 69 Alden Street (men's, women's, and children's sweaters and sportswear), open Monday-Saturday; Fall River Dress Discount Center, 69 Alden Street (women's dresses, skirts, slacks, blouses, remnants), open Monday-Saturday; Darwood Manufacturing Co., 18 Pocasset Street (men's and young men's clothing, outerwear, slacks), open Monday-Saturday; Fashion Outlet, 305 Pleasant Street (women's apparel, dresses, slacks, skirts, blouses), open Tuesday-Saturday; M & G Sportswear, 451 Quarry Street (boys' and girls' clothing, jackets, coats, slacks, suits, yard goods), open Monday-Saturday.

GLOUCESTER

30 miles north of Boston

Train: B & M from North Station, Tel. 227–5070. (Note off-peak rate information, p. 28.)

. . . Out of season visitors have a chance to park at choice beaches (p. 209).

. . . If you come into town from Rt. 128 and Rt. 133, turn right for Stage Fort Park, left for the harbor and the town.

. . . East Gloucester with Beauport and the scenic shore drive is along Rt. 127A.

. . . On the way along Rt. 128, near Exit 15 in West Gloucester, stop at Mt. Ann Park for a short (15-minute) climb to the top of the highest point on Cape Ann. Great view. Shady glen two-thirds way up with picnic tables. No admission charge. No rest rooms.

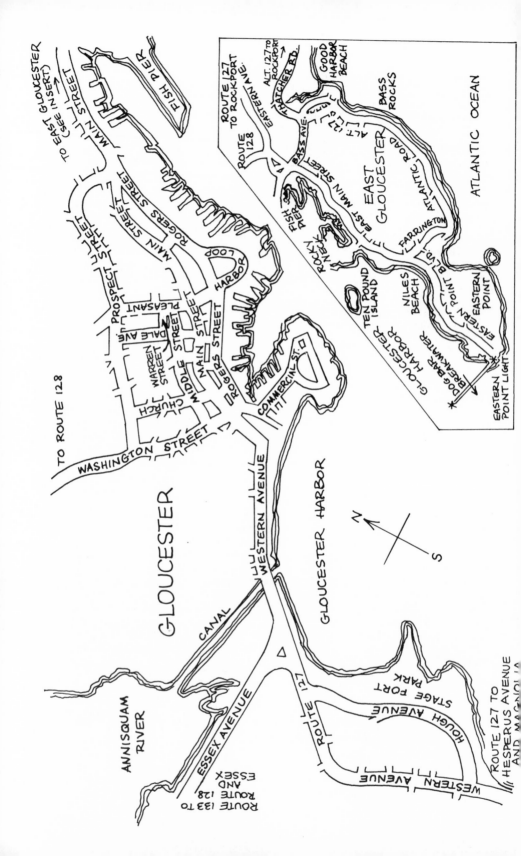

... You are more likely to go to specific places in Gloucester rather than browse through the town.

... Hammond Museum could be the (indoor) lure to find the outdoor exploring possibilities in spring or fall when traffic is not so heavy.

... DOGTOWN is an area that had about 100 families in the 1700s. It was deserted and never developed again. Remains of foundations can be found along the twisting paths. Unless you have a strong sense of direction or lots of time, it is recommended that you go with a leader from an outdoor group (p. 67) that schedules such ventures from time to time. Every path seems to fork every hundred feet!

Restaurants: Bob's Clam Shack on East Main Street is open early April-November. Closed Mondays pre- and post-season. Can eat inside or out. Sawyer's Lobster Pool—on ocean in back of Fitz Hugh Lane house. New porch restaurant. Eat outside only. Summer 11 A.M. –9 P.M., fall and spring 11–6.

Picnicking: Stage Fort Park is essentially right in town.

IN TOWN

STAGE FORT PARK. Plenty of room for flying saucers, picnicking, and rock climbing. The site was used as a defense fort during the Revolution and the War of 1812. A tablet announces that this was the first permanent settlement of the Massachusetts Bay Colony. (For parking fees in summer, see p. 209.)

There is nothing "to do" at the FISHERMAN STATUE, but this memorial to those who have "gone down to the sea in ships" is important to the area. As you look out to sea, there is a stretch of land to the left; that is Dog Bar Breakwater on Eastern Point. Although it is possible to walk on it, because of high tides and winds it is not recommended. Follow Western Avenue to the area of Gloucester House Restaurant and a public parking area. There are plenty of fishing boats in the HARBOR even though the industry is seeing hard times. The fish plants are now principally distribution centers for frozen blocks received from other countries. (Gloucester is where Clarence Birdseye developed the first method of freezing and cutting fillets into controlled portions for breaded fish sticks.) Walk onto the HARBOR LOOP, which has a small park near the Fitz Hugh Lane house, once the home of the artist and later used as a jail. At this writing restoration of the Lane house has just been completed, and plans to open it to the public have not been formulated. On the Harbor Loop is the GLOUCESTER MARINE RAILWAYS CORPORATION. (It also has a location in East Gloucester.) It is the nearest facility of its kind to Boston. Work is done mostly on wooden boats, occasionally on steel. If the exterior is being repaired, you may be able to see rib cages and all; if it is interior work, you may see nothing at all. Once in a while there may be hauling or launching of a boat; take your chances. It is an unusual out-of-water close-up view.

Two historic houses in the area
are open during the summer:

CAPT. ELIAS DAVIS HOUSE   27 Pleasant Street
Open: June 15-September 15, weekdays 1 –4.

Admission: $1.

The home of the Cape Ann Scientific, Literary and Historical Association has many exhibits of Gloucester's history, including a display of fishing boats, models and fishing gear, scale models of brigantines, schooners, and other vessels, and 33 Fitz Hugh Lane paintings and drawings.

THE SARGENT-MURRAY-GILMAN-HOUGH HOUSE (1768)   49 Middle Street   Tel. 283 –4505

Open: July-September 15, weekdays 11–5.

Admission: $1.

As a child John Singer Sargent played and painted here. The hand carving of the interior is highlighted by an unusual balustrade. The rare antiques are in paneled rooms and the garden is complete with sundial.

A little beyond the harbor loop is Prospect Street on your left. It leads to the CHURCH OF OUR LADY OF GOOD VOYAGE, where the first carillon bells were installed in the country. Visitors are welcome to go inside to see the stained glass windows. It has been years since you could obtain a fresh fish directly from the boats. While you are near the church, you may want to stop in to the WHITE STAR FISH MARKET at 139 Prospect Street, open Monday-Saturday 8:30 –4:45, where there are fresh fish kept in a homemade lift-top pulley chest.

Beyond this area along Western Avenue:

RAVENSWOOD PARK with its immense trees, mostly pine and hemlock, un-paved paths for walking and cycling. Autos banned. No charge. No picnicking allowed. Or go to:

HAMMOND MUSEUM   80 Hesperus Avenue   Tel. 283 –2080

Directions: Rt. 128 North, Exit 14, go down ramp, turn right, follow Rt. 133 to Rt. 127 and view of Gloucester Harbor. Turn right onto Rt. 127 for about a mile to Hesperus Avenue on left.

Open: June 15-September 15 daily, weekdays 10 –3:30, Sundays 1:30 –4. After October 1: Weekdays 11 A.M. and 2 P.M. Sundays and holidays 1:30 –4. Closed Thanksgiving, Christmas, and New Year's Day.

Admission: Adults, $2; children 12 and under, $1.

Drawbridge and moat are here, but you enter through the small iron door to see a 100-foot hall, a 10,000-pipe organ, with many of its parts from ancient churches, and art and religious exhibits. John Hays Hammond, Jr., inventor, placed his collections in the castle that he designed and built (1926 –1928), overlooking the Reef of Norman's Woe, described in Longfellow's "Wreck of the Hesperus," in Gloucester Harbor. It was built with portions of dwellings and churches from abroad to resemble not one particular castle, but the structures of Europe in medieval times.

Special Events: Free mailing list for a schedule of children's programs, concerts, silent films, and classes (drama, dried flowers, sketching).

Gift and Coffee Shop: Open same hours as museum.

Nearest Picnic Area: Stage Fort Park (5-minute drive).

EAST GLOUCESTER

FISHING   Yankee Fleet sport fisherman take passengers from Rocky Neck

Sport Fishing Dock in the summer. Leaves 8 A.M., returns 1 P.M. Adults, $5; children, $3.25.

BEAUPORT   Eastern Point Boulevard toward tip of East Gloucester
Tel. 283–0800

Open: June-September, Monday-Friday, except holidays, for guided tours at
   2:30, 3:30, and 4:30 P.M.

Admission: $2, children 8–12, $1.

It is a 1-hour tour through what has sometimes been called the most fascinating house in America. It is a vast assemblage of rooms, each completely decorated and architecturally representative of a different period of American life. Some of the rooms were moved here from pre-Revolutionary houses. Henry Davis Sleeper, a Boston architect and interior decorator, originally built it as a small summer house. He enlarged it over the first three decades of this century. (From here turn right onto Farrington Avenue to Atlantic Road for the Scenic Shore Drive.)

SCENIC SHORE DRIVE   No real parking here. Spectacular ocean views along Bass Rocks. Drive slowly and enjoy. You are near Good Harbor Beach— turn right on Nautilus Road—where you can go on to see the different coastlines in a very short stretch: Long Beach, and Pebble Beach that is covered with smooth stones once used as ballast on Gloucester fishing vessels.

LEXINGTON

12 miles northwest of Boston

(Could be combined with Concord, Sudbury, or Fruitlands.
The oldest flag in the country is in nearby Bedford, p. 123.)

No picnic facilities in town. Most people go on to Concord
and use Fiske Hill, p. 72.

Directions: Via Rt. 128 or Rt. 2 to Waltham Street exit to Lexington Center.
   Bus: From Harvard Square. Change at Arlington Heights. No Sunday
   service.

Stop #1 seems to be the Green (the Battleground), site of the first battle of the Revolution, a small triangular shaped area bordered with trees and monuments. Many camera fans stand near passing traffic to photograph the famed Minuteman statue of Captain John Parker, and the bench near the boulder with Parker's famous command is a popular resting place. During the summer there are usually Sunday afternoon demonstrations of musket firing accompanied by fife and drum music.

Near the Green across from the Minuteman Statue can be found: VISITORS'
   CENTER, 1875 Massachusetts Avenue, Tel. 862–1450. No charge. Open
   year round, 7 days a week. April-October 9–5, until 8 P.M. in summer.
   Winter hours 1–4. Drinking fountain and sanitary facilities are here. The
   center has a diorama of the Battle of the Green. Other exhibits include
   some of the hundreds of shards and artifacts found (many by children)
   in the 1960s when the Lexington Historical Society conducted an archaeological project to unearth the foundation of the original site of the Hancock-
   Clarke House (see below). Take Clarke Street to reach the OLD BELFRY, a
   reproduction of the original; its bell called the Minutemen together. Just
   beyond the Green and the First Parish Unitarian Church is Ye Olde Bury-

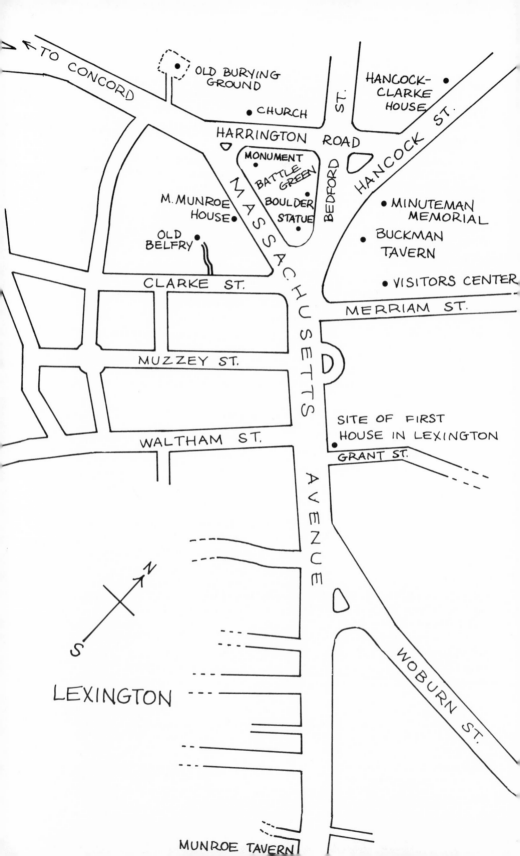

ing Ground with the graves of Captain Parker, Governor Eustis, Reverend John Hancock, and Reverend Jonas Clarke. The oldest stone is dated 1690.

Just opened:

MUSEUM OF OUR NATIONAL HERITAGE   33 Marrett Road (corner Massachusetts Avenue, very near Munroe Tavern)   Tel. 861–6563

Open: Year round Monday-Saturday 9:30–4:30, Sundays 12–5:30.

Admission: Free.

This history museum is establishing a growing collection of prints, maps, manuscripts, clocks, and furniture. It has 4 galleries, an auditorium, and library. Traveling exhibits come from other organizations and institutions. Call for current information.

HISTORIC HOUSES

Buckman Tavern is opposite the Battle Green.
Hancock-Clarke House is about a half mile down Hancock Street.
Munroe Tavern is about a mile away (toward Arlington).

Open: April 19-October 31, weekdays 10–5, Sundays 1–5.

Groups: Supervised, one adult for every ten children. Organized groups should make arrangements with the Lexington Historical Society, Box 514, Lexington. Try to schedule trips before June 1 or after September 1. Special rates available.

Fees: Each house: Adults, $1; children under 12, 25¢. Combination ticket for all three for adults: $2.25.

HANCOCK-CLARKE HOUSE (1698)   35 Hancock Street

This is the house where John Hancock and Samuel Adams were slumbering when Paul Revere arrived the night of April 18, 1775. Not only is it filled with eight rooms of interesting furnishings (including a family room with rotisserie), but there is a small museum with displays where you can browse and find treasures of the Revolutionary days. The house was spared demolition in 1896 and moved across the street. In the 1960s the original site was excavated and four foundations were found. In 1975 the house was moved back onto the original foundation.

BUCKMAN TAVERN (1690), opposite the Battle Green, is where the Minutemen met on April 19, 1775. You are guided through seven furnished rooms.
Handicapped: 2 steps. Once in, you are fine.

MUNROE TAVERN (1690), 1332 Massachusetts Avenue, a hostelry used as a hospital on April 19, 1775, has four furnished rooms.
Handicapped: Slight hill, 2 steps, once in you are fine.

MARBLEHEAD

17 miles north of Boston

Directions: Rt. 128 north to Rt. 114 to Marblehead or Rt. 1 to Rt. 114 at Peabody to Marblehead.

Bus: 55 minutes via Ⓣ. Leaves from Haymarket Square.

Where to Eat: Fort Sewall, Chandler Hovey Park, or Redd Pond for picnics. Brown's Bakery, 9 Atlantic Avenue, open Monday-Saturday 6 A.M.–3 P.M., may be open on Sundays this year; everything homemade.

Boat Rentals: See p. 216.

The entire town is 4 square miles in all; when caught on a one-way street, you are not going very far off course. Parallel (sort of) to Washington Street and the shopping center are Front Street and the harbor.

Walkers will find the town filled with charm as they amble along winding streets with hidden lanes, interesting doorways, and old-fashioned gardens. If you can stay until dusk, you may be rewarded with silhouettes of yachts, masts, and sails against the sunset. If you wish a 3-hour guided tour, rent a taped tour cassette ($3) from the Lee Mansion.

Maps are available at the INFORMATION CENTER in Abbot Hall, the spired building with clock in tower. Bring the whole family in to see the original painting of *The Spirit of '76*, given to Marblehead by General John Devereux whose son was model for the drummer boy. And open the chest on the wall to see the original deed to Marblehead dated 1684. Abbot Hall is closed July 4 and Labor Day, but open year round Monday-Friday 8 A.M.–9 P.M. and Saturdays 8 A.M.–12 noon; June-September, Monday-Saturday 8 A.M.– 9 P.M., Sundays 1–5 P.M.

A good vantage point for this yachting center is FORT SEWALL (1724) at the far end of Front Street. Not too far from Fort Sewall is OLD BURIAL HILL, with gravestones of Revolutionary soldiers, and REDD'S POND where model sailboat races are held in the mornings starting at 10. Picnicking is allowed on the shores of this former Marblehead reservoir and you may walk around the pond.

HISTORIC HOUSES

JEREMIAH LEE MANSION (1768)   161 Washington Street   Tel. 631–1069, open May-October, Monday-Saturday 9:30–4 (closed Memorial Day), provides a half-hour tour through the three floors of this outstanding building of Georgian architecture with exquisite eighteenth-century furnishings and original wallpapers.
Admission: Adults, $1; children 10–16, 50¢; age 10 and under and accompanied by an adult, free.

HOOPER MANSION (1728)   on Hooper Street charges 50¢ for admission and is open 2–5 daily except Mondays. There is no charge to view the art exhibition in the ballroom on the third floor.

MYSTIC SEAPORT
Mystic, Connecticut
Tel. 203–536–2631

Located 100 miles from Boston, 7/10 mile south of I-95 on Connecticut Rt. 27. If the distance is beyond your usual day trip, consider making a special effort for this. As with other major attractions, summer attendance is heavy, particularly on weekends, when lines form at some of the exhibits.

Open: Daily year round except Christmas and New Year's Day.

Exhibit Hours: April-late November 9–5; late November-March 10–4. The

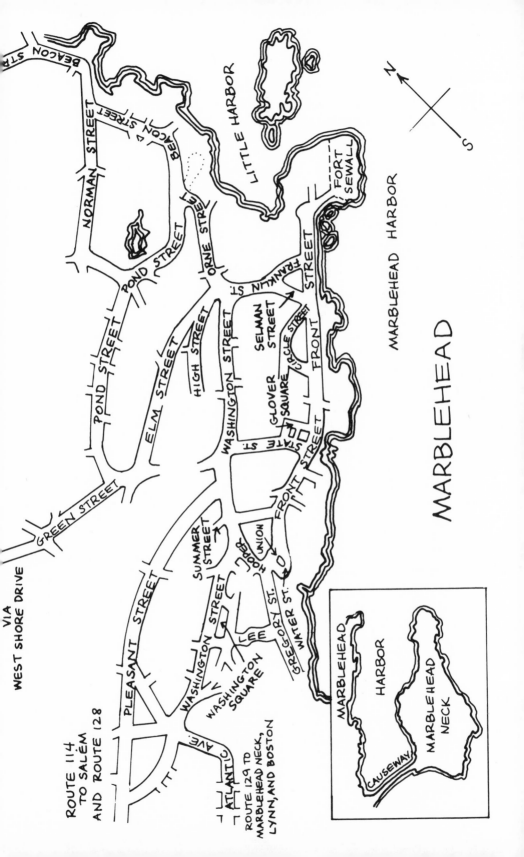

MARBLEHEAD

grounds close 1 hour later. All exhibits are open year round, but in the winter months some exhibits do not have interpreters in them. Best time of year to visit: spring or fall.

Admission: Summer: Adults, $4.25; children, $1.75. Winter: Adults, $3.75; children, $1.50. Under 6 free year round. Two-day tickets available. Admission includes parking and all exhibitions.

Stroller or Wheelchair Rentals: $2 plus deposit.

Eating: Picnic areas provided. Snack bar (summer season) and restaurant.

Groups: Arrangements must be made at least 3 weeks in advance. Day visits, study tours, and overnight programs are offered to youngsters by reservation only. Write or call Monday-Friday 9–5. Although there are no guided tours, schools may arrange for special self-guided tours that are integrated with the classroom curriculum. Tour-related materials provided to teachers; a resource center has been established in the Education Department.

Special in Summer: Visitors may help make chafing gear and nets. Demonstrations in sail setting and furling, breeches buoy descent, chantey singing, fish drying, and small boat sailing.

All Summer plus Fall Weekends: Whaleboat demonstrations (5 oarsmen and 1 steerer). The nation's last coal-fired passenger-carrying steamboat runs on the Mystic River: Adults, $1.75; children 6–16, $1.

All ages can enjoy this delightful nineteenth-century seaport village, which has been re-created with buildings and shops that have been moved from other locations. The greatest attractions seem to be the ships that are docked at the seaport. The *Joseph Conrad* is a training ship built in 1882. You may board the *L. A. Dunton*, one of the last great Gloucester fishing schooners, with its nests of dories once used with long trawl lines. When you explore the restored *Charles W. Morgan*, the only American wooden whaler in existence, you will be on a floating ship that was embedded in sand from 1941 to 1974.

The Children's Museum has an adult watch walkway above the cabin room where youngsters climb onto a quilt-covered bunk to see out of a porthole, play with toys (reproductions) or a gingham cat, try on clothes that are copies of an earlier time, don a period hat and look in the mirror—all in a rather luxurious environment that reproduces what was once a child's life on a ship.

Everywhere interpreters are happy to explain the activity. Walk the cobblestone street and stop in at the doctor's office, the Apothecary Shop, the Tavern, the General Store complete with potbellied stove, step along the old ropewalk to see how rope was made—and smell the oakum used for caulking in the Chandlery. The fires are burning in the Shipsmith Shop to make hoops for casks or tools such as harpoons or lances. The Buckingham House has foods cooking in its fireplace made from recipes of the 1800s. And there are furnished homes of the period and a large museum filled with ship models, figureheads, paintings, and navigational equipment.

All maintenance and restoration work is done at the seaport. The rigging loft produces hemp and wire stays; the sailmaker stitches canvas for sails and other articles. Replicas of wooden boats are sometimes built to demonstrate to visitors how they would have been sailed, while the originals remain ashore on display.

Wear comfortable shoes, bring a jacket, and become immersed in a grand change of pace.

NEWPORT

about 73 miles from Boston

Directions: Rt. 128 to 24 to 114 to Newport.

Where to Eat: Dozens of picnic places with ocean views. Restaurant: Leo's Family Restaurant, 142 Long Wharf (far side of Treadway), very informal, reasonably priced. Everything from spaghetti to lobster.

Information Booth: Located next to Brick Market on Long Wharf Mall. Operated by Chamber of Commerce.

. . . There is a lot to see and do here. In one day it is necessary to pick and choose, chance it, explore and see what happens! Much depends upon the age and interests of the visitors—and maybe the weather of the day. It is possible to spend all your time out of doors and get a strong feeling of the unique (often lavish) environment around the ocean. Or try a combination of activities.

. . . Attention cyclists: If 10 miles of moderate cycling is within reason, that is the best way to do Ocean Drive.

. . . If it is Sunday, plan to arrive in the morning. Traffic does pick up in the afternoon.

The following suggestions are guidelines for a taste of Newport: As you drive into town, just beyond Brick Market, there is a semicircular road (America's Cup Avenue) that leads to BOWEN'S and other wharves. Find a parking place (possibly on some side street), walk around the wharves with cobblestones, craft shops, and a candy shop, too. Meander over to King's Dock and at least look at, if not go on, the sailing frigate H.M.S. *Rose*, open daily April-December, 10 A.M.–sunset. Admission: $1. It is the only ship of the Revolutionary War afloat. Her principal role was to clamp down on smuggling operations, and she was reconstructed in 1970, using as much material from the original ship as possible.

Ahead (south) along Thames Street is CHRISTIE'S YARD (on right), which offers a dockside view of yachts and a distant view of Newport shipyard (where visitors are *not* allowed) where Cup boats come and go. On the left at 380 Thames Street is 10 SPEED SPOKES, which rents only full-size bikes—several speeds as well as tandems. (Rates: 3-speed—$5 day, $1 hour; 5- or 10-speed—$6 day, $1.25 hour; tandem—$8 day, $1.75 hour.)

OCEAN DRIVE is not to be missed! Follow along Thames Street, through town, passing restored frame houses, and you will see Ocean Drive (and bicycle route) signs. In minutes you will come to a park, pier, and small beach with a slide in the water. No charge for parking or use of beach. Great view of waterfront. If you continue—by the rear of the estates and onto great ocean views and rocky beach areas with available parking—there are many places for picnicking and exploring. Or wait until you get to Brenton State Park, which has grass and sand. There is a radical change as you go along Bellevue Avenue with its *sumptuous mansions*. There are all sorts of *combination tickets*, but one of the mansions may be enough in a day (if indeed you feel the children are old enough to enjoy the experience). Each tour takes about an hour. Some possibilities:

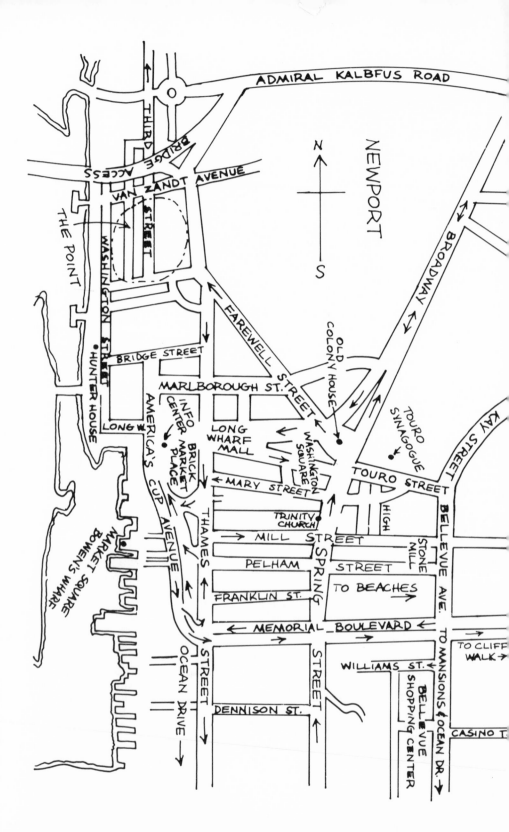

MARBLE HOUSE, sumptuously built with marble and gilt.

Open: Memorial Day-October 31, 10–5, Friday evenings until 9, open weekends throughout the winter.

Admission: Adults, $1.75; children 6–15, 75¢.

THE BREAKERS, former home of the Cornelius Vanderbilt family.

Open: Memorial Day–October 31, 10–5; Sundays until 9, July–mid-September.

Admission: Adults, $2; children 6–15, 75¢.

THE ELMS, built in 1901 for coal magnate Edward J. Berwind.

Open: Memorial Day-October 31, 10–5; Thursdays and Saturdays until 9 July-mid-September. Open weekends throughout the winter.

Admission: Adults, $1.75; children, 75¢.

Go on into town with shopping mall on left and a welcome ice-cream cone at Newport Creamery.

You are minutes from other Newport specials. There is CLIFF WALK (from Bellevue Avenue turn right on Memorial Boulevard at light). Walk starts just after Cliff Manor. (FIRST BEACH with extensive swimming and surfing is here on Memorial Boulevard.) The walk is about a mile of uninterrupted view of ocean; height (and drop) may not be what you wish with young children.

If you do not turn on Memorial Boulevard, straight ahead at #8 Bellevue is the MT. ZION BLACK MUSEUM with an exhibit of black history and culture in the foyer of the Mt. Zion A.M.E. Church. Bellevue Avenue becomes Truro, and Truro Park on the left has the OLD STONE MILL with bases on true compass points. Its origin is controversial. Further down on the right is the oldest synagogue (1763) in America, TRURO SYNAGOGUE, open late June-Labor Day, Monday-Friday 10–5 and Sundays 10–6; other Sundays 2–4. No admission charge.

From this area you continue onto Long Wharf and The Point if you did not cover that territory while you were in town earlier.

THE POINT, one of the oldest sections of Newport, is located on the other (north) side of the Brick Market. First you come to Treadway Inn, then a small park and playground, and Long Wharf (where you will find Leo's Family Restaurant). The Point is the residential area that is north and west Long Wharf. On the bay side is HUNTER HOUSE, 54 Washington Street, open Memorial Day-October 11, 11–5; tour of the house: Adults, $1; children 6–15, 50¢. The exterior has a widow's walk and beaded clapboards, and a pedimented doorway with pineapple (Newport's symbol of hospitality). From here you can weave your way through the close blocks and easily tell which homes have been or are in the process of being restored. There is a strong feeling of spirit. The signs with "OC-acorn" mean that the house was a private restoration, and its history has been researched and documented by Operation Clapboard. This organization bought options on eighteenth-century houses that were architecturally worthwhile and held them until a sympathetic buyer who would restore them was found. The Newport Restoration Foundation sign means that the house was or is being restored by Doris Duke's very active organization. These houses may be rented but not sold; the restored interiors include modern bathrooms and kitchens.

OLD STURBRIDGE VILLAGE

Sturbridge, Massachusetts

Tel. 347–3362

Located at the junction of Rts. 86 and 20 and
the Massachusetts Turnpike.

Bus: Continental Trailways, Tel. 482–6620, can give you details about a round
trip 1-day package arrangement that includes admission.

Open: Year round, April-October 9:30–5:30, December-February 10–4, March
and November 9:30–4:30. Closed Christmas and New Year's Day.

Admission (all inclusive): Adults, $4; children 6–14, $1.25; under 6, no charge.
Group rates available; make advance reservations. Strollers may not be
taken into buildings; few buildings are extensive.

Where to Eat: Picnic areas in pine grove, Tavern on the Green offers buffet
weekends mid-April–May, daily and weekends June-October. Cafeteria
open year round; box lunches available summer only.

Thanksgiving Dinner: Reservations accepted anytime. Usually filled by
March. Adults, $8.50; children 8 and under, $4.75. Price does not include
admission to the village. Three servings.

Slide Lecture: "A Tour of Old Sturbridge Village" may be borrowed by groups.
Advance reservations necessary. Contact Public Information secretary.

Plan to arrive early as there is really more than a day of fun and fascination for
everyone at this living regional museum of early New England life. Forty buildings of the 1790–1840 period have been moved from various sections of New
England and reconstructed on 200 rolling acres of meadow and woodland.

The costumed village craftsmen, e.g., the miller, candlemaker, and printer
(as he pulls a historic newspaper from a 200-year-old press), are all willing to
peer over their small old eyeglasses (if they wear them) to explain their activities. The farmer, too, loves visitors and animals (oxen, cows, sheep). Take a seat
on the horse-drawn Carry-All for a ride through the covered bridge and around
the millpond. You may buy fresh warm cookies at the bakery, rest on the village
green, and see a potter shape utensils from native clay.

Special in Summer: Historical drama presentation, ballad singing on the Common, fife and drum concerts by the Sturbridge Martial Band, parlor music
recitals daily in the Ladies' Parlor of the Tavern, interpretation and demonstration of muzzle-loading guns twice daily near the Gun Exhibit.

Special in Winter: Sleigh rides offered, weather permitting, on weekends and
during Washington's Birthday week. Christmas week tours (p. 300). Maple
sugaring, p. 284.

Museum Education Building: Located outside the historical exhibition area.
The open space multilevel building is designed to allow students to pur-
sue history studies in direct, participatory, in-depth experiences. (A
theatre and orientation facility is scheduled to open this year.) The Education Building accommodates students from third grade through college,
adults, retarded, handicapped, and other special education students, and
offers teacher-education programs that focus on the use of museum and
community resources in social sciences curriculum development. The Education Materials Program prepares primary historical resources, mainly
involving the lives of "ordinary" people, for classroom use.

PLYMOUTH

37 miles southeast of Boston
45 minute drive via Rt. 3

Bus: From Greyhound Terminal, Tel. 423–5810. Some summers there is boat service.

> There is a long list of attractions in the town, but first visit Plimoth Plantation—and then you will know what time, energy, and absorption power are left. For those with an early start and/or yen to "see everything," there are combination tickets—good all season and sold at a considerable saving—for Plimoth Plantation, *Mayflower II*, and 7 historic houses.

Eating: It is worth a detour to picnic at Standish Monument Reservation, Duxbury, on the way home. (Rt. 3, 3A, right at Dory Restaurant, Standish Street from Duxbury Center.) Picnic sites, fireplaces, and fantastic views of the harbor. Parking $1.

If it is Friday or Saturday and you feel like a 10-minute walk from the waterfront—and fresh Portuguese sweetbread—walk to the Danforth Bakery at 26 Main Street.

Restaurants: The Lobster Hut on the wharf uses its own potatoes for fish and chips. Eat on benches outside. The Mayflower Restaurant on the Town Wharf has a cafeteria and takeout area. The natives often eat at the Colonial Restaurant, 39 Main Street.

PLIMOTH PLANTATION
Box 1620   Tel. 746–1622

Consists of Pilgrim Village and Indian Camp, *Mayflower 11*, and the nearby two early houses.

PILGRIM VILLAGE. Two miles south of Plymouth Rock on Rt. 3A. Admission: Adults, $1.75; children under 13, 60¢; children under 5, free.

Groups: Special rates available for a minimum of ten. Much orientation material sent on request. Allow 1½ hours for a visit and make appointments as early as possible.

Open: April 1 through the Sunday after Thanksgiving. Spring and fall 10–5 (some weekends until 6). Mid-June–Labor Day 9–7. Although no tickets are sold after 1 hour before closing, allow 2 hours for leisurely looking. Indian Camp open May 15-October 15.

Eating Facilities: Snack bar (vending machines) open until 1 hour before closing. Picnic tables limited to those who have paid admissions and available on a first-come basis. Group picnickers who come with their own lunches are asked to eat in their cars or buses.

Strollers: Allowed on the grounds (but not in the buildings); the going is rough on those early paths.

Each season has its own rewards for a visit to this replica Pilgrim colony of 1627. It is worth a special trip. If you have a choice, you may prefer to avoid the busy summers; however, the village can handle large numbers. DRESS

PLYMOUTH

FOR THE SEASON for this outdoor museum; it is often cool by the ocean in spring and fall. Wear comfortable shoes to cope with the rough paths.

There is an excellent brief orientation program and, as you tour the village and the fort meetinghouse, you will find helpful guides of all ages who are happy to meet curious visitors: men at work cutting planks, thatching a roof, or making a barrel. The crops are being tended and the women are in the kitchen gardens cooking or sewing. What you see depends upon when you visit. Seasonal activities are posted in the Reception Center.

In the Indian Summer Camp, directed, researched, and staffed by native Americans, you pass through fields planted with enough vegetables to last a family for a year. The activities vary through the season and day: there is harvesting of reeds from a dugout canoe, processing of clay for pottery, smoking fish for storage, and the playing of a dice game. The furnishings of the wigwam include a display of Indian crafts: mats, basketry, and quillwork.

Everything else is near the Plymouth waterfront near the center of town (in an almost honky-tonk atmosphere):

MAYFLOWER II   a replica berthed near Plymouth Rock.

Open: April 1-December 1, spring and early autumn. Tickets sold 9–5 weekdays, until 6 weekends. Late autumn: Tickets sold until 5 daily. In July and August tickets sold until 8:30 P.M. daily.

Admission: Adults, $1.25; children under 13, 60¢; under 5, free.

In 20 to 30 minutes you get the feeling of the cramped quarters that the Pilgrims had during their 1620 voyage. During most of the summer there are dockside demonstrations of crew duties.

WATERFRONT HOUSES

Admission: 10¢ per person. If you haven't been to Pilgrim Village, you may want to see First House, which represents the earliest permanent type of house built by the Pilgrims, and the 1627 House, which shows refinements in building at a later date.

Other attractions in the center of town

PLYMOUTH ROCK   During busy days you have to wait to step inside the portico to see this comparatively small treasure. The imagination has somehow been at work and the usual reaction is one of disappointment. No charge.

You can climb Cole's Hill—across from Plymouth Rock—where the Pilgrims buried the dead in unmarked graves. Vistascopes (10¢) give a better view of the harbor.

On Cole's Hill:

PLYMOUTH NATIONAL WAX MUSEUM (air-conditioned)   Tel. 746–6468

Open: March-June 1 and Labor Day-December 1, 9–5. June 1-Labor Day, 9 A.M.–9:30 P.M.

Admission: The extensive gift shop is open to the public. If you step into the shop, you may get a peek at a sample museum display. Adults, $1.50; children 5–12, 75¢; under 5, free.

The life-size vinyl figures are arranged in 26 scenes that depict the time in England, escape to Holland, the Mayflower voyage, and the rain before the landing at Plymouth. The Pilgrims' first washday—on a Monday—is part of the story that unfolds as visitors push buttons that release the lighting and narrative for each scene. Average visit: 45 minutes.

BREWSTER GARDENS (often overlooked by tourists), next to Cole's Hill, is a small, peaceful, charming park at the site of the Pilgrims' first gardens. You are welcome to have a refreshing drink from the spring.

Still more places:
HARLOW OLD FORT HOUSE (1677)   119 Sandwich Street   (Rt. 3A)
Tel. 746–3017
Open: May 25-September 15, 10–5 daily.
Admission: Adults, 75¢; children under 14, 25¢.

Half-hour tour in house, which has hostesses in authentic Pilgrim dress and demonstrations in spinning, carding, dyeing, weaving, and candle-dipping. Informal visitor participation is encouraged, but a group should make special arrangements.

PILGRIM HALL, the Pilgrim Society Museum on Court Street (Rt. 3A)
Open: Year round 10–4:30, winter Sundays 1–4:30.
Admission: Adults, 75¢; children, 50¢.

ANTIQUARIAN HOUSE (built 1809–1830), 126 Water Street
Open: Mid-May–mid-September 10–5.
Admission: Adults, 75¢; children, 25¢.

Octagonal rooms, nineteenth-century costumes, a furnished nursery in a gracious home.

THE JABEZ HOWLAND HOUSE (1677), Sandwich Street
Open: May 25-September 15, Monday-Saturday 9:30–5, Sundays 10–5.
Admission: Adults, 75¢; children, 25¢.

NATIONAL HEADQUARTERS OF THE GENERAL SOCIETY OF MAY-FLOWER DESCENDANTS
Open: May 25-September 15, 10–5 daily.
Admission: Adults, 75¢; children, 25¢.

SPARROW HOUSE, Summer Street
Open: May 25-September 15, Monday-Saturday 9–5. Closed Sundays.
Admission: Adults, 75¢; children, 25¢.

Perhaps the oldest house in Plymouth, and now the home of the Plymouth Pottery Guild, whose workshop occupies the rear of the house.

SPOONER HOUSE (1750), 27 North Street, near Plymouth Rock
Open: Mid-May–mid-September, 10–5 daily, Sundays 1–5.
Admission: Adults, 75¢; children, 25¢.

Portraits, china, and fine furniture used in the house by generations of the Spooner family.

JENNY GRIST MILL on Town Brook at Spring Lane
Open: Weekends in April-late June. Daily late June-Thanksgiving, 9–5:30.
Admission: Adults, 50¢; children 6–12, 25¢; 5 and under, free.

An early American waterpowered mill grinds corn as the Pilgrims did over 300 years ago. Cornmeal for sale. (No charge for watching candlemakers at work in the neighboring Candlecraft Center.)

ROCKPORT
36 miles north of Boston

Train: B&M from North Station, Tel. 227–5070. (Note off-peak rate information, p. 28.)

There are many appealing aspects: Open spaces, vistas, and dozens of small shops. Rockport has its photographed and painted motif #1, rock-lined shores, inviting lanes, and historical background. *But be forewarned:* Crowds will greet the day tripper. As a matter of fact, the town is coping with traffic and parking by providing a bus from a parking lot 1 mile out of town. The parking lot is on Main Street, Rt. 127. Service is offered weekends during May, June, September, and October, and daily during the summer 10 A.M.–7 P.M. Parking fee $2. No charge for bus, which leaves about every 15 minutes.

Eating: Picnic areas—no place right in town. Granite Pier Wharf has a summer parking fee of $1. Take Granite Street to Wharf Road on the right. Park on jetty. Or go to Halibut Point, p. 188.

Suggested restaurant in center of town: Oleana, 23–27 Main Street, a restaurant and coffee shop with Norwegian decor and an American menu. Open April-December, closed Mondays. Delightful atmosphere, good cooking, moderate prices. Smorgasbord luncheon daily except Sunday. Children's menu. Fantastic fish or clam chowder on Friday. Homemade bakery specialties. Coffee shop is small, but great if you do not want to linger.

Most BEARSKIN NECK shops don't open until 1 on Sundays; as many of them now seem to be carrying more commercial products rather than handcrafted items, you might consider walking the Neck on fall or spring Sunday mornings, have an early lunch at Oleana, and then head out to Halibut Point to complete the day. The ROCKPORT PUPPET THEATER, located in Masonic Hall, has rotating puppeteers during the summer. Admission $1. Artists can be seen all over town and along the shore. Bring your sketch pad. Old tombstones can be seen in the OLD FIRST PARISH BURYING GROUND, right on Main Street, and the SEWALL-SCRIPTURE HOUSE, 40 King Street, is open 2–5 daily in July and August. The TOAD HALL BOOKSTORE at 51 Main Street gives all proceeds to environmental groups.

If you do not want to walk:
BICYCLE RENTALS available from L. E. Smith, 17 Railroad Avenue, Tel. 546–6518. Full-size bicycles only. Large groups should make reservations. Open until 8 Thursday and Friday evenings, 5 P.M. other days. Closed Sundays.

BOAT TRIPS FROM T WHARF. Captain Ted's (546–2889) has 1-hour island

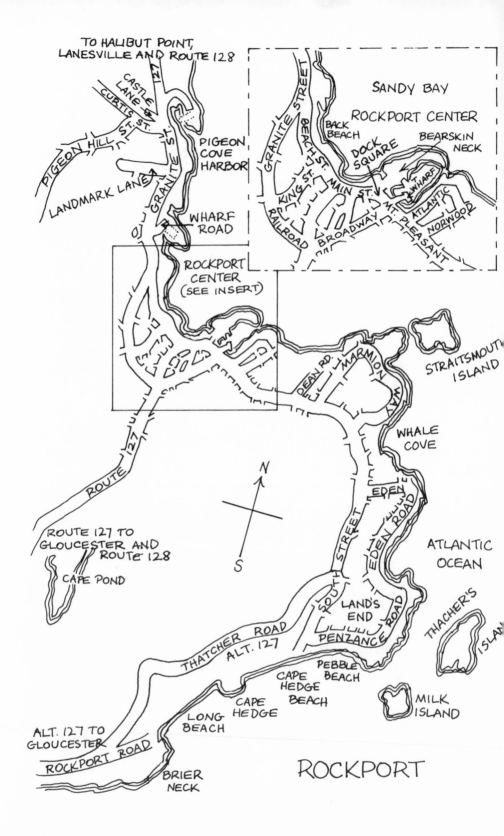

trips at 11 A.M., 1, 2:30, and 4 P.M. Adults $1.50, children $1. Captain Otto's (546–6752) offers daily trips around Cape Ann from 2:15–4. Adults $4, children $2.

DEEP-SEA FISHING. Leave from T Wharf. Offered summer months. Captain Otto's (546–6752) leaves at 8:30 A.M. and returns at 1 P.M. Captain Ted's (546–2889) leaves at 7:30 A.M. and returns at 12:30 P.M. $6 per person, including bait, rod, and reel.

HORSE-DRAWN SURREY RIDES from Dock Square on good days, May-October, Monday-Saturday 10–4:30. It is a 3-mile ride (almost an hour) along the shoreline. Reservations accepted: Laurence Swan, 25 Curtis Street, Rockport, 546–2364.

PIGEON COVE

An area preferred by some: Pigeon Cove is a 10-minute drive along Rt. 127 or a healthy cycle from the center of Rockport. Turn at the Tool Co. if you want to see the unloading and weighing of lobsters at THE NEW ENGLAND LOBSTER CO. It retails fish, clams, and lobsters. THE OLD CASTLE, corner of Granite and Curtis streets, built in 1678, has early American utensils and furniture, and a large locomotive bell. It is open from 2 to 5 Saturdays and Sundays in July and August without charge. THE PAPER HOUSE, not far from the Pigeon Cove post office, is open May 30-October 12 every day 9–5 for a 15-minute tour of a 20-year effort, in which everything is made of paper, including walls of 215 thicknesses, lamps, chairs, table, grandfather's clock, fireplace mantel of rotogravure sections, and a writing desk made of newspaper reports of Lindbergh's flights. After years of 25¢ admission, the entrance fee may go up a little this year. Preschoolers admitted free. Mrs. Curtis, hostess, may point out any unusual birds bathing in the shallow spot near the ledges.

Many people bypass these sights and head straight for HALIBUT POINT RESERVATION, the outermost tip of Cape Ann (p. 188).

SALEM

20 miles northeast of Boston

Train: Leaves from North Station, Tel. 227–5070. (Note off-peak rate information, p. 28, for the 35-minute ride.) Salem station is 6 blocks from center of town.

Bus: Ⓣ from Haymarket Square.

Directions: Rt. 95, C1 in Revere, Rt. 1 North to Rt. 128 East in Lynnfield to Exit 25 and Rt. 114 to downtown Salem.

Information: The Chamber of Commerce is located in the Hotel Hawthorne.

> Along Rt. 1 in Danvers you may watch candy
> being made at Putnam Pantry, p. 258.

Eating: Bring a picnic lunch and go to Salem Willows Park, 1 mile from town. Informal restaurants are along Rt. 1A toward Beverly.

Beaches: At Salem Willows Park or Forest River Park.

Suggestions: There is more than a day's worth of places to visit. And there may be more gift shops than you care to face. If you are with young children, drive to Pioneer Village first, then go into the center of town for the Peabody Museum, the John Ward House, or the Bonded Warehouse. Those with some literary knowledge can enjoy the House of the Seven Gables. Many of the sites are within walking distance of each other. Any necessary driving is very short. If you have been going from one guided tour to another, take a break by seeking out CHESTNUT STREET, which is lined with magnificent houses once owned by sea captains and considered one of the most distinguished streets in the United States.

SALEM WILLOWS PARK   (follow signs from Historic Salem)   Tels. 744–2989, 744–3328. Beaches on the ocean, picnic grounds, shaded grass areas, open-air concerts, an amusement park (separate charge for each ride such as the merry-go-round or dodgem). Large groups may reserve baseball diamond, tennis courts, and basketball court by writing the Recreation Department, Broad Street, Salem, or calling 744–0733. Admission free. Plenty of free parking.

FOREST RIVER PARK   adjoining Pioneer Village. Sundays: Nonresident parking area limited. A lovely wooded picnic area. You may bring your own barbecue. Pool and beach are heavily used.

HARBOR EXCURSIONS. Pier Transit Company leaves for Marblehead from pier at Salem Willows Park. One-hour round trip 7 days a week, weather permitting, during the summer months. Lower deck enclosed, upper deck exposed. Some variations on this excursion may be forthcoming. Present rates: Adults, $1.25; children under 12, 75¢; under 5, free. Senior citizen rates available.

PIONEER VILLAGE   Clifton Avenue   (10-minute drive from Salem Center)

Open: June 1-Labor Day 9:30–6:30; after Labor Day–mid-October 10–5.

Admission: Adults, 50¢; children under 12, 25¢.

This reproduction captures the atmosphere of the Salem of 1630 with thatched-roofed houses and bark-covered wigwams, dugouts, pillory, and stocks, and evidences of industry—the bellows in the blacksmith shop, the saltworks (evaporation of seawater in shallow pans), and a brick kiln. You will probably spend an enjoyable and educational half hour here. The printed signs on exhibits are helpful, but young children sometimes get impatient while you are reading.

CUSTOM HOUSE   Derby Street   744–4323

Open: 8:30–5 daily year round (until 7 P.M. June-August).

Admission: Free.

Salem's old waterfront, a National Historic maritime site, once had 45 wharves. The area is hardly reconstructed, but it is possible to feel the importance of shipping to Salem's past. The Custom House once housed the collector, surveyor, weighers, gaugers, measurers, inspectors, boatmen, and clerks, all of

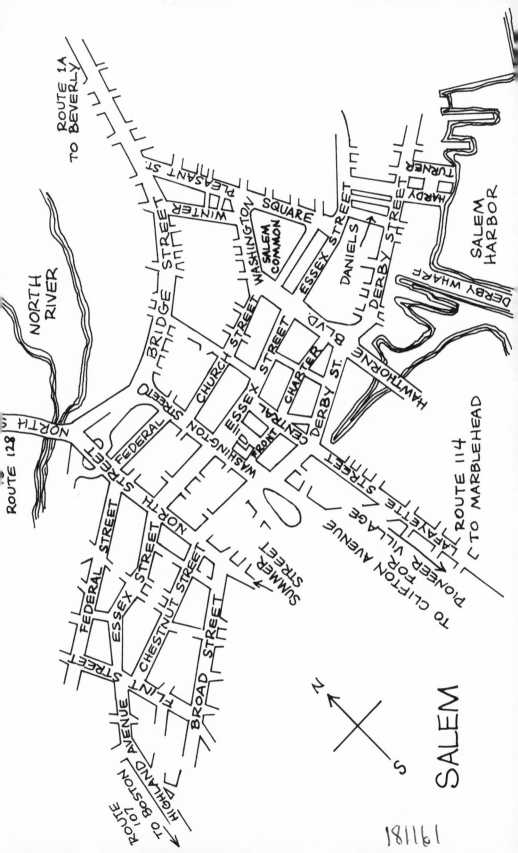

SALEM

whom were very busy when a boat would appear on the horizon. Some of the offices are restored, including one used by Nathaniel Hawthorne. The cupola atop the building is open by special arrangement for some groups.

Behind the Custom House is the BONDED WAREHOUSE, which was used for the storage of cargoes awaiting export or payment of custom duties. The original hoisting winch and other pieces of equipment are still in operation. Tea chests, rum barrels, spices, silks, coffee, and dried cargoes can be seen. Visitors may operate the hoist as well as the tall steelyard scales on which cargoes were weighed.

School Groups: Tours offered. Two weeks' advance notice. Length depends on size and age of class.

HOUSE OF THE SEVEN GABLES   Turner Street (off Derby)   Tel. 744–0991

Open: July-Labor Day 9:30–4:45 three buildings, 4:45–7:30 Gables only; other months—tour of Gables 10–5 except Thanksgiving, Christmas, and New Year's Day.

Admission: Adults, $3 in summer and on fall weekends, summer evenings $2 for the one house, $2 in winter; children 13–18, $1; 12 and under, 50¢. Proceeds go to the House of the Seven Gables Settlement Association.

Tearoom (shaded garden setting) serves lunch 12–2 and dessert until 4:30.

Those who have read Nathaniel Hawthorne's novel will enjoy the 20-minute tour through the six rooms. The guides tell of the relation of particular items and rooms to the story. Most memorable is the winding climb to Clifford's room via the narrow secret staircase. The summer tour includes the Hathaway House (1682), Hawthorne's Birthplace, moved to the present site in 1958, and the little Counting House. The gardened grounds look out on Salem Harbor.

WITCH HOUSE   Essex and Summer streets

Open: May 1-October 13, 10–6 daily.

Admission: Adults, 75¢; children under 12, 25¢.

If you want to see the place where the trials of persons accused of witchcraft were held, there are guides in the first-floor rooms, antique items, and accounts to be read upstairs. This turns out to be a very brief visit. Some visitors would appreciate other than a few memorized sentences by each guide.

PEABODY MUSEUM   161 Essex Street   Tel. 745–1876

Open: Year round Monday-Saturday 9–5, Sundays and holidays 1–5. Closed Thanksgiving, Christmas, and New Year's Day.

Parking: Municipal garage under construction across street.

Admission: Adults, $1; children 6–16, 50¢; senior citizens, 50¢; Salem residents, free.

Guided Tours: By appointment. Two weeks' notice. Minimum age: 5th grade. 1–1½ hours.

If your children are museum-goers, this is worth a special trip. The collections of maritime history, ethnology, and natural history have been growing ever since the East India Marine Society was organized by a group of Salem captains and merchants in 1799. There are ship models—in and out of bottles—a corridor filled with nautical instruments, paintings, and a natural history diorama with sound. Upstairs you can step inside the reproduction of the saloon, and see the full-size cabin from Cleopatra's Barge built in Salem in 1816, and an enormous tusk said to have come from 150-year-old elephants. There are also Japanese, Chinese, Siamese, East Indian, Tibetan, and Korean ethnological collections with everything from flower holders and costumes to armor and ornate saddles.

A new air-conditioned wing is scheduled for completion late this year. It will provide more space for the education department and permit the museum to provide many more programs.

ESSEX INSTITUTE HISTORIC HOUSES

The historic houses that are owned and operated by the Essex Institute are all staffed by volunteer guides who are schooled in the period of "their home." Consequently, they give a very informative tour that is geared to the interests of the visitor.

Summer package ticket includes museum and all five houses: Adults, $4.50; children under 16, $1. Individual admissions: Adults, $1; children 6–15, 50¢.

All the houses are CLOSED Mondays, holidays, including January 1, July 4, Thanksgiving, and Christmas.

THE JOHN WARD HOUSE (1684)   132 Essex Street (in back of Essex Institute)

Open: June-October 15, Tuesday-Saturday 10–4 and Sundays 2–4:30.

This is ideal for a family visit. It is a small seventeenth-century house with old parlor, kitchen, apothecary shop, and "cent shop" (nothing for sale).

CROWNINSHIELD-BENTLEY HOUSE (1727)   126 Essex Street (across from Hotel Hawthorne)

Open: June 1-October 15, Tuesday-Saturday 10–4:30, Sundays 2–4:30.

This furnished eighteenth-century house has a child-minder (confining maypole affair), and a darling third-floor child's room with treasure-filled cubbyholes. (Average visit: 30 minutes.)

ESSEX INSTITUTE   132 Essex Street   Tel. 744–3390

Open: Tuesday-Saturday 9–4:30, Sundays 2–5. Closed Mondays, January 1, July 4, Thanksgiving, and Christmas.

Use of Library: 75¢.

Exhibits include old dolls and toys, early costumes and uniforms, portraits, furniture, silver, and pottery.

School Groups: 10-minute introductory slide lecture and guided tour. One week's notice. Adults, 50¢; children, 25¢.

OPEN FREE DURING THE SUMMER are buildings in the rear gardens: THE DOLL HOUSE, probably the original seventeenth-century Salem Quaker meetinghouse, and since 1946 the home of a unique collection of dolls, doll furniture, and toys. And the 12' by 14' LYE-TAPLEY SHOE SHOP, which represents the shoe industry during its handcrafting period, 1750–1850.

THE ASSEMBLY HOUSE (1782)   138 Federal Street

Built in 1782 as a hall for social assemblies, this house was remodeled by Samuel McIntire as a residence in 1876. A rare Chinese parlor and a Victorian parlor are included in the eighteenth–twentieth-century furnishings.

Two examples of wealthy merchants' homes both designed by Samuel McIntire:

GARDNER-PINGREE HOUSE (1804)   128 Essex Street

Open: Tuesday-Saturday 10–4:30 year round. Also open Sundays June-October 2–4:30.

All rooms are roped off in this elegant home. The third floor has a nineteenth-century children's playroom.

PEIRCE-NICHOLS HOUSE (1782)   80 Federal Street

Open: Year round Tuesday-Saturday 2–4:30.

The period furnishings do not offer something special for children, but an old counting house and stable are in back.

SANDWICH
60 miles from Boston via Rt. 3

Ashumet Holly Reservation (p. 196) is 6 miles south via Rt. 130.

Picnicking: Along the Canal at Bourne Scenic Park (fairly populated), and at beaches. Please note that Shawme Crowell State Forest is only for overnight users.

Beaches: Scusset (state), p. 211, the most accessible in the area during the summer months. Parking $1.

PLANK WALK BEACH. Town Neck Road. (From Rt. 6A left on Jarvis Street, left on Factory Street, right on Harbor Street.) Has a real plank walk across marsh and creek. Parking $1. Some dunes, but not as pretty as SANDY NECK BEACH (possibly limited to residents during the summer), off Rt. 6A, about 20-minute ride toward Barnstable from Sandwich Center.

There are enough things to do and see in this area so that groups with a span in ages could divide according to

interests and then meet later. The area has survived the threat of commercialism, and maintains the atmosphere that one would like to think of when Cape Cod is mentioned. There is much discussion about planning and marking scenic roads. (This may be done soon.)
Special note: PAIRPOINT GLASS WORKS visit (p. 257) is a highlight.

As you approach Sandwich you get a close look at the CANAL by taking Rt. 6 at the Sagamore Bridge and stopping at the herring run (p. 286), or drive about 3 miles beyond it to rent bicycles (see below). The only vehicles allowed on the 6-mile service road along the canal are government cars and bicycles. It is possible to ride up one side of the canal and back along the other. (It is 4 miles between bridges.) Only hangup: It means riding on the sidewalk of the bridge, an experience in itself—frightening to some adults. The level service roads offer several places along the way where you can picnic. You may choose to walk and maybe push a stroller along the road, or just sit on the banks of the canal for a view of passing freighters or tankers.

Along Rt. 6A (through the center of town and turn right on 6A): A 5-minute ride from the center of Sandwich brings you to the STATE FISH HATCHERY on the right on Rt. 6A. Drive through the tree-lined path to see the troughs and different sizes of fish. (Some are sizable indeed.) No admission charge. Pellets (10¢) are sold for those who want to feed the fish. If you are coming with a group, write to the manager and he will show you the progression of growth from egg to fish. There is no charge for walking the paths of BRIAR PATCH (second right after hatchery onto Chipman Road, follow signs). It is the site of Thornton Burgess stories, now marked as a woodland and conservation area.

The small TITCOMB'S BOOKSHOP is good for browsing or finding a treasure: an old map, magazine, or book. Open year round. The Titcombs love children and the shop. It is worth the extra drive to SANDY NECK BEACH (on the left on Rt. 6A after you have gone over the creek). The huge sand dunes are in a location with an unusual view of Cape Cod Bay. There is room in the parking area in the spring and fall.

Bicycles: Available at The Fisherman's Friend, 341 Scenic Highway (at Bourne Bridge), Buzzards Bay, Tel. 759–7656. Open April 1-September 30, 7 days a week and just weekends in February, March, October, and November. Three-speed rates: 2 hour minimum $2, each additional hour 75¢, one day $4.50. Tandem and 3 wheel-3 speed available. RODS AND REELS may be rented here too.

Bourne Scenic Park (across the street from The Fisherman's Friend): Open daily April 15-October 30. Day users: $1.50 includes use of fireplaces. 352 campsites (some rather close to each other) in this popular area, so you will not be alone. Run by town of Bourne.

A major attraction:
HERITAGE PLANTATION   Pine and Grove streets   Tel. 888–3300

Directions: From Rt. 6A, right into Sandwich Center, Rt. 130 to Plantation.

Open: May 1-October 15 10–5 daily. Tickets sold until 4 P.M.

Admission: Adults, $2.50; children 6–11, 75¢; children 5 and under, free.

Picnic Grounds: In pine grove. No fires allowed.

Acres of rhododendrons (best in May and June), with species and hybrids representing three continents, azaleas and laurel, and nature trails allow for an indoor-outdoor experience. Buildings (air-conditioned): The Round Barn, a reproduction of an original design of the Shakers of Hancock, Massachusetts, houses a collection of early American automobiles dating from 1893 to the mid-1930s; the old East Mill, which ground cornmeal for the Union forces during the Civil War; a restored carousel on which you may ride; and a military museum containing collections of antique firearms and miniature soldiers. Cultural events held throughout the summer.

In the center of town:

The PUMP with the most delicious water. Bring your picnic jug. Free.

SANDWICH GLASS MUSEUM   Main Street   Tel. 888–0251

Open: July and August 9–6 daily; 10–5 in May, June, September, and October.

Admission: Adults, $1.50; children 5–16, 25¢; under 5, free.

If you want to introduce children to the beautiful glass collections, there are lovely shapes, colors, and rare pieces handsomely displayed in well-lighted cases or set in windows to allow natural lighting. Exhibits of the famous glass manufactured at Sandwich are arranged in chronological sequence of Sandwich production from 1825 to 1888. A scaled diorama of the Boston and Sandwich Glass Works depicts the various stages of glassmaking.

DEXTER'S GRIST MILL   across the street from the Glass Museum

Open: Mid-June through late September 10–5 daily, opens Sundays at 1.

Admission: Adults, 75¢; children, 50¢.

The mill has been restored so that you may see the old machinery with modern gears in full operation grinding corn. Most visitors spend 5 minutes here. Freshly ground meal is sold at the ticket booth, and there is no charge for enjoying the lovely white ducks and swans in the pretty setting of Shawme Lake.

> Combination fees for Grist Mill and Hoxie House:
> Adults, $1; children, 75¢.

HOXIE HOUSE (1637), a restored saltbox said to be the oldest on Cape Cod.

Open: Mid-June through late September 10–5 daily, open Sundays at 1.

Admission: Adults, 75¢; children, 50¢.

If you have never taken the children to a colonial house, this may be a good introduction. Most visitors spend no more than 15 minutes looking at utensils by the fireplace, an early convertible bed, the Indian board lock, and the place where children slept.

YESTERYEARS MUSEUM has two floors with hundreds of beautifully costumed dolls in labeled glass cases.

Open: May 30-October 15 daily 10–5, Sundays 1–5; just weekends in May.

Admission: Adults, $1; children under 12, 50¢.

There are Oriental dolls and accessories obtained from rich and noble families of Japan and never made for export, many Nuremberg kitchens, some dating from 1730 and completely furnished with ancient copper and brass utensils, tiny shops, and miniature rooms. Students of dress design and Oriental background are particularly fascinated. Unless you and/or the children have a special interest in this exceptional collection, there may be just "too much" to hold a youngster's attention.

SAUGUS IRONWORKS NATIONAL HISTORIC SITE (p. 131)

STRAWBERY BANKE, INC.
Portsmouth, New Hampshire
56 miles from Boston
Tel. 603–436–8010

Directions: Rt. 1 and Interstate 95. Once in Portsmouth, follow strawberry signs. Entrance and parking area on Hancock Street.

Open: May–October daily 9:30–5.

Admission: $2.75; under 16, 75¢; under 6, free.

Guided Tours: By arrangement only. Minimum age: Grade 1. Length: 2 hours.

Picnicking: No area designated, but picnickers could be accommodated. Restaurant on premises.

As restoration progresses, shops and homes of merchants, captains, shipbuilders, cabinetmakers, and other craftsmen will be re-created. Originally settled in 1630, this community, which had riverbanks lined with wild strawberries, became important during the clipper ship era. Six buildings now restored and furnished include the Governor Goodwin Mansion (1811), the Chase House (1762), and the Joseph Sherburne House (1660), with exposed hewn timbers and leaded glass casements. The Dunaway General Store has a pickle barrel and old-fashioned candy. The "before" of buildings can be seen when you view architectural and art exhibits and (most appealing to youngsters) craftsmen at work. Currently there are leatherworkers, a blacksmith, a boatbuilder, a limner (a portrait painter using techniques of the early nineteenth-century itinerant artist), and a craftsman who makes Windsor chairs; more are expected in the coming years.

The 10-acre project is separated into two sections: one with buildings erected on their same sites two hundred and more years ago and the second with important landmarks moved from other parts of Portsmouth. An archaeology exhibit shows what was found when a partial excavation of Puddle Dock was made about 10 years ago—after being filled in since 1899.

It is a good 3-hour visit or a leisurely paced full day.

SUDBURY
20 miles west of Boston

The Wayside Inn area could be combined with the Country Store (p. 46), with bison as the main attraction, or go on to the Toy Cupboard Theatre (p. 54) or maple sugaring (p. 284).

Directions to Wayside Inn Area: Follow Rt. 20 and you will be there.

Just off what is now the main road is an area that is pleasant for meandering, though it could hardly be called a Sturbridge Village.

First stop should be the GRIST MILL, just beyond the Wayside Inn. The miller is on duty April-November 8:30–12 and 1–5; grinding hours vary. He offers a 5-minute explanation of the operation of the mill. Admission: 10¢ per person. Outside follow Hop Brook, which provides water to power the mill-stones in the eighteenth-century reproduction, watch the water splash over the huge wheel, and cross a bridge to the snow remaining in the woods in late spring.

When you cross the Boston Post Road to the other buildings built or restored by the Ford Foundation, it takes some imagination to think about the carriages that once traveled these paths. The MARTHA MARY CHAPEL, open by appointment, was built from timber that was felled on that hill in the 1938 hurricane. The RED SCHOOLHOUSE, attended by Mary and her little lamb, built in Sterling, Massachusetts, in 1798, and in actual use until 1952, is open from approximately noon to 5 P.M. 5 days a week during the summer.

WAYSIDE INN   Boston Post Road   Tel. 443–8846

Guided Tours: By arrangement, 45 minutes.

Admission: Adults, 50¢; children in family groups, free; high-schoolers, 15¢.

Having known time and fire, the operating Wayside Inn is part original (1686) and part restored. It has the Old Bar Room, old kitchen, and early American bedrooms. Dinner guests are welcome. The formal garden is presided over by a bust of Longfellow. (From October to May a small group of Longfellow devotees meet here regularly to read his works.) If you are in the area at dusk, you may see the outside oil lamps being lit. The inn is open 9–6 year round (closed Christmas); dinner guests may look through, but after 6 the light is not good.

A short drive westward brings you to the COUNTRY STORE, open 7 days a week, in Marlboro, at the Sudbury border. This complex has been very popular since the store, originally built in 1790 in Sudbury Center, was moved and restored by Ford in 1930. Outside are hens, chickens, roosters, ducks, geese—and Republican and Democratic benches. Soldier beans (baked beans) and barrel pickles are sold inside. There is a CANDY SHOPPE complete with penny (2 for 5¢?) candy, and mechanical machines that do respond to coins. Upstairs and down and here and there are nickelodeons that will open the curtains and exhibit a band if you deposit 10¢.

In the CIRCUS ROOM, open during fall and spring weekends and daily in the summer, circus buffs may reminisce a bit while a guide explains the 160-square-foot model with its hundreds of figures, animals, and wagons. Admission: 25¢ per person.

HISTORIC SITES
AND EXHIBITS

... Unless it is a designated children's day, historic houses request (or require) that youngsters be accompanied by adults.

... The early houses with few rooms are a good introduction. If enough interest is shown, take on an estate.

... Group leaders are reminded that orientation is a help.

... Most guided tours tend to focus on things rather than particular people who lived there. When this is done in relation to space, there is the added benefit of visual awareness. The most successful guides may be those who have anecdotes to relate.

... Check locally for walking tour material. (Dedham, Milton, and Quincy are among the communities that have such information.)

... The most visited site in Boston is *The Constitution* (p. 122).

... The most asked-for site is that of the Boston Tea Party (p. 112).

... Gravestone rubbing is often a part of field trips. It is necessary to check with the local city or town hall. Boston and some surrounding communities have discontinued permission to record tombstones via this art.

BOSTON NATIONAL HISTORICAL PARK

Although the sites that the newly established park will work with have been on the "places to see" list for a long time, they will now be preserved, and interpretation services will be provided through federal funds. Most of the changes will not take place until after the Bicentennial. The sites involved are the Boston Naval Shipyard, Bunker Hill, Faneuil Hall, The Old State House, Old South Meeting House, Paul Revere House, and the Old North Church. A downtown National Park Service Visitor Center is planned. When the program takes full effect, it is likely that some hours and prices will change. For current information, check with the National Historical Park office, 150 Causeway Street, Boston, Tel. 223–2915.

THE FREEDOM TRAIL

(See p. 117 for Black Heritage Trail.)

Suggestions:

. . . Those with limited energy—or young children—may be reminded that many find the North End most fascinating. (Those sites are in Loop Two of the new arrangement of Freedom Trail sites.)

. . . The other arrangement—now called Loop One—covers sites between and includes Faneuil Hall and Boston Common. If you start at the Common on a Friday or Saturday, the end of your walk could be combined with the market district suggestions (p. 148). If you start at Faneuil Hall and end at the Common, you are in a large outside area with a place to sit down, grass, entertainment, and the Park Street subway station.

. . . CLOSING TIMES: These hours refer to the hour when you are asked to leave. Arrive at least a half hour before at most sites.

. . . Many visitors enjoy just walking the Trail—even when some buildings are closed—and noticing the blend of old and new.

. . . Wear comfortable shoes.

General Information:

HOURS: Bicentennial bonus: For years the hours for the various sites have been quite individual. Most Freedom Trail sites are open 10–6 daily during Bicentennial years. Perhaps such benefits will remain after 1976.

MAPS are available from the Information Booth on Boston Common, from other information booths (p. 22), and at any of the sites along the Trail. Printed information is available in French, Spanish, Italian, and German.

EXPENSES: Only three places charge admission. PAUL REVERE HOUSE: 50¢ for adults; school groups of 10 or more over 14, 10¢; children under 14 with adults, free. OLD SOUTH MEETING HOUSE: Adults, 50¢, accompanied children under 12, free. OLD STATE HOUSE: Adults, 50¢; children over 6, 25¢. Massachusetts schoolchildren in groups are free. Out of state schoolchildren in groups 10¢ each if teacher collects.

The Freedom Trail: Loop One (Downtown)

FANEUIL HALL ("Cradle of Liberty")   Dock Square. (The building has a grasshopper weather vane made in 1742 by Shem Drowne, maker of many colonial weather vanes.)

Ⓣ**Stop:** Haymarket on Orange or Green Line.

Open: Monday-Friday 9–5, Saturdays 9–12, Sundays 1–5. Closed Thanksgiving, Christmas, and New Year's Day. Special note: *The Armory is closed on weekends.*

Armory: A good climb to the third floor; open Monday-Friday 10–4. If groups (suggested minimum age: junior high) would like a talk, please make advance arrangements with Sidney M. Abbott, Curator, Tel. 227–1638.

By the time most tourists reach the famous second-floor auditorium, they take a seat to rest. Think about what the town of Boston was like when its town meetings were held here. The building was built in 1742, burned in 1763, and enlarged in 1803, and the hall is still available for open meetings.

Those who climb to the third floor will visit the place where the Ancient and Honorable Artillery Company, chartered "as a nursery for soldiers and a school for officers" in 1638, has had its home for over 200 years. The museum is fairly child-proof. On display are early flags—some with 15 stripes; after Vermont and Kentucky were admitted to the Union, the narrowing stripes were considered a problem and the flag was changed to the original 13. Many uniforms, arms, and possessions of colonial military men are on display.

To comply with the wishes of donor Peter Faneuil, the ground floor still has markets. Stop in to see the activity.

Handicapped: Plenty of steps to cope with.

QUINCY MARKET   faces Faneuil Hall

Open: Monday-Saturday, all day starting very early.

Admission: Free.

This is a "must" for a walk-through to see the stalls that sell produce, cheese, poultry, and meat. Each area is small; you can see whatever activity there is. Mornings are best. Those who man the stalls are friendly and helpful.

BOSTON MASSACRE SITE   Congress and State streets (near the Old State House)

If you stand on a corner of this busy intersection and look beneath the policeman directing traffic, you will see a ring of cobblestones in the center of the circular traffic island. The first bloodshed of the Revolution was here, when, on March 5, 1770, a jeering Boston crowd clashed with a British guard of nine soldiers.

OLD STATE HOUSE   206 Washington Street (actually located in the middle of State Street)   Tel. 523–7033

Ⓣ **Stop:** State Street (located right underneath the building).

Open: Year round, Monday-Saturday 9–4. Closed Thanksgiving, Christmas, and New Year's Day.

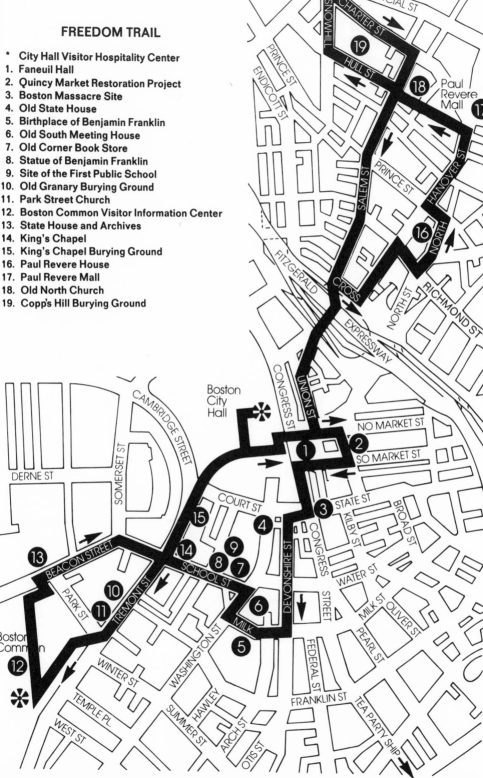

FREEDOM TRAIL

* City Hall Visitor Hospitality Center
1. Faneuil Hall
2. Quincy Market Restoration Project
3. Boston Massacre Site
4. Old State House
5. Birthplace of Benjamin Franklin
6. Old South Meeting House
7. Old Corner Book Store
8. Statue of Benjamin Franklin
9. Site of the First Public School
10. Old Granary Burying Ground
11. Park Street Church
12. Boston Common Visitor Information Center
13. State House and Archives
14. King's Chapel
15. King's Chapel Burying Ground
16. Paul Revere House
17. Paul Revere Mall
18. Old North Church
19. Copp's Hill Burying Ground

Admission: Adults, 50¢; children over 6, 25¢; Massachusetts schoolchildren in groups, free; out of state schoolchildren in groups, 10¢ if teacher collects.

Groups: Arrange for a guide in advance. No more than 30 in a group please.

Built in 1713, the building that was the seat of the Colonial government is essentially a museum now. Exhibitions have just been redesigned, and new lighting allows visitors to see the exhibits in late afternoon hours. There are shop signs, pictures of early Boston, and Revolutionary relics. Labeled treasures include a doctor's kit, ship models, and surveyor's instruments of early days. Browsers are welcome; bare feet and food are banned.

After climbing to the second floor via a circular staircase, visitors may stand near the balcony where laws were proclaimed with the beat of a drum. It is a good vantage point for looking at the site of the Boston Massacre.

On many historic house tours, guides point out the difference in height of the early settlers and twentieth-century Americans. This is evident when you see John Hancock's embroidered velvet outfit located in the room where he was inaugurated as first governor of the Commonwealth.

Outside, the gables are among the most photographed features in Boston. They still bear the lion and unicorn emblems of England.

Handicapped: Steps make it generally difficult.

BIRTHPLACE OF BENJAMIN FRANKLIN   17 Milk Street (around the corner from the Old South Meeting House)

Look up to the second story to see the bust of Franklin on the exterior of the building. A plaque designates the site of the house where he was born, the fifteenth in a family of 17 children.

OLD SOUTH MEETING HOUSE   Washington Street between School and Milk streets   Tel. 482–6439. (The building with the centuries-old tower clock and Goodspeed's Basement Book Store is 2 blocks from Filene's.)

Ⓣ **Stop:** State on Orange and Blue Lines.

Open: April 1-August 31, 10–6 daily; fall Monday-Saturday 10–5; winter Monday-Saturday 10–4. Closed Sundays. Closed Thanksgiving, Christmas, and New Year's Day. (Sunday services are at the Old South Church, Copley Square, 11 A.M. and 7:30 P.M.)

Admission: Adults, 50¢; accompanied children under 12, free. All school groups admitted free.

Groups: 10-minute guided tour. Minimum age: 10.

Visitors are allowed to sit in pews of the church, but most exhibits are under glass here where the Boston Tea Party was conceived during a town meeting that was too big for Faneuil Hall. After the citizens resolved that the tea should not be landed, those attending the meeting left from this point. During the siege of Boston its pews were used for firewood and the building was used as a riding academy.

Once you step inside the tower front door, now bordering the sidewalk of a heavily populated business district, you see the numbered pews and a plan that shows the families who owned them when the building was a church. (The "New" Old South Church was built in Copley Square in 1872.) Now a museum, occasionally used for meetings or concerts, its exhibits include a model of Boston as it was in 1775, the tricornered hat of the Continental army, paper currency, and photographs of the great Boston Fire. Reproductions of historical documents are sold for 15¢.

Handicapped: Low threshold. Assistance available.

You may be tempted to browse among the sidewalk stalls of GOODSPEED'S BASEMENT STORE at #2 Milk Street, Tel. 523–5970, a side entrance to the Old South Meeting House building. There are few books for the very young at this organized used book store. Prices start at 25¢ and they are open 9–5 Monday-Friday and 9–12 Saturdays. Closed Saturdays during summer. Their rare books, autographs, and old prints are at 18 Beacon Street.

> **Hours of historic sites may now be coordinated. Places may also be open 7 days a week. Call to check. Most are open 10–6 during Bicentennial years.**

OLD CORNER BOOK STORE   Washington (formerly Cornhill) and School streets   Tel. 929–2602

Open: Monday-Friday 8:30–6.

Admission: Free.

Average Visit: 10 minutes.

The building has a varied history: private home, apothecary shop and home, printing establishment—before it became a bookshop and gathering place of many important literary figures including Holmes, Longfellow, Lowell, Whittier, and Hawthorne. Changes continued and before recent restoration it was a pizza parlor. The ground floor, now the *Boston Globe* intown office, has an old interior with first editions (behind glass), period furniture, a Franklin stove, and an old Willard clock.

Handicapped: Double doors open.

Across Washington Street is SPRING LANE. For over two centuries the Great Spring gave water to the people of Boston.

STATUE OF BENJAMIN FRANKLIN   Old City Hall grounds   School Street

Franklin's involvement in many areas is recognized by the four bronze panels at the base of the statue, which was erected in 1856: they show him signing the Declaration of Independence, signing the Treaty of Peace with France, in his role as a printer, and experimenting with lightning and electricity.

SITE OF THE FIRST PUBLIC SCHOOL   School Street

A plaque on one of the fence posts outside the Old City Hall designates the site of the first public school in the country. It was here that the Boston Public Latin School, now located on Avenue Louis Pasteur, originated in 1635. (If you are following the trail, you may wish to insert King's Chapel here, so that you terminate at the Boston Common.)

GRANARY BURYING GROUND   Tremont Street (next to Park Street Church)

Ⓣ**Stop:** Park Street.

Open: Daily 8–5.

Originally the site of the town granary. Included are the graves of John Hancock, Robert Treat Paine, Samuel Adams, "Mother Goose," and those killed in the Boston Massacre.

Note: No gravestone rubbing allowed.

Handicapped: 4 steps to enter.

PARK STREET CHURCH   corner of Tremont and Park streets   Tel. 523–3383

Ⓣ **Stop:** Park Street.

Open: Monday-Friday 9–4:30, Saturdays 9–12, Sundays 9–1. Closed July 4 and
Labor Day. Young people with parents or group leaders are welcome.

It is a two-flight climb to the auditorium in the church where the spire and
clock have been landmarks since 1810. When the town granary occupied the
site, the sails for the frigate *Constitution* were made here. Brimstone for gun-
powder was stored in the crypt of the church for use in the War of 1812.
Parishioners of 1829 heard William Lloyd Garrison give his first antislavery
address. And the first public singing of "America" took place two years later
in 1831.

When the church bells announce noontime, an almost village-like feeling
is created in the area.

Handicapped: Side door, not always open, has an elevator.

BOSTON COMMON   bounded by Park, Tremont, Boylston, and Charles
streets

Ⓣ **Stop:** Boylston or Park.

Parking: Underground parking garage, entrance on Charles Street.

The oldest public park in the country continues to have a variety of uses. In
the past it has been used for hangings, stocks and pillory sites, pasturelands,
and as a station for British troops during the Revolution. Today it is frequented
by demonstrating groups and those who "wish to have their say." You can be
sure of finding benches among the labeled (some in Latin) trees, a potpourri of
architecture and facades nearby, and a bandstand concert on most summer
weekdays. There is plenty of running space. The playground (near the Frog
Pond) has plenty of climbing possibilities. Wading is allowed in the Frog Pond
during the summer months, and ice skating is possible in winter (p. 230). You
can count on seeing hundreds of hungry pigeons. Many a child has been
photographed with pigeons atop head and shoulders. Peanuts and popcorn
are sold by the vendors near the Charles Street entrance.

The plaza near Park and Tremont streets has become the area where
"most goes on." Hari Krishna members may be chanting; a dulcimer player
may be performing to one audience while a banjo and guitar team gathers
still a different group; there may be a demonstration for a cause, food vendors,
newspaper hawkers—it is lively.

Although people-watching is a favorite pastime here, there are some monuments and memorials worth seeing. Near the State House is the Robert
Gould Shaw Monument (p. 118). Closer to the Park Street subway entrance is
tall ornate Brewer Fountain; its original was made for the Paris Exposition of
1855. Along Boylston Street, opposite West Street, is the bronze plaque of the
monument that honors those who fell in the Boston Massacre. The Central
Burying Ground (entrance on Boylston Street) has some tombstones with
young ages on them—reminders of the hard times of the colonists. In 1974
with the help of pennies from Boston schoolchildren, a new Liberty Tree, a
successor to the original that served as a symbol of the Revolution, was
planted near the corner of Tremont and Boylston streets.

STATE HOUSE   Beacon Street (and Park)   Tel. 727–2121   Archives Museum, Tel. 727–2816

Depending upon interests—and follow-through possibilities—this could be a major stop taking 1½–2 hours.

Open: Monday-Friday (except holidays) 9–5. (During the Bicentennial it will be open on weekends.) Visitors may sit in the gallery to observe the legislature in session. Call 727–2356 for schedule.

What was once John Hancock's pastureland now has this gold-domed building with impressive marble staircases. The *Sacred Cod* still hangs in the Senate Chamber as a reminder of an initial major industry in the state; Bulfinch architectural details are everywhere; the Hall of Flags displays battle flags from Civil and Spanish-American wars as well as some from World Wars I and II.

If you would like to see the role of the legislators today, you may spend some time in the House or Senate; even if they are not in session, you may see the roll board and consider procedures. Perhaps a group could hold its own mock session with the help of a legislator; advance arrangements should be made for this. Meetings of the legislature and committee hearings are open to the public; call the Clerk of House for a schedule. For follow-up educational activity, copies of any of the bills under consideration can be obtained from Room 428, the Legislative Document Room. The Public Document Room, 116, Tel. 727–2834, has copies of the recent gubernatorial proclamations (days and weeks often unheard of by the general public).

Guided Tours: State House tours (45 minutes–1 hour) are available year round (holidays excepted) Monday-Friday. Groups should make advance arrangements for tours; individual visitors are welcome to join a group. The Information Desk in Doric Hall will have the day's schedule. It is possible to arrange for tours in Spanish, French, Portuguese, and Italian. For appointments and information, call 727–3676 or write to Room 179, State House, Boston 02133.

Self-guided Tours: Pick up printed information in Doric Hall.

THE ARCHIVES MUSEUM has its own entrance from outside—just to the left of the main exterior stairway—or it can be reached from the State House. This can be an exciting visit for those who want to see original documents (which are encased for proper humidity control). Parents may help read the script or older children may like to read for themselves the "Muster Role" of men who responded to a call to arms on April 19, 1775, the details of how far they marched, and how much they were paid. There is the request of Captain Kidd's wife to be allowed to visit him in jail, seals of wax with the writer's ring pressed into them, and inkblots on some of the papers that have been preserved for over 300 years. Treaties made with the Indians during the seventeenth and eighteenth centuries are on display, as is the oldest constitution still in effect—that of 1780.

KING'S CHAPEL   58 Tremont Street (corner of School Street)   Tel. 523–1749
     Ⓣ **Stop:** Park Street.

Open: Year round Monday-Friday 10–4. Sunday services at 11.

Guide: Sometimes provided for a 15-minute tour. Minimum age for guided groups: 12. Maximum size: 20–25. Minimum age: Elementary school.

As you walk up and down its central aisle, there is a feeling of beauty and history in a living church. You are in a place that has a history of many "firsts" —the first Church of England in the Massachusetts Bay Colony, the first Unitarian Church in America, and the first church to use organ music. Its bell was made by Paul Revere, the governor's pew was used by George Washington, and it is the oldest stone (Quincy granite) church in Boston. The 4-foot thick walls were built around the original wooden church when the church was still in use.

Handicapped: Threshold low. Accessible.

As the adjacent BURYING GROUND was the first cemetery in town, many of the markers are not legible today.

The Freedom Trail: Loop Two (North End)

(See p. 151 for combination suggestions.)
You may wish to finish the routing at City Hall (p. 250)
and the adjacent market district (p. 148.)

Please note that the hours may now be 10–6 daily. (See p. 113.)

PAUL REVERE HOUSE   19 North Square (between Richmond and Prince, both streets run from Hanover)   Tel. 227–0972

Ⓣ**Stop:** Haymarket on Green or Orange Lines.

Open: Monday-Saturday 9–3:45, closed Sundays and most holidays. Open April 19.

Admission: Adults, 50¢; school groups of 10 or more over 14, 10¢. Children under 14 with adults, free.

It was from this point that Paul Revere started his ride to Lexington in April 1775. Built around 1660, it is the oldest house in Boston, and was about 100 years old when Paul Revere acquired it. His 16 children—by two wives—were all born here. You are welcome to linger over the exhibits, but most groups hear a short talk and go in and out of the 4 rooms in less than 15 minutes. As this is a stop for tour buses, it is particularly busy in the summer. Allow time for children to sign in and look at some of the tools representing Revere's versatility, the rare coattail chair, and wide floorboards.

Handicapped: 1 step into house, second floor difficult.

PAUL REVERE MALL is a small park with benches occupied by residents, and it has 13 bronze tablets set in the surrounding walls that tell the part played by the North End and its people in the history of Boston from 1630 to 1918. Visiting children—and all those carrying cameras—usually focus their attention on Cyrus Dallin's equestrian statue of Paul Revere.

Handicapped: A few steps on each end of mall.

Steps at the far end of the mall lead to

OLD NORTH CHURCH (Christ Church)   193 Salem Street   Tel. 523–6676

Ⓣ **Stop:** Haymarket on Orange and Green lines. Ten-minute walk.

Directions: If driving directly, take Causeway Street to Hull, go up over the hill, and at the bottom is the church. If walking on Hanover Street, find St.

Stephen's Church, distinguished from a distance by its white spire, cross the street, walk through the Paul Revere Mall to the church.

Open: Year round, daily 9–4:30.

Admission: Free.

Tours: 10–20 minutes for groups if advance notice given.

While the guide may point out the 1724 brass chandelier, the 1726 clock (the oldest working one in a United States public building), or on rare occasions even play the 1759 Johnston organ, everyone will recall the role of this church in the Revolution. Children may hear familiar details, learn some new ones, and be inspired to ask some questions. This gracious and well-maintained structure, Boston's oldest church building still standing, was built in 1723. Visitors may sit in the box pews marked with names of Revolutionary parishioners, but the path to the narrow steeple is not open to the public. The old bells in the steeple, still rung every Sunday at 10:45, were rung by Paul Revere at the age of 15 when he was a member of the boys' Bell Ringers' Guild, and they signaled Cornwallis's surrender at Yorktown.

Replicas of the two lanterns that were hung in the steeple to signal that the Redcoats were leaving for Lexington and Concord can be seen in the small MUSEUM adjacent to the church.

Handicapped: Use the main entrance rather than the mall.

COPP'S HILL BURYING GROUND   corner of Snowhill and Charter streets, 1 block from Old North Church. From the front door of the Old North Church it is a 3-minute uphill walk on Hull Street.

Directly across the Hull Street gate is the narrowest house in Boston—only 9 feet 6 inches wide.

Open: July and August daily 8–4, other months Monday-Friday 8–4.

Thousands of early Bostonians are buried here. Some gravestones show bullet marks from the muskets of the British who used them as practice targets during the siege of Boston; weather-worn names are now difficult to discern. From this site you can see Old Ironsides in the harbor. (Copp's Hill is part of the Black Heritage Trail, p. 119.)

BLACK HERITAGE TRAIL

A walking tour of downtown Boston and Beacon Hill. All sites relate to the development of Boston's Afro-American community in the eighteenth and nineteenth centuries. Note the Black Heritage Trail logo—a red, black, and green marker—outside buildings. Brochures with map are distributed by the Museum of Afro American History (p. 168) at the starting point on Smith Court (Beacon Hill) and at information booths (p. 14). Conducted tours of the trail are given periodically, often on weekends. Length: 1–2 hours. For current schedule telephone 723–8863 or 495–7400.

THE AFRICAN MEETING HOUSE   built by members of the African Free Society in 1805. It is the oldest existing church building in North America built by black Americans for their own use. Its renovation is scheduled to be completed this summer. Exhibits and programs planned for the public.

SMITH COURT RESIDENCES   Number 3 is the only structure that ante-dates the Meeting House. From 1851 to 1856 Number 5 was the home of William C. Neill, the black activist who initiated the movement to integrate the public schools. Numbers 7, 7½, and 10 are typical styles of the homes occupied by nineteenth-century Afro-American families.

THE SMITH SCHOOL   adjacent to the Meeting House. Built by funds left by Abiel Smith for the education of black children in 1830 when the schools were legally separated. It currently houses an American Legion Post.

COLONEL GEORGE MIDDLETON HOUSE   5 Pinckney Street, home of the leader of the Massachusetts Bucks, a black volunteer unit during the Revolution.

JOHN J. SMITH HOUSE   86 Pinckney Street

John J. Smith was born in Virginia, moved to Boston at age 20, and had a barbershop that served as a front for antislavery activities all over New England. In the Civil War he was stationed in Washington, D.C., and worked as a recruiting officer for the all-black 5th Cavalry. He also served in the Massachusetts Legislature and was the first black man appointed to the Boston Common Council.

LEWIS HAYDEN HOUSE   66 Philips Street

The plaque on the house tells you that this was the home of a leading black abolitionist, a slave who escaped to Detroit and bought his freedom. The house was a "station" on the Underground Railroad.

GEORGE GRANT HOUSE   108 Charles Street

George Grant was a talented inventor and recognized dentist, the first black graduate of Harvard College, a graduate of Harvard Dental School, the first black instructor at the Harvard Dental School, an expert in treatment of cleft palate and cognate diseases—and inventor of the golf tee.

THE CHARLES STREET MEETING HOUSE   Charles and Mt. Vernon streets

Built by blacks for a white congregation. After the Civil War, the African Methodist Episcopal Church bought the building where its members worshiped until the 1930s. The congregation was the last black institution to leave Beacon Hill.

STATE HOUSE   Beacon Hill

Records in the Archives detail the history of the state's black citizens. Slavery was finally declared unconstitutional in 1783 by the Massachusetts Supreme Court. In 1780 the state had a system of taxing the personal income of blacks even though they could not vote in Massachusetts elections. In the State House library is the medal awarded Senator Charles Sumner by the Haitian government in gratitude for his efforts toward the United States' recognition of the black nations of Liberia and Haiti. The banner of the 54th Regiment and the flag saved by Sergeant William Carney at Fort Wagner are in the Hall of Flags. The first black state representative, Edwin Walker, took office in 1867.

54th REGIMENT MONUMENT   corner of Beacon and Park streets on Boston Common across from the State House

The Massachusetts 54th Regiment, which had its drilling grounds in Readville (present-day Hyde Park), was the first black division from the North to serve in the Civil War. The leader, Robert Gould Shaw, was white. This monument was designed by sculptor Augustus Saint-Gaudens.

BOSTON MASSACRE MONUMENT   Tremont Street side of the Common, opposite West Street

Erected by black citizens of Boston. Crispus Attucks, a former slave from Framingham, was the first to fall in what became known as the Boston Massacre on March 5, 1770.

OLD GRANARY BURYING GROUND (p. 113)   next to Park Street Church

The common grave of Crispus Attucks and the other four victims of the Boston Massacre is to the right of the entrance gate.

OLD SOUTH MEETING HOUSE (p. 112).   Judge Samuel Sewall, a member of the congregation, was one of the first to protest the African slave trade. Here in one of the oldest churches in the city is a copy of George Washington's will in which he freed his own male slaves and provided for their education—and explained his attitude toward slavery.

BOSTON MASSACRE SITE   in front of the Old State House

The place where Crispus Attucks (see Boston Massacre Monument above) and four others were slain by the British in 1770 is marked by a cobblestone ring in the middle of a traffic island.

COPP'S HILL   Hull and Snowhill streets (North End)

Boston's second oldest cemetery contains the bodies of over 1,000 pre-Revolutionary War blacks, including Prince Hall, the founder of the Masonic (African) Lodge. A monument to him is on the Snowhill Street side of the cemetery.

THE EMANCIPATION GROUP   Park Square

Its nearest Black Heritage Trail site is the Boston Massacre Monument, but with a location at the center of Park Square, recognition is mostly by motorists. The model for the "kneeling slave" was Archer Alexander, a fugitive slave from Missouri. This is a duplicate casting of the sculpture by Thomas Ball, the original being commissioned by the Freedman's Memorial Society in Washington, D.C.

OTHER PLACES OF HISTORIC INTEREST IN BOSTON

BEACON HILL MANSIONS (1818)   39–40 Beacon Street

Open: Wednesdays (except holidays) 10–4.

Admission: Adults, $1; children under 12, 50¢. (Not many children come here.)

A guided tour with an opportunity to view the Boston Common through purple glass windows. These lovely furnished Federal mansions are preserved and maintained by the Women's City Club of Boston.

BOSTON TEA PARTY SHIP (p. 160).

BUNKER HILL MONUMENT on Breed's Hill   Charlestown   Tel. 242–9560

Ⓣ **Stop:** From Haymarket Square take Sullivan Square via Bunker Hill bus.

Directions: The natural way to approach the Monument seems to be via Park, Commons, and Adams streets. For a dramatic approach it is worth going a minute out of your way. Go around Winthrop Square, which has memorials to Charlestown men who fought at Bunker Hill, come down the hill via Winthrop Street, turn right onto Warren, and then take a right onto Monument Avenue, a hill that is lined with historic brick residences.

When leaving, go along Warren to Main to see some of the changes (restorations) that are taking place right under the elevated structure that is scheduled to come down soon.

Open: Year round 9–5 daily. Closed Thanksgiving and Christmas.

Admission: Adults, 75¢; children under 12, 50¢; school groups, 25¢. Fee includes audio tour and admission to small museum.

At the base of the mall you can follow the battle in its proper sequence with your headset by going to marked locations and listening to appropriate audio at each location. You hear both the British and Colonial sides of the battle.

The granite for the monument came from Quincy via horse-drawn railroad cars from the quarries to the Neponset River, and then by barge to Charlestown. As the railroad was built for this contract, it is known as America's first commercial railway. But the site is more remembered for the command "Don't fire until you see the whites of their eyes." (The museum includes a diorama of the battle.) When General Lafayette laid the cornerstone in 1825, Daniel Webster delivered the dedication address.

A highlight for many visitors is the 294-step climb around the shaft inside the monument for a good view of the harbor and city. Younger ones may appreciate adult accompaniment up the narrow passageway.

GIBSON HOUSE (1859)   137 Beacon Street   Tel. 267–6338
Open: Year round, Tuesday-Sunday 2–5. Closed legal holidays.

Admission: $1.

It is real Victoriana—from the cat's bed upstairs to the kitchen in the basement. The home, originally built and always occupied by members of the Gibson family, is as the bachelor son Charles Hammond Gibson left it in 1956. The guide will take you through the four floors open to the public in less than a half hour.

This is a museum that appeals most to antique buffs and "Upstairs-Downstairs" fans. Young children are not usually too interested.

MASSACHUSETTS GENERAL HOSPITAL Ether Dome   Fruit Street
Open: Monday-Friday, sometime between 9 and 5; hospital personnel use it about 50 percent of the time.

Both the Bulfinch building and the Ether Dome atop the building are National Historic Landmarks. Climb the graceful staircase and enter the Ether Dome, an amphitheatre still used for medical rounds and conferences. Here in the operating room of the hospital (1821–1867) was the first public demonstration of the use of ether in a surgical operation. Light enters through the window in the dome (which opens with the push of a button). Around the room are cases with artifacts, including an operating chair, (a copy of) an ether inhaler, some instruments, and an Egyptian mummy. A slide presentation of the past, present, and future has been prepared for the Bicentennial; it may continue to be available for visitors.

NEW ENGLAND LIFE INSURANCE BUILDING   501 Boylston Street
Tel. 266–3700

Ⓣ **Stop:** Arlington (use Berkeley Street stairs) or Copley.

Open: Monday-Friday 8:45 A.M.–4:45 P.M. Closed weekends and holidays.

If you are in the Copley Square area, it is worth stopping in to see Charles Hoffbauer's murals of colonial New England. Included are depictions of George Washington taking command of the Continental army in Cambridge, Samoset bidding welcome to the Pilgrims at Plymouth, the Declaration of Independence being hailed in Boston, Paul Revere's Ride, and the launching of the U.S.S. *Constitution.* Picture postcards of the murals are provided free to visitors upon request.

In the rear lobby are dioramas of important milestones in the history of Boston's Back Bay.

NEW ENGLAND TELEPHONE HEADQUARTERS BUILDING   185 Franklin
Street (corner Congress), is 2 blocks from Old State House, 5 blocks from Filene's, and 1 long block from Post Office Square

Open: Monday-Friday 8:30–5.

The actual attic workshop of Alexander Graham Bell has been reassembled in the lobby on the first floor. See the world's first switchboards, replicas of the very first telephones, and telephone history depicted in a mural.

NICHOLS HOUSE MUSEUM (nineteenth century)   55 Mt. Vernon Street
(Beacon Hill)   Tel. 227–6993

Open: Wednesdays and Saturdays 1–5.

Admission: Adults, $1.

Guide service is provided through the furnished rooms in this Bulfinch-designed building that now houses the Boston Council for International Visitors. "The house has been carefully and lovingly preserved as it was lived in for 80 years. There is really a no-touch rule. We could not handle groups of children."

HARRISON GRAY OTIS HOUSE (1796)   141 Cambridge Street   Tel.
227–3956, is on the "other" (back) side of Beacon Hill almost midway between Massachusetts General Hospital and the Government Center.

Open: Monday-Friday. Guided tours only at 10, 11, 1, 2, and 3. Closed weekends and holidays.

Admission: Adults, $1; children under 12, 50¢. Doesn't appeal to children.

This Federal-style mansion is the first of three houses in Boston designed by Charles Bulfinch for Otis, a lawyer, congressman, and mayor of Boston.

Tours take you through the magnificent period rooms of the first two floors, which have recently undergone a thorough scholarly analysis to reflect the taste and decoration of Boston townhouse living from 1790 to 1820.

The house has a varied history. At one time it was a Turkish bath for women. Currently, it serves as museum and headquarters for the Society for the Preservation of New England Antiquities. The society's library houses extensive architectural and photographic archives.

U.S.S. CONSTITUTION   Boston   Naval   Shipyard   Charlestown   Tel.
242–3734

> As this receives the heaviest attendance of all Boston's
> historic sites, residents may choose to visit in fall or
> spring when lingering is more possible.

Ⓣ **Stop:** From Haymarket Square take Sullivan Square via Bunker Hill bus.

Open: 9:30–4 every day of the year except one day in June for the turnaround
cruise and during blizzards.

Admission: Free.

Average Visit: 45 minutes.

"Old Ironsides," the 44-gun frigate launched in 1797 and undefeated in forty
battles, is still an officially commissioned flagship of the U.S. Navy. You will
have a feeling of the navy of another century as you note the towering masts,
cannons, hammocks that were beds for the crew, dentist and surgeon chairs,
and the galley where soups and stews were cooked for over 400 men. Crew
members (in 1812 uniforms) are helpful with young children on the steep
narrow stairways that connect the three decks.

Although the ship is once again open to the public, complete restoration
(the fifth in 177 years) is not scheduled until 1976. Little more than 5 percent
of the original craft remains.

Note: You can see the Bunker Hill Monument from here. One-way streets make
driving difficult. It is about a 10-minute walk.

SOME HISTORIC SITES IN
NEARBY COMMUNITIES

(Many of these offer special programs for local schoolchildren.)

Arlington

JASON RUSSELL HOUSE   7 Jason Street   Tel. 648–4300 (Located 1
block from Pleasant Street along Massachusetts Avenue)

Open: April 1-November 1, Tuesday-Saturday 2–5.

Admission: Memorial Day-Labor Day: Adults, 50¢; children under 12, 10¢.

Length of Tour: 30 minutes.

Minimum Age: Kindergarten.

Within the six rooms can be found holes made by the British on April 19, 1775,
and Revolutionary period guns, dolls, and cradles.

Just a block away, bordering the Robbins Public Library, are the TOWN
GARDENS where you may take a short stroll or read. The Indian statue designed by sculptor Cyrus Dallin and dedicated to the Massachusetts Indian
tribe from which Arlington took its original name of Menotomy is on the top
level of a very pretty waterfall. But if it is running space you need, drive about
a mile up Jason Street to Menotomy Rocks Park (p. 194). Cooke's Hollow, just
off Mystic Street near Arlington Center, is an example of a community project
that changed the neglected, weedy shores of Mill Brook into a landscaped park.

THE OLD SCHWAMB MILL   17 Mill Lane at Lowell Street   Arlington Heights   Tels. 643–0554, 643–0640

Contact: Mrs. John A. Fitzmaurice, Director

Ⓣ **Stop:** Lowell Street on Arlington Heights bus from Harvard Square.

Tours: Offered year round, Monday-Friday 9–4:30. Length: 1¼ hours. Minimum number: 4 including one adult. Minimum age: 8. Maximum number: 15.

Tour Fees: Adults, $2; through high-school age, 50¢.

"It is like going through a time tunnel to go down Mill Lane and into the Mill."

Adjust to the abrupt change in environment just minutes from Massachusetts Avenue traffic in this charming historic landmark. This is the site of the Revolutionary battle of the Foot of the Rocks on Mill Brook and the location of a 1650 grist and saw mill. The nineteenth-century working mill, saved through the efforts of the director, now houses several potters and woodworkers, framemakers, a furnituremaker, and a violinmaker. All use traditional tools and stop to talk with visitors. (This is the only mill in the United States making museum quality, hand-turned oval wooden frames.)

As a guide takes you through a barn and the four floors of the mill, you feel the pulse of another era. Craftsmen are making a living in an occupation where care and creation are important. All over the building are messages and news and weather reports. (The windows were washed on December 31, 1901; the first major snowstorm of the season took place on . . . and more.)

Classes: Fine arts and crafts classes for young people (minimum age) and adults are open to the public for registration.

For Sale: A supply of kiln-dried, rare hardwoods. Products and services of resident craftsmen are available.

Slide Presentation: Call the mill for information.

Picnic: Menotomy Rocks Park (p. 194), 1½ miles away.

Bedford

THE OLDEST FLAG IN THE COUNTRY is on display at the Bedford Public Library, Mudge Way (off Great Road), Tel. 275–9440

Open: Monday-Friday 9–5; evenings and weekends by appointment.

The only Minuteman flag carried at Concord Bridge on April 19, 1775, was made in England in 1660–1670 for the militia of the Massachusetts Bay Colony before the Revolutionary War.

Beverly

BALCH HOUSE (1636)   448 Cabot Street   Tel. 922–7076

Open: June 15-September 15, Monday-Saturday 10–4. Closed holidays.

Admission: Adults, $1; children, 50¢.

It is a half-hour tour through what is said to be the oldest wooden house in America. Complete restoration dependent upon funds.

Braintree

GENERAL SYLVANUS THAYER BIRTHPLACE (1720)   786 Washington Street   Tel. 843–6044

Open: April 19-October 12, Tuesdays, Thursdays, Fridays, Sundays 1:30–4, Saturdays 10:30–4; October 13-April 18, Tuesdays, Saturdays 1:30–4. Closed Thanksgiving, Christmas, and Easter.

Admission: Adults, 75¢; schoolchildren, 25¢.

Groups: Please make advance arrangements. Minimum age: 5.

The 1-hour tour with a guide—sometimes in costume—takes you through the parlor, hall, kitchen, and two bedrooms. Old phonographs of Thomas Watson and a detailed replica of a country schoolhouse are part of the museum in the basement. The house is completely furnished in pre-1785 antiques—those of a well-to-do farmer of the period.

Brookline

EDWARD DEVOTION HOUSE (1750)   347 Harvard Street (near Coolidge Corner)

Open: Tuesdays, Thursdays 2:30–5. Closed holidays.

Admission: Adults, 50¢. No charge for children under 12; must be accompanied by an adult.

Guided Tours: By appointment only for groups at least in 4th grade.

Black kettles are in position in the fireplace of the large original kitchen. Other rooms open to the public are the parlor, buttery, and an upstairs bedroom complete with trundle bed.

JOHN FITZGERALD KENNEDY NATIONAL HISTORIC SITE   83 Beals Street

Directions: Going west on Beacon Street, run right on Harvard Street (Coolidge Corner) to sign at Beals Street.

Open: Daily, except Christmas and New Year's Day, 9–4:45.

Admission: Adults, 50¢; children under 16 and educational groups, free.

Groups: Guided tour on request.

Parking: On adjacent streets or in municipal parking lots (the nearest is 3 blocks away on Fuller Street).

The thirty-fifth president of the United States lived here from his birth, May 29, 1917, until 1920. The house has been restored to that period, and has many original furnishings and some reproductions. A short walk through the halls of the house gives a view of the three rooms on the first floor and four on the second (20 minutes).

National Park Service personnel distribute informational leaflets, which direct you on a 45-minute walk to nearby places that played a part in the president's early days.

PUTTERHAM SCHOOL   Larz Anderson Park

Open: May-September, Tuesdays, Wednesdays, and weekends.

Admission: Contributions.

Formerly known as the Newton Street School when located elsewhere, the schoolhouse has been moved to this location just outside the Museum of Transportation. The school, built in 1768 and in use until 1920, is intended as an educational museum to show how a one-room school was set up. Of unusual interest is a portion of plaster painted black on which a "number work lesson" was written with white chalk and dated October 18, 1897; it was revealed when many layers of repair cloth were removed.

Cambridge

Heritage Trail information: The route that was established in 1965 with 15 points of interest has been enlarged. All the new sites are included in the current brochures. Free brochures with map may be obtained from the Historical Commission, City Hall, Central Square, or at the Information Booth in Harvard Square.

Some trail sites near Harvard Square:

CHRIST CHURCH   Zero Garden Street   Tel. 876–0200

Open: Year round, every day. September-June 7:30–6; July and August 7:30–5. "Children are always welcome. During a wedding ceremony that may be in progress we do prefer that visitors wait at the back."

Guide: One will be on duty during the Bicentennial.

The oldest church building in Cambridge was used as a barracks by George Washington for his troops in 1775, and the pipes of the organ were melted to provide ammunition for the army. You can see a bullet hole "made by a stray shot fired by the British soldiers marching to Lexington, April 19, 1775." Next to the church is the Old Burying Ground where many early settlers are buried.

LONGFELLOW NATIONAL HISTORIC SITE (1759)   105 Brattle Street Tel. 876–4491

Open: Year round, daily 9–4:30. Closed Christmas and New Year's Day.

Admission: Over 16, 50¢; under 16, free if accompanied by an adult.

Guided Tour: This is a theme-oriented rather than furniture-oriented tour, using objects and rooms to relate stories and events concerning people and ideas. Length: About 25 minutes.

Programs for Children: In the developmental stage. Check current status.

The tour is through the house where most of Longfellow's poems were written and will appeal to children familiar with Longfellow's writings. Visitors also learn about the role of the house in early American history. The house, as Longfellow left it when he died in 1882, has reminders of "The Children's Hour" and "The Village Blacksmith," as well as drawings by the Longfellow children and toys they played with. A formal garden is in the rear of the house.

VILLAGE SMITHY   56 Brattle Street

Once the home of Dexter Pratt, Longfellow's "Village Blacksmith," and now a part of the Cambridge Center of Adult Education. The Blacksmith House has light meals and Viennese pastries. Stop to see the huge gnarled wisteria vine (in bloom in June).

CAMBRIDGE CENTER FOR ADULT EDUCATION   42 Brattle Street

When it was built in 1736, this was a country estate setting. It is now a bustling center of activity with more than 200 on the faculty.

ANCIENT BURYING GROUND (1631) at the corner of Massachusetts Avenue and Garden streets, next to the First Parish (Unitarian) Church (1833). Among the many tombstones are those of the first eight presidents of Harvard, and Cato Steadman and Neptune Frost, two Negro soldiers of the American Revolution.

WADSWORTH HOUSE (1726) is the yellow colonial mansion on the edge of Harvard Yard along Massachusetts Avenue. Harvard presidents occupied the residence for more than 100 years. It now houses the Alumni Association and is not open to the public.

HARVARD YARD (1636) is included on the Harvard tour (p. 255). This is the original campus with Massachusetts Hall (1720)—to the right of the main gate —as the oldest surviving building. Harvard Hall (1766) is the other eighteenth-century weathered red-brick building near the gate.

OLD HARVARD YARD, cornered by Cambridge Street and Massachusetts Avenue, has the largest group of existing eighteenth-century college buildings in this country.

MEMORIAL HALL (1870—1888). This Victorian building that occupies a complete triangle (bordered by Kirkland, Cambridge, and Quincy streets) was built as a Civil War memorial. If you ever have the opportunity to attend a lecture or concert here, it is an experience just to sit in the wood-adorned-with-wood hall. (Audiences would not think of being elsewhere for some events, even though it is cold in the winter.)

Two historic houses open to the public:
COOPER-FROST-AUSTIN HOUSE (1691)   21 Linnaean Street

Open: May-October, Tuesdays, Thursdays, Saturdays 1–5.

Admission: Adults, 25¢; children accompanied and under 12, free.

The oldest house now standing in Cambridge is a representative of saltbox architecture. The side view with its steeply pitched seventeenth-century roof offers a contrast to surrounding structures.

LEE NICHOLS HOUSE   159 Brattle Street

Open: Mondays and Thursdays 3–5.

Admission: 25¢.

Built in 1657, later a Tory mansion. Excavation exhibit shows original 12-foot chimney with oyster shell and clay mortar.

And all by itself (with not too much to see):
FORT WASHINGTON, located sort of midway between the Charles River and Central Square. From Brookline Street take Allston toward MIT. Fort Washing-

ton is at the end of Allston across Waverly Street. Signs are in the area.

This is the site of the only original earthworks remaining from those built by George Washington during the siege of Boston.

Danvers

GLEN MAGNA FARMS   57 Forest Street   Tel. 774–9165
(Just off Rt. 1 between Rt. 114 and Rt. 62 exits)

Open: June 1-September 30 or by appointment, Tuesday-Friday 1–4.

Admission: Adults, $1; under 16, 50¢. Group rates for 25 or more.

Guide Provided: 45-minute tour.

Minimum Age: 6th grade.

Enter the grounds through the stone wall opening and tour the exquisite mansion. The McIntire doorways and the hand-painted wallpaper in the dining room are particularly beautiful. Formal gardens lead up to the McIntire Summer House (1792); this is a two-storied, twenty-foot square building with two small rooms downstairs and a large room on the second floor, decorated in the Oriental manner, where tea used to be served. There is also a nineteenth-century shoe shop on the grounds.

Dedham

FAIRBANKS HOUSE (1636)   511 East Street (corner Eastern Avenue)
Tel. 326–1170

Open: May 1-October 31, Tuesday-Sunday 9 A.M.–5 P.M..

Admission: Adults, $1.50; children under 12, 50¢. Group rates available.

Tour: 45 minutes. Guide provided.

Visitors are taken through eleven rooms filled with treasures that belonged to some of the eight generations (84 members) of the family that occupied the house from 1636 to 1903. Children may sit where the Indians sat (on the floor) in this oldest frame dwelling in existence in the United States. You can see how each addition was made (with its own stairway to the second floor), notice the change in ceiling height from period to period, a fireplace beam lintel, an enormous piece of American oak over 400 years old, and notice a three-cornered hearth, a blanket crane, a foot dustpan, old maps, the careful penmanship of an eleven-year-old, and a cradle that rocked 47 babies.

At least 11 trenches have been dug around the house in the search for the escape route that led from the house to the safety of the barn.

Haverhill

HAVERHILL HISTORICAL SOCIETY   240 Water Street   Tel. 374–4624

Open: September-May, Tuesdays, Thursdays, and Saturdays 2–5; June-August, Tuesday-Saturday 1–5.

Admission: Adults, 50¢; teen-agers, 25¢; children under 10, 10¢.

TENNY HALL has a large display of Indian artifacts, including one of the country's best collections of Indian arrowheads. Three other places seen during the 1½-hour guided tour: the seventeenth-century (furnished) JOHN WARD HOUSE, oldest frame house in the city; the Cobbler Shop; and BUTTON-WOODS (1814), with Haverhill heirlooms; nineteenth-century shoes made in Haverhill; the original Haverhill deed from the Indians in 1642; hatchet and scalping knife used by Hannah Duston; old glass and china and period furnishings.

JOHN GREENLEAF WHITTIER HOMESTEAD   305 Whittier Road (Rt. 110) Tel. 373–3979

Open: Daily Tuesday-Saturday 10–5, Sundays 1–5. Closed Mondays, Thanksgiving, Christmas, and New Year's Day.

Admission: 50¢.

Guided Tour: 30 minutes.

Groups: Age 8 and up. "We welcome young people at all times."

Located on its original site, it is substantially the same as when it provided the setting for the famous poem "Snowbound." The kitchen has a large fireplace, the elevated Mother's Bedroom is built over a rock too large to move, there is the desk at which Whittier worked, and outside you can see the original bridle post.

Hingham

OLD SHIP CHURCH (1681)   107 Main Street   Tel. 749–1679

Open: July and August 12–5 for half-hour guided tours. Other tours by arrangement.

This oldest wooden church building in continuous use has roof beams similar to those in a wooden ship's hull. Although the church has been altered a few times, original characteristics can be seen due to a 1930 restoration.

Lynn

LYNN HISTORICAL SOCIETY, INC.   125 Green Street   Tel. 592–2465

Open: Year round Monday-Friday 9–12 and 1–4, closed holidays.

Admission: Free. Children should have adult accompaniment.

A guided tour is given through the early nineteenth-century house, which is furnished completely from Lynn homes. In the JOHNSON MUSEUM are dolls, toys, a colonial room of 1775, and on the lower level are high-wheel bicycles, colonial household utensils, a shoe shop set up as typical of those many Lynn men worked in from 1750 to 1850, and an exhibit of fire buckets and hats.

Medford

ROYALL HOUSE   15 George Street (at Main)   Tel. 396–9032

Open: May 1-October 15, daily 2–5 except Mondays and Fridays.

Admission: Adults, $1; children under 12, 25¢ (must be accompanied by an adult).

Governor John Winthrop owned the site on which the original house was built in the seventeenth century. Colonel Isaac Royall enlarged it in 1732. The guided tour, not really youth-oriented, is a minimum of 30 minutes, and, depending upon interest, could be an hour. The completely restored house—with four furnished rooms on each of three floors—has formal gardens of 1732.

PETER TUFTS HOUSE (c. 1678)   350 Riverside Avenue near Spring Street

Open: June-September, Tuesdays and Thursdays 2–5.

Admission: 50¢. Children up to 12 must be accompanied by an adult.

This is believed to be the oldest surviving brick house in New England. Original seventeenth-century features include exposed oak beams, staircase, and a curved fireplace with oven.

Newton

JACKSON HOMESTEAD (1809)   527 Washington Street (between Newton Corner and Newtonville Square)   Tel. 332–3920

Open: September-May, Monday-Friday 2–4; July and August, Wednesday afternoons 2–4. Closed all holidays.

Admission: Free.

Minimum Age for Groups: 2nd grade.

It is a 45-minute tour through the house that once played a part in the underground railway. There are six fireplaces with hand-carved mantels, a kitchen fireplace and oven used for cooking, a costume collection, and a 300-year-old well in the laundry room.

Quincy

Maps of the HISTORIC TRAIL are available from Quincy–South Shore Chamber of Commerce, 36 Miller Stile Road, from Quincy City Hall, or at the Adams birthplaces. ALL THE HISTORIC HOUSES ARE CLOSED IN THE WINTER. Quincy is a busy city and parking can be difficult; walk wherever possible.

Directions: From Boston take Southeast Expressway to Neponset exit, go over bridge, along Hancock Street to Quincy Square.

Historic Houses along the Trail:

ADAMS NATIONAL HISTORIC SITE   135 Adams Street   Tel. 773–1177

Ⓣ **Stop:** Quincy Center. Ten-minute walk.

Directions: Southeast Expressway, Exit 24, Furnace Brook Parkway, right on Adams Street (3rd set of lights), 1½ miles to site.

Open: April 19-November 10, 9–5 daily.

Admission: Adults, 50¢; under 16, free.

Guided Tour: 25 minutes.

Built in 1731, enlarged several times, this was the home of four generations of the Adams family from 1787 to 1927. The ever-changing style and taste of its occupants is seen during the tour.

In one corner of the lovely eighteenth-century garden is a stone library, the surprise of the visit. It is floor to ceiling—and balcony too—with books.

Large Groups: Please make reservations.

BIRTHPLACES: JOHN ADAMS   133 Franklin Street (1681)   and **JOHN QUINCY ADAMS**   141 Franklin Street (1663)   Tel. 773–1770

Open: April 19-October 15, 10–5 daily except Mondays. Also open both 3-day October holiday weekends.

Admission: Two houses, 75¢; one house, 50¢. Children under 16 must be accompanied by an adult: 15¢, one house; 25¢, two houses.

A guide is provided for a half-hour tour through each of these neighboring saltboxes, oldest presidential birthplaces in the United States. Groups should be at least school age. Both houses have a questionnaire for children. The John Quincy Adams Birthplace has a secret hiding place in the chimney.

DOROTHY QUINCY HOMESTEAD   1010 Hancock Street   Tel. 472–5117

Open: April 19-October 31, 10–5 every day.

Admission: Adults, $1; children 12 and under, 50¢.

Minimum Age for Groups: 6. "Children are welcome at any time."

An outstanding feature is the architectural evolution of this house, which was built in the seventeenth century and enlarged in the eighteenth. The house has been recently renovated, and there are plans to provide an audio-visual program touching on the history of the local area as well as that of the house.

COLONEL JOSIAH QUINCY HOUSE (1770)   18 Muirhead Street   Wollaston   Tel. 472–1587

Open: June 1-September, Tuesdays, Thursdays, Saturdays 1–5.

Admission: 50¢.

Groups: Guide provided, minimum age 8, tour about 45 minutes.

It is possible to spend from 10 minutes to more than an hour during a personalized tour. There are no ropes across doorways, and explanations to children are geared to their level. Not only can certain items be touched, but there is the opportunity to try on old-fashioned glasses and hats.

Other Places along the Trail:

ADAMS ACADEMY, Newport Avenue, near Hancock Street, site of John Hancock's birthplace. FIRST PARISH CHURCH at Hancock and Washington streets in Quincy Square, built with hammered Quincy granite, and site of the tombs of John Adams, John Quincy Adams, and their wives. HANCOCK CEMETERY at Hancock and Granite streets, where many patriots are buried. ABIGAIL ADAMS CAIRN on Franklin Street—a stone monument, erected in memory of John Adams's wife at the top of the hill where she and John Quincy Adams watched the Battle of Bunker Hill. FIRST IRON WORKS (West Quincy) at Crescent Street off Copeland, off Furnace Brook Parkway. A small park has been established near the resurrected ruins of the blast furnace of 1644 (which preceded Saugus). A diagram shows the original construction. FIRST COMMERCIAL RAILROAD, the site of the single-rail railroad used to carry granite for Bunker Hill, has not had recent attention. It can be seen from the Southeast Expressway, but you will never recognize it. Restoration possibilities are being studied.

Saugus

SAUGUS IRONWORKS NATIONAL HISTORIC SITE   Central Street Tel. 233–0050 (9 miles north of Boston)

Directions: Driving north on U.S. 1, turn right at Main Street (Saugus), and left onto Central, and follow signs 1½ miles to Restoration.

Open: Daily year round, April-October 9–5. Guided tours given every half hour. November-March 9–4, self-guiding arrangements.

Admission: Free.

Average Length of Visit: 1 hour. Suggested for 5th grade and up.

The original plant, built by John Winthrop in 1650, began America's iron and steel industry, and was in operation on the banks of the Saugus River for 20 years. Stones from the original structure were used in the rebuilding of the blast furnace, a replica of the 300-year-old forge where cast iron "sow" bars from the furnace were reheated and "beaten" into usable wrought iron.

It will be several years before the power waterwheels, the bellows, and giant forge hammer are again used in demonstrations at the rolling and slitting mills. While work is being done on them, you may see some craftsmen on the premises. Eventually this will be a living history museum. At the moment there is a blacksmith making nails and a carpenter repairing a roof. The Iron-master's house has two furnished floors, and the museum has relics found during the excavation of the old ironworks.

Scituate

It is a pleasant town for cycling. Four Scituate Historical Society sites are open by appointment and on specific dates each year (1975—June 8, July 13, August 23, September 14; 1976—June 7, July 12, August 22, September 13 1–5). For information: 545–0474.
Admission: Adults, 25¢; children 5–12, 10¢.

THE CUDWORTH HOUSE   First Parish Road and Cudworth Road (1797), furnished as a home in the early American tradition. Weaving demonstrated on old loom.

Open: Wednesday-Saturday 2–5 from mid-June–mid-September and on open house days.

HISTORIC LAWSON TOWER, an American water landmark, with a height of 153 feet, encloses a water tank, and has a bell room and clock room. When open visitors may climb to the bell tower; bells are played during the afternoon.

MANN FARMHOUSE AND HISTORICAL MUSEUM (1700s)   Greenfield Lane and Stockbridge Road. Construction spans nearly three centuries.

Open: Same hours as the Cudworth House.

STOCKBRIDGE MILL (1640)   Country Way and Driftway. The first water-driven gristmill in the Old Colony was restored in 1970. Corn is ground during open house days.

Waltham

AMERICAN JEWISH HISTORICAL SOCIETY on the campus of Brandeis University   Tel. 891–8110

Open: Winter: Monday-Thursday 9–5:45, Fridays 9–2, Sundays 2–5. Summer: Monday-Thursday 9–4:45.

Two exhibit areas are in the building that houses volumes and manuscripts on American Judaica. Everything from Yiddish theatre posters to paintings from Colonial times is included in the material that relates to the settlement, history, and life of the Jews in the United States.

Slide-tape: A 20-minute color presentation is set up for use in the library; it is also available for rental.

GORE PLACE (1805)   52 Gore Street (Rt. 20)   Tel. 894–2798

Open: April 15-November 15, Tuesday-Saturday 10–5, Sundays 2–5. Closed holidays.

Admission: Adults, $2; children 12 and under, 50¢.

Tours: Special arrangements may be made for groups.

Minimum Age: 8.

All 22 rooms of this outstanding house of the Federal period are covered during the 1-hour tour. Young people usually are attracted to the flying staircase, which spirals up for three full flights, the delightful nursery, and Governor Gore's shower room. The acres of grounds include a restored herb garden, apple trees that have been planted to reestablish the orchard, and the stable.

LYMAN HOUSE   "The Vale"   corner of Lyman and Beaver streets, off Rt. 20 near the center of town   Tel. 893–7232

Open: July and August, Thursdays, Fridays 11–2.

Admission: House, $1.25; greenhouse, 50¢.

One of Samuel McIntire's most ambitious houses, with notable ballroom and bow parlor, it has some McIntire pieces designed especially for certain rooms and a large antique dollhouse. Visitors may see the entire first floor and two upstairs bedrooms. The house has extended lawns, vistas, and magnificent gardens. The grounds include a stable designed by the architect.

Two early nineteenth-century greenhouses are known for their camellias and muscatel and black Hamburg grapes.

Watertown

ABRAHAM BROWNE HOUSE (c. 1698)   562 Main Street (Rt. 20)

Open: June 1-October 31, Mondays, Wednesdays, Fridays 2–5, closed major holidays.

Admission: Adults, 50¢; children under 12, 25¢. Group rates available.

Reclaimed from near ruin and carefully restored under the direction of William Sumner Appleton, this house has a seventeenth-century parlor and a photographic record of structural and documentary evidence compiled during restoration.

"This house is essentially for scholars in the field. While young visitors aren't discouraged, it is not a children's house."

Wenham

WENHAM HISTORICAL ASSOCIATION AND MUSEUM, INC.   Main Street (Rt. 1A)   Tel. 468–2377

Open: Monday-Friday 1–4, Sundays 2–5. Mornings by appointment. Closed legal holidays and in February, day before Thanksgiving, Christmas, and New Year's Day.

Admission: Adults, $1; children 6–14, 25¢.

Minimum Suggested Age: 10. "This is not a children's museum, but supervised young people are welcome."

Guided Tours: By appointment.

Minimum Age: 3rd grade.

It is a charming setting for a 1350 B.C. doll with beads made from mud of the River Nile, dolls of colonial days to the present, and costume dolls from all over the world. The toy room houses a farmstead representing colonial days, dollhouses of the nineteenth and twentieth centuries with appropriate furnishings, a variety of games of the 1800s, and mechanical and iron toys. The Claflin-Richards House, with two rooms c. 1600 and two more added in 1673, shows furnishings of the period with special collections of fans, quilts—including one with girls' names on it—well-preserved children's dresses, and magnificent Parisian and domestic gowns. One dress, made in 1845, has a dozen pockets. In the Thomas Pickering Library room, furnished by the Massachusetts Society for Promoting Agriculture, there are publications, medals, trophies, and paintings. There is an exhibit of Wenham Lake ice tools. And the garden has a "ten-footer" completely equipped shoe shop of 1860.

. . . Look up! Tops of buildings often have the original architecture.

. . . The wrecker's ball, common in the 1960s, resulted in several parking lots. Notice signs of days gone by or the contour of a neighboring building.

. . . Play the identification game before or after a trip. From pictures (there are several collections on Boston) see who can identify this doorway or that weathervane.

LOOKING AT THE CITY

Viewpoints

CUSTOM HOUSE OBSERVATION TOWER   1–8 McKinley Square   Tel. 223–6565 (State Street entrance near India Street, within walking distance of the Aquarium)

> ⓣ **Stop:** Aquarium on Blue Line. (Those steep single-width 42-foot escalators are an adventure in themselves.)

Open: Monday-Friday 9–11:30 and 1:30–4. Closed holidays and in inclement weather. (Bicentennial hours: 9–3.)

Admission: Free.

Take two elevators—the tower was built in 1915 on top of the building of 1847—for a most exciting view of the waterfront. (And unless you know one set of buildings from another, children may appreciate this observation site more than any other.) The Tobin Bridge, excursion boats, freighters, tugboats, all can be seen without field glasses as you stand on the open-air balcony of the twenty-fifth floor. A protective high caging does not obstruct the view. Proposed changes—and those that are being implemented—on the waterfront and surrounding area provide construction activity for years to come. As you circle the tower, you will see the expanse of the nearby Government Center bordered by Faneuil Hall. In clear weather Blue Hills is about the farthest point that can be spotted.

Groups: As the second elevator can accommodate 6 adults, plan to separate and allow extra time. It is possible to walk from the eighteenth to the twenty-fourth floor.

Handicapped: State Street side without steps. Second elevator very narrow; assistance needed.

JOHN HANCOCK TOWER OBSERVATORY   John Hancock Mutual Life Insurance Co.   Hancock Place   Tel. 421–2632

Note: At this writing the "old" observation tower at 200 Berkeley Street is still open 9:30–4 every working day. Admission is free. Plans for the future are undecided.

The observatory at Hancock Place, Copley Square, is expected to open this year.

Expected Admission: Adults, $1.50; children 5–16, 75¢; under 5, free.

> ⓣ **Stop:** Copley.

Directions: Massachusetts Turnpike, Exit 22, Copley Square.

Open: Monday-Saturday 9 A.M.–11 P.M., Sundays 12 noon–11 P.M. Closed Christmas.

We will have a new "highest" when this opens—the highest observatory point in New England. It will offer a panorama of eastern Massachusetts from New Hampshire to Cape Cod. Its major exhibits: 20-foot animated topographical historical map of Boston in 1775; *City Flight,* a filmed helicopter ride around Boston; *Skyline Boston;* and *Photo-Rama,* an exhibit of 170 back-lit color transparencies of familiar landmarks.

LOCKS AND DRAWBRIDGE (MDC)   Charles River Dam at Museum of Science, Science Park (p. 173)

Although there are other locks in the area, the operation can best be seen from the embankment—with protective fence—alongside the Museum of Science. See all the gates for 5 compartments as the water is made level (according to the tide) connecting the Charles River with the harbor. The locks operate 24 hours a day, but the busiest times are weekends and warm summer weekdays. At the sound of the horn the bridge will open, but not between 6:15 and 9:10 A.M. or between 4:15 and 7:40 A.M. on weekdays.

LOGAN INTERNATIONAL AIRPORT   East Boston   Tel. 567–5400
Special note: Avoid going the Friday before the February and April school vacation weeks. For several years it has meant hour-long waits on the expressway because traffic is so heavy.

Directions: Via the Maurice J. Tobin Bridge (formerly Mystic River) or the Callahan Tunnel. Toll for each facility: 25¢.

Parking Garage: Alleviates the parking problem at most times. Rates: 60¢, first hour; $1.25, 1–8 hours.

For a panoramic view, go to the sixteenth floor of the Tower Observation area— open daily 10 A.M. to 9 P.M. There is no charge and visitors have the unusual experience of hearing live traffic reports.
    The nation's closest major airport to a city center has observation areas in all terminals. Charge 10¢. If the children are not seasoned travelers, they may enjoy seeing the luggage arriving on the carousels in the baggage pickup areas. Plan to spend at least an hour for a visit.

Note: The International Terminal is the last one along the driving loop. Beyond that it is a full loop back to the terminals. The parking garage may be the best idea.
Tours: See p. 255.

THE SKYWALK   Prudential Tower   Tel. 236–3313

Ⓣ **Stop:** Prudential, Auditorium, or Copley on Green Line.

Open: Monday-Saturday 9 A.M.–11 P.M., Fridays and Saturdays 9 A.M.–midnight, Sundays 1–11 P.M.

Admission: Adults, $1; children 6–12, 50¢; under 6, free; senior citizens 65 or over, ½ price. Special group rates available.

Nights offer a spectacular view. At any hour the 32-second elevator ride to the fiftieth floor may be the most memorable aspect for young children. For appreciation of the panorama, try to go when it is clear. Some repeat visitors favor sunset time. The vistascopes (10¢) give a few minutes of magnification so that you can better see the nearby harbor, river, and highways (or the ballgame at Fenway Park!), and possibly Cape Cod or the southern tip of Vermont.

At the Center: In the south lobby of the tower building is Alfred M. Duca's enormous sculpture *Boston Tapestry.* Four tons of white-hot molten iron, poured in molds of hardened sand, emerged into the shapes and forms that were combined with fragments of Sandwich glass for this interpretation of the city. There is a special exhibit area in the lobby of the Prudential Tower. For more information about possible art showings or other exhibits call 236–3041. At this writing it is not known what will happen in or with the Bicentennial Pavilion after 1976; it is a multimedia show of Boston in the twentieth century (admission charged). In the PLAZA of the Prudential Center you may find a carol sing or outdoor band concert depending upon the season. There is a wide variety of stores but BRENTANO'S is best for browsing; this emporium that nurtures a great desire to spend money has many departments with books and books, museum reproductions, sculpture, and adult games. In the lobby of the Sheraton Boston Hotel (on the second level—the same one that the plaza is on) there is a pink, green, and white canopied window that sells yogurt and soft freeze CONES for 30¢ and up. Note that the STAR MARKET is open 24 hours a day. If you make an appointment, a tour of the store (p. 259) can be arranged.

Nearby: The MAPPARIUM (p. 265) and reflecting pool of the Christian Science Center are a few minutes away. And NEWBURY STREET (p. 141) can offer some interest. It is about a half-hour walk along COMMONWEALTH AVENUE to the Boston Public Garden and the Swan Boats (or two stops on the Ⓣ to Arlington Station). Between the Prudential Center and the Swan Boats: If it is hot and you are ready to sit down, the courtyard of the BOSTON PUBLIC LIBRARY (p. 272) is cool and lovely. During the summer there may be noontime performances outdoors in Copley Square (in front of the BOSTON PUBLIC LIBRARY). One block beyond the library is the NEW ENGLAND LIFE BUILDING with paintings of historic events, three-dimensional exhibits, and gift packets for visitors (p. 121).

Bus Tours

THE GRAY LINE   Tel. 426–8800

COPLEY MOTOR TOURS   Tel. 266–3500

Both companies have daily trips around Boston, Boston and Cambridge, and to some day-trip communities. Rates vary. Children are half fare. Generally the tours are offered spring through fall. *They leave from* Copley Square area hotels: Statler-Hilton, Copley Plaza, and Sheraton-Boston.

FREEDOM TRAIL TOUR . . . BICENTENNIAL SHUTTLE . . .

The name has changed according to its route, but it is probably the best bet whatever it is called. The driver offers a narration as you travel to most of the major historic sites in the city. The fare (around $2) allows you to get off at one site and board the next bus to go on to another site. Some years there is a discount on admission fees to the places on the route. Presently it is offered by The Gray Line, Tel. 426–8800.

Walking

Reminder: One area often borders another. The waterfront and Cambridge are within a few subway stops of most Boston "looking" places.

. . . Wear comfortable shoes!

. . . Try the Freedom Trail (p. 110) on a Sunday.

. . . Parking: Difficult in just about every area.

. . . Although it is common for youngsters to have things pointed out to them, many children note sights that adults tend to overlook.

. . . The areas covered here include suggestions in compact territory rather than give information on every marker and significant place.

. . . A Bicentennial bonus is the focus placed on neighborhoods. The South End offers strong community action groups, a mixture of races and backgrounds, and some restored townhouses; the Fenway is an area where garden plots can be rented for $3, and East Boston may be noted for the Italian chef who cuts off the tie of a customer who does not finish a meal. Boston is a city of surprises.

. . . Parking lots and new buildings have replaced some treasures that were not appreciated. Now that recycling is "in," and there is not likely to be too much more demolition, look for a few cast-iron facades or for a frieze on some old existing building. (Elaborate friezes are on the Tremont Street Baptist Church located next to the Parker House and King's Chapel; the symbols of Time by Solomon Willard are on the front of the Old Granary Burying Ground.)

. . . There has been concern about open spaces and you will find them in all walking areas. They may offer the opportunity to people-watch. Whenever, wherever, it is often the conversations with people that remain the most memorable part of a day.

. . . Some sections of the city that are architecturally interesting are being re-developed, have been overdeveloped, or are not really territory for children unless they are in a group that has had a strong orientation to topographical or economic changes, or perhaps some historical background to offer perspective.

. . . The Victorian Society, 137 Beacon Street, Tel. 267–6338, has Boston-area spring and fall walks on Sunday afternoons, relating to nineteenth-century Boston: architecture, women, literary activity, and landscape architecture. Nominal fees. No advance registration necessary. (Group leaders may find these walks helpful—before taking a group of youngsters through an area.)

. . . Children's Boston Tours, 3 Dartmouth Place, Tels. 536–1692, 536–0106. This new organization has skilled guides who give tours for ages 4–14. The focus may be museums and historic sites, sketching, photography, or the harbor. Most trips are on foot, about 3 hours in length, and average $5 per child. Group and family rates available.

BACK BAY

In a city with paved cow paths, here is filled-in land that has Commonwealth Avenue and parallel Newbury, Beacon, and Marlborough streets in a section where eight perpendicular cross streets do progress alphabetically from Arlington at the Boston Public Garden to Hereford, just before Massachusetts Avenue and the Ⓣ Auditorium Station.

Done in leisurely fashion, the Back Bay walking possibilities could easily fill a day—recommended only for the serious sight-seer.

Restaurants (p. 32).   John Hancock Tower (p. 136).

Walking Suggestions:

. . . From the Boston Public Garden to the Charles River (accessible via the footbridge at Arlington Street) OR

. . . From Copley Square to the Charles River OR

. . . Use Berkeley Street as the "cross street" to get a good feeling for the area, and have the opportunity to see some interiors that give a feeling for the life-style of another era.

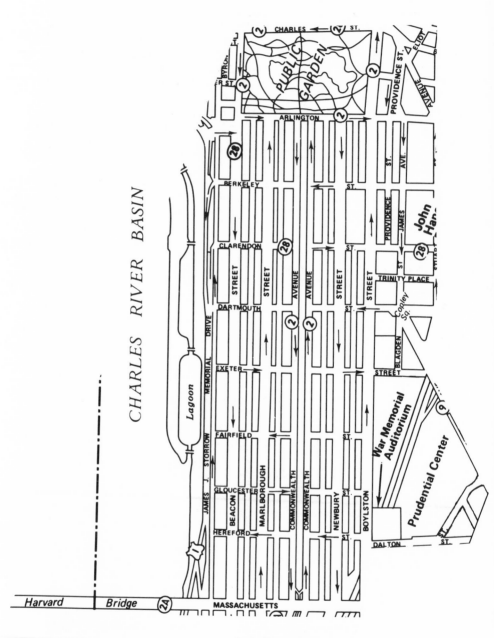

BACK BAY

WHAT'S INSIDE?

Just looking at exteriors is a tease. Within a block of Berkeley Street are several possibilities for seeing inside: The GIBSON HOUSE (p. 120) is true Victoriana. Also on Beacon Street, but offering more splendor, is FISHER JUNIOR COLLEGE (p. 254). The FRENCH LIBRARY (p. 273) on Marlborough Street is in a lovely building. The children's room on the second floor is particularly charming; this part of Marlborough Street has gas lamps, plenty of trees, and is directly across the street from the oldest church in Boston, THE FIRST AND SECOND CHURCH IN BOSTON. Very little of the old building is left from the devastating fire of 1968, but you have an opportunity to see several views: From Berkeley there is the rose window frame, porch, and steeple. The surprise is on Marlborough where you can see a sunken amphitheatre (picnicking allowed if you take your trash with you). Inside it is a warm modern building with split-rib concrete block and two views through windows where you can see the old and new. With advance notice, a tour may be arranged. THE BOSTON CENTER FOR ADULT EDUCATION at 5 Commonwealth Avenue would appreciate advance notice if you want to see its magnificent ballroom with floor of note, chandeliers, mirrors, and elegance; it is a busy place.

BOSTON PUBLIC GARDEN   (bounded by Arlington, Boylston, Beacon, and Charles streets)

Traffic jams and the hurried pace of the city are forgotten as you stroll on the winding paths amidst fountains, the old trees of rare varieties with well-weathered labels, and colorful formal flower beds. But there will be no peace with the children if you don't head for the Swan Boats (p. 218) first. If you have not brought bread crumbs, peanuts may be available from the vendor on Charles Street. And near the vendor there may be a photographer with tripod and black curtain willing to frame "a picture for the kids." In the garden are plenty of ducks, pigeons, and squirrels to be fed. Walk on and then under the oft-photographed bridge. (The children will find the pigeon nests.) Sometimes a mounted policeman is around; the conversation with rider and horse could be a highlight. There are statues throughout the garden, but you are most likely to be asked to identify the four along the Boylston Street side: Kosciusko, from Poland, a colonel in the American Revolutionary Army; Thomas Cass, an Irishman who organized and commanded an all-Irish regiment in the Civil War; Charles Sumner, abolitionist; and Wendell Phillips, champion of the slave. The recognizable figure is George Washington on his horse, facing Commonwealth Avenue.

NEWBURY STREET

The four blocks between Arlington and Dartmouth streets offer some pleasant distractions (wearing apparel, antiques, crafts, china), but the street is most noted for its ART GALLERIES. Enter the former town houses by stairs that go up or down half a flight for perusal of the contemporary and traditional. If your child has had the opportunity to try different media, he or she may be interested in the sculpture, paintings, and prints of a "real artist" (or may be inspired to try his/her own.) Gallery owners have listened to some uninhibited comments.

Interspersed among the galleries and of interest to all ages: Near the corner of Berkeley Street is F.A.O. SCHWARZ at #40, which offers a change of pace. Chances are you won't stop in—with children—to see the interior of BONWIT TELLER, which occupies a Berkeley Street block (at Newbury), but you might

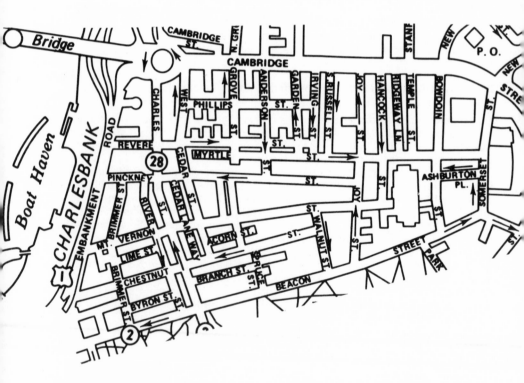

BEACON HILL

mention that this was the first home of M.I.T. and later the Museum of Science (then known as the Museum of Natural History). The SOCIETY OF ARTS AND CRAFTS (p. 63) is at #69.

Beyond the corner of Clarendon on the right is the ARTISANS (closed Saturdays in summer), which sells everything from donkey beads to old musical instruments. Next door at #167 is THE WANDERING PIPER; it sells bagpipes (and clothing), but beginners should first practice fingering on the chanter with the help of a tutor book. You may be attracted to other intriguing windows and shops, but if you are ready to sit down, walk 1 block along Dartmouth Street to the mall of Commonwealth Avenue. (One block in the opposite direction would bring you to COPLEY SQUARE for the Boston Public Library, p. 272, and Copley Square Station of the Ⓣ.)

"Way up" near Massachusetts Avenue is the BOSTON CHESS STUDIO at #335 with a large assortment of chess sets, manuals, and books, and a public playing room (40¢ an hour) in the back.

COPLEY SQUARE has two landmarks: Trinity Church (p. 260) and the library (p. 272); nearby is the New England Life Building (p. 121), and on blowy days there is a wind tunnel created by the John Hancock Building. The square has been recently renovated and is the source of much controversy. It has a sunken unlandscaped area that many consider unappealing. There is room to sit, a fountain that tries to give a sense of coolness on hot days, and there are some performances and/or exhibits during the summer. For the past few years folk dancing has been a popular weekly summer evening occurrence.

Two brownstone lions, formerly in front of the Kensington Hotel (razed in 1967), are now located at the James Street entrance of the Copley Plaza.

BEACON HILL

. . . So named because of the beacon once erected at the top to warn the residents of any oncoming danger. It was never used.

. . . For walking tour purposes we will say it encompasses the area bounded by Bowdoin Street, Beacon Street by the State House down to the Esplanade, along Storrow Drive by the Charles River, and Cambridge Street.

. . . The Abolitionist Movement started here. Now the Museum of Afro American History (p. 168) has tours of the Black Heritage Trail on the hill.

. . . Wander up, down, and across the Hill (which was at least 60 feet higher before its dirt was part of the fill for Back Bay), and discover your own views of city living. You could start at the State House and wind your way to the river (overpasses are at Beacon or Charles Circle) or circle round and return via Government Center.

You may still find quaint gaslights, footscrapers at the doorsteps, stables now converted into homes, interesting doorways, underpasses of the State House, purple windowpanes (the original content of the glass affected by the sun), which can be seen from inside out at 39–40 Beacon Street (p. 119), and several dead-end lanes called Places.

Some particulars you have heard about: ACORN STREET, bordered by West Cedar and Willow, is a narrow sloping street about one car wide and paved with river stones. Early residents were coachmen who served nearby families. (West Cedar runs off Chestnut near Charles Street.) Follow Willow, with its iron railings that have seen use as support during icy weather or as hitching posts, to MOUNT VERNON for one of the entrances (Pinckney is the other) to LOUISBURG SQUARE, with its plain doorways, bowfront three- and four-story brick dwellings, and the central park open only to the proprietors of the square. You may like to find #10, once the home of Louisa May Alcott, or #4 where William Dean Howells, an editor of the *Atlantic Monthly*, lived, but the children may still be looking for an entrance to the iron fence of the oval-shaped park, which has a statue of Aristides the Just on the Mt. Vernon side and Christopher Columbus on the north side. Both were a gift of Joseph Iasigi, a Boston merchant; they came as ballast in ships from Italy. Before frustration sets in, turn up MT. VERNON STREET to see some elegant homes with elaborate iron fences. One, #55, is open to the public at certain hours (p. 121). Number 85 is the second of three homes built for Harrison Gray Otis, a prominent attorney involved in real-estate development of the hill; the driveway still has cobblestones. That 13-foot-high #50 was once stables for three horses, and some say it was planned that height so that the gentleman across the street could see his cattle grazing on the Boston Common.

One short left on Joy Street will bring you to PINCKNEY and one of the greatest delights—the view of the Charles River framed by the buildings on each side of the Hill. These buildings often have tunnels that lead to more doorways. Investigate Places, Lanes, and Courts that add to the flair of the area. Follow the designs on brick sidewalks or make your way over to the upper part of Revere Street (parallel to Pinckney), because facing #24 is a house at the end of ROLLINS PLACE; those closed green shutters hide only a brick wall—a house front that does not have a house. Walkers with the energy to cross the hill for one more block will find Phillips Avenue; near Charles Street off Phillips is PRIMUS AVENUE with an iron grillwork entrance and an ascending path with a series of steps with interesting doors at each level.

During the summer the entire scene is splashed with the color of flower boxes. The merchants along CHARLES STREET may exhibit bouquets during a January thaw. The antique shops or others with elegant wares may not be of the "touch" variety. Refresh yourself with an ice-cream cone (the homemade variety) at Fred's (located at #47), or lunch from one of the eateries. (Romano's Bakery and Coffee Shop at 89 Charles is open daily 8 A.M.–11 P.M. and serves reasonably priced soups and sandwiches, as well as French and Italian pastries, in an intimate atmosphere.)

Charles Street has had a turnover of businesses in recent years. But the area will basically remain as is; in 1963 the National Park Service designated it a Registered National Historic Landmark.

CAMBRIDGE

Historic Cambridge: p. 125.

Cycling: p. 212. (Note that cyclists are fearless here!)

Tours of Harvard: p. 255, and M.I.T., p. 256.

Some Restaurants: p. 35.

Bookstores: Located every few feet in Harvard Square, and used to those who stand (and in some cases sit) to read on the spot.

Information: When the HARVARD SQUARE INFORMATION CENTER is open, it is very helpful; there is a possibility that its hours will improve. A good source of information in the square is the HARVARD INFORMATION CENTER located in the Holyoke Center, 1353 Massachusetts Avenue, open Monday-Saturday 9–4:45, closed Thanksgiving and Christmas.

> Herewith are thoughts for browsers. If it is a nice day, you are within minutes of the banks of the Charles River, a good place for picnicking and relaxing.

HARVARD AREA. With its historic background and cultural resources, Cambridge has many charming areas. As the circumference of what is commonly referred to as the Harvard Square area widens—by demand and rehabilitation—interesting streets increase. Some are grand avenue types with estates, while others are narrow passageways lined with intriguing structures of attractive color combinations and windows filled with hanging plants.

It is a great place for people-watching. Have a seat on the HOLYOKE CENTER PLAZA where there are crafts vendors (when allowed), maybe a food wagon, and musicians too. You can see the world go by. For some this area even offers a first view of trackless trolleys. The OUT-OF-TOWN NEWSPAPER STAND offers a touch of home with local newspapers from dozens of places.

The international flavor of the community is reflected in the shops and restaurants. Children's toys from all over the world, antiques, art galleries, furniture stores, gourmet cooking utensils—what is your desire? Even Woolworth's has unusual stock. A great recycled building is THE GARAGE on the corner of Boylston and Mt. Auburn streets; walk up the ramp and explore the goods that are attractively displayed in a mall that has the warm feeling of a neighborhood; some folk musicians may be adding to the atmosphere. The brick building behind this—on the corner of Dunster—has a new old-fashioned ice-cream parlor, CIBO'S, serving homemade ice cream, fudge, and goodies. ELSIE'S (p. 35) and its sandwiches is right here. And that triangular-shaped building with red, yellow, and blue door, with stork atop, is home of the humor publication THE HARVARD LAMPOON; attached to it at 29 Plympton Street is the STARR BOOK CO., a favorite for many who seek used books. PHILLIPS-BRENTANO'S BOOK STORE is at #7 Holyoke Street with a good selection of children's books; the HARVARD BOOKSTORE at 1256 Massachusetts Avenue has an inviting cushioned window place for a child to curl up in. At this "end" of the square is Quincy Street with the FOGG ART MUSEUM (p. 164) and the CARPENTER CENTER FOR VISUAL ARTS, the first structure designed by Le Corbusier in this country. Beyond the center you will have a chance to see more of Harvard's varied architecture as you come to the area with the BUSCH-REISINGER MUSEUM (p. 161), the Graduate School of Design's GEORGE GUND HALL, with its sloping structure that allows the best use of natural light, and the recently opened Harvard Science Center.

If you choose to walk in the "other" direction from Harvard Square—down Brattle Street, there is THE SPA with yogurt cones and granola topping, the Harvard Cooperative Bookstore (THE COOP) with its Palmer Street entrance that leads to three floors of books and posters and records; its children's department on the first floor is about the best in town. The PAPERBACK BOOKSMITH is in large quarters and open Monday-Thursday 8 A.M.–1 A.M., Fridays and Saturdays 8 A.M.–2 A.M., Sundays 9 A.M.–1 A.M. TRUC has a surprising shopping mall with specialty areas, all beneath the ground. READING INTERNATIONAL has newspapers and magazines in several languages, bargain books on remainder tables, as well as a selection of new titles. The CAMBRIDGE CENTER FOR ADULT EDUCATION, a historic red house, retains its charm while being utilized by Greater Boston residents who enroll in more than 200 courses offered year round. In addition the center now has #56, once the home of Dexter Pratt, Longfellow's "Village Blacksmith." Here you may see a magnificent wisteria vine on the terrace that is used by the WINDOW SHOP in good weather for serving light lunches and Viennese pastries. DESIGN RESEARCH's glass walls suggest a visit, and you won't be disappointed as you climb from one level to another—from kitchen utensils to fabrics to clothing to home furnishings.

Just beyond and still on Brattle Street is the LOEB DRAMA CENTER at the corner of Brattle and Hilliard streets. Exhibition lobbies are open, and the doors may be open to the main and experimental theatres (although the lights may not be on). The main theatre is designed to allow flexibility for productions on a proscenium, or three-sided arena, stage. A system of electronic and hydraulic controls moves the front section seats to the sides of the theatre, and elevators then lift a projected stage apron to the desired level. Performance information is available through the box office, Tel. 864–2630, 12–6 P.M. Productions in the experimental theatre, offered most weekends during the academic year (Thursday-Sunday), are interesting student work; free tickets are issued the day before the scheduled performance.

If you continue along BRATTLE STREET, you will be in an area that has lovely old homes including the Longfellow House, p. 125.

MASSACHUSETTS INSTITUTE OF TECHNOLOGY AREA

Parking: A problem, particularly on weekdays.

Tours: p. 256.

Information Board: Just inside main door of Student Center.

Maps: Available from the Information Office, located on the first floor of the main building at 77 Massachusetts Avenue, open Monday-Friday 9–5.

The CHAPEL at M.I.T., designed by Eero Saarinen, is surrounded by a shallow moat and has an aluminum bell tower by the sculptor Theodore Roszak. Enter the chapel to see the light reflected from the moat make changing patterns on the walls.

A few steps from the chapel is KRESGE AUDITORIUM with its single concrete dome supported primarily at its points. The glass walls stand independently, sealed to the roof by rubber gaskets. At the top of the roof the concrete measures only 3½ inches thick. The large concert hall has an unusual shaped stage with a wide projected curved apron. The stage can seat 250 and faces more than 1,200 seats, each one intended to give front seat vision.

The nearby STUDENT CENTER on Massachusetts Avenue has such diverse facilities as a library, bowling alleys for students, and a grill room that is well patronized.

The CREATIVE PHOTOGRAPHY GALLERY often has interesting exhibits on the third floor of the Armory Building on Massachusetts Avenue. If you turn left at Memorial Drive, walk a short distance, and look left you will see Alexander Calder's largest American stabile, *La Grande Voile*, which may give the illusion of moving or changing shape as you approach it. The HAYDEN GALLERY in the nearby library has exhibits of paintings and sculpture, and across the drive is the Charles River with sailboats (whenever the ice is gone) and tree-shaded benches.

CHINATOWN

It is within walking distance from the Boston Common, the theatre district, and not too far from Jordan Marsh and Filene's. A few of its 28 restaurants are mentioned on p. 33.

The pagoda atop the CHINESE MERCHANTS BUILDING acts as a landmark from the Southeast Expressway. Although Boston's Chinatown centering on Beach, Hudson, and Tyler streets is quite small and not very Old World-like, there are still 4,000 members of this ethnic group living here; 7,000 living in the suburbs and New England call it "home." English is spoken by most, but the primary language is Chinese. The bulletin board (in Chinese) on Oxford Street (corner of Beach Street) serves the purpose of a community newspaper.

The GIFT SHOPS, each with a "no fireworks" sign on the door, sell hundreds of items, some from mainland China, others from Japan, including dolls, scrolls, tea sets, and chopsticks.

The visitor can feel a sense of community in the markets where Chinese is spoken by both shopkeepers and residents; on warm summer evenings the full range of generations on the sidewalks and stoops also contributes to the feeling of family.

EASTERN MARKET at 48 Beach Street is a mini-supermarket; in addition to the Chinese vegetables or packaged products such as Bijon, Chinese vermicelli, you will see notices that give information on available lessons in Chinese cooking, calligraphy, and brush painting. HO YUEN BAKERY at 54 Beach Street is open 9–9 daily and has mixed nut pastry (delicious), fish-shaped cookies, black bean cakes, moon cakes, huge walnut cookies, and more. Some pastries are filled with meats and are not really desserts. BO-SHEK COFFEE HOUSE at 63 Beach Street has a smaller selection of pastries, but they are all marvelous—and here you may stay and eat in a very informal atmosphere.

In the SMALLER GROCERIES you will see fresh Chinese vegetables, suspended dried meats, dried fish, dried shrimp in apothecary jars, litchi nuts, dried lotus roots, and bamboo leaves. If you buy several items—plain salad oil and canned goods are sold too—the merchant may use his abacus. If it is the right season (wintertime), perhaps someone at Wing Wing, 79 Harrison Street, will cut open a fresh water chestnut for you. There is a difference between that and the canned variety!

FANEUIL HALL AREA
(Government Center)

Note the corner markers outside Faneuil Hall: They have such names as Corn or Sheep Market.

. . . This is the hub of a fascinating area. Once you have spent some time here, you have innumerable choices for adjoining areas—including the North End and the Waterfront.

People—the focus of this area where you can feel the pulse of the city. Historical exhibits (p. 110) and a variety of architecture offer a very special environment, but it may well be that you remember the people most.

If you go on a Friday or Saturday, the PUSHCARTS are "parked" along Blackstone Street; there you will be tempted to "come and buy" quantities of fresh fruits and vegetables at low prices from vendors who have inherited their pushcart positions once occupied by horse-drawn wagons. The vendors arrive at 4 A.M. to set up and sell until about 8 or 9 P.M. Bring a carryall or buy one here so that the family can help carry, and eat. Some seasoned buyers examine the prices as they walk in one direction and buy on the way back. (No secrets for a parking place—wherever you can find a spot.) The area is busy year round. Friday mornings (especially before 10) are not too crowded. Real bargains can be found around closing hours on Saturday night. If you step into one of the wholesale meat markets, the youngsters may have a chance to see meat before it reaches the wrapper. (Have your children ever seen the grinding of hamburger?) Along the block you will come to AL CAPONE'S CHEESE SHOP with cheeses from all over the world. On weekends you often have to wait a half hour before being served. The aroma is worth a visit, and you may decide to wait so that you save over supermarket prices; somehow the cheeses always seem better than prepackaged goods. You will hear many languages spoken in the line waiting for Al's personal service at the small meat counter—complete with cooking instructions, if you would like. Al's other enterprise on the block is a hole-in-the-wall PIZZA place that has the drippiest, tastiest, largest pieces of pizza in town. They are about 35¢ a slice and are well worth it. There is no place to sit down and it is a waiting situation on weekends, but the crowd knows what it wants. In warm weather the area has a SLUSH (flavored ice) vendor.

The existence of markets on the ground floor of FANEUIL HALL complies with the wishes of the donor Peter Faneuil. Stop in to see the occupied areas, which are busiest in the mornings. E. M. Niles at #25 has a tying machine, which bundles a roast in quick order. Across the street from Faneuil Hall is the granite Quincy Market with dozens of stalls of retailers and wholesalers. At #61 DOE, SULLIVAN AND CO. has more than 200 kinds of cheeses from all over the world.

From Faneuil Hall, as you face the new City Hall, take CHANGE AVENUE for a short walk on a footpath. Be sure to look skyward for a city view framed by close surrounding buildings.

Or turn the opposite way for a potpourri of suggestions: Follow the Freedom Trail path along Union Street. As you pass OLDE UNION OYSTER HOUSE you are likely to see Tommy Butt shucking oysters at the U-shaped mahogany bar—where he has for over 50 years. Just beyond this is Marshall

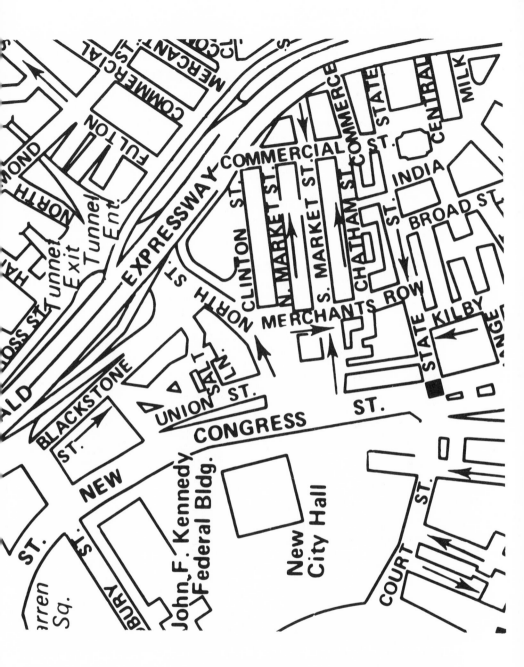

FANEUIL HALL

Street with the BOSTON STONE that was brought from England to grind pigments in the trough. The pigments were mixed with linseed oil to make paint. Legend says that the stone was used as a starting point for surveyors. Facing the stone is a small shop, THE EAST INDIA TRADING COMPANY, located in the oldest brick building in Boston and filled from ceiling to floor with items of all sizes and ages. Just stand outside and look at your surroundings: There is a picture to be framed in every direction. A few more steps and turn to your right for one of the KENNEDY'S & CO. stores at #153, open Monday-Thursday, 8:30–6, Fridays and Saturdays 8:30–8:30. Here the man in the big white apron will scoop pure peanut butter into a carton or cut a slab of butter from a refrigerator full. A short walk along Blackstone Street will bring you back to Faneuil Hall.

The stretch from City Hall to the ocean is being renovated. Architects argue whether it is a restoration or a reconstruction; the result is a mall to the sea. At the moment there are shells of BRICK WAREHOUSES ALONG SOUTH AND NORTH MARKET STREETS. Together with Quincy Market, the area is planned to attract people day and night with eateries, shops facing car-free streets with benches, plants, play areas, and pushcarts.

> If you are looking for a pleasant place to sit (and picnic), you might find the waterfall near the JFK Building (at one end of City Hall Plaza) in nearby

GOVERNMENT CENTER The plaza may have lunchtime and evening entertainment in the summer, plenty of people to watch, very few trees, and some vendors (depending upon the rules of the year). CITY HALL has tours (p. 250), and if you go into the JFK BUILDING, you will find a government information desk (that knows the answers or can lead you to someone who does), some free pamphlets available round the corner of the desk; the passport office is nearby (some groups stop in to see what is involved in obtaining a passport), and it is an escalator ride down to the GOVERNMENT BOOKSTORE, open Monday-Friday 8–4, with more than 1,000 publications for sale. Some are inexpensive pamphlets (about birds, food, home repairs, or whatever). A mail-order service is available for the thousands of titles stocked in Washington, D.C. The cafeteria (p. 32) is open to the public.

Near City Hall is the SEARS CRESCENT, the curved brick building that was saved from demolition when this part of the city was "done over." This was once lined with bookstores and was the center of Boston's literary world. The ORIENTAL TEA COMPANY has its steaming kettle here; it serves sandwiches—and you may wish to try its muffins. It is all a stand-up arrangement.

Cross Cambridge Street and take the broad staircase at One Center Plaza to find the new urban space in PEMBERTON SQUARE, where reverse curves are bounded by the new plaza buildings, and the late nineteenth-century Suffolk County Courthouse, which is still being considered for renovation or replacement. (If you want to go in, it may be possible to observe a trial. Inquire at the clerk's desk.) Outside you are in open unshaded space, which offers peace and a respite for the eyes. At #2 Center Plaza is the BOSTON VISUAL ARTISTS UNION GALLERY (closed Mondays), which has ramps for the handicapped, very high ceilings, and interesting exhibits.

Architecture buffs should seek out nearby LINDEMANN MENTAL HEALTH CENTER. Its split-rib concrete circular staircase and curved theme inside and out gives a feeling of warmth to what could have been a sterile structure.

NORTH END

The Italian section, now separated from the rest of the city by a maze of highways, has a cohesive community atmosphere. Those who come to dine in the area often miss the sights that are clustered. Even when it is not election time, groups of every age gather on the street corners, at Paul Revere's Mall, and in playgrounds; several generations watch the activities from windows above or from portable chairs on the sidewalks. The shops centering on HANOVER STREET represent all needs; but the visitor may be most interested in coffee-makers or windows of decorated pastries (elaborate wedding cakes seem to be a mile high). Enter a bakery for the aroma—and perhaps a bag of goodies for your walk. Specialties include marzipan (almond paste) and the huge round mountain bread. In the window of the HAYMARKET COOPERATIVE BANK is an unusual map of Italy that shows all the villages and towns in the country.

One block over on SALEM STREET, closed to traffic Monday-Saturday 8–6, vegetables are sold from sidewalk stalls in good weather. There are barrels of live snails and squid, hanging meats, olives (in bulk), drums of olive oil and cheeses; there are many shoppers, neighborhood-type dry-goods stores, and plenty to see. Meats are custom cut by "a friend."

You can buy homemade egg noodles and ravioli and see the trays they are made in just a few steps off Hanover Street at V. BIAGI'S, 143 Richmond Street (1 block from the expressway), open until 7 Fridays and Saturdays. Opposite Richmond Street on the other side of Hanover Street, again just a few steps away, is the marvelous NORTH END BRANCH OF THE BOSTON PUBLIC LIBRARY. Even if you are not yet ready for a rest, stop in at one of the most inviting libraries you will ever see. A small pool is bordered with chairs and ceiling-high plants; there is a lovely children's area, complete with steps before a bubbler; near the section of Italian books is the very large diorama of the Ducal Palace in Venice in a colorful sixteenth-century setting with figures of the Doge in his state gondola, merchants, monks, ladies of the court, peasants, and beggars. Library hours vary; at present it is closed on weekends. Just beyond the library on the corner of Salem Street is POLCARI'S where you will find five varieties of coffee beans (in old copper bins) waiting to be custom ground, about 300 kinds of spices sold in bulk, cheeses, cold cuts, and wooden boxes filled with about 25 different dried beans. It is open 8–6, 6 days a week.

When looking for the OLD NORTH CHURCH, find the white spire (illuminated at night) of ST. STEPHEN'S CHURCH at 401 Hanover Street; the Old North can be reached by walking through Paul Revere's Mall opposite St. Stephen's. (Just inside the door of St. Stephen's is a before-during-after photographic exhibition of the 1965 restoration. The entire church was lowered almost 7 feet by hydraulic lifts to the original entrance level; historical and architectural details include the original bell made by Paul Revere placed in

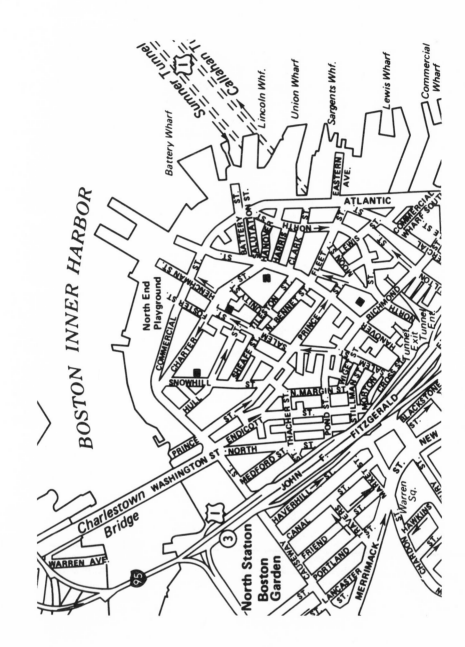

NORTH END

the steeple reproduction.) When you walk through the PAUL REVERE MALL, you are very much part of a neighborhood scene: men playing cards, children playing tag, others conversing—and some residents maybe even watching the tourists. If you want to see bocce, the older men of the neighborhood are usually playing on the courts located next to the Police Station on Commercial Street.

Although there is talk of major real-estate changes (some rather disturbing), it is hoped this special area will retain its character appreciated now by residents and visitors alike.

WATERFRONT

(Reminder: Parking is difficult.)

Ⓣ **Stop:** For Atlantic Avenue area—Aquarium Station. For Fish Pier—bus from South Station.

Beaches: p. 209.

Boat Trips: p. 219.

Boston Tea Party Ship: p. 160.

> There is a feeling that years of talk have indeed resulted in many changes—some not yet completed. Along Atlantic Avenue are the many recently opened restaurants (most with brick walls and hanging plants), luxury apartments, converted warehouses—and traffic, along with views of tugboats, tankers, boats, freighters, fishing and, occasionally, ocean liners.

> . . . Below are suggestions for a close look at the waterfront. For an outstanding panoramic view of the harbor, walk to the nearby Custom House and ride to the (free) observation tower. Check the hours (p. 136) carefully.

To Get to the Fish Pier: Drive on Summer Street, alongside South Station, go over the railroad bridge, and take a left on Viaduct Street, the sign says "To Commonwealth Pier." Follow the ramp to the fish pier. (It is also possible to take Northern Avenue to Atlantic. Turn right at the James Hook lobster sign.)

Park your car in the nearest available spot, hold the hands of the little ones, and walk to the end of the pier, which is probably lined with fishing boats, possibly unloading after weeks at sea. (This is also a marvelous observation point; you can see planes taking off and landing, and there is usually very little company on the pier.) Modern technology has produced innovations in the fishing industry, and the Boston fleet is seeing hard times; there are still many wooden boats in use that were built quite awhile ago. The daily early morning fish auctions are not what they used to be, but you may wish to enter the Boston Fish Exchange at the end of the pier and see the postings of the day's catch. Some school groups have held their own mock auctions here.

You are in the neighborhood of two of Boston's large established seafood restaurants, JIMMY'S HARBORSIDE and ANTHONY'S PIER 4, but if it is a weekday, you may want to try the more casual establishment at 15½ (p. 35) right on the pier. Even if you are not eating at Anthony's Pier 4, you will want to park near it for a close view of the former Hudson River Day Liner *Peter Stuyvesant*. It served New York and Hudson River Point from 1927 to 1964. Everything gleams from fresh paint and polish on the boat that sits on a spe-

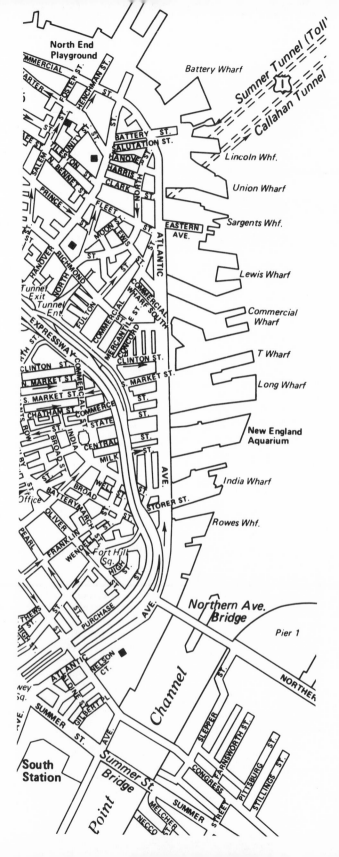

WATERFRONT

cially constructed cradle that allows it to rise and fall with the tide and still be on a vertical plane. It has the unique feature of one stack, and there are four decks that are now used as cocktail lounges and special function areas. The interior, sumptuously outfitted with objects gathered from Europe, provides a turn-of-the-century effect. The gift shop on board (not really a place for finding trinkets) opens at 2 P.M.

ATLANTIC AVENUE AREA, 1½ miles from fish pier. Go along Northern Avenue and take a right on Atlantic. (This area is about a 15-minute walk from Faneuil Hall.)

This is the area of the NEW ENGLAND AQUARIUM (p. 43), LONG WHARF with its boat excursions, the GREEN DOLPHIN at #67 where the sign clearly indicates that children are not invited to explore antiques, the Custom House block with its sign painted on the brick end of the building ("Established 1831, Martin L. Hall Co."), and the CHART HOUSE, a moderately priced restaurant in a former warehouse. COMMERCIAL WHARF has apartments, flower-filled white barrels on the pier, and a marina. LEWIS WHARF has shops on the first floor, a Japanese restaurant, a nautical supply house—and landscaping that tourists sometimes abuse; if you do have a sandwich here, please take your trash with you.

By the spring of 1976 there will be a plaza with a terraced lawn area visually oriented to the harbor. The PARK, located between Long and Commercial wharves, the expressway, and Commercial Street, is planned to accommodate spontaneous festivals and vendor-related activities. Look for the 350-foot-long-trellis rose arbor, one of the longest ever designed.

MUSEUMS

. . . Going by school or chartered bus with a group? Such vehicles are barred on MDC parkway roads, but permission may be granted if you write at least 2 weeks in advance to the Commissioner, Metropolitan District Commission, 20 Somerset Street, Boston 02108. Include information on the number of people going, where and when (day and hours).

. . . Try to become aware of a child's attention span.

. . . Special programs for children may be scheduled.

. . . Since so many people converge on Boston institutions on Sunday afternoons, museums in surrounding communities may present a pleasant change. Several outstanding institutions that are not overwhelming in size are mentioned here and in the chapter on Day Trips.

. . . Reminder: Many museums are closed Mondays.

. . . Outdoor museums (e.g., Mystic Seaport, Old Sturbridge Village, Plimoth Plantation, Strawbery Banke) are included in the chapter on Day Trips, pp. 65–106.

. . . Museum memberships often include free or reduced admission, a newsletter, special events, preferred enrollment for courses, and savings in the gift shops.

ADDISON GALLERY OF AMERICAN ART   Phillips Academy (on Rt. 28)
Andover   Tel. 475–7515

Open: Monday-Saturday 10–5, Sundays 2:30–5. Closed New Year's Day, Memorial Day, Labor Day, Thanksgiving, and Christmas.

Admission: Free.

Special exhibitions are often scheduled at the gallery, which has American works of art from colonial times to the present. The permanent collection includes paintings, sculpture, graphic arts, furniture, glass, textiles, eighteenth-century silver, and models—built to uniform scale—of famous American sailing ships.

Also at Phillips Academy:
R. S. PEABODY FOUNDATION FOR ARCHAEOLOGY   corner of Phillips and Main streets   Andover   Tel. 475–0248

Open: Monday-Friday 8:30–4:15, Saturdays 9–5, Sundays 2–5. Closed January 1, Memorial Day, Thanksgiving Day, Labor Day, Christmas.

Parking: Free.

The Peabody Foundation features: Archaeological exhibits focusing on New England and nearby Canada; shards from various locations clearly marked in uncluttered displays; exhibits on general anthropology outlining the physical and cultural evolution of man over a period of 2 million years; a study on the comparative evolution of three cities—Boston, Mexico City, and Baghdad.

BLUE HILLS TRAILSIDE MUSEUM (Massachusetts Audubon Society)
1904 Canton Avenue   Milton   Tel. 333–0690

Located on Rt. 138, 10 miles south of Boston, adjacent to Blue Hills Ski Area.

Directions: Southeast Expressway to Rt. 128, Exit 64 north, short drive to museum.

Bus: Red Ⓣ Line to Mattapan Square. Brush Hill bus to museum.

Open: Tuesday-Sunday 10–5. Closed Mondays except on state holidays; closed Thanksgiving, Christmas, and New Year's Day.

Admission: Adults, 50¢; children 3–11, 25¢; MDC District school groups, free.

The location of this museum allows for a pleasant combination of indoor and outdoor activity. Trailside is an institution of manageable size for families.

River otter in action offer one of the most animated outdoor exhibits. Red and gray foxes, quail, pheasant, hawk, and deer are year-round examples of life in the immediate territory. Inside at a "Planter's table" are living wild flowers transplanted from the reservation outside, live animal demonstrations (announcements for them are made inside and out), and displays including plants, trees, minerals, meteorites, birds, mammals, amphibians, reptiles, and fish. Ground has been broken for a new auditorium that will allow for larger group capacity and a more flexible and varied program.

Regularly Scheduled Programs: Includes hikes into the Blue Hills and animal talks on many Saturday afternoons.

Guided Tours: Available by arrangement only. Spring and fall require many months' notice. Minimum age: 4. Length: About 1 hour. The tour could include museum exhibits, live animal demonstration-lectures, outdoor animal trail exhibits, and a hike to the top of Big Blue.

Courses: Held for all ages on a variety of nature topics. Call for current information.
Handicapped: Special arrangements can be made for a program.
Animal Loan Program: Available for qualified persons.
Speakers and Slide Programs: Available for age 10 and up.
Junior Curator Program: Minimum age: 14.
Chair Lift: May be in operation during fall foliage season.

Eating: Winter visitors may walk to the base lodge of the Blue Hills ski area to purchase refreshments. No picnicking is allowed at the museum (although a small area is planned), but fireplaces and a playground are at Houghton's Pond, about a mile away.

Hikers: Marked trails: Red—¼ mile (15 minutes) or green trail (30 minutes) to the observation tower atop Big Blue. Those who climb the tower can view many Boston landmarks. The museum sells a nature trail guide (25¢), which identifies the growth near numbered posts along the way. The Blue Dot Trail (Skyline Trail) joins the green trail at the public lookout tower. It crosses only three paved roads and is about 10 miles long through (urban) wilderness.

BOSTON TEA PARTY SHIP   Congress Street Bridge (off Atlantic Avenue)
Boston 02210   Tel. 338–1773

Ⓣ **Stop:** South Station on Red Line (3-minute walk).
Open: Every day except Thanksgiving, Christmas, and New Year's Day. Winter 9–5, summer 9–8.
Parking: Free 2-hour parking permitted on Congress Street Bridge. Two commercial lots available on Atlantic Avenue if necessary on weekdays.
Free Shuttle Bus: From Old State House daily June-September and off-season weekends.
Admission: Adults, $1.50; children 5–14, 75¢. Group rates available.

Griffin's Wharf, now covered by the Southeast Expressway, was the site of the Boston Tea Party, Now, 200 years later, you can go to the nearby Congress Street Bridge for a different view of the city and see *Brig Beaver II*. This two-masted brigantine, a privately owned replica of a ship involved in the Boston Tea Party, was constructed in Denmark and sailed to Boston in 1973. You can go above and below the (small) ship, inspect the rigging and galley, see work being done on the ship below, and throw tea into the harbor—if you wish to create your own Party.

In the museum, exhibits portray the economic and political conditions of pre-Revolutionary Boston. There are audio-visual presentations, one historical on the Tea Party, one contemporary on the 1973 voyage of the *Brig Beaver II*, historical documents, and a three-dimensional model of Boston in 1773. *Length of average visit:* 45 minutes.

All sorts of plans and dreams for new programs (some possibly participatory) are in the thinking stage. Call for current details.

Guided Tours: Available year round for school and youth groups. Reservations required. A month's notice suggested. Minimum age: 5. Tea Party Reenactment (p. 300) and Annual bending of the sails (p. 285).
Speakers and Slide Shows: Available for traveling.
Junior Curator Program: Minimum age: 14.

BROCKTON ART CENTER   Oak Street on Upper Porter's Pond   Brockton 02401 (about 25 miles from Boston)   Tel. 588–6000

Directions: Rt. 128 south to Rt. 24, Exit 28W. First right onto Oak Street. Art Center is 1 mile on left.

Bus: Chateau Westgate from Park Square and South Station. Weekdays only. Plymouth-Brockton Street Railway Co.

Open: Tuesday-Sunday 1–5, Thursdays, 1–10 (except July and August). Closed July 4, Thanksgiving, Christmas, and New Year's Day.

Admission: Adults, $1; children under 16, free; senior citizens, 50¢.

Parking: Free and plentiful.

Air-conditioned.

This weather-shingled contemporary structure has loan exhibitions, a permanent collection of nineteenth-century American works, and appealing showings of contemporary work by area artists and craftsmen.

The art center is on the edge of the pond in a very large, beautiful, wooded public park. You can walk around Upper Porter's Pond to the Observation Tower (½ mile) and climb for a good southerly view. Or pick up the 4 miles of bicycle trails (shared with motor vehicles) near the art center. Or fish in the stocked (trout and bass) ponds. Something for everyone.

Guided Tours: Tuesday-Thursday by arrangement only. Three weeks' advance notice. Written requests preferred. Minimum age: 5.

Programs Regularly Scheduled: Plays, theatre, films, puppet shows, lectures, craft fairs.

Mailing List for Nonmembers: $2.50.

Memberships: Individual, $12; family, $20; students and senior citizens, $5.

Courses: Offered for children in arts and crafts, theatre, dance, painting, drawing, sculpture.

Traveling Speakers Available for Groups: 4 weeks' notice. Fee.

Library: extensive collection of art reference materials.

Gift Shop: No admission fee to museum required for entrance.

To Schools within a 20-mile Radius: Volunteer instructors are available to visit a school and prepare a class for their visit. No fee.

Art Rentals: Available to anyone. Rates based on a sliding scale of value of painting. (About $5–$15 for a 2-month period.)

Eating: Cafeteria available to accommodate box lunches only. Please give advance notice. Picnicking: Many tables and fireplaces throughout the park.

BUSCH-REISINGER MUSEUM   29 Kirkland Street   Cambridge   Tel. 495–2338

Open: June-September 1, Monday-Friday 9–4:45; September 2-June, Monday-Saturday 9–5. Closed holidays.

Parking: Very difficult near museum.

Admission: Free.

The museum, which could be covered in one visit, has sculpture, paintings, and decorative arts of Austria, Germany, the Low Countries, Scandinavia, and Switzerland from the Middle Ages to the present day. Young children may enjoy going through just a few galleries (passing from one gallery to another through plaster-cast reproductions of fifteenth-century gates). Near the entrance is a surprise—a small courtyard complete with large colorful goldfish in the pool, and roses, irises, and other flowers in season.

Guided Tours: By advance arrangement only. For adults only.

Organ Concerts: On the famous classic-style organ, given every Thursday afternoon at 12:15 during the academic year.

Picnicking: Tables set up in garden but groups are not encouraged. Young children, too, may be happier at the nearby Cambridge Common.

CHILDREN'S MUSEUM   Jamaicaway (Rt. 1)   Boston 02130   Tel. 522–4800, taped information 522–5454

A new large facility on the waterfront (Congress Street) has just been acquired. It will probably open in 1977.

Ⓣ **Stop:** Burroughs Street on Arborway-Huntington car (Green Line), 2-block walk.

Parking: Free.

Memberships: Boston families, $8; double, $6; individual child, $2; individual adults, $4. Nonresidents: twice all stated fees.

Eating: No restaurant. Picnicking not allowed on grounds, but you are across the (busy) Jamaicaway from the pleasant banks of Jamaica Pond. Or you are 10 minutes away from the business center with many eateries.

The Museum Has Three Major Divisions:
VISITOR CENTER (the one youngsters know and enjoy)
RESOURCE CENTER (often undiscovered by visiting adults)
COMMUNITY SERVICES

VISITOR CENTER

Open: All months except September. October-June, Tuesday-Friday 2–5; Saturdays, Sundays, Boston school holidays, and vacation days 10–5. November-August free (to all) Fridays 6–9 P.M. Summer hours: late June-August, Monday-Friday 11–5, Saturdays and Sundays 10–5. Closed January 1, July 4, Labor Day, Thanksgiving, and Christmas.

Admission: Adults, $2; children 3–15, $1; under 3, free. Free when open Friday evenings 6–9.

Handicapped: Steps between many levels difficult to maneuver during regular museum hours. Help available.

The former theatre building offers nine levels of exhibits that invite participation: Climb up to Grandmother's Attic under the eaves, and rummage through trunks and dressers and try-on clothes, discover funny and wonderful things—early gramophones and crystal sets, old schoolbooks, toys, household items, and intriguing dollhouses. The intimate amphitheatre sometimes has demonstrations of museum materials. Make your own movies, see a silent one, or turn the old zeotrope. Play with colors and mirrors and discover how a kaleidoscope works. Work a computer and play games with one. Spend some time in a Japanese home. Touch a rabbit or snake. See what's in the "What's New" area. In the summer: Try a furry seat in the outside wigwam, while considering demands of such an environment. It is all meant to arouse and satisfy curiosity.

The exhibits are enhanced by those marvelous staffers who appear everywhere. They understand young people and their need to touch, to talk (it is not a quiet place), and to discover for themselves useful information about the world in which we live. It is geared for preschool through elementary school-aged youngsters.

Visitor Center Shop: Even the cash register has exposed works here. The stock has the child purchase in mind. Small slates, 5-foot balloons, marbles . . . items for 5¢ and up.

Small Groups: Visits booked for mornings October-June. Call immediately after Labor Day. Usually filled for entire year within 1 week: Visits allow for a 20-minute program and 1 hour's exploring time. Minimum age: preschool.

Special Education Program: 1 hour, every Wednesday, October-June, when staff members provide a one-to-one situation.

Afterschool Clubs: Offered during school year. Various interests represented (art, science, cooking, math). Fees charged.

Junior Curator: Age 12–15.

Museum Helpers: Age 10–12.

RESOURCE CENTER

. . . Open for adult browsing and workshops.
. . . Children may come in if accompanied by an adult.
. . . Home of circulating materials and "Recycle."

Admission: Free.

Hours: Vary from season to season. Generally closed Sundays and Mondays. Open: Tuesday-Saturday and Thursday evenings. Check on current schedule.

Inside the rambling stucco mansion is a gold mine of information and ideas. There are tables with batteries, wires, and bulbs, Eskimo tools, balance scales, sandals and robes from Afghanistan, saltwater aquariums, a library with books, magazines, and hundreds of periodicals. One thing leads to another; plan on plenty of time for browsing.

Workshops: Offered year round Thursday nights on a drop-in basis. Fee: $3 per session. Scope: Uses of three-dimensional materials in teaching, crafts, arts, and more. Always changing and expanding to meet needs.

Small animal loans are available.

Circulating Materials: Loan exhibits are boxes of real objects, labels, illustrations (in some cases books and filmstrips are also included), organized so the teacher can set up a classroom exhibit on a selected topic. MATCH boxes (Materials and Activities for Teachers and CHildren) are 2- to 3-week lesson sequences organized through teachers' guides into self-contained kits of artifacts, models, audio-visual materials, equipment, and references.

Recycle: Open generally the same hours as the Resource Center. Located in the Resource Center building. It is an area that has a wide variety of by-products of industry. Experts in art, preschool education, mathematics, science, language arts, and music are constantly contributing ideas on how to use recycled materials. Memberships available. Individual bags of materials: $2.25.

Teacher Shop: Hours same as Resource Center. Items for 2¢ up. All sorts of hard-to-find things that are designed for counting games and imagination: Dice, small plastic boxes, eyedroppers, and more.

COMMUNITY SERVICES

This department assists neighborhood houses, multiservice agencies, community centers, day-care centers, Headstart programs, youth clubs, and community schools to develop materials and activities for education in the visual arts, crafts, music, natural and physical sciences, and early childhood education. It trains leaders of children's programs, acquires, trains, and supervises student interns; designs and adapts space for educational and arts uses; runs summer arts and science programs; and obtains assistance from other cultural institutions in metropolitan Boston.

DECORDOVA AND DANA MUSEUM AND PARK   Sandy Pond Road   Lincoln   Tel. 259–8355   (15 miles northwest of Boston. Could be combined with a visit to apple country, p. 297.)

Directions: Rt. 2 to Rt. 128 North to 47 West (Trapelo Road)—until end, across to Sandy Pond Road.

Open: Tuesday-Friday 10–5, Saturdays and Sundays 1:30–5. Closed July 4, Thanksgiving, Christmas, New Year's Day, and Easter.

Admission: Adults, $1.50; under 21, 50¢.

Parking: Free and no problem.

Drive up to the turreted psuedocastle structure along a road surrounded by a variety of lovely old trees and beautiful lawns. Since this estate and art collection were given to the town as a museum in the 1940s, it has become a cultural center for the performing and visual arts. Rotating exhibits emphasize more recent periods, with examples of antiquity. Each has a slide presentation, which gives perspective. You may easily tour the museum in one visit. For those members of your party not keen on gallery stepping, there are large sculptures on the grounds. Plenty of roaming and running space. The paths in the park (open 9 A.M.–5 P.M.) are lined (in season) with wild flowers and fields of daisies leading to the pond below. Five new studio units offer a pleasant atmosphere for creativity.

Courses: Many for all ages in a wide variety of art media. Classes offered year round. Fees charged. Museum members allowed to register before nonmembers. Most film and lecture series and musical concerts open to nonmembers for a fee.

Summer Sunday Afternoons: p. 294.

Borrowing Materials: Art slides available to teachers. No charge.

Speakers: On various subjects (fee charged) for audiences that are at least junior high age.

FOGG ART MUSEUM   Quincy and Broadway   Cambridge   02138   Tel. 495–2387 (2 blocks from Busch-Reisinger Museum, p. 161)

Ⓣ **Stop:** Harvard Square on Red Line.

Open: Summer weekdays 10–5; after Labor Day through school year: week-days and Saturdays 10–5, Sundays 2–5. Closed Federal and State holidays, Thanksgiving, and Christmas.

Admission: Free.

The extensive university-owned collection, ranging from classical to modern, represents all fields of Occidental and Oriental art, Degas drawings, prints, sculpture, paintings, seventeenth- and eighteenth-century silver. Special loan exhibitions are shown in addition to the still-growing collection. With orienta-tion and follow-up this could be a fascinating place for youngsters. Recom-mended for those with art and/or museum appreciation.

Lectures by visiting art authorities open to the public.

FRUITLANDS MUSEUMS   Prospect Hill   Harvard   Tel. 456–3924

30 miles northwest of Boston. This is apple country; the orchards have blossoms or country stands with cider and fruit for sale, depending on the season.

Directions: Rt. 2 to Harvard exit (Rt. 110), turn right on Old Shirley Road, cross intersection where Old Shirley Road becomes Prospect Hill Road, continue less than a mile to museum.

Open: May 30-September 30, Tuesday-Sunday 1–5. Closed Mondays except when a holiday.

Admission: Adults, $1; children under 16, 25¢.

Parking: Provided in 3 lots. Drive down to middle parking lot at Reception Center to purchase tickets.

Strollers: Allowed. (Good place for them.)

Although many of the exhibits are not meaningful to some young children, the setting makes this a popular place for families. Instead of spending the after-noon in one museum, visitors view exhibits in six structures situated along a rolling hill, with Mount Wachusett and Mount Monadnock in the background. On very busy days (Sundays after 2) there may be a wait for some of the houses. (And it is hot in the summer sun.)

Because Fruitlands has so much to see, you may wish to visit that first—while attention span is greatest. Memorabilia of Emerson and Thoreau are here along with possessions and furnishings of the Alcott family. Smell the spices in the restored colonial kitchen, find the mouse in the trap, take the steps to see drying herbs and the toy collection, read of Joseph Palmer who was persecuted for wearing a beard, and notice the framed locks of hair of Louisa and Anna Alcott.

SHAKER HOUSE, built in the 1790s, forms the setting for a particularly good representative collection of furniture and products of Shaker handicrafts and community industries such as weaving and shoe repairing. The INDIAN MUSEUM includes prehistoric implements and specimens of Indian arts and industries. See a ceremonial buffalo robe, a buffalo skull, arrowheads, all sorts of beading and basketry—with Indian music adding atmosphere to the mu-seum. The PICTURE GALLERY has collections of paintings by itinerant por-trait artists of the nineteenth century, American folk art, and landscape painting.

Groups: Helpful attendants are available in each of the houses, but groups of 50–100 people may make an appointment a week in advance for a 1½–2-

hour tour of all the buildings, including a 50-minute program at the Indian Museum.

Eating: No picnicking allowed on premises. Snack Bar located in Prospect House, which has a marvelous observation terrace overlooking the valley with Mount Wachusett and Mount Monadnock in the distance.

ISABELLA STEWART GARDNER MUSEUM   280 The Fenway   Tel. 566–1401   Concert schedule: Tel. 734–1359

Ⓣ **Stop:** Ruggles Street on Arborway-Huntington Green Line. Three-block walk to the museum.

Open: September-June, Tuesdays 1–9:30 P.M., Wednesday-Sunday 1–5:30 P.M. Closed Mondays, all national holidays, and Sunday before Labor Day. July and August, Tuesday-Sunday 1–5:30 P.M. Closed Mondays and July 4.

Admission: Free except Sunday, $1.

Recommended for children over 8. Thirty unusual display areas show a collection, formed by Mrs. Gardner, of renowned paintings, sculpture, tapestries, stained glass, furniture, and other objects. The building is of Italian style with a central court that has magnificent seasonal displays of flowers. It is a particularly peaceful atmosphere on weekdays. The trailing nasturtiums are usually in bloom (from the third floor to the ground) late in March and most of April.

Taped Tour Units: 50¢ per person, 75¢ for 2 people.
Guided Tours: Available for adults with advance notice. Fee charged.
Music: Free programs Tuesdays at 8, Thursdays and Sundays at 4. No music in July and August. Performers range from students to well-known musicians. The room is long, narrow, and without elevation. Tends to fill up on Sundays. No seat-holding allowed.
Strollers: With rubber wheels allowed inside. (Long flights of stairs between floors.)
Eating: Light refreshments sold in garden in summer. Nearest picnic area— across the street in the Fenway. No tables.
Handicapped: One wheelchair available. Elevators on request.

HAMMOND MUSEUM   (p. 80).

FRANCIS RUSSELL HART NAUTICAL MUSEUM   Massachusetts Institute of Technology   77 Massachusetts Avenue   Cambridge 02139   Tel. 253–5942

Ⓣ **Stop:** Kendall Square or Central Square plus 1-mile walk. Dudley-Harvard bus stops at 77 Massachusetts Avenue.

Open: 9–5 daily. The 55 Massachusetts Avenue door (near Memorial Drive) is open 9–5 Monday-Friday. At other times—including weekends—entrance can be made through the main rotunda at 77 Massachusetts Avenue.

Admission: Free.

Parking: Difficult.

Recommended for children over 8.

More than 100 ship models displayed in glass cases are chronologically arranged in this small museum. Here you may trace the history of shipbuilding with rigged models of merchant ships and warships ranging from a Viking ship to those of the present. The larger models include handsome examples of a Danish warship of 1700, an Elizabethan galleon of 1590, and an American frigate of 1800.

JOHN WOODMAN HIGGINS ARMORY, INC.   100 Barber Avenue   Worcester 01606   Tel. 853–6015

See Index for other Worcester suggestions.
(Could be combined with trip to Southboro Country Store, p. 46.)

Directions: I-290 west to Exit 20. Turn right onto Burncoat Street, then left onto Randolph Road.

Open: Tuesday-Friday 9–4, Saturdays 10–3, Sundays 1–5. Closed national holidays.

Admission: Adults, 75¢; children, 10¢; under 5, free. Group rates available.

Mounted knights in full panoply line the main exhibit hall, a reproduction of a medieval Austrian castle. Over 100 complete armors (not encased—no touching allowed) are chronologically arranged to tell the story via displays of steel plates, mail, full armor, Maximilian corrugated armor, decorated armor more useful for parade than battlefield, and finally the thicker half suits of the seventeenth century. The collection, dating from pre-Christian to modern times (a bullet-proof vest), includes primitive Stone Age weapons, chests with great locks, surgical instruments, tools of the armorer, as well as stained glass windows from European cathedrals, paintings, wood carvings, and tapestries.

Groups: 20-minute audio-visual program emphasizes the relationship of the collection to art and history.

Library: Students may use it on request. Books, monographs, clippings, and prints on armor and related subjects.

INSTITUTE OF CONTEMPORARY ART   955 Boylston Street (across from the Prudential Center—Hynes Auditorium   Boston 02115   Tel. 266–5151

Open: September-June, Monday-Saturday 10–5, Sundays 2–5. Possible summer hours.

Admission: Adults, $1; children under 17, 50¢. Group rates available.

Many locations have been called home since the Institute was established in 1936. Only recently has a permanent site been acquired. There are 2½ spacious floors of gallery space in the renovated former Back Bay police station. The third floor will be available for educational programs. In addition to having exhibits of contemporary art in all media, ICA is involved with VALUE, a program for high-school seniors in which they study the city through Visual Arts. The PUBLIC ART PROGRAMS project may schedule bus tours or arrange to have artists work in public places. Contact ICA for its present programming of film series and lectures.

LONDON WAX MUSEUM   179 Tremont Street (opposite Boston Common) Tel. 542–6882

Open: Monday-Saturday 10 A.M.–9:30 P.M., Sundays and holidays 1–9:30 P.M. Closed Christmas.

Admission: Adults, $1.95; children under 12, $1. Group rates available.

For those who are tempted by the sample scene in the window, the museum has forty scenes of famous people of past and present, life size in wax, displayed in historically accurate settings. Among the wax figures created in the Josephine Tussaud factory in London are Paul Revere, John F. Kennedy, the Battle of Bunker Hill, Snow White, Pinocchio, and Batman. And then there is a Chamber of Horrors—not really a young child's paradise.

MERRIMACK VALLEY TEXTILE MUSEUM   800 Massachusetts Avenue
North Andover   Tel. 686–0191

> Rt. 93 to Rt. 495 north, exit at Massachusetts Avenue, North
> Andover, east on Massachusetts Avenue for 1½ miles. Museum
> is on left, ½ mile beyond second traffic light.

Open: Monday-Friday 9–5, Saturdays and Sundays 1–5. Closed New Year's Day, Easter Sunday, Thanksgiving, and Christmas.

Admission: No fees Monday-Saturday except for prearranged tours. Sundays: Adults, $1; children under 18, 50¢.

Two galleries of artifacts and machinery depict the history of wool textile manufacturing—from raw wool to finished cloth. Signs, illustrations, and actual equipment (only one piece is a reproduction) are well arranged, but the guided tour that accompanies the Sunday demonstrations provides a memorable and exciting visit.

The exhibits illustrate the steps of sheep shearing, raw material preparation, spinning, weaving, and finishing. With each process, hand-operated implements alternate with power-driven machinery to emphasize the transition from handicraft to factory production during the Industrial Revolution.

Guided tours and continuous **demonstrations** of the textile machinery are given Sunday afternoons.

Groups: Guided tours by arrangement with two weeks' advance notice.

Borrowing Materials: "Textiles for the Classroom," a resource kit on woolen manufacturing. Rental: $10 week. Film available.

MUSEUM OF AFRO AMERICAN HISTORY   African Meeting House
Smith Court, off Joy Street on Beacon Hill   Boston   Tel. 723–8863

Roxbury Center: 90 Warren Street, Tel. 445–7400

The Smith Court location, built entirely by Afro-Americans in 1805 as the first church building for blacks in New England, is being restored. It is the oldest extant church building built for blacks in the country and has seen several uses, the most recent as a synagogue. When it is open this year, its appearance will resemble that of 1850, with space allocated for a museum gallery. Behind the Meeting House will be a research library and archives for the museum.

The Roxbury branch will continue, but it will be in the Dillaway-Thomas House in John Eliot Square, Roxbury.

Roxbury Center Hours: Sunday-Friday 11–5. Closed Saturdays. Special school group hours arranged.

Admission: Adults, 50¢; students and senior citizens (with ID's), 25¢. Educational group rates available.

Exhibits change about every 6 weeks. They portray "a sense of community and how black people survive in a given period of time" and include documents, photographs, and paintings on various themes.

Special Sunday Afternoon Outdoor Programs: Call for the present schedule.

Films (on education, integration, historical themes): Available for group showings.

Tours: Historic sites in Roxbury conducted by the staff.

Traveling Exhibits: Black Education in Boston, Roxbury Puddingstone.

Black Heritage Trail (p. 117): Conducted tours, 1–2 hours, given periodically. Brochures on the trail distributed by the museum (and Boston 200 visitor centers).

MUSEUM OF THE AMERICAN CHINA TRADE   215 Adams Street   Milton 02186   Tel. 696–1815

Directions: Southeast Expressway to Exit 22 (Squantum Street) to stop sign, right on to Adams Street for a mile.

Open: Year round, Tuesday-Saturday 2–5. Closed holidays.

Admission: Adults, $1.50; children under 12, 50¢.

This early nineteenth-century Greek-Revival mansion, built on the oldest road in the Commonwealth, atop Milton Hill, features many furnishings brought back from China. Marble-topped tables, elaborately carved chairs, a butler's pantry filled with priceless china, a Document Room, the spiral staircase, and changing exhibits are included in the 1-hour tour. (Many exclaim over the Chinese silk wallpapered parlor.) Visitors may walk on the grounds and enjoy the view.

Group Arrangements: Minimum age—12. Summer day school for elementary school children.

MUSEUM OF FINE ARTS   479 Huntington Avenue   Tel. 267–9300 For recorded information, which includes events of the day: 267–9377 or ANSWERS.

The staff is working on new programs and possibilities for children, groups, and families. Check with the Education Department for latest developments.

> If you are bringing young children with short attention spans, everyone may enjoy the Fenway (p. 186) for picnicking, feeding ducks, relaxing, or running.

Ⓣ**Stop:** Arborway-Huntington car on Green Line.

Open: Tuesdays 10–9, Wednesday-Sunday 10–5. Closed Mondays, New Year's Day, July 4, Labor Day, Thanksgiving, Christmas eve, and Christmas.

Admission: Age 16 and over, $2.50; members and children under 16, free. Free Sundays 10 A.M.–1 P.M.

Note: Eating at the restaurant or attending a film or lecture does not require museum admission fee; such admission limited to specific activity.

Parking: Near Fenway entrance (off Museum Road) without charge.

Handicapped: Use employees' entrance on Museum Road. Elevators and staff assistance available.

Strollers: Allowed, but not in special exhibition galleries. Carriages not allowed.

Membership: Single $20, double $30, family $30. Yearly student admission cards for college and university students $5.

Calendar of Events: Subscriptions to the complete monthly calendar (summer events are included in the June edition) are available to nonmembers through the membership office for $1.50 annually.

Among the almost 200 galleries: The finest OLD KINGDOM sculpture exhibit outside of Cairo, the result of a museum-supported 40-year expedition, includes mummies, altars, and hieroglyphics in renovated galleries that take advantage of natural and concealed light. The ORIENTAL COLLECTION has elegant screens and a Japanese-fashioned garden adapted for inside. The ANCIENT MUSICAL INSTRUMENTS ROOM has lovely-to-look-at pieces that may be handled (note information below). All are kept in playing condition whenever possible. You may see a glockenspiel from the Harriet Beecher Stowe estate, a snakewood violin bow from 1800, a Swedish viola da gamba with carved monster head, and eighteenth-century hunting horns. The early nineteenth-century European 32-glass-bell armonica (made to be played by a seated musician who moistens the rims of the glass cups) is the type invented by Benjamin Franklin. The DECORATIVE ARTS WING has a 1695 room from Britain's Hamilton Palace and a 1760 Louis XVI salon complete with rococo mirrors, tapestries, and chandeliers. The museum has an authentic CATALO-NIAN CHAPEL on the second floor of the Fenway side. The GREEK AND ROMAN GALLERIES include a coin collection. The newest wing contains TWENTIETH-CENTURY SCULPTURE AND PAINTINGS. The work of Paul Revere, a master silversmith before he became a legend, is an important part of an AMERICAN SILVERWARE COLLECTION that dates from 1640. There are special galleries of primitive and twentieth-century art. On the Court Floor are EARLY AMERICAN FURNISHED ROOMS, including the entire framework of an Ipswich House with a four-poster bed with curtains used for warmth. One of the best collections of FRENCH IMPRESSIONIST ART in this country is exhibited in the painting galleries on the second floor. There are thirty-four paintings by Monet; also shown are paintings by Van Gogh, Renoir, Gauguin, and Matisse.

Musical Instruments Room (follow the down staircase near the Museum Shop): Open: Tuesday-Friday 2–4. Minimum age suggested: 8, with adult. Youngsters who either play an instrument or have some background knowledge —and most adults—will be fascinated by this room, which is really a living textbook of instrument history. Advanced music students may play the instruments in this open working collection.

Courses: Call for information on ADULT courses. For children 8–18 there are Saturday classes in several media. The 2-hour sessions require registration and a fee of $31 for each (fall or spring) semester. Registration for the 7-week summer series opens late in the spring. Call if you wish to be on the mailing list for course announcements; classes fill quickly.

Children's Room Classes: Grades 1–6. October-May without charge, includes lectures with slides, photographs or films, trips to the galleries, and correlated creative work. Weekday classes are held 3:15–4:30 P.M. on Tuesdays, Wednesdays, and Fridays and from 10:15–11:45 A.M. on Saturdays.
    There is no registration. Children may attend just once or come once a week through the season. Classes are limited to 30, and tickets are available on a first-come, first-served basis 15 minutes before each class at the Fenway desk. Preschool class on Thursdays, 1–2 P.M., limited to 20.

Eating: GARDEN COURT. *Open:* Mid-June–August. Visitors may bring their own lunch or buy it from the snack bar (just outside restaurant entrance). Light lunches are available Tuesday-Sunday 11:30–4. Greenery, statuary, and a fountain make a delightful setting. Tea (35¢) is served in the Crypt area Tuesday-Friday 3–4:30.
RESTAURANT. *Open:* Monday-Friday 11:30–2:30 and 5–7:30 Tuesday and Thursday evenings. A large pleasant facility in the new wing. Sandwiches and full meals served.

Museum Library: *Open:* Tuesday-Friday 10–4:30; also open Saturdays 10–1 September-May. Open to public. Graduate students may use the library for course work; undergraduates must have a note from their professors.

Group Visits: All groups should schedule visits with the Department of Public Education. Teacher orientation workshops, held once a month without charge, are for anyone who plans to bring a group. Guides are available for elementary and secondary levels by appointment only. All scheduled organized groups admitted without charge. At least 2 weeks' notice needed.

On-own Tours: Printed materials for "guideless tours" are available from the Department of Public Education.

Research Laboratory: Minimum age: Junior high school. Groups of 10–30 people may make an appointment with William J. Young, ext. 467, for a 1-hour visit.

Youth Programs: Held on weekends and school holidays. They are creative and fun. Check on current activities.

Borrowing Materials: Slides available without charge to elementary and high-school teachers. Others may rent or purchase slides. Please contact Education Department for the current list of available resources.

Gallery Lectures (no charge): Offered by volunteer guides of the Ladies Committee Tuesday-Friday at 11:30 October-May.

MUSEUM OF SCIENCE   Science Park   Tel. 723–2500, taped information: 742–6088

Ⓣ **Stop:** Science Park on Green Line.

Open: Every day in the year except Thanksgiving, Christmas, New Year's Day, and Labor Day. Monday-Saturday 10–6, Friday evenings until 10, Sundays 11–6. Suggestion: Call taped information number to check on hours and prices.

Admission: Adults, $2.50; children 5–16, senior citizens, students 17 and over with ID, $1.25. Group rates available; advance notice necessary.

Parking: Garage charges—first ½ hour, no charge. Over ½–3 hours: 50¢ museum members, $1 nonmembers. 3–4 hours: $1 museum members, $1.50 nonmembers. Over 4 hours: $2 members and nonmembers.

Air-conditioned and not usually crowded on hot summer weekends. Nursery available for Project Eye-Opener volunteers only. Special courses and programs for young people are of particular note.

From the moment you enter the foyer and see the spectacular view looking up the Charles River and showing Boston's skyline, curiosity is piqued, questions are answered, and there are views of "the real thing," but in many cases children may appreciate a personal explanation. Everyone—young children in particular—enjoys the periodic animal demonstrations; announcements while you roam the museum tell you where and when. Other demonstrations and exhibits are geared for various levels and cover a wide range of subjects.

SPOOKY the Owl will follow your movements, the snake BLACK BEAUTY may rest in your hands, or play with a slinky. Climb into the APOLLO CAPSULE or find your way on the moon scale. Hear your own telephone voice, play ticktacktoe with a computer, listen to the TALKING TRANSPARENT WOMAN, make a sand pattern, let push-button exhibits tell you about your skeleton, or activate models of early wagons, locomotives, and an automobile engine. There is a 20-foot-high dinosaur model and you can examine some ancient rocks. When you crank the generator, mechanical energy is converted to electrical energy lighting electric bulbs. There are also many large beautiful and technological exhibits that may or may not have child appeal.

Hayden Planetarium: Children under 5 not admitted but welcome in the museum. (Age restriction may be waived for special Christmas program, p. 301.) 50¢ for all plus museum fee. Lecture-demonstrations (45 minutes) with a very realistic depiction of the skies, past, present, and future. Programs, featuring celestial phenomena, natural and man-made, are changed 7 times during the year; the traditional Christmas program is the only one repeated each year.

Schedule: Varies. Given several times daily and at 8 P.M. Fridays. Buy tickets when you first enter the museum; they may be sold out by program time.

Memberships: Many categories available including individual $20, family $30, and student (for school year) $5.

Shop Hours: Usually set in June for the summer and September for the school year, but likely to be Monday-Saturday 9:30–5:50, Friday nights until 10, Sundays 11–5:50.

Lyman Library: Open same hours as museum. Although borrowing privileges (loan period is 4 weeks) are limited to members, and those currently enrolled in courses, the library is open to all. The many film loops, intended for in-museum use only, offer an exciting experience. While children operate the simple projecting equipment for these single-concept motion picture segments, they may hold a certain view (e.g., as the wings unfold on a butterfly) by the push of a button. Special children's picture book section. Something for all ages here.

Junior Curator Program: Animal Room Aides—must be at least 12. Other volunteers: Age 14 and up.

Speakers Available for Groups: Suggested for junior high through adult. Programs adapted to group's needs. There is no fee, the only expenses are travel and meals, if necessary. Two weeks' notice. Contact Service League Office, ext. 258.

Group Visits: Recommended for fall or winter. Spring is heavily booked. All public, private, and parochial school children are admitted free, provided they come during the school year in organized school groups and with advance reservations. Other groups should make reservations with the Visitor Services Section and plan to spend 2–3 hours at the museum. No guided tours are offered. Groups are encouraged to linger at those exhibits that capture their attention. There are several possibilities for programs during a group visit, however, and arrangements can be made when booking. If groups wish to eat in the cafeteria, arrangements must be made in advance.

Taped Tour: Available in English and Spanish. 75¢ for one earphone, $1.25 for two.

Courses: Offered fall, winter, and spring for preschool through adult. Registration for fall sessions starts in late summer. K–3 classes fill very quickly. Fees: $30 per child with family membership, $35 for others. Summer possibilities change annually.

Handicapped Youngsters: Animal programs available with advance notice. (Wheelchairs may be used in museum. Elevators available in west wing by request. Elevators in central building open to all.)

Spanish: Guidebook of exhibits available at admission desk. Taped tour (see above).

Eating: The Friendly Ice Cream and Sandwich Shop is on the second floor. Open daily ½ hour after museum opens to ½ hour before closing. Skyline Room Cafeteria (admission to museum required) offers panoramic view of the Charles River Basin; open during school year, Monday-Saturday 11–2, Fridays 11–2, Friday nights 5–8, Sundays 1:30–2. Minimum: Adults, $1.75; children with adults, $1.25. No picnic facilities.

No charge for looking outside:

Steam Locomotive: Climb into the cab and see what's what. Touching allowed. Everything is labeled. Hours vary; usually spring through fall. Closed in inclement weather.

Locks and Drawbridge (MDC): Although there are other locks in the area, the operation at the Charles River Dam can best be seen from the embankment —with protective fence—alongside the museum. See all the gates for 5 compartments as the water is made level (according to the tide) connecting the Charles River with the harbor. The locks operate 24 hours a day, but the busiest times are weekends and warm summer weekdays. At the sound of the horn the bridge will open, but not between 6:15 and 9:10 A.M. or between 4:15 and 7:40 P.M. on weekdays.

MUSEUM OF TRANSPORTATION   15 Newton Street   Larz Anderson Park   Brookline 02146   Tel. 521–1200

The museum plans to move to a new waterfront facility (together with the Children's Museum) in 1977.

Ⓣ**Stop:** Cleveland Circle—take bus #51. Get off at Newton and Clyde streets, 2-block walk.

Directions: Jamaicaway south to Pond Street west to Newton Street.

Open: Tuesday-Sunday 10–5; closed Mondays, July 4, Thanksgiving, Christmas and New Year's Day. Open Monday holidays.

Admission: Adults, $2; children 6–15, $1; 3–5, 25¢; senior citizens (60 and over), $1. Group rates available.

Membership: Children, $5; individual adult, $10; family, $15. Announcement mailing list for nonmembers: No charge.

Parking: No problem. No charge.

An expanding collection and focus have changed the antique automobile museum to one that is designed to involve visitors so that they think about life-styles through transportation. You may wish to tempt youngsters with the old cars by walking through those areas, and begin viewing in the hayloft where there is a collection of country buckboards, depot hacks, sleighs, carts, and more. A slide show puts the collection into context. As you walk through the nineteenth-century carriage house, modeled after a French castle, you will find a large motor vehicle collection. Participation is invited through a suspended Model T; visitors are encouraged to explore the engine, crawl under the car, turn the crank, and blow the horn. The "Great Steam Machine" is a model designed to allow youngsters to get into the exhibit and "become" water molecules that change into steam molecules in the machine. The collection shows all kinds of body styles, starting with a steam road machine of 1866. There is a picnic car with a silk umbrella top, fenders, rumble seats; Franklin D. Roosevelt's 1939 presidential touring car; and extensive fire engines and equipment. The bicycle collection, about to be expanded, has a wide variety dating from 1830. How does one sit, pedal, and stop?

The Education Department is initiating a participatory program for school groups and families. Some outdoor possibilities involve a fire pumper and a car that needs cranking.

Groups: Guided tours available year round Tuesday-Friday by arrangement only. Minimum age: 5. Minimum number: 10. Length of tour: 1–1½ hours.

Special Education Program: Available in many areas, including for the blind, deaf, and emotionally disturbed.

Bridge Unit: Being developed. Children will be able to construct various types of bridges from preformed parts, and then walk on the completed bridge.

Average Visit: 1–1½ hours.

Rides: On some museum vehicles: Available by advance request to small groups of children.

Strollers: Allowed.

Handicapped: Wide doors for entrance. Difficult to get to second floor.

PEABODY MUSEUM (Harvard), p. 178.

PEABODY MUSEUM (Salem), p. 100.

ROSE ART MUSEUM   Brandeis University   Waltham   Tel. 647–2402

Open: Tuesday-Sunday 12–5. Closed Mondays.

Admission: Free.

Drivers: Stop at information booth for special guest parking pass.

Air-conditioned.

Guided tours if advance arrangements are made.

Early ceramics, primitive art, lithographs, twentieth-century American art, and glass are among the permanent collections exhibited during the summer. Outstanding rotating exhibits in many media predominate during the academic year. Call for information on the current exhibit. (The campus is architecturally interesting. You may choose to walk up and down the hills and in and out of buildings.)

SEASHORE TROLLEY MUSEUM   Log Cabin Road   Kennebunkport, Maine 04046   Mail Address: Box 220   Tel. 207–967–2712

Unless you are a trolley buff, live on the North Shore, or just want to head for the coastline, this is a long trip for just the museum.

Directions: Rt. 1 or Turnpikes to Kennebunk, 2 miles north on Rt. 1 to yellow flasher at Log Cabin Road. Two miles east.

Open: Daily June 15-September 15 10–6; Saturdays and Sundays May 30-June 15 and September 15-October 30 12–5.

Admission: Adults, $2; children 6–12, $1; children under 6, free.

Parking: No problem.

A different kind of museum—an outdoor place with a collection of scores of trolleys, from the horsecar to the modern streamliner, open and closed cars, from the years 1873 to 1942 from near (Boston) and far (Japan). Many are waiting for attention from hardworking volunteers. But until they are restored, you may climb aboard and "touch." Sit in the driver's seat, swish the windshield wiper, crank the bell, or change the direction of the seats. Be sure to stop into the car shop to see the restoration work in progress. An elaborate parlor car from Manchester is among 15 cars that are now completely restored.

Rides: Scheduled every half hour. Admission fee gives unlimited rides on a variety of cars. Trolleys used during rides are changed during the day. Two miles round trip.

Groups: Guided tours May 1-November 30. Written requests preferred. Minimum age: 6. Minimum number: 15. Length: 2 hours. Two rides in different streetcars, tour of exhibit buildings, transit history from horsecars to high-speed intercity cars.

Museum Slide Show: Available. Several weeks' notice required.

Picnicking: In pine grove.

SEMITIC MUSEUM (Harvard)   6 Divinity Avenue   Cambridge   Tel. 495–4631

Used for research projects, this Harvard University Museum is generally closed to the public. However, if groups wish to arrange for an appointment, they may view ancient Palestinian collections. Among the exhibits—representing nothing later than the Romans—are pottery, weapons, glass, and tablets.

Tours: Arrangements should be made about one month in advance with Dr. C. E. Gavom. A 1-hour lecture tour on requested topics (aspects of Near Eastern cultures) will be given. Minimum age: 7. Offered September-December, March-June by appointment only. Groups will see some results of archaeological work in progress and artifacts from throughout the ancient Near East.

Special Programs: For handicapped youngsters, particularly blind children and "difficult learners."

Archaeological Kits: Are being developed for schools; trained archaeologists will take objects into schools and lecture on them.

Borrowing Materials: In the process of being arranged. Check on current status.

THE SLATER MILL HISTORIC SITE   Roosevelt Avenue   Pawtucket, Rhode Island 02861   Tel. 401–725–8638

Directions: Rt. 95 South, Exit 20, right off exit ramp, right on Exchange Street, left on Roosevelt Avenue. (It is ½ mile from Rt. 95.)

Open: Memorial Day-September 30, Monday-Saturday 10–5, Sundays 1–5; October 1-Memorial Day, Monday-Friday for group reservations only; Saturdays and Sundays 1–5. Closed July 4, Thanksgiving, and Christmas.

Admission: Adults, $1.25; children 6–14, 50¢.
Parking: Free space available.

The SLATER MILL shows textile history through exhibits that include many periods. This is where the first successful waterpowered textile machinery to be built in this country was set in motion, and an assembly line successfully adapted to produce cotton yarn. The historic building, built in 1793 and recently restored, stands on the original site overlooking the Blackstone River; it is now in the heart of a business district. Factory methods that were the beginning of a new industrial system were introduced and developed here. With the exception of the cotton gin and the mule, which are crank-operated for demonstration purposes, all the machines are electric powered. The WILKINSON MILL shows a re-created nineteenth-century machine shop space complete with turning lathes (metal and wood), planing machines, drill press, jigsaw, circular ripsaw, and more; here is where Oziel Wilkinson and his five sons were among America's most important early machinists. The SYLVANUS BROWN HOUSE is restored and furnished in strict accordance with a 1924 inventory of the house's furnishings.

Average Visit: 2 hours.
Mobile Program: "Growing the Clothes We Wear" focuses on production and
    use of natural fibers. Available to schools.
Handicapped: With advance notice special tours arranged.
Picnickers: Directed to Slater Park.

CARDINAL SPELLMAN PHILATELIC MUSEUM   235 Wellesley Street
Weston 02193 (located on the grounds of Regis College)   Tel. 894–6735

Directions: West on Rt. 30 to signal lights at Wellesley Street, right on Wellesley Street. Museum is first driveway on the left on grounds of Regis Campus. OR West on Rt. 20, left at lights at School Street, bear right on Wellesley Street. Driveway is on right after entrance to Regis.
Open: Tuesdays and Thursdays 9:20–2:30, Sundays 2–5; except second Sunday of the month when 11–5 are dealers' hours. Other times by appointment only. Closed holidays.
Admission: Adults, 50¢; family, $1; children 15 and under, 25¢. No charge to school groups. Memberships available.
Parking: Allocated area. No charge.

Air-conditioned.

This is the only museum in the United States designed and built expressly for the display and preservation of stamps. The nucleus of the museum is the internationally famous personal collection started by Cardinal Spellman in his youth. Among the exhibits are the Dwight D. Eisenhower Collection (received by Eisenhower when he was president of the United States), Papal States stamps and covers, Lincoln memorabilia, including a letter pardoning Wilburn Bybee for robbing the mails, tributes to the late President John F. Kennedy, a collection of British Commonwealth stamps and covers, and an airmail collection.

Regularly Scheduled Programs on Philatelic Subjects: Second Sunday of the
    month 3:30–4:30.
Guided Tours: Year round, Tuesdays and Thursdays 10–2:30 by arrangement
    only. One week's notice. Written requests preferred. Minimum age: 8.

Length: 1½ hours. An additional 1 hour workshop is included for stamp clubs.

Mailing List: Interested persons may phone or send self-addressed stamped envelope.

Courses: Offered for children.

Loans: Books and periodicals on stamps and stamp collecting.

Speakers and Films: Available. Fee charged.

Post Office and General Store: No museum admission fee charged to enter. Shop carries current U.S. mint stamps, philatelic supplies, and gifts.

UNIVERSITY MUSEUM
(Harvard)

Houses 5 museums under one roof. They are just off Kirkland Street. The Oxford Street entrance brings you to the Botanical Museum. The entrance to the first floor of the Peabody Museum is on Divinity Avenue.

Open: Monday-Saturday 9–4:30, Sundays 1–4:30. Closed most holidays.

Admission: Free.

Parking: Difficult!

Strollers: Not allowed.

Handicapped: Wheelchairs are allowed; with special notice, elevators are available.

Gift Shops: Considered "special" and "worthwhile." *Peabody* has constantly changing ethnographic items. *Comparative Zoology* has rocks, minerals, books, shells, and peacock feathers. *Botanical* has slides and postcards. Inquire about *treasure hunt game* that leads you to some of the more spectacular exhibits.

MUSEUM OF COMPARATIVE ZOOLOGY (Agassiz Museum)   Tel. 495–2463, includes a 42-foot fossil Kronosaurus "Sea Serpent" found in Australia in 1932, dinosaurs, rhinoceroses, elephants, kangaroos, and a balcony where you may get an unusual view (close-up) of a whale skeleton. Look up, down, and around you. The largest turtle carapace ever found is taller than visitors (6 by 8 feet) and weighs 200 pounds.

Many recent changes have been made and more are to come. There is a new fossil invertebrate hall; a living invertebrate hall will have displays of major groups plus exhibits detailing life histories and ecological relationships. Ant hills and insect nests will demonstrate the complexities of insect social behavior.

BOTANICAL MUSEUM   The first and second floors include a comprehensive exhibit on America's principal food plant, corn, and a display of fossil plants, the oldest exceeding 100 million years. Your climb to the third floor is rewarded by the famous Ware Collection of hand-blown glass flowers that appear real in every detail. *Glass Flower* admission: 50¢, under 16 and students in a class accompanied by an adult admitted free. The few cases of glass flowers outside the main exhibit may be enough for young children. The wonder of this art is heightened by the fact that Leopold Blaschka and his son developed the process and shared it with no one. Their sole customers, the Ware family, gave the collection to Harvard.   Tel. 495–2358

MINERALOGICAL MUSEUM   24 Oxford Street   Tel. 495–2356

Over 15,00 specimens of minerals in the world are in the collection, which is used for teaching purposes, but the third floor display includes a systematic collection of known mineral species, a comprehensive display of gemstones and minerals from New England, and a meteorite exhibit. Push the button to turn off the lights, and watch the colors and timing with the exhibit of fluorescent minerals.

PEABODY MUSEUM   11 Divinity Avenue   Tel. 495–2248

The main entrance is on Divinity Avenue but if you have entered from Oxford Street, go to the third floor, the only floor that connects Peabody to the other museums, walk through the large exhibit of minerals, and continue onto Peabody.

In this museum, devoted to archaeology and ethnology, may be seen outstanding collections of native and prehistoric cultures of several continents. Among these is a fine sampling of Middle and South American materials, including casts of stone stelae and the ceremonial altar of Copán. Although teaching and research are the primary functions of the museum, the abundant material is often used by other than Harvard groups, and enjoyed by the casual visitor. Totem poles, canoes, ethnological material from Africa, and dioramas of Algonquin family life are distributed on five floors.

Special Visits for the Blind: Advance arrangements necessary. Minimum age: 5th grade. Touch-oriented sessions, often on a one-to-one basis, allow for contact with objects from all over the world (instruments, masks, spears, metals, woods, basketry), complete with background information. No charge.

A Thumbnail Directory:

First Floor: Northwest Coast Indians, North American Indians, American Indian portrait gallery

Second Floor: Primitive arts and industries, textiles, ceramics, musical instruments, Southwestern United States

Third Floor: Archaeology—North America west of the Plains, North America east of the Rockies, Mexico, Central and South America, Central America and the West Indies

Fourth Floor: Europe, Neolithic and Bronze Ages; Europe, Late Bronze Iron Ages; Pacific Island

Fifth Floor: (It is a long walk up, but worthwhile) Old World Paleolithic, Asia, Africa

WHALING MUSEUM   18 Johnny Cake Hill   New Bedford   Tel. 1–997–0046

> 53 miles south of Boston, about a 90-minute worthwhile drive if children have an interest in the whaling era.

Directions: Rt. 128 to Rt. 24 to Rt. 140 to Rt. 195E, Exit 21.

Open: June-September, Monday-Saturday 9–5, Sundays 1–5. Closed Mondays October-May. Closed Thanksgiving, Christmas, and New Year's Day.

Admission: Adults, $1.50; children 6–14, 75¢.

Walk the decks of the one-half-scale ship model, the 1850 *Lagoda*, then climb to the balcony of the museum for a topside view. Exhibits include the most comprehensive collection of artifacts and relics from the American whaling industry: tools and equipment necessary for whaling in the nineteenth century, scrimshaw (intricate carving on whalebone and teeth), ship models, paintings, dolls and toys, and early household items. Children may have the satisfaction of completely touring the museum during one trip.

Guided Tours: Two weeks' advance notice required. Minimum age: 4th grade. Length: 1½ hours.

No strollers allowed.

Other Stops while in New Bedford:

THE SEAMEN'S BETHEL, opposite the Whaling Museum, has wide plank floors and a ship-shaped pulpit. This church, built in 1832, open daily July–September and on request at the Mariner's Home, is described in Herman Melville's *Moby Dick*. It is a short walk from the Whaling Museum to COMMONWEALTH STATE PIER, where you may see a freighter loading or unloading. Nearby is a close-up view of a key fishing port (once the whaling port known around the world). If the fishermen are not unloading and working on the boats, the piers may be actually "blocked in" with the fishing fleet. THE NEW BEDFORD PUBLIC LIBRARY, located at Pleasant and William streets, has the country's most extensive collection of manuscript and printed material dealing with the American whaling industry. Closed Sundays.

Running space, a small zoo, and simple PICNICS allowed at BUTTONWOOD PARK (10-minute drive from the museum along Rt. 6 toward Fall River) at Rockdale Avenue. It is an equally short drive in the opposite direction for a picnic at the state beach, FORT PHOENIX (parking fee $1 for cars), along Rt. 6 toward Cape Cod; as you drive over the Fairhaven Bridge, look to the right to see the HURRICANE BARRIER, the most formidable flood protection device in this country.

Eating: If you are not picnicking, you could drive a short distance to Me & Eds at 30 Brock Avenue, Tel. 993–9922. It is open daily 11:30–11:30 and serves everything from pizza to seafood.

Note

New Bedford and Fall River (p. 77) have many manufacturers who have factory outlets: Cape Cod Clothing Co., 1 Coffin Avenue (men's suits and sports coats) open Monday-Saturday; Valor Factory Retail Outlet, 671 Belleville Avenue (pants coats, slacks, pants suits, outerwear, skiwear, knitwear, sweaters, skirts, sportswear, beachwear, fabrics, patterns) open Monday-Saturday; Eastern Sportswear Factory Outlet, 94 Sawyer Street (girls' sizes 3–14, sportswear and play wear) closed Mondays; Fairhaven Corporation Factory Outlet, 358 Belleville Avenue (ladies' handbags and belts) open Monday-Saturday; Berkshire Hathaway, Inc., Gifford Street (curtain and drapery material, ready-made curtains and draperies) open Monday-Saturday; Revere Copper & Brass, Inc., 24 N. Front Street (cooking utensils) open Tuesday-Saturday; Normandie Bedspread Mill Outlet & Needlepoint Center, 21 Cove Street (woven and quilted bedspreads, sizes crib to king) open Monday-Saturday; Pierce Mill Factory Outlet, Sawyer Street (men's suits, sports coats, slacks, yard goods) open Tuesday-Saturday; Elco Factory Outlet, 330 Collette Street (dresses, pants suits, slacks) open Friday evenings and Saturdays 10–5.

In Dartmouth: Kay Windsor Outlet, 375 Faunce Corner Road (½ price on Kay Windsor items) open Monday-Saturday.

WORCESTER ART MUSEUM   55 Salisbury Street   Worcester   Tel. 799–4406

Directions: Massachusetts Turnpike west to Grafton exit. At end of street turn left onto Grafton Street to Lincoln Square, Rt. 9. OR take I290 for about 15 miles to Exit 18, Lincoln Square, Rt. 9. Museum is located 2 blocks west of rotary on Rt. 9.

Open: Tuesday-Saturday 10–5, Sundays 2–6. Closed July 4, Thanksgiving, and Christmas.

Admission: Free.

Parking: Free in two lots on Tuckerman Street.

Memberships: Start at $12.

Art of fifty centuries, ranging from a 3000 B.C. Sumerian stone figure to paintings by Gauguin, Matisse, and Picasso. History of art through the centuries is exhibited chronologically—allowing for a methodical tour—and includes a noteworthy collection of Egyptian, classical, pre-Columbian, Oriental, and medieval sculpture; mosaics from Antioch in the central court; frescoes from Spoleto, Italy; a Romanesque chapter house removed stone by stone from France and rebuilt here; Italian and other European paintings of the thirteenth to twentieth centuries; English and American collections from the eighteenth century to the present day. It is very much a traditional museum setting, but it is lovely—and of manageable size.

Strollers: Allowed.

Programs: Free public concerts, gallery talks, and films for adults and young people. Auditorium is air-conditioned.

Guided Tours: September-June, possibly July and August. Tuesday-Saturday 10–4, Sundays 2:30–5. By arrangement only, 3–4 weeks' notice required. Minimum age: Preschool. Can accommodate 12–60. Length: Varies with age and interest. Tours can be a general introduction or specialized.

Regularly Scheduled Tours: Sundays at 2:30, Tuesdays and Saturdays at 10:30.

Courses: Offered for preschool through high-school age, summer, spring, and fall. Younger age group courses fill quickly.

Borrowing Materials: Art slides. $3 per time.

Picnicking: Institute Park is 1 block away.

WORCESTER SCIENCE CENTER   Harrington Way   Worcester 01604   Tel. 791–9211

Directions: Rt. 9 to Plantation Street. Follow yellow signs.

Open: Monday-Saturday 10–5, Sundays 12–5. Closed national holidays.

Admission: Adults, $2; children 16 and under and senior citizens, $1; Explorer Express tickets, 50¢.

Parking: Free and plentiful.

Air-conditioned.
Picnic area provided.

The museum has several participatory exhibits and appeals to various age groups. Walk through a human heart . . . sit in a human sized bird nest . . . visit the working power plant . . . see snakes, turtles, and lizards. The building is of "manageable" size; the average visit is about 1½ hours. Much depends upon interests and programs being conducted by the staff.

The Alden Omnisphere (no additional charge) offers various programs in its multimedia theatre: live demonstrations, special effects, planetarium programs, and films. The Omnisphere can have the effect of taking you into space, placing you in the world of a tiny microbe, or into the ocean depths. Groups may request a program with special emphasis. Minimum age: 5.

The museum is in a 50-acre park, which allows for an inside-outside experience, so that confinement is not the rule. An unusual outdoor exhibit allows you to have a close-up view (through a window) of a swimming polar bear. There are also mountain lions, wolves, raccoons, and rabbits, and a meandering stream through woodlands. Immediate plans include a Friendship Corral, an animal contact area for children.

Explorer Express: A miniature railroad that runs daily, weather permitting. A 20-minute, 1¾-mile guided tour of the grounds.

Regularly Scheduled Programs: Omnisphere and live animal demonstrations.

Handicapped: Special programs can be arranged for handicapped youngsters. Help is available for getting from one level to another.

Strollers: Allowed.

OPEN SPACE

Islands

(See pp. 219–21 for all ferry information.)

More BOSTON HARBOR islands will be open for recreation and conservation within the next few years. Included here are those that are available now.

Resources have only recently been opened to the public. BUMPKIN and GRAPE have limited camping, GALLOPS is open for day use and has a sandy beach, BREWSTER is open for day use and intended for conservation and environmental education. These islands have much poison ivy and are, in some cases, receiving a badly needed control program. Private transportation is necessary. For access information, see p. 222.

The following are operated by the MDC and are available for day use:

GEORGE'S ISLAND in Boston Harbor

Open: Memorial Day weekend-October 15, 10–7.

If you do not have your own boat, use commercial transportation (p. 220).

Groups: For 25 or more, arrangements should be made by writing to the Metropolitan District Commission, Attn. James Whalen, 20 Somerset Street, Boston, Tel. 727–5250.

First opened to the public in 1961, this is an unusual place for an outing, with plenty of open space, shade, playground for young children, picnic areas, barbecue pits, baseball field, volleyball court, and areas for badminton and horseshoes. No swimming allowed.

The adventuresome explore old Fort Warren—used as a defense of Boston Harbor in all U.S. wars and as a prison for military and civilian personnel during the Civil War—and find the chapel with murals concerning the writing of the marching song "John Brown's Body," which was composed at the fort in 1861. With tunnels, parapets, and steps to investigate, depending upon curiosity and fortitude, it can be a long hike.

Taped Walking Tour: Adults, 75¢; children, 50¢; groups, 25¢.

Snack Bar: Open daily during summer.

Clambake: Offered by Robert Industries, Inc., of 762 Nantasket Avenue, Hull, Tel. 925–1558, weekends and holidays 10–5 for the public. $1.75–$11 a la carte. Special arrangements made for groups. Lobster, corn on the cob, chicken, stuffed clams, and spareribs served.

PEDDOCKS ISLAND

Permit needed. Obtain from MDC, James Whalen, Director of Recreation, 20 Somerset Street, Boston.

Limited docking facilities for private boats. Commercial boats go to Peddocks occasionally. No sanitary facilities. Groups are limited to 25. About 25 World War II buildings are on the island and badly in need of repair.

PLACES IN OR VERY NEAR BOSTON

THE ARNOLD ARBORETUM (Harvard University)   The Arborway   Jamaica Plain   Tel. 524–1717 (located near the Children's Museum)

Ⓣ **Stop:** Arborway on Green Line (4 blocks to Jamaica Plain gate), Forest Hills on Orange Line (2 blocks to Forest Hills Gate).

Directions: Rt. 1 south to the Arboretum, Rt. 203.

Open: To pedestrians from sunrise to sunset every day of the year. Automobile passes (no charge) are issued at Administration Building weekdays 9–5. Greenhouse (near Centre Street gate) open Wednesdays 12:30–4.

Admission: Free.

A beautiful place for a leisurely walk among 6,000 different kinds of ornamental trees and shrubs on 265 acres. Many think that the Arboretum is most colorful from about the second week in May through mid-June. Each plant is labeled with its common and scientific names, age, and origin. Sorry, no picnicking allowed, and driving through the grounds allowed by special permit only—obtained at the Administration Building. Some groups visit in late winter in hopes of seeing "footprints in the snow."

A map (free), postcards, and guidebooks (for sale) may be obtained Monday-Friday at the Administration Building at the Jamaica Plain gate 8:30–4:30 in July and August and 9–5 September-June.

Guided Tours: Available for adult groups by appointment only.

BEAVER BROOK RESERVATION (MDC)   located on each side of Trapelo Road, Belmont (parts are in Waltham)   Tel. 484–0200

Parking and Admission: Free.

The duck pond area (parking at the crest of the hill on Mill Street): After you walk the bridge over a waterfall, find a perching rock for fishing, or continue on the short path through the woods around the duck pond. (Skating allowed here in the winter.) Perhaps a carrot from your lunch could be fed to the rabbits, and the ducks may accept some bread. Picnic tables in shaded spots, swings, seesaws, a push-go-round, and a fantastic slide complete this pleasant site.

The Trapelo Road area is larger (though neither area is expansive), and in the summer has a wading pool (for children up to 10 years old), good playground equipment, a ball park, woodlands with a brook, picnic tables, and fireplaces (first come, first served). This area also has tennis courts, two softball fields, wooden footbridges over the ponds, and shade trees.

BOSTON COMMON (p. 114) and **BOSTON PUBLIC GARDEN** (p. 141).

CASTLE ISLAND (MDC)   Day Boulevard   South Boston (located just after Pleasure Bay, p. 209, swimming beach)

Parking and Admission: Free.

Recently renovated, it is a pleasant place with grass, barbecue pits, passing freighters, and a fishing pier that juts out into the ocean. Fort Independence, built in 1801, is currently being restored. If groups wish to tour the site, call 727–7250 for details.

CHARLES RIVER RESERVATION (MDC)   both sides of the Charles. Excursion boat (p. 217) from the Hatch Memorial Shell.

If you walk from the area across from Massachusetts General Hospital, starting at Community Boating, along the Boston shore, you will pass the lagoon (presently the location of an experimental project designed to make the river swimmable) where there may be a model sailboat or two and dozens of sailboats on the river. There are several enclosed well-equipped MDC children's playgrounds in this area before the Harvard Bridge (Massachusetts Avenue). This is a 2½-mile stretch. Suggestion: Take a footbridge across Storrow Drive into Back Bay (p. 139).

On the Cambridge side near Harvard University there are some open spaces. Although the marvelous sycamore trees are along this section of Memorial Drive, there is little to shade the open weed and grass area.

For information on cycle path, see p. 212.

FENWAY (more accurately: Back Bay Fens)   established 1877

The area bordered by the Museum of Fine Arts and Gardner Museum has hungry wild ducks, short rustic bridges crossing the muddy river, paths, benches, and dog walkers. The Rose Garden has a seasonal display, the Fenway gardeners will chat with passersby, and spectators' seats are available for the show of local competition in the ball park (flooded for skating in the winter).

Boundaries of the area are difficult to set. The area winds its way from Charlesgate, goes along Park Drive and to Brookline Avenue (near Sears). The Riverway to the overpass at Huntington Avenue is an extension of this.

Fenway Gardens: Located near the ball field along Park Drive, has hundreds of 15-by-30-foot plots, which are thriving vegetable and flower gardens. The city of Boston allowed some residents to have "victory gardens" during World War II, and the nearly 5 acres has been tilled ever since. Most of the planting is done in late May and early June. Depending upon your time of visit, you may see blossoms or ripening beans, tomatoes, corn, pumpkins—and even peanuts—along with magnificent flowers. The gardeners combine a variety of backgrounds with a common interest and are happy to share their enthusiasm with you.

FRANKLIN PARK   main entrance at intersection of Blue Hill Avenue and Columbia Road

Directions: See p. 42.

Admission and Parking: Free.

Vehicular traffic is banned on all but two roads. New direction and information signs indicate what is where. Three hundred acres of wooded and open land, golf course (p. 228), and zoo (p. 42). Elma Lewis Playhouse in the Park has free nightly summer performances. The park, an important part of Olmsted's park and open space design, "Emerald Necklace," has seen much use and abuse and is currently receiving some attention.

FRESH POND PARK   Fresh Pond Parkway at Rt. 16   Cambridge

Ⓣ **Stop:** From Harvard Square take bus No. 74.

Located near the water department. In the summer it offers shaded areas, picnic sites, swings for the children, and a large open area good for ball tossing or just plain running. (Many joggers use this area.) The only drawback is the lack of sanitary facilities. Closing hour: 8 P.M. The slopes are good for skiing (no tows) and sledding in the winter.

JAMAICA POND   junction of Pond Street and Arborway (across busy Rt. 1 from the Children's Museum)

A beautiful 65-acre expanse of fresh water is encircled by 55 acres of parkway. The area near the Children's Museum offers limited (sloping) land, benches, and shade trees. Good place to picnic or explore water life. Refreshment stand is open in summer. Children are allowed to fish the stocked water (no license required under age 15) from certain designated areas on shore. Rowboats for rent (p. 216).

LARZ ANDERSON PARK   entrances on Goddard Avenue and Newton Street
Brookline   Tel. 232–9000

Directions: Rt. 1 to Jamaicaway Rt. 203, right on Pond Avenue to Newton Street, right off Newton to Goddard Avenue.

Open: 8:30 A.M.–8 P.M. Closes at 5 in winter.

Sixty acres of beautiful fields and hillside with panoramic views of Boston. Plenty of running space. Facilities include well-equipped tot lot (near Goddard Avenue entrance), extensive picnic and barbecue area, baseball diamond, and rest rooms. Good kite-flying area at top of hill, which is used for sledding in winter. Bring bread for the beautiful white ducks in the picturesque pond.
Groups: Reservations required. Nonresidents should apply 1 week in advance. Fees charged.

MOUNT AUBURN CEMETERY   580 Mt. Auburn Street   Cambridge
Tel. 547–7105

On the Watertown-Cambridge line, near Brattle Street, opposite Mount Auburn Memorials, Inc.

Open: Daily 8–7 summer; 8–4:30 winter. No cycling allowed.

From the first crocus to the last chrysanthemum, these 164 acres blossom with about a thousand varieties of flowers, shrubs, and trees. A map indicating the graves of noted persons is available from the office near the main gate (and the markers are certainly of a different proportion from those on the graves of colonists), but many people come just to walk along Tulip, Honeysuckle, Hollyhock, and Camellia paths, among azaleas, dogwood, beech, Japanese cherry, and other labeled trees, to climb a slope or turn a corner and discover a lake or pond bordered by a velvet lawn.

The collection dates back to 1831 when the Massachusetts Horticultural Society established an experimental garden on what was to become the first garden cemetery in this country. Hundreds of bird watchers have their own keys to the Egyptian gates.

The greenhouses on the Grove Street side are open Monday-Friday and on some summer Saturdays.

STONY BROOK RESERVATION (MDC)   along Turtle Pond Parkway
West Roxbury and Hyde Park

Acres of comparatively flat land, a picnic area, fishing, and skating at Bajko Rink (p. 231). Cycle paths are planned for the late 1970s.

PLACES NORTH OF BOSTON

BREAKHEART RESERVATION (MDC)   Saugus and Wakefield Headquarters: 145 Pond Street, Stoneham   Tel. 438–5690, Police: 396–0100

Directions: Take Rt. 1 north, left onto Lynn Fells Parkway, Saugus entrance to reservation is on your right. For Wakefield entrance, take Farm Road off Rt. 129, left toward Northeast Regional Vocational School, through school's parking lot to reservation entrance.

This is one of the loveliest wooded areas in the Boston area. Some of the picnic sites have shelters that are large enough to drive your car under, the bathing beach at the lower pond tends to be crowded on warm days, a flume flows between ponds, there is fishing and also an ice-skating rink (p. 231). Camping allowed (p. 222). Plenty of trails for hiking. Some of the climbs are strenuous.

Fireplace Permits for Cookouts: Obtained at headquarters.

Camping Arrangements: Made with headquarters. Sites on a first-come first-served basis. Available year round. Maximum stay: 2 nights, 3 days.

Maps of Area: Available at headquarters, 10¢ each.

HALIBUT POINT (Trustees of Reservations) between Folly Cove and Andre's Point   Rockport

Directions: Rt. 128 to 127 to Gott Avenue at Old Farm Inn Restaurant.

Open: April 1-November 30.

Parking: Monday-Friday, 50¢; Saturdays, Sundays, and holidays, $1.

Picnicking: Allowed. Fires allowed on rocks.

Here at the outermost tip of Cape Ann you have an expansive uncluttered ocean view from huge sheets of granite rock. The 10-minute walk along a path lined with blueberry bushes (blueberries may be picked in late July) brings you to a summer scene of lobstermen hauling traps, dots of sailboats on the coastline of Plum Island, New Hampshire, and Maine. The air is filled with white spray in winter. At low tide there is a small natural pool good for children. Tide pools are magnificent. (Look for them over to the right; some are under rocks that you can crawl under.) Wear sneakers. Fishing (perch and mackerel) is done from the rocks. Great for spring and fall trips if the sun is warm; always bring jackets.

IPSWICH RIVER (Massachusetts Audubon Sanctuary)   Perkins Row Topsfield   Tel. 887–8649, taped information: 887–2241

Directions: Rt. 1 North to first stoplight in Topsfield, right onto Rt. 97, first left to sanctuary.

Open: Tuesday-Sunday, Monday holidays. Closes 8 P.M. in summer.

Admission: Car, $2 for nonmembers.

Picnicking: Allowed; no formal picnic area. No cooking allowed.

Walk on paths of pine needles, pebbles, moss, wood chips, see large gnarled trees (labeled), cross water over bridges (are there two alike?), plenty of wild flowers, a partially frozen pond (still) in spring maybe, a magnificent rockery that the youngsters will go under, in, and around, rhododendrons, yews, greenery, a duck pond, forests, and acres of waterfowl nesting grounds . . . 10

miles of well-marked trails. A fantastic place. Somewhat buggy on warm May and June days.

Full programming includes courses for all ages.

Canoeing: Limited to members. $1 per hour.

LYNN WOODS   Lynn

Directions: Rt. 1 to Walnut Street toward Lynn, left at lights onto Penny Brook Road. Or Rt. 1 to 129 (Lynnfield Street) to Great Woods Road.

Parking and Admission: Free.

Paths without trail markers. Not many people. Very pretty large (2,000 acres) area. Observation tower about a mile's hike. Path around reservoir is about 5 miles. Picnicking allowed; bring litter out.

MIDDLESEX FELLS RESERVATION (MDC)   located in Winchester, Stoneham, Medford, Malden, and Melrose

Headquarters: 145 Pond Street, Stoneham, Tel. 438–5690 (Open Monday-Friday 9–5); MDC Police: 396–0100

Parking and Admission: Free.

Plenty of trails (in 3,500 acres) for hiking, not all are well cleared. Terrain fairly level.

Fireplace Permits: For cookouts, obtained at headquarters.

Horses: May be rented (p. 230) for use on trails here.

There are several entrances to this reservation of over 3,500 acres.

Maps: 10¢, available at headquarters.

Entrances:
SHEEPFOLD: Main entrance off Rt. 38 on the Stoneham-Medford line. Large meadowlike recreation areas, parking facilities, fireplace area (bring your own barbecue here). Obtain permits at headquarters.

BELLEVUE POND AREA: Enter from So. Border Road in Medford. Fireplaces, picnic tables, parking facilities. Walk up to WRIGHT TOWER and take a marked trail known as the Skyline Trail.

JERRY JINGLE: Entrance from Fellsway East in Malden. Skyline Trail is marked from this point.

FROM LYNN FELLS PARKWAY in Stoneham (near Crystal Spring area): Here you have Hall Pool (adults 25¢, children 10¢). From area behind pool you can walk to BEAR HILL OBSERVATION TOWER, children's playgrounds, and tots' wading pool. Walk around Spot Pond to the zoo (p. 46).

WINCHESTER ENTRANCE: Off South Border Road. As you travel, northwest entrance is on right opposite Myrtle Terrace. Skyline Trail included here.

BRADLEY W. PALMER STATE PARK   Rt. 1   Topsfield   Tel. 887–5931

Parking: Picnic area, $1. Walk-in, 25¢ for everyone over 12.

Interesting terrain, beautiful trees, flowering bushes, brooks to follow, hiking trails, and footpaths. A paved auto road takes you through variegated flora that is a botanic delight. Watch the Ipswich River flow as you fish. Plenty of room for ball games. A beautiful picnic area set in a pine grove. It is an extensive place that is well kept.

HAROLD PARKER STATE FOREST   Rt. 114   North Andover   Tel. (Lawrence) 686–3391

Parking: Cars, $1 (p. 203).

Trails for hiking and cross-country skiing. Popular in summer for picnic and beach facilities (p. 209), tent and trailer sites (p. 223). Large open areas for ballplaying as well as extensive woods.

PARKER RIVER NATIONAL WILDLIFE REFUGE   Plum Island   Newburyport (32 miles northeast of Boston)   Tel. 465–5753

Directions: Signs near Newburyport along Rt. 1 lead you onto Hanover Street to Newburyport, to Plum Island Turnpike, and to a 7-mile gravel road through the refuge.

Open: Year round, dawn to dusk.

Admission: Free.

Greenhead Fly Season: Late July and August. Least troublesome on cool, cloudy, windy, dry days.

Hike on nature trails, walk along the beach, sunbathe, swim, picnic, barbecue, go surffishing, or take a 7-mile drive through the area that is used year round by bird watchers. (The gravel road can offer a dusty ride in dry weather; it is an hour round trip in the refuge.) The peak migration period for ducks and geese would be in March and again in October. The refuge, thousands of acres, is a resting and feeding area for migrating waterfowl, and includes 6½ miles of sandy beach, dunes, freshwater bogs, and fresh and tidal marshes. Ripe beach plums and cranberries may be picked in August and September.
  Information stop with leaflets is at the entrance to the refuge.

Rules: No vegetation picking. No alcohol, no dune climbing, please—and no pets allowed Labor Day-Memorial Day.

PLACES WEST OF BOSTON

ASHLAND STATE PARK, reached from Rt. 135, is small, but has a particularly lovely wooded setting for picnics and good (small) swimming facilities. Can be crowded. Located in Ashland.

Parking: Car, $1. (See p. 203 for other arrangements.)

BROADMOOR SANCTUARY (Massachusetts Audubon Society)   South Street   South Natick   Tel. 655–2296

Directions: Rt. 16W to Natick. One mile past South Natick is sanctuary sign on left.

Closed: Mondays, except holidays.

Parking: Car, $1; bicycle, 50¢; bus, $10.

No sanitary facilities. No drinking water.

Several "manageable" trails that go through a variety of habitats and vegetation —uplands, wetlands, different woods, fields—with many birds, mammals, and insects. Of particular interest are the stone foundations of one of the first grist-mills in America—and a sawmill. A full trail could be covered in an hour, several could be done in a day. This area is the last of once Indian-owned land that remains undeveloped.

Picnicking: Not allowed, but a very nice area on the Charles River at South Natick Dam is 1 mile toward Boston on Rt. 16.

Note: Parking is somewhat limited so it is difficult to leave your car here, but you are in a great area for cycling around Farm Pond (p. 212) and the town of Sherborn.

CARLISLE   STATE   PARK   Lowell   Street   Carlisle   369–6312
18 miles from Boston. Take Lowell Street out of Carlisle Center for 2 miles.

The state has just acquired the Farnham Smith estate, which has about 860 acres of woods, brooks, and farmland. The dairy farm is to remain private, but groups may be able to have tours.

Meanwhile, as you wander through the paths, there is plenty of wildlife, swamp, marshland—and grazing cows. A beautiful place. Plans for development, if any, are not yet complete. It is planned as a passive recreational area.

CASE ESTATES OF ARNOLD ARBORETUM   Wellesley Street   Weston
Information: 524–1717   Barn phone: 894–0208
Located between Rts. 20 and 30.

Open: Sunrise to sunset year round for walking. No picnicking.

Parking and Admission: Free.

An outdoor laboratory atmosphere pervades Harvard University's 112-acre estate of nurseries, display planting of ground covers, small street trees, and perennials. Guided tours arranged for 25 or more adults. For self-guided tours obtain a brochure outside the barn, 135 Wellesley Street.

Children may enjoy reading the labels with botanical and English names. Special open house in May on a Sunday, when staff is available to answer questions. Call for information on spring and fall walks led by staff members.

COCHITUATE STATE PARK   on Rt. 30 near Massachusetts Turnpike exchange   Tel. 653–9641

Used mostly for boating (p. 216); some swimming and picnicking. Located in Natick. Parking for cars: $1.

CUTLER PARK (encompasses what was formerly called Newton-Brookline Waterlands)   Rt. 128 between Exits 56 and 57. Enter on Newton-Needham line, Kendrick Street. Canoe launch being built (p. 225); paths to walk near but not really along the banks of the Charles.

DRUMLIN FARM NATURE CENTER   South Great Road (Rt. 117)   South Lincoln   Tel. 259–9807

Directions: Rt. 128, Exit 49 toward Waltham, Rt. 117 (doubles back west). Or Rt. 2, Rt. 20 to 117.

Train: Boston and Maine train from North Station or Porter Square in Cambridge. Possible to walk to farm, but not with very young children in tow.

Open: Year round, Tuesday-Sunday, open Monday holidays. Closes 8 P.M. in summer.

Admission: Nonmember adults, $1.50; nonmember children under 16, 50¢; under 3, free.

This large demonstration farm, also headquarters for the Massachusetts Audubon Society, is one of those places that you and the children will want to return to again and again. (It is particularly good for preschool and elementary school youngsters.) There are a typical New England farm garden, grapevines, horses, pigs, cows, raccoons, owls, night animals, chickens (see if you can find a freshly laid egg), New England plants, birdhouses everywhere, fields to run, tall grass to hide in, short trails to follow, and ponds to explore.

Picnicking: Not allowed.

Tours: By arrangement only. Two weeks' notice required. Spring tours should be booked the previous fall. Offered year round. Farm tours for grades K–3 include a tractor-driven hayride.

Handicapped Youngsters: Can be accommodated.

Youth-oriented Programs: Held Saturdays and Sundays at 3 P.M. year round—films, lectures, and family walks. A bird-banding demonstration is given once a month.

Strollers: The paths can accommodate them.

Classes: For children age 4 and older, teen-agers, and adults. Special sessions for young children and parents who accompany them. Topics range from wild edible plants to astronomy. Call for spring and fall schedule.

Gift Shop: Open Tuesday-Saturday 10–5, Sundays 1–5, closed holidays. Located in building near main parking area. A marvelous place that has bird feeders, gifts with a natural history theme, toys, books, and handcrafted items.

GARDEN IN THE WOODS   Hemenway Street   Framingham   Tels. 877–6574, 237–4924

> . . . Feet should be kept on the narrow paths;
> this may be difficult for young children.
> . . . This is the headquarters of the
> New England Wild Flower Society.

Directions: Rt. 9 or Massachusetts Turnpike to Exit 11, Framingham Center. Right on Edgell Road, about 1½ miles to right turn onto Water Street, left on Catherine Road, which winds around to one-way Hemenway Street. Woods are on right.

Open: April-October, Monday-Saturday 8:30–5. Closed Sundays.

Admission: Adults, $1; children, 50¢.

More than 400 species and varieties of native American plants grow in this rare and beautiful wild flower garden. On the 30 acres can be found 4 miles of woodland paths, dry wooded slopes, shady brooks, sunny bogs, open spaces for field flowers, interesting geology, and even a hemlock dell; it is an encyclopedia of local natural history. Tall azaleas and numerous lady slippers appear during May and June, the most colorful months. Bring insect repellent for May-September visits. Walking shoes and long sleeves may be good suggestions.

Library: It is small, but available.

Plants Sold: A few native wild flowers, May-September 10–4.

Groups: Information on suggested areas will be sent prior to a trip.

Guided Tours: By reservation only. School groups: 50¢ per child.

Children's Programs: Age 4–grade 2 include walks, games, crafts, and plant experiments.

GREAT MEADOWS NATIONAL WILDLIFE REFUGE   191 Sudbury Road
Concord   Tel. 369–5518

Directions: To Concord entrance—take Rt. 62 from Concord Center toward Bedford for about a mile, turn on Monsen Road, and enter refuge between two homes. To Wayland entrance—Rt. 126 to Wayland Center, turn right on Rt. 27, and take first left on Pelham Island Road to Heard Pond.

Open: Year round, sunrise to sunset.

Parking and Admission: Free.

As you walk along the 1.7-mile dike, constructed to provide a freshwater habitat for waterfowl, you may see several species of ducks, Canada geese, and muskrats in their natural surroundings. You can climb the tower to see all the birds that use the impoundments, including various shorebirds, terns, and gulls. Late in the summer the presence of duck weed gives a strong odor that some children and adults may object to. Trail guides available at entrance.

From the Concord entrance it is about a 1½-mile bicycle ride to the Minute Man National Park; you are on your own without signs.

The Wayland entrance area is just being "developed," and it has a very short (¼-mile) trail that takes you over a boardwalk to a high point overlooking a marsh, by an Indian burial ground where some excavation has been done— and back to the parking lot.

HAMMOND POND   Chestnut Hill (Brookline and Newton)

Park in the Chestnut Hill shopping area and walk around the pond. The land surrounding the pond is owned by the Metropolitan District Commission and the city of Newton. In parts there are paths into the woods.

HARVARD FOREST   Rt. 32   Petersham   Tel. 724–3285

Could be combined with maple-sugaring (p. 284) or apple country (p. 297) visits.

Directions: Rt. 2, exit Athol-Petersham, drive 3 miles south on Rt. 32.

Open: Daily. Museum open 10–5 7 days a week, office open Monday-Friday.

Parking and Admission: Free.

Seventy-three miles seems like a long drive for a walk in the woods, but several *In and Out* readers have suggested that it is among the missing. It is a research center (botany, forest economy, soil science) for Harvard University. Spring through fall self-guiding marked trails offer pine groves, a meadow surrounded by birches, and peace and quiet. The museum has 20 dioramas that show the changes that have taken place in land use.

No picnicking allowed.

HEMLOCK GORGE—Echo Bridge   Newton

A small area. Rt. 9 west, Chestnut Street ramp on right, cross Chestnut Street, take left onto Ellis Street (Quinnobequin is on your right), to small parking area. It is the bridge (aqueduct) that you have come for. Take the steps to the platform below the bridge and call out. Result: An echo! Then walk over the bridge to the other side of the Charles River to a wooded section. Picnicking allowed.

LAUGHING BROOK EDUCATION CENTER AND WILDLIFE SANCTUARY
(Massachusetts Audubon Society)   789 Main Street   Hampden   Tel. 413–566–3571

Directions: From Turnpike take Exit 8, follow signs to Monson, turn sharp right at High Street, follow to Hampden (6.7 miles) bearing left as indicated.

Open: Tuesday-Saturday 10–5, Sundays 1–5, closed Mondays and holidays.

Admission: Car, $2; bus, $10; bicycle or pedestrian, 50¢.

Wind through Green Forest on Green Forest Trail and the Striped Chipmunk Trail. The Crooked Little Path follows Laughing Brook and the Scantic River to the Deer Exhibit—here at the home of the children's author Thornton W. Burgess. The animal and nature centers have outside exhibits constructed to simulate the natural habitats of Reddy Fox, Jimmy Skunk, Peter Rabbit, Hooty-the-Owl and Blacky-the-Crow. The Barn Studio by the banks of Laughing Brook is now a museum open to the public.

The 1742 Burgess Home: Open by appointment only. Furnished as it was when the author lived here. Adults, $1; children, 50¢.

MENOTOMY ROCKS PARK   off Jason Street   Arlington Heights

Directions: Massachusetts Avenue to Arlington Center, left on Jason Street, about ¼ mile beyond Gray Street—on right.

Admission and Parking: Free.

Trails through woods, rocks to climb on, fireplaces provided, picnic area, baseball and soccer fields, and a children's playground. Skating on pond in winter.

Groups: Permits required; restricted to Arlington residents in the summer. Available from Recreation Department, 643–6700.

PROSPECT HILL PARK   Totten Pond Road   Waltham   Tel. 893–4837

Directions: Rt. 128 north, Winter Street exit, turn right for short drive to park entrance on your right.

Parking and Admission: Free.

If you want good exercise, walk (otherwise drive), bearing left along the paved road, to almost the top of the large wooded reservation. Next to Blue Hill, this is the highest point in Greater Boston. Picnic tables available. Call for fireplace reservations. Blueberry picking in August. Skiing (p. 237) in winter. At the base of the hill is a small farm that could be covered in 15–30 minutes, depending upon the time you spend with the horses, goats, sheep, deer, donkeys, ducks, geese, raccoons, and rabbits.

PURGATORY CHASM   Sutton (50 miles west of Boston)

Directions: Massachusetts Turnpike to Exit 11, Rt. 122 north to Rt. 20 west to Rt. 146 south. There are signs on Rt. 146.

Open: Every day from dawn until dusk year round.

Admission: Free. No parking fee.

The park, surrounding the chasm on two sides of the road, has marvelous equipment of a type they hardly make anymore. One playground is for young children and the other is a challenge for any age. The picnic sites are spread throughout the pine-groved area, which is extensive and has interesting topography. Wood is supplied (free) for the fireplaces.

Bring insect repellent!

The unusual and historic rock formations have paths that twist and turn and test foot skill. Ice remains in some sections until late in the spring. The chasm, awesome and beautiful, is about ½ mile in length and at least 60 feet deep in parts; climbing and exploring may be limited to those who are at least 9 or 10. Some scouts may be seen with flashlights, used for finding one's way in discovered caves; but the uninitiated could follow a suggested route designated by a white line. New trees are sprouting through the walls of parts; others have huge exposed roots. On the hottest of days this is a cool spot.

A 1-mile trail through the woods (the Dudley Memorial Trail) seems to be little traveled. It is well marked and appealing.

Also provided: a pump for spring water (cool and delicious), a refreshment stand, rest rooms, and campsites for Boy Scouts.

Groups: Make reservations with Charles H. Gravelin, Boston Road, Sutton 01527, Tel. 865–2506.

QUABBIN RESERVOIR   Winsor Dam   Belchertown   65 miles from Boston   Tel. 413–323–6921

Directions: Massachusetts Turnpike, Palmer exit. Follow signs to Belchertown. Rt. 9 toward Ware. Signs are on Rt. 9.

Open: 7 A.M.–7 P.M.

Observation Tower: Open Memorial Day–mid-November.

Parking: Free. Fishing area, $1 (p. 226).

It is a complete change for the eye and mind. Quabbin, the source of Metropolitan Boston's water supply, offers a drive over Winsor Dam, hiking on several marked trails 1–2 miles in length, the view of 60 islands from an easy-to-climb enclosed tower for a magnificent view of three states, Mount Wachusett, and Mount Monadnock, maybe a peek at a beaver (try water hole 57), and plenty of picnic tables scattered among thousands of acres. No fires allowed. About 8 miles of (difficult) cycling is possible.

Guided Tours: p. 259, include Quabbin Park Cemetery where the bodies from 34 cemeteries were reinterred when Quabbin was constructed.

WALDEN POND STATE RESERVATION   Rt. 126   Concord

Parking: Car, $1.

Heavily used. The wooded area offers pleasant hiking opportunities that are not overwhelming. There is a path, almost 2 miles long, that completely encircles the pond, and the site of Thoreau's hut is marked near the north end.

Picnic tables available. Boating (p. 215), swimming (p. 212), and fishing are allowed.

PLACES SOUTH OF BOSTON

ASHUMET HOLLY RESERVATION (Massachusetts Audubon Society)   Rt. 151   East Falmouth

Closed: Mondays except holidays.

Parking: Car, $1.

Quiet. Possible to walk all its paths in an hour or two. One path is completely around pond. Others take you among noted hollies (in early winter), or heather, wild flowers, dogwood, and rhododendrons. There is bamboo growing near the greenhouse.

BLUE HILLS RESERVATION (MDC)   Canton, Quincy, and Milton

Headquarters: 685 Hillside Street, Milton, Tel. 698–5480

Directions: From Boston, expressway to 128 North, Exit 65 marked "Houghton's Pond, Ponkapoag Trail," and turn right at top of ramp.

Admission and Parking: Free. Many parking areas including Trailside Museum (p. 159) and Houghton's Pond (p. 211).

This is a huge (6,000 acres) reservation that has the highest ground in the metropolitan area. There are woodlands, open spaces, well-marked nature and hiking trails from Blue Hills Trailside Museum (p. 159), picnic areas, bridle paths (rentals, p. 230), natural ice skating areas, artificial rink (p. 231), ski slopes (p. 237), and cross-country trails (p. 239). Houghton's Pond area offers children's playgrounds, swimming and fishing, tennis courts, two athletic fields, tables, fireplaces, and rest rooms. Maps available from the Appalachian Moutain Club (p. 200) or the MDC Police Station on Hillside Road.

BORDERLAND STATE PARK   Massapoag Avenue   Easton   Tel. 238–6566

Directions: 45 minutes of twists and turns that are worth it—Southeast Expressway to Rt. 128 to 24 to 123 in Brockton. Take 123W toward Easton, right at light onto 138N, left at light onto Main Street, No. Easton to end. Lincoln Street ahead to end, right on Bay Road, left on Allen Road to end, right on Rockland Street, right on Massapoag Avenue. Parking lot is a mile up Massapoag.

This new state acquisition is very special. There are 1,250 unspoiled acres of oak, beech, and pinewoods, ponds, cedar swamps, glacial rocks, and upland meadows. A gravel road leads onto sweeping lawns, decorative shrubbery, hidden garden pools, and the imposing mansion of the Oakes Ames estate. Someday (soon) there may be a program of nature interpretation and a tour of the garden and mansion. Meanwhile, the area is open for hiking, horseback riding, and about 4–5 miles of cycling on multiuse roads. Much of what you see is man-made: Ponds, fields, stone walls, and roadways. Picnicking allowed; please carry your litter out.

CAPE COD NATIONAL SEASHORE   South Wellfleet   Tel. 349–2785
90 miles from Boston

Note: If it is not a beach day on the Cape, almost every summer visitor takes to the road.

Directions: Rt. 3 to Rt. 6.

Open: Year round, daily. Salt Pond Visitors Center, Eastham, and Province Lands Visitor Center, Provincetown: Summer: mid-June–Labor Day, 8–6. Other times 9–5.

Beaches: (Bathhouses) open mid-June–Labor Day, lifeguards on duty 9–5:30. Beach parking lots close at midnight. No fee to use bathhouse.

Parking: Fee at beach areas: car, $1 daily. Golden Eagle Pass (p. 204) accepted. No parking problem at nonbeach areas. On every road that is walking distance to the beach, there is a problem. Beach parking lots frequently filled on good beach days.

Summer Interpretive Program: July-Labor Day. Printed schedule of activities available mid-June. Evening programs presented at 8:30 in July and 8 in August. Shellfishing, surf casting and lifesaving demonstrations frequently presented.

Guided Walks: Conducted each day during the summer. A few special walks require advance reservations; majority of walks do not. The walks are led by Seashore interpreters who explain the natural and human history of the area. Most walks begin at 9 or 10 A.M. and at 2 P.M. Evening sunset campsite walks also presented.

Dogs: Those on short leashes allowed on self-guided trails.

Caution: Lots of poison ivy!

Miles and miles of uninterrupted beach, dunes, and some forests and ponds are part of the more than 26,000 acres from Nauset Beach at Chatham north to Provincetown. Since its opening in 1962, the area has become increasingly popular. Four areas now open to the public are:

EASTHAM

Visitors' Center, off Rt. 6, at Salt Pond, with an automatic orientation program, information desk, interpretive publications, summer evening programs. Coast Guard Beach has a special area for surfing; Nauset Beach has limited parking, bicycle trail, 2 miles, and self-guiding walking trails.

A ¼-mile trail (starting at the Visitors' Center) has texts in Braille and large print. There is also a guide rope.

NORTH TRURO

Head of the Meadow Beach in dune country, Pilgrim Heights area with picnic tables, exhibits describing activities of the Pilgrims and Indians; two self-guiding trails, one to the site believed to be where the Pilgrims found their first drinking water on the Cape; bicycle trail, 2 miles.

PROVINCETOWN

Province Lands at the tip of the Cape. Exhibits describe Lands' history. Herring Cove Beach on bay side, thus a little warmer; Race Point Beach with spectacular dunes. Bicycle trails (p. 213) 8 miles over dunes.

SOUTH WELLFLEET

Seashore headquarters, the Marconi Station where exhibits describe the location of the first wireless station in the United States. Some consider this area the one with the most spectacular views of ocean from high points. White Cedar Swamp Trail leads you partially over a boardwalk through a swamp.

MOOSE HILL SANCTUARY (Massachusetts Audubon Society)   Sharon
Tel. 784–5691

Directions: From the intersection of Rts. 1 and 27 turn east on Rt. 27, take first right .2 mile to Moose Hill Street for 1.5 miles.

Open: Tuesday-Sunday year round, plus holiday Mondays.

Parking: Car, $1.

Four self-guided nature trails, a museum room, and activity shelters are here at one of the oldest sanctuaries in the United States. It is a delightful upland woods area of wild flowers, ferns, fields, brooks, and bogs. A good hiking place.

Sunday Programs: Held on alternate weekends spring and fall.

Sugaring-off Days: Held in early spring.

School Walks: Conducted by appointment in spring and fall.

MYLES STANDISH STATE FOREST   in Plymouth is used principally for camping (p. 224) and cycling (p. 212).

ROCKY WOODS   Hartford Street   Medfield   Tel. 359–6333

The most "developed" of the Trustees of Reservations sites.

Directions: Rt. 128, Rt. 109 for 1½ miles to Hartford Street on your right, 3 miles to reservation.

Open: Year round. Closed Mondays except holidays and skating days.

Parking: Tuesday-Friday: Car, 50¢; bus, $3; Saturdays, Sundays, and holidays: Car, $1; bus, $5.

Fireplace: 2-hour limit, 50¢ per fireplace.

Ice Skating: Monday-Friday: Adults, $1.50; 17 and under, $1. Weekends and holidays: Adults, $2; 17 and under, $1.50. Warming house with rustic fireplace near pond.

Boating: Paddle boats, 50¢ for 15 minutes; $1, half hour; rowboats available for use on the 6-foot-deep man-made pond.

Memberships available.

Once on the short trail you are away from any sound of road traffic; you will come upon the site of an old quarry, climb to an observation tower, and find chipmunks among the rocky woods. There are skunk cabbage and budding trees in the spring, ducks and geese to be fed, shaded picnic areas by the pond, and swings and a sandbox for children.

STONY BROOK NATURE CENTER (Massachusetts Audubon Society)
North Street   Norfolk   Tel. 528–3140

Directions: From Norfolk Center follow Rt. 115 1 mile south to North Street. Sanctuary is south on North Street.

Open: Tuesday-Sunday year round, plus holiday Mondays.

Admission: Free.

A long winding boardwalk leads visitors over a marsh and alongside King-fisher Pond during a 1-hour walk that has appeal for all ages. Near the smaller clean Stony Brook Pond, part of the Charles River Watershed—and home for a resident family of geese—are parts of foundations of several mills.

WOMPATUCK STATE PARK   Union Street   Hingham   Tel. 749–7160

Directions: Rt. 3 south to Rt. 228 Hingham, Nantasket exit, turn left onto 220, 4.2 miles to Free Street on right. Take Free Street to first right to park.

Parking: Cars, $1.

Once a military station and now a wooded area open to the public. Good for hiking. Very popular with cyclists on Sundays as there are 15 paved miles where vehicles are not allowed. Special areas are designated for minibikes and horses. A 2-mile road passes through the park; if you follow it for about 1½ miles, you will come to a constantly running natural spring where everyone drinks and fills containers. The acres are rich in geological formations dating back to the Glacial Period. A visitors' center with interpretive program is planned for the near future. Camping (p. 224). No fireplaces. Picnicking allowed; bring your litter out please. Rest rooms provided.

WORLD'S END   14 miles from Boston in Hingham

For information: The Trustees of Reservations, 224 Adams Street, Milton, Tel. 698–2066

Directions: Rt. 3A through Hingham, go around rotary to road that branches to the left (to Nantasket) for ¼ mile to set of lights; turn left and drive slowly on Martin's Lane. If that route did not please you, try coming back by crossing Rt. 3A onto Summer Street, right on East Street to Main Street to Rt. 228 to Rt. 128. (Reminder: Nantasket traffic is extremely heavy on weekends.)

Open: Sunrise to sunset. Carriages allowed. No sanitary facilities. No picnicking, swimming, fires, firearms, or camping allowed. No organized sports or games. Dogs must be under owner's control.

Admission: 15 and over, 50¢. Annual ticket, $5 per person.

From the shores of this beautiful peninsula, which extends into Hingham Bay, you may see the Boston skyline, a panorama of the South Shore, views of harbor islands, sailboats (possibly racing), yachts, and unusual birds.

The water is just a short walk from the parking area; the entire shoreline, however, offers an extensive hike. (Reminder: Energy may have waned when it is time to return to the parking area.) Put on walking shoes and explore some of the 8-foot-wide gravel winding trails located on the 248 acres where wildlife abounds and magnificent landscaping dates back to 1890. The peninsula is composed of two drumlins, the outer elevation known as World's End and the inner elevation called Planter's Hill. You may find tall grass to hide in or freshly mowed hay. Connecting the two hills is a narrow strip of lowland (possibly 30–45 minutes' walk from the entrance) almost at water level; this may be the favorite place of some youngsters as they observe horseshoe crabs in the water or note various shells on the shore.

Interpretative Trail: Booklet available at entrance. There are 22 marked points of interest as you walk through the area and become more aware of the plants and animals in a wet meadow.

Notes to hikers looking for "other" open spaces:

. . . TOWN FORESTS. There are more than 150 in the state. They were originally set up for wood production, but now are considered multiple-use areas (hiking, bird watching, and in some places swimming). Check with town hall to see if there is one locally or in an adjoining community. Chances are that there are paths throughout.

. . . CONSERVATION LAND. Many towns and cities are acquiring land before it disappears. The intent is not to develop it, but often paths are cleared for hiking.

. . . BEACHES. Many that are filled on hot summer days offer new vistas during spring and fall and mild winters. See "Town Beaches in Outlying Communities" (p. 209). Another suggestion is to notice the varied coastline within a few miles. That is possible by seeing the rocks at Halibut Point (p. 188), driving from Rockport along South Street to Penzance Road (on your left) to Pebble Beach, which is lined with layers of smooth stones said to be used as ballast on Gloucester fishing vessels. You can take a long hike on the stones to the footbridge, which brings you to sandy Long Beach. (Driving is a little tricky. Go back to South Street, turn left on Thatcher Road—Rt. 127A—and double back to the coast on Rockport Road to Long Beach.) Long Beach is actually in Rockport and Gloucester.

Reminder: It often seems longer on the return trip of a hike.

Note: Appalachian Mountain Club (below) publishes hiking maps for specific areas.

Organizations
(Resources, Services, Places, Information . . .)

AMERICAN YOUTH HOSTELS, INC. (p. 213).

APPALACHIAN MOUNTAIN CLUB   5 Joy Street   Boston 02108   Tel. 523–0636

Open: Monday-Friday 9–5.

Excellent guidebooks, mountain climbing, canoeing, snowshoeing, skiing, camping, or just being outdoors are all aspects of this programming that may be enjoyed by all ages. Training programs in rock climbing, mountaineering, and white-water canoeing are among its activities. Instruction is available for beginners and leaders. Extensive map and photographic collections as well as one of the largest libraries on mountaineering are all available at the Joy Street office.

Membership is not essential for many of the benefits, such as participation in outings, excursions for the day, weekend, week, or for more extended periods. Call for current schedules.

Their Hut System in New Hampshire provides hikers and climbers with lunches and beverages. (See p. 233.)

Membership: $4–$15, depending upon age.
Vacation Facilities and Base Camps: See p. 244.

THE CHARLES RIVER WATERSHED ASSOCIATION, INC. 2391 Commonwealth Avenue Auburndale 02166 Tel. 527–2799

Ⓣ **Stop:** Riverside (about a mile walk).

Open: Monday-Friday 9–5.
Parking: Use the space in duck-feeding area and take stairway to the sidewalk level.

As a clearinghouse of information on the Charles, the CRWA lives up to its purpose and aim through study and follow-through on all aspects of the river.

Educational Programs: A wide range offered at its headquarters and in the field, including slide shows, bus tours with personal guides, and seminars in schools.

Resource Library: Open to the public. It has considerable material on environmental areas and complete files on the Charles River.

Schools: Bus tours may be available. Printed information available for schools to take a tour on their own.

Biweekly Briefing Meetings: Held to inform anyone who is interested. Call for schedule.

THE ELBANOBSCOT FOUNDATION, INC. Weir Hill Road Sudbury Tel. 443–9931

Open: Monday-Friday 9–4, weekends by arrangement.

As an environmental education center Elbanobscot offers the public self-guiding nature trails, trails for hiking, snowshoeing, and cross-country skiing. A library of environmental materials is available. Classes for children and adults: Natural history, outdoor skills, canoeing, crafts, and local Indian culture.

Membership: $5 for the first year.

Programs: Summer day camp (ages 4½–12), Junior Environmental Aides Training Program (13–15), Canoe Camp (14–16), winter and spring school vacation camps (ages 7–10), swimming program for all ages including junior and senior lifesaving, Day and Resident Environmental Education programs for school classes.

Groups: Primitive and dormitory overnight facilities, group programs (participatory) in local Indian culture, orienteering, map making, ecology, water life, sensory development, nature study, outdoor cooking.

Publication: *Environmental Education Manual*, $3.95. It has lesson plans and guides, elementary natural history data, and ideas for incorporating environmental education into many areas of the educational process.

ROBERT SEVER HALE RESERVATION 80 Carby Street Westwood Tel. 326–1770

Directions: Rt. 128 to Rt. 109 to Dover Road on your right.

This private reservation, run by a nonprofit organization, has 1,000 acres of unspoiled land, ponds for swimming and skating, picnic areas, woodland trails, and drilled wells.

Handicapped: Braille nature trail for the blind.

Programs: Environmental education to schools, community education courses and workshops, wilderness camping programs. Courses are open to the general public. Several summer camps operate on the reservation.

Family use is through membership, which opens annually in December.

MASSACHUSETTS AUDUBON SOCIETY   Headquarters: Great South Road
Lincoln 01773   Tel. 259–9500

A nonprofit educational organization dedicated to the conservation of the Commonwealth's natural resources. Clear driving directions to each sanctuary are included in the descriptive folder available from headquarters.

Sanctuaries: Enjoy the outdoors in the more than 15 sanctuaries with different assets—the hiking path in the forested area in Sherborn, the blueberry hills and swamp at Princeton, and the rustic bridges, floral displays, and interesting topography in Topsfield.

Those with family weekend programs present bird-banding or sheep-shearing demonstrations, show how to make an aquarium, and conduct a manageable guided walk.

Open: All are open 6 days a week sunrise to sunset Tuesday-Sunday. Open Monday holidays.

Picnicking: Not allowed at any sanctuary, except in the case of organized groups who may be given permission at some sanctuaries.

Group Arrangements: Field trips may be arranged at most sanctuaries by special arrangement. Tours given at Drumlin Farm (p. 192).

Special Programs and Summer Camps: Held at many sanctuaries.

Taped Reports on Birds: Tel. 259–8805.

Membership: Individual, $10; family, $15.

Curious Naturalist Subscriptions: Published for young people 10 times a year, $3.

Audubon Ark: A traveling arrangement for 2–5 animals who are "interviewed" by staff. Call headquarters for details.

In-school Programs: In conservation and natural science for grades 4–6 are offered through local organizations or school departments. A trained staff member comes to the class October-May.

Films (most are rented $7.50–$10): Annotated list available from Pamphlet Department.

Library: Unusual, complete, helpful with natural history and environmental subject areas. Film strips, charts, slides, games, records, and books to borrow. Open to the public. An informational gold mine.

Courses: Offered by several sanctuaries for various age groups.

MASSACHUSETTS 4–H CENTER   466 Chestnut Street   Ashland
Tel. 881–1243

Youth programs conducted here: Workshops on Saturdays and during school

vacation. Single summer programs for youth groups and day camps mid-June–
August, ages 7–17; fees $1–$2.

As this is a statewide conference facility with programs for youth and
those who work with them, there are many training programs for adults in
natural resources, environmental education, nutrition career information, and
leadership development. All are open to the public.

MASSACHUSETTS STATE PARKS AND FORESTS   Massachusetts
Department of Natural Resources   Bureau of Parks and Recreation
100 Cambridge Street   Boston 02202   Tel. 727–3180

There are over 60 state parks and forests in Massachusetts. Almost all have
picnicking and hiking. Almost all have heavy attendance during summer
months, particularly on weekends. The Recreation chapter (p. 205) includes
some of the places near Boston. Harold Parker (large) in Andover and Ashland
(smaller) are two nearby pleasant areas. Write for a complete list of all areas
with facilities. They are currently in a brochure, *Camping in Massachusetts.*

Fees (allow use of facilities): Parking: Car, $1; bus, $10 (includes 8 picnic
tables and fireplaces for 2 hours); $10 for seasonal pass (available at gate
of parks). No charge when rest rooms are closed.

Season: Varies according to weather and personnel. Generally April–mid-
October.

Day Hours: 9 A.M.–sunset.

Boating: See p. 216.

Camping: See p. 222.

Groups: There is a $1 bus parking fee permit issued for nonprofit organiza-
tions; arrangements for this must be made at least 2 weeks in advance by
writing to the office in Boston. It is then recommended that you notify the
supervisor of an area of your plans. Some locations tend to be filled on
weekends.

Interpretative Program: Few in eastern part of state. Check with office for
current programming.

METROPOLITAN DISTRICT COMMISSION (MDC)   Headquarters: 20
Somerset Street   Boston   Tel. 727–5250

The MDC constructs, operates, develops, and maintains several systems for
Boston and other municipalities. For instance, the MDC Parks District, which
now includes 37 towns and cities, "secures and maintains open spaces more or
less in their natural state until such time—if ever—as artificial development
seems necessary." Telephone numbers are listed with particular references in
this book. Their recreational facilities booklet (p. 243) is available without
charge.

MIDDLESEX CANAL ASSOCIATION   58 Monument Avenue   Charles-
town   Tel. 242–3323

The Middlesex Canal was the forerunner of 2,500 miles of canals in this country. The association is concerned with the history and present condition; members discover, record, explain, and interpret facts about the canal. Wherever
possible they are hoping to re-create sections of the canal; there is a restored
section in Wilmington. A museum and archives are open in Lowell.

A detailed guide to Middlesex Canal has history, geography, minute directions, and exact route by car and on foot.

Lectures and slide programs available to schools.

NATIONAL PARKS SERVICE   150 Causeway Street   Boston   Tel. 223–3777

Golden Eagle Pass: $10 year; over 65, issued free. Admits holder to any national park and historic site without charge. Pass does not cover camping fees.

OUTWARD BOUND, INC.   165 West Putnam Avenue   Greenwich, Connecticut 06830   Tel. 203–661–0797

This is the national address that can give you information about all the courses and programs scheduled in various locations in the United States. Applicants must be at least 16½ years old. There is no upper age limit. Most people who apply have little or no previous wilderness experience. The not-meant-to-be-easy courses are vehicles for personal growth that require an applicant in good health.

SIERRA CLUB   14 Beacon Street   Boston   Tel. 227–5339

It is not necessary to be a "working member" of the club in order to enjoy the wide variety of day and overnight trips offered year round. Backpacking, canoeing, cycling, bird watching, beach walks, and city (may be issue-oriented) tours of the waterfront and Logan Airport are all announced in the newsletter, a bimonthly publication that also has informative concerns of the club: environmental awareness, conservation, and education. The club also operates an environmental bookstore.

Minimum Age: Depends upon trip and specifications of the leader. Urban walking tours have no age limitations.

Memberships available. Cost of receiving newsletter only: $3 per year.

TRUSTEES OF RESERVATIONS   244 Adams Street   Milton   Tel. 698–2066

Since this charitable corporation was founded in 1891 for conservation purposes, it has acquired 53 places of natural beauty and historic interest throughout the Commonwealth of Massachusetts. It is a privately administered, nonprofit organization that has different admission and/or parking fees and policies for each location. Some of the reservations (e.g., Rocky Woods, The Old Manse, Crane's, Halibut Point, and World's End) are included in this book.

RECREATION

Amusement Parks

For those who relish the hoopla, lights, and cotton candy, you can find them all at many agricultural fairs, p. 291. Whatever, it is not really an inexpensive adventure. Permanent locations:

CANOBIE LAKE PARK   Salem, New Hampshire (Rt. 93 to Rt. 111 East in New Hampshire)   28 miles from Boston. Forty-five-minute drive.   Tel. 603–893–3506

Open: Sundays only, April, May, and September, 1–6. Daily June-Labor Day 10–10. Amusements open at noon; at 1 on Sundays.

Admission: 25¢. Separate charges for all sorts of rides, including a roller coaster and boat ride around lake. Friday is Kiddies Day when children's rides are half price. Group rates for 25 or more. Outdoor swimming pool, $1. Roller skating, 50¢ an hour.

Pleasant setting, lots of shade. Perhaps the most attractive of all amusement parks. Fireworks Wednesday nights, free circus acts daily in summer. Picnic facilities in grove; fireplaces available.

LINCOLN PARK   State Road (Rt. 6)   North Dartmouth   Tels. 636–2744, 999–6984   Boston tel. (weekdays): 289–3300

Directions: Rt. 128 or Southeast Expressway to Rts. 24, 195, Rt. 88 east via Dartmouth to Rt. 6 toward New Bedford.

Open: Weekends Palm Sunday-end of June, and Labor Day-October 7–11 P.M. Saturdays and 1–11 P.M. Sundays. Summer schedule: Amusements open at 1 P.M. unless arrangements have been made for a special group.

Admission: Free. Huge parking area. Amusements are individually priced. Most of the summer there is a flat day rate—good on almost all rides. One day a week there is usually a special rate Kiddies Day in their own ride area.

Roller Skating: Skates rented. General public sessions just about every night.

Bowling (duckpins): 50¢ string Sundays, holidays, evenings after 6; 25¢ days Monday-Saturday.

Groups: Special rates and package arrangements available. Advance notice should be given.

Two roller coasters, two ferris wheels, dodgems, Tilt-a-whirl, and many more rides are here. There are 20 kiddie rides, a picnic area with shaded tables, barbecue facilities, flowers and grass, an enclosed pavilion with shows given on Sundays, two baseball fields (which may be reserved), and miniature golf.

PARAGON PARK   175 Nantasket Avenue   Hull   Tel. 925–0114

Ⓣ **Stop:** Green Line to Quincy, bus to park.

Directions: Along Nantasket Beach. 16 miles southeast of Boston. Rts. 3, 228. By boat, p. 219.

Open: Weekends Easter Sunday-May 30, every day May 30-Labor Day, 1–11 P.M.

Admission: Separate price for each amusement. Reduced rate on Bargain Days; call for this year's schedule.

Miniature rides for smaller children. Size rather than age determines admission on the other rides. Everything from a shooting gallery and merry-go-round to a roller coaster that is considered one of the best—and steepest—around. A large popular place that has a few new chilling rides each year. Picnic across the street on the beach.

Atlantic Aquarium (p. 38) nearby.

ROCKY POINT AMUSEMENT PARK   Warwick, Rhode Island   Tel. 401–737–8000

Directions: Rt. 95 south to Rhode Island, Exit 10 east to 117 east to park.

Open: Decoration Day-Labor Day, from noon until 8 in spring, until 11 in summer.

Admission: 50¢; under 5, free. Group rates for 50 or more.

Parking: No charge. Bus, $15.

Specials: Wednesday is Kiddies Day when all tickets are 5¢. Friday night after 6—admission and rides: $2.50. Fireworks on holidays. Acts on midway stage daily.

Recently renovated, the park has 29 major rides (that's a lot), 10 kiddieland rides, an olympic-sized saltwater pool, and large dinner hall that serves an all-you-can-eat shore dinner for a set price (around $2.50). No picnic facilities.

SHAHEEN'S FUN-O-RAMA PARK   26 Ocean Front   Salisbury   Tel. 465–0801

35 miles from Boston, on Salisbury Beach, p. 210.

Open: June 20-Labor Day daily at 1. Open Friday and Saturday evenings. Spring: Open Sundays at 1 starting May 1. Will open especially for groups.

Admission: Free.

Parking: Municipal facilities, 50¢.

Specials: Kiddies Day with reduced fares on Wednesdays. Fireworks every Friday night.

A small park with a wide variety of amusements. Combined with the beach, it is a full day.

WHALOM PARK   Rt. 12   Lunenberg   Tel. 342–3707

Directions: Rt. 2, Rt. 13, right (north) on Rt. 13 to park (about an hour's drive).

Admission and Parking: Free.

The main attraction seems to be the combination of swimming in Lake Whalom and the amusements—all in one place. The park hasn't had constant careful care.

Separate charges for the 30 rides, miniature golf, games, bowling, roller skating, an arcade, and boat rides on the lake. Reduced rates for groups. Picnic groves with tables and barbecue pits throughout the park.

Ballooning

If you would like to watch, help (inflate and deflate), and/or go up on a tether, it can be arranged with Ralph Hall, 1656 Massachusetts Avenue, Lexington, Tel. 861–0101 (who flies out of Acton), or Dr. Clayton Thomas, Balloon School of Massachusetts, Balloon Port, Dingley Dell, R.F.D., Palmer, Massachusetts, Tel. 413–245–7013. There is no charge for observing, assisting, or explanations. If you arrange for lessons or to go on a flight, there is a charge.

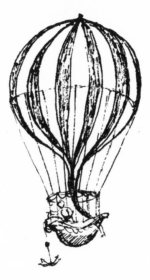

Beaches

General Information: North Shore Atlantic waters tend to be much cooler (sometimes colder) than the South Shore areas. There may be many smaller beaches in your locality, some limited to town residents. Although those listed here may be miles long, parking areas are sometimes filled on weekend or holiday afternoons. Try to get an early start. Bring a kite!

STATE BEACHES, PARKS, AND FORESTS   Operated by the Massachusetts Department of Natural Resources, Bureau of Recreation, 100 Cambridge Street, Boston 02202. Tel. 727–3180.

Open: Year round. Lifeguards on duty and bathhouses open 9–6 mid-June–Labor Day.

Fees: No charge for bathhouses. Parking charge when personnel on duty; generally it is spring-fall for parks and forests and mid-June–Labor Day for state beaches. Car, $1; bus, $10, includes 8 picnic tables and fireplaces for 2 hours. $10 for seasonal pass. In many parks and forests there is free fireplace wood for day users.

MDC BEACHES   Lifeguards on duty June 15-Labor Day at saltwater beaches. Bathhouse lockers: 25¢, towels 10¢. PARKING free at most places; 50¢ at Nantasket, Nahant, and Revere.

TOWN BEACHES IN OUTLYING COMMUNITIES   Many have lovely areas that are essentially restricted to residents during the summer months. If you would like to take a long walk in off-season, try Duxbury Beach (good for several miles), which is reached via its Powder Point Bridge (said to be the longest wooden bridge in the country). If you just want some sun in spring or fall, there are beaches in the smaller communities of Scituate and Marshfield (both south of Boston) and Manchester (north of Boston)—where parking would not be such a problem.

BOSTON AREA

Frog Pond, Boston Common (p. 114) has sprinkler in operation (for wading) June 15-September 15.

MDC Saltwater Beaches: ALL CAN BE VERY CROWDED. ALL ARE ACCESSIBLE.

DORCHESTER   MALIBU BEACH (has bathhouse and tot lot) and SAVIN HILL BEACH (not much sand, but there is grass to lie on) are on Morrissey Boulevard. Ⓣ *Stop:* Savin Hill Station on Red Line. TENEAN BEACH, off Morrissey Boulevard, can be reached by trackless trolley from Field Corner Station. Tel. for all: 436–1116.

EAST BOSTON   CONSTITUTION BEACH has bathhouse and children's playground. Ⓣ *Stop:* To Wood Island Station, then Orient Heights bus. Near airport. Noisy. Tel. 569–2800.

REVERE   REVERE BEACH, Revere Beach Parkway, Tel. 284–0038. Rt. 1 and C1 or Ⓣ to Revere stop on Blue Line. Some semblance of sand, plenty of water, and crowds. Some tired amusements. Scheduled band concerts. Parking 50¢.

SOUTH BOSTON   CASTLE ISLAND—recently renovated, exploration possibilities at fort, picnic area, fishing pier; CITY POINT (pleasant with small park), PLEASURE BAY and M STREET BEACH are all on Day Boulevard (Exit 17 from Southeast Expressway, left onto Columbia Road to rotary, halfway around rotary onto Day Boulevard). City Point Bus from Broadway, South Station, or Dudley Station. CARSON BEACH on Dorchester Boulevard has a bathhouse. Ⓣ *Stop:* Columbia on Red Line.

BEACHES NORTH OF BOSTON

ANDOVER   Harold Parker State Forest, Rt. 114, North Andover, Tel. 686–3391. Picnic areas, fireplaces, and beach (freshwater) facilities. Entrance on Rt. 125 (Andover State Police Barracks). Sundays extremely busy. Arrive early.

GLOUCESTER   All saltwater swimming. Nonresident parking $4 per car June 15-September 15. All these areas are popular, and parking areas fill early.

STAGE FORT PARK (Rt. 128 to Exit 13). Playground equipment, old fort to explore, rocks to climb. Closed fires allowed. Shaded and grassy picnic area. Bathhouse. Beach not all that spectacular.

WINGAERSHEEK (Rt. 128, Exit 13 to long ride on Atlantic Street). Small and lovely. White sand and dunes at mouth of Annisquam River. At low tide exposed sandbar allows you to walk almost to lighthouse. No barbecue pits. Parking fees may be waived for nonprofit organizations who write to Gloucester City Hall in advance.

GOOD HARBOR BEACH. Small, sandy, populated. Rt. 128, Rt. 128 extension to lights at bottom of hill, left onto Eastern Avenue to First National Store on right, just after store take right on unnamed street to beach.

IPSWICH   CRANE'S BEACH (saltwater) on Argilla Road. 30 miles north of Boston. Rt. 128, Exit 18 or about 6 miles from Rt. 1A at Ipswich South Green.

Lifeguards on Duty: May 1-May 30, weekends only. May 30-Labor Day daily 9 A.M. to sunset.

Parking (when lifeguards are on duty): Weekdays: Car, $2; Saturdays, Sundays, and holidays, $3.50. Bus, $10.

The beach can handle crowds, but on some weekends the parking lot is so filled that it is necessary to turn people away. Saltwater swimming and 5½ miles of beautiful sand. Late July–mid-August a bottle of insect repellent may help with the greenhead (very bothersome) flies. Public bathhouse, refreshment stand. Walking possibilities: It is a good hour round trip to the Castle Hill estate for a magnificent view of sea, sand, and marshlands. Rolling lawns and sculpture. Pine Hollow Interpretative Trail: Booklet (25¢) available from office during summer and patroling ranger in winter; leads you to ½-mile trail over sand dunes into pine hollows and onto a boardwalk in a red maple swamp.

LYNN   LYNN BEACH (MDC water), Lynn Shore Drive. Rts. 1A and 129.

NAHANT   NAHANT BEACH (MDC) on Nahant Road, Tels. 595–0063, 593–2120. Rts. 1A and 129. Take Ⓣ bus near Haymarket Station. Fireplaces, band concerts Sunday afternoons, children's playground, surfing in restricted area. Parking: 50¢.

NEWBURYPORT   PLUM ISLAND, Parker River Wildlife Refuge (directions on p. 190). No admission charge. Open ocean, strong surf, 6½-mile beach. Lifeguards on duty in summer in area where swimming is permitted. Surf fishing allowed. Parking lot fills early on hot summer weekends. Late July and early August is greenhead fly season. Surf occasionally has dangerous undertow. Good beach for walking, picnics. (Note refuge description, p. 190.)

SALEM   FOREST RIVER PARK. No parking fee. Fills by late morning.

SALEM WILLOWS PARK has more parking. No parking fee. Small amusement area and a big pier from which excursion boats (p. 98) leave. Pleasant park with grass and trees on a stretch overlooking water.

SALISBURY   SALISBURY STATE BEACH, 40 miles north of Boston. Rt. 1, 95, 110, 1A to beach. Amusement park, p. 207. Clean sandbar beach. Four miles of surf swimming, fireplaces, barbecue pits, picnic tables, horseshoes, play equipment for children, shuffleboards. Boat ramp. Camping area (p. 224). No surfing or open fires allowed. Undertow when heavy surf. No parking problem!

SAUGUS   PEARCE LAKE (MDC freshwater swimming) in Breakheart Reservation, Lynn Fells Parkway, near Rt. 1. Bathhouse, recreation building, picnic area. Crowded. Tel. 233–9883.

SWAMPSCOTT   KING'S BEACH (a good one!) MDC. On Lynn Shore Drive. Tel. 595–0063. Rts. 1A and 129.ⓣ bus from Haymarket Square.

WINCHESTER   SANDY BEACH (MDC freshwater), Mystic Valley Parkway (Upper Mystic Lake, off Mystic Valley Parkway). Tel. 729–9819. Bathhouse, picnic areas, tot lot. Crowded.

WINTHROP   WINTHROP BEACH. Large, very nice. On Winthrop Parkway. Rt. 1A via Revere. Rt. C1 via East Boston, Rt. 145.

ⓣ**Stop:** Orient Heights on Blue Line.

Reminder: See p. 208 for general information and parking fees.

BEACHES SOUTH OF BOSTON

CAPE COD NATIONAL SEASHORE (p. 213).

HULL   NANTASKET BEACH (MDC), Tel. 925–0054, 25 minutes from Boston. Large. Usually crowded on warm days. Children's playground, amusement park (p. 206), band concerts Wednesdays, weekends, and holidays. Surfing in restricted area. Often a bumper-to-bumper situation (weekends) along the road. Boat leaves from Boston (p. 219) orⓣ bus from   Fields Corner. *Directions:* Southeast Expressway to Rt. 3, Rt. 228 exit. Parking 50¢.

MILTON   HOUGHTON'S POND (MDC), Hillside Street, Blue Hills Reservation. Rts. 128 and 138 north; at first set of traffic lights take a right to pond. Freshwater swimming in an area that tends to get very crowded. Tot lot provided. New bathhouse, picnic areas, tennis courts, and baseball field.

PLYMOUTH   MYLES STANDISH STATE FOREST, Tel. 295–2135

Directions: Rt. 128 south, Rt. 3 south, Rt. 44 west to sign for Myles Standish.

Two good ponds open to public for day use. Sandy beach. Filled to capacity on warm days. Parking $1.

QUINCY   WOLLASTON BEACH (MDC), Morrissey Blvd., Tel. 436–1116. Bus from Ashmont Station or Quincy Station. Considered a better beach—long, not as crowded as some.

SANDWICH   SCUSSET STATE BEACH (cool water) reached from Rt. 3 at the South Sagamore Circle of Sagamore Bridge, 59 miles from Boston. Play enclosure for small children with wading pool, swings, seesaws, few cookout fireplaces, snack bar, and a fishing facility which juts out into Cape Cod Canal. Parking fees, p. 203. Tel. 888–0859.

SOUTH DARTMOUTH   DEMAREST LLOYD STATE PARK. Rt. 6 (Rt. 128–24–6 toward New Bedford, follow sign). Small saltwater beach. Shallow for quite a distance. Excellent for young children. Not too crowded. Shaded picnic area. Lifeguards in summer.

WESTPORT   HORSENECK STATE BEACH, 55 miles south of Boston. Rt. 128 or I–195 to 24 to Rt. 6, then 12 long miles of single-laned Rt. 88. Surf, slight undertow, barbecue facilities, and some picnic tables. Plan to have supper among the protective dunes. Warm water. Highly recommended with caution: At low tide there can be a sharp drop. Watch young children. Parking fees, p. 208. (If it rains suddenly, you are not far from the Whaling Museum, p. 178, or Fall River attractions, p. 76.) Tel. 636–8816.

WESTWOOD   HALE RESERVATION (p. 201) for members.

WOLLASTON   WOLLASTON BEACH (MDC), Quincy Shore Drive. By public transportation take bus from Quincy Center, get off at Vassal Street, 2-minute walk. Considered one of the best of Boston-area beaches.

BEACHES WEST OF BOSTON

SHERBORN   FARM POND. Rt. 16 to Rt. 27 toward Medfield. Left on Farm Road to pond. Nonresidents apply for 50¢ permit (required for parking) at town hall in May. Parking 50¢ per person. Small, quiet; fills early.

State Beaches (all freshwater swimming): For regulations, see p. 203:
ASHLAND   ASHLAND STATE PARK, Rt. 135. Small swimming area in a lovely setting surrounded by woods and picnic and barbecue facilities.

CONCORD   WALDEN POND STATE RESERVATION, Rt. 126, south of Rt. 2. When the water level allows the area to be used for swimming, the pond is available Memorial Day-Labor Day and tends to be very crowded. Adjacent woodlands, p. 195.

HOPKINTON   HOPKINTON STATE PARK, Rt. 85 south of Rt. 9. New facility with a long straight beach. Bathhouse and picnic tables available. Rest rooms equipped for handicapped.

NATICK   COCHITUATE STATE PARK on Rt. 30 near Massachusetts Turnpike Interchange. A very busy area with picnic tables in wooded areas around a small swimming hole.

Bicycling

Although the area has a growing number of cyclists, Boston does not have bikeways in the European sense. Bicycle routes challenge the best of riders. However, there are a few

CYCLE PATHS

Along the Charles River: Between Eliot Bridge and Longfellow Bridge in Cambridge. Also between Boston University Bridge and Charles River locks in Boston.

Under Design: Stony Brook Reservation, Charles River between Eliot Bridge and Watertown Square, and along the Charles River between Watertown and North Beacon Street.

State Areas with Paved Paths:
Myles Standish State Park (p. 198), 15 miles of mostly wooded trails, some crossroads.
Wompatuck State Reservation (p. 199), 15 miles of trails without crossroads. R. C. Nickerson State Forest, Brewster, 8 miles of wooded trails through cedar swamp and around a pond.

Bike paths are also in Martha's Vineyard State Forest, Martha's Vineyard, and Chicopee State Park in Chicopee.

Cape Cod National Seashore:
Nauset Trail, Eastham, 2 miles—moderate grades.
Head of Meadow Trail, North Truro, 2 miles, relatively flat.
Province Lands Trail, near Provincetown, 8 miles. Labeled "difficult sections with steep grades and sharp curves." It is a ride that is well worth the effort through forests, ponds, bogs, and sand dunes.

CYCLE ROUTE MAPS

The AMERICAN YOUTH HOSTELS (below) has maps with route sheets (15¢ each) that detail the best routes for traveling from one eastern Massachusetts hostel to another. The office wall has a 4- by 6-foot topographic map of New England showing hills and river valleys, as well as the exact locations of the 41 New England hostels.

There is a set of 35 mileage-marked maps that is distributed by the MASSA-CHUSETTS DEPARTMENT OF NATURAL RESOURCES, Division of Forests and Parks, Leverett Saltonstall Building, 100 Cambridge Street, Boston 02202. These routes have been designed and cyclist-tested by local bicycle groups (mostly by the Charles River Wheelmen). Family groups with small children may find the distances a bit difficult to tackle, although several rides offer shortcuts that provide loops of only 15 miles in length.

CYCLE REPAIRS

Finding a place that repairs bicycles is not difficult. (No satisfaction guaranteed, however.) Repair clinics are held by some organizations (below) and stores. (Laughing Alley Bicycle Shop, 51 Harvard Street, Allston, has free clinics every Wednesday 6–9 P.M., weather permitting.) A place that may be of particular interest:

BICYCLE REPAIR COLLECTIVE   351 Broadway   Cambridge   Tel. 354–9891

Open Monday-Saturday. The hours vary according to the season. There are three price levels: for space and tools, for mechanics' help, for work done by them.

BICYCLE RENTALS

Although there are many places on Cape Cod and in Day Trip communities (p. 65) that rent bikes, there are very few in the Boston area. THE BICYCLE PEDDLER, 832 Commonwealth Avenue (near Boston University), Tel. 731–3550, and BEACON HILL BIKE SHOP, 303 Cambridge Street (near Massachusetts General Hospital), Tel. 523–9133, rent three-speeds and are open Sundays. In Cambridge check with Herson Cycle Co., 1250 Cambridge Street, Tel. 876–4474.

CYCLE ORGANIZATIONS

AMERICAN YOUTH HOSTELS, INC.   Greater Boston Council   251 Harvard Street   Brookline   Tel. 731–5430

Open: 12–6 Monday-Friday.

Call for information concerning group trips, hosteling, and hostels here and abroad. Activities include cycling, mountain climbing, skiing, sailing, and canoeing. Trips are patronized by all ages. Trips planned through the national office have a minimum age of 14 for trips in this country and 16 for trips abroad. National Office: Delaplane, Virginia 22025.

Day Trips: 15 miles or more round trip, take place in the Boston area almost every Saturday and Sunday all year. There is no set minimum age for these trips. Membership is not necessary.

Hostels: $2–$2.50 a night depending on season and place. Family rooms (one for all members of a family) are available in many locations. Reservations necessary. Kitchen facilities exist in hostels and some duties are expected of hostelers. New hostels constantly being added. There are hostels in all New England states. In Massachusetts they are located in Brookline, Buzzards Bay,* Charlestown,* East Bridgewater,* Granville, Hyannis,* Littleton,* Martha's Vineyard,* Milton, Nantucket, Newburyport, Orleans, Pittsfield,* Sheffield, Springfield, Sunderland, and Truro.

Introductory Pass: $1.

Memberships: Family, $12 (valid in U.S.A. and Canada only); junior (under 18), $5. Group memberships available for 10 or more. Membership card recognized in any youth hostel in the world. Senior (18 and up), $10.

BAY STATE WHEELMEN   79 Garnet Road   West Roxbury 02132   Tel. 327–5886
Membership Fee: $2.

Sunday afternoon bicycle rides. Also offers extended rides in summer. In addition there are bus trips to distant areas such as the Pennsylvania Dutch country. Families welcome.

CHARLES RIVER WHEELMEN   131 Mt. Auburn Street   Cambridge 02138   Tel. 876–8636

Minimum Age for Membership: 16. No minimum age for participation. Trips open to nonmembers and entire families.

Membership Dues: $15. Includes a subscription to the CRW monthly newsletter plus annual membership dues in the League of American Wheelmen, the national bicycling organization.

"We call ourselves a club, but we really enjoy bicycling, good friends and have found we learn a lot from each other by comparing equipment and riding techniques, swapping advice and sharing good times." Everything from leisurely rides to hundred-mile jaunts included in trips scheduled early spring to late fall.

Day, weekend, and extended trips are also offered through PONKAPOAG OUTDOOR CENTER, p. 245, SIERRA CLUB, p. 204, APPALACHIAN MOUNTAIN CLUB, p. 200, and:
LINCOLN GUIDE SERVICE   Lincoln Road at railroad track   Lincoln Tel. 259–9204. For adults and teen-agers. Spring through fall.

BIKING EXPEDITION   R.D. #2   Hillsboro, New Hampshire   603–478–5783

* Open year round.

Trips for 13–17-year-olds. Offered late June-August. Varying lengths.

STUDENT HOSTELING PROGRAM OF NEW ENGLAND, INC.   Maple Hill   Rochester, Vermont 05767   Tel. 802–767–3297

Trips for 14- to 17-year-olds. Offered June-September 1.

VERMONT BICYCLE TOURING   R.D. 2   Bristol, Vermont 05442

Age 9 and up. Overnights spent at Vermont country inns. Mid-May–end of October. Special family trips.

Boat Launching Areas

Some towns have their own rules for their residents. The following places are open to the public (most without charge):

IN THE BOSTON AREA   BRIGHTON: Charles River, on Nonantum Road, parking area and launching ramp (near skating rink). CAMBRIDGE: Charles River, Magazine Beach, off Memorial Drive (near Stop & Shop), natural beach, cement pads for ramp. CHARLESTOWN: Little Mystic Channel on Terminal Street. From City Square take Chelsea Street to Medford Street to Terminal. WESTON: Charles River, Riverside Recreation Grounds, Rt. 128, Exit 48, shallow draft only, natural grade. WEST ROXBURY: Harvey's Beach, Charles River, natural beach, across street from Veterans' Hospital. WINTHROP: Winthrop Harbor paved ramp on Veterans Road and Shirley Avenue; off street parking.

A SHORT DRIVE FROM BOSTON   CONCORD: Walden Pond, rowboats and canoes (muscle-powered only). HOPKINTON: Whitehall Reservoir on Rt. 135, 3 miles west of the intersection with Rt. 85 in Hopkinton Center. IPSWICH: At the town pier on East Street. As you come into town go straight ahead instead of turning on Rt. 1A. MARSHFIELD: Plenty of signs in town. Launching from recreation area in Brant Rock near old lighthouse. NATICK: Lake Cochituate. Boat-trailer parking area and launching ramps on state park land. Parking fee: $1 per car. Special area on north side of Rt. 30 set aside for sailboat launching. No charge. SALEM: Danvers River near Kernwood Country Club on Kernwood Avenue leading to the old bridge to Beverly. Parking: $1.50. WEYMOUTH: Turn off Rt. 3A opposite the doughnut shop and beside the supermarket. Ramp is on the right just after the first curve. Access to Back River and Hingham Bay. (Good fishing.) WOBURN: Horn Pond. Town recreation area on Lake Avenue, just off Main Street (Rt. 38). No power boats allowed.

Boat Rentals

Canoes . . . Rowboats . . . Paddle boats . . . Motorboats . . . Sailboats (Special note to sailors: The best "deal" may be with Community Boating, p. 235.)

CONCORD   SOUTH BRIDGE BOAT HOUSE   Main Street   Tel. 369–9438

Located just beyond Concord Center on the Concord River.

Open: April 1-November 1, 9 A.M.–dusk. Closed Monday mornings.

Rentals: *Canoes* (up to 2 adults and 3 children allowed in one)—weekdays: $2.50 per hour; $10 per day. Weekends and holidays: $3.00 per hour, $15 per day. *Rowboats* available at same rates. Small outboard $5 per hour, $25 per day. Reservations are taken up until 11 A.M.

It is possible to visit at the Old North Bridge (p. 72) and Great Meadows Wildlife Refuge (p. 193). You can paddle up to 24 miles and lunch along the river. (No fires allowed.)

Reminder: Return trips are against the current.

EAST BRIDGEWATER   Paddle boats and canoes (see p. 74).

HINGHAM   MULTIHULL ASSOCIATES INC.   349 Lincoln Street (Rt. 3A)   Tel. 749–0100

Sailboat Rentals: 11'–30' boats available. Rates start at $10 for a morning, $15 for an afternoon, $20 all day.

JAMAICA PLAIN   JAMAICA POND BOAT HOUSE   507 Jamaicaway Rt. 1 near Children's Museum   Tel. 522–4944

Rowboats: For rent. Rate: $1 per hour ($5 deposit required).

Season: Early April-October 1, every day sunrise to sunset. Reservations not necessary. Must be able to swim. Life jackets supplied. Pond (50 feet deep) is stocked by State Fish and Game Division.

MARBLEHEAD   MARBLEHEAD RENTAL BOAT CO.   81 Front Street Tel. 631–2259

Sailboats for Rent: May-October, 7 days a week.

Rates: $3–$10, depending upon class of boat for first hour. Half price second hour. Ten percent less on weekdays. Telephone reservations accepted.

MEDFIELD   ROCKY WOODS RESERVATION has paddle boats and rowboats for use in 6-foot-deep small pond. (See p. 198.)

NATICK   COCHITUATE STATE PARK   Rt. 30   Tel. 653–9504
Canoes $2.75 hour, catamarans and sailboats: 2 hours for $9.50; paddle boats (holds 2 people) $2 for ½ hour; motorboats $6 hour. Water-skiing boats available. Open May–mid-September. Popular and busy area.

WINTHROP   WINTHROP SAILBOAT RENTAL   11 Moore Street   Tel. 846–2497

Ⓣ**Stop:** Blue Line to Orient Heights and then bus to Winthrop, Shirley Street stop. Two blocks to marina.

Day sailers from 10 to 17 feet are available.
Some Sunfish.
New: A youth program with enrollment fees. Call for details.

Note: See Canoeing (p. 225).

CANOES (ONLY) ARE AVAILABLE AT:

CAMBRIDGE   CAMBRIDGE CANOE RENTAL   Memorial Drive (opposite Stop & Shop) $3 hour, $10 day.

IPSWICH   HAROLD FOOTE CO.   Topsfield Road   Tel. 356–9771
Directions: Rt. 1, past Topsfield Fairgrounds, at second light take Ipswich Road, which becomes Topsfield Road to landing.

Open: Whenever weather permits.

Rates: $2 hour, $6 day, $10 overnight during week, and $15 weekends.

Reservations accepted; needed for spring and summer weekends particularly.

Overnight Camping Arrangements: Inquire. It is possible to camp on an island that is a wildlife sanctuary.

NEEDHAM   RED WING BAY CENTER   58 Fisher Street   Tel. 444–6400

Located on the Charles River. From Needham Center take Chestnut Street for about 2 miles, right on South Street for about 2 miles to Fisher Street.

Open: Mid-April–late June and Labor Day–mid-October, weekends 9–6. Summer season: Monday-Friday 12–6, Saturdays and Sundays 9–6. Late August is particularly beautiful. If you are willing to portage around a waterfall (upstream), it is possible to paddle as far as Wellesley or Natick.

Rates: $2 an hour, $10 per day. Group rates available.

Minimum Age for Use: 10 with proof of swimming ability and parents' permission slip (needed for anyone under 16 who is taking a canoe out without an adult). Picnic facilities, open field and wooded area nearby.

NEWTON   CHARLES RIVER CANOE CENTER   2401 Commonwealth Avenue   (There may be additional Charles River sites in the future.) Auburndale   Tel. 527–9885

Located in the boat berths at MDC Police Station, Rt. 30 (Commonwealth Avenue) near Norumbega Duck Feeding Station. About a 15-minute walk from Riverside stop on Ⓣ Riverside (Green) Line.

Open: April (or late March if warm)-October, 7 days a week. 11 A.M.–dusk on weekdays; 9 A.M.–dusk weekends and holidays.

Fees: $3 hour; $6 for 3 hours, $10 day. Groups should make advance reservations. Those under 16 and unaccompanied by an older person must have a signed permission form.

Car Rack Rentals (their canoes may be taken to another site if you wish): $1 day, 75¢ each additional day.

Guided Tours: Offered on Charles and other rivers. By reservation. $6 per person per ½ day. Tours include history of New England, ecology of land and rivers, animals, plants, and wildlife in commentary given while canoeing. Group rates for 1-, 2-, and 3-day river trips.

Canoes can take 3 people, 4 if two are young children.

You may paddle up and downstream for about 3 miles before portage is necessary. There are three dams between the Canoe Center and the Larz Anderson Bridge in Cambridge; that is as far as you can go in that direction. Upstream you could paddle 75 miles as far as Hopkinton. Most day trippers will find the specified 3-mile limitation reasonable.

Boat Rides in Boston

CHARLES RIVER EXCURSION leaves from behind the Hatch Shell at Charles River Embankment near Revere Street. It is about a 45-minute ride to the Harvard area and back along the Charles River. For this year's arrangements, check with the Metropolitan District Commission, 20 Somerset Street, Boston, Tel. 727–5250, Monday-Friday.

SWAN BOATS   Boston Public Garden   Tel. 323–2700

Ⓣ **Stop:** Arlington.

Season: First Saturday before April 19 through the last Saturday of September. Open except on rainy or windy days. If in doubt, call.

Open: June 20-Labor Day 10–6. From opening day through June 20 10–4 and from Tuesday after Labor Day until the closing date 12–4.

Fare: 40¢; children 12 and under, 25¢. Group rates available.

A young man pedals as he sits between the wings of a swanlike form in back of benched passengers on these well-known boats. Bring feed for ducks and try to spot Mrs. Mallard and her ducklings (made famous by Robert McCloskey's *Make Way for Ducklings*) during the 15-minute ride.

HARBOR EXCURSIONS in boat trip information (p. 220).

Boating Education

Recorded marine weather: 569–3700

SMALL CRAFT SCHOOL held at Kiddie Kamp in Sharon.
Contact: Greater Boston Red Cross, Safety Services, 99 Brookline Avenue, Boston 02215. Tel. 262–1234.

Three-day Memorial Day weekend training offered in outboard boating, rowing, sailing, canoeing.

Eligibility: At least 17 and pass certain swimming tests.

Expenses: $30 all inclusive.

MASSACHUSETTS DIVISION OF MARINE AND RECREATIONAL VE-HICLES   64 Causeway Street   Boston 02114   Tel. 727–3900

Many courses in safe boat handling, with emphasis on motorboats and rules of the road, given through the fall, winter, and spring, and occasionally in the summer. There is no charge, but recommended books may be sold through the course. Call the above number for a schedule of classes near your community.

Children are welcome at the 6-week series. Classes are once a week, usually 7–9 P.M.

THE UNITED STATES COAST GUARD AUXILIARY   150 Causeway Street Boston 02114   Tel. 223–3608

Entire families are encouraged to attend its basic seamanship classes. Two-hour evening classes, held once a week for a 12-week series usually on Tuesdays or Wednesdays in various communities. Call for present schedule.

THE UNITED STATES POWER SQUADRONS   P.O. Box 102   Auburn-dale 02166   Tel. 1–800–243–6000

Offers a 10-class series to anyone who is at least 16. The schedule of locations and months varies. A few have junior squadrons for ages 9–16.

Boat Trips That Leave from Boston's Waterfront

(Bring a sweater or jacket!)

Parking: Few free street spaces. Parking areas: $2–$2.50.

The wharves along Atlantic Avenue have had several companies that service trips. The two mainstays:

MASSACHUSETTS BAY LINE
Rowes Wharf (344 Atlantic Avenue)
Tel. 542–8000
Ⓣ**Stop:** Aquarium (2-block walk).
In addition to trips listed below, there are commuter boats Monday-Friday and cocktail cruises Tuesday-Thursday at 5:30 P.M.

BAY STATE-SPRAY & PROVINCETOWN STEAMSHIP CO.
20 Long Wharf
Tel. 723–7800
Ⓣ**Stop:** Aquarium (you are right there).

TO GEORGE'S ISLAND (p. 184). For boat information, see weekend and holiday details under Bay State Spray excursion boat (below).

SAILBOAT RIDE   THE SPRAY (capacity: 49 passengers)

Bay State Spray & Provincetown Steamship Co. (above).

Schedule: May 1-October 15 (possibly longer on both ends). Two-hour sailing leaves at 10 and 2 Saturdays and Sundays. Cruises after 5 P.M. are for reserved groups only. Arrive early for Sunday afternoon trips. Always verify sailing schedule before coming to the wharf.

Fare: Adults, $5; children under 12, $4.

The Spray carries an authentic rig and design typical of vessels used a century ago. Launched in 1963, she is a larger replica of the boat in which Captain Joshua Slocum of Boston single-handedly circumnavigated the globe in 1897. There are many repeat guests for the peaceful sail through Boston Harbor. Charts with points of interest are distributed to passengers. As you sit on the cushions on the main deck, you will sail near several islands, Winthrop, Logan Airport in the outer harbor, and in sight of the Constitution, Coast Guard base, and the Maurice J. Tobin Bridge in the inner harbor. Refreshments sold on board. If the wind gives out and it is time to return, an auxiliary motor will bring you back on schedule. On calm days children find this trip a bit confining. When there is wind, however, the changing sails and waves provide plenty to watch.

LUNCH BOAT (Memorial Day-September depending on the weather). Both Massachusetts Bay Line and Bay State Spray leave at 12:15 for ½-hour cruise Monday-Friday. $1 per person.

TO NANTASKET
Massachusetts Bay Line sails late June-Labor Day at 10, 1, 4, 5:30. Round-trip

fare: Adults, $4.75; children under 12, $3.25. Babes-in-arms, free.

One-hour and 20-minute ride to Nantasket Beach and Paragon Amusement Park. On warm Sunday afternoons this is a means of transportation rather than a relaxing cruise; they are busy!

BOSTON HARBOR TOUR with commentary about the islands and landmarks:
Massachusetts Bay Line (p. 219): 1½-hour trips 7 days a week Memorial Day–September. Leaves at 1 and 2:45. Adults, $3; children under 12, $2.
Bay State Spray (p. 219) excursion boat: Monday-Friday: 1½-hour tour leaves at 10, 1, 3. Adults, $3; children under 12, $2. School groups, $1.50 per student. Saturdays, Sundays, and holidays: Morning trip leaves at 10, is 3 hours long, and includes a 1-hour tour of George's Island with Edward Rowe Snow. Afternoon trips are 2–4 and 4:30–6:30. You may get off at George's Island on the 2 o'clock boat and leave on a 5:30 pickup. Passengers stay on the 4:30 boat.

TO PROVINCETOWN
Bay State Spray & Provincetown Steamship Co. (p. 219) sails Saturdays and Sundays in May, June, and September. Daily in July and August. Two galleys on board. Live band for entertainment. Leaves Boston at 9:30 for a 3½-hour trip. You have 2½ hours in Provincetown before leaving at 3:15. Round trip: Adults, $12; children 2–12, $8; children under 2, free; senior citizens, $8. Bicycles: $1 each way.

Boat Trips to Block Island

This small (7 by 3 mile) village-like island is serviced by the Interstate Navigation Company. Boats leave from Port Judith, Rhode Island (Tel. 401–783–4613) year round. (Port Judith is about a 1½ hour ride from Boston.) Summer trips are also available from India Street in Providence, R.I. Boat trips are about 1 hour. Day trippers have about 6 hours for exploring and/or swimming. Bring a lunch and consider spring or fall bicycling. One day round trip: $4.75, under 12, half fare; bicycles, $2.

Boat Trips to Martha's Vineyard and Nantucket

The islands are serviced from Hyannis, Falmouth, and Woods Hole. Schedules vary from season to season. No reservations for passengers. The companies that service the islands are:

WOODS HOLE STEAMSHIP AUTHORITY (only year-round service)
Box 284, Woods Hole, Massachusetts 02543
Tel. Boston 426–1855; Woods Hole 548–5011; New York 966–1929
    Automobiles: Reservations essential. Auto rates do not
    include passengers.

HY-LINE, a division of Hyannis Harbor Tours (May-October),
Ocean Street Dock, Hyannis
Tel. 775–1885 for island trips, 775–7185 for sight-seeing

ISLAND QUEEN, Island Commuter Corporation (May-October),
Falmouth Heights Road, Falmouth
Tel. 548–4800

TO MARTHA'S VINEYARD (all fares are round trip):

FROM FALMOUTH via Island Queen. Docks at Oak Bluffs. Adults, $5; children 5–12, $2.50. Bicycles, $2.

FROM HYANNIS via Hy-Line. Adults, $8, for excursion that gives you maximum of 4 hours on island. Children under 12, $4. Longer time on island same as overnight rates: Adults, $10; children, $5, Bicycles, $2. One-way trip is 1 hour, 45 minutes.

FROM NEW BEDFORD the Cape Island Express Lines, Inc., P.O. Box J4095, Tel. 997–1699, leaves from the foot of South Street 3 times a day during the summer. $8, under 12, half fare; under 5, free; bicycles, $2.

FROM WOODS HOLE (74 miles from Boston) via Steamship Authority. 45-minute trip. Adults, $4.75; children 5–15, $2.40. Bicycles, $2. Maximum time on island for 1-day excursion: 12 hours. Overnight rates: Adults, $5; children 5–15, $2.50.

TO NANTUCKET

FROM HYANNIS via Hy-Line. One hour, 50 minutes. Excursion rate allows maximum of 4 hours on island: Adults, $8; children under 12, $4. Bicycles, $2. Via Steamship Authority: 2-hour trip. Adults, $8; children 4–15, $4. Bicycles, $3.

FROM WOODS HOLE via Steamship Authority: 2½-hour trip. Adults, $8; children 5–15, $4. Bicycles, $3. Maximum time on island for 1-day excursion: 5 hours. Overnight rates: Adults, $10; children, $5.

Boat Trip to Star Island

It is 10 miles at sea. Leaves from Portsmouth, New Hampshire.

Directions: See p. 105, 1½ hours from Boston.

Bus: Greyhound Bus depot is 4 blocks from the Portsmouth dock.

Ferry Season: Late June-Labor Day. For current schedule contact Viking of Yarmouth, Tel. 603–436–9839. Ferry ride takes 1 hour, 10 minutes. Advance reservations advised for day trippers.

Considered special by many. It is "different" with a vast turn-of-the-century hotel and a spired meetinghouse built of native stone in 1800. Guided tour fills you in on historical details (Isles of Shoals noted by Samuel Champlain in 1605; Captain John Smith carefully mapped them in 1616; dried fish once common occupation here; see a small cemetery that dates back to fishing village days). Treeless island with rocks (no swimming), birds, plants, places to think. Bring lunch or eat on boat at snack bar.

Star Island is now the home of summer Unitarian Conferences, which include programs for high schoolers and entire families. Activities include marine biology, astronomy, sketching, crafts, talks, and discussions. For information: Star Island Corporation, 110 Arlington Street, Boston 02116, Tel. 426–7988.

Bowling

Most bowling alleys which are members of the Massachusetts Bowling Association (and most large alleys are) have Little Leagues September-March. Special prices and free instruction are offered to boys and girls in two age groups: 7–11 and 12–14. Check the Yellow Pages for facilities near you.

Some alleys have Sunday morning specials, many offer lessons, and some have package arrangements that include lunch.

Handicapped: Many have special programs for youngsters with special needs.

Camping

. . . Places vary in beauty and space; all fill early.

. . . Arrive early in the day, mid-week if possible. Some areas such as Nickerson on Cape Cod are almost impossible to get into during the summer.

. . . Better private campgrounds accept reservations. Not all are necessarily scenic but can act as a good base.

CAMPING ALLOWED IN MDC AREAS

BLUE HILLS RESERVATION   Headquarters: 685 Hillside Street   Milton Tel. 698–5840

Camping is allowed—for those who don't mind "roughing it"—in the wooded area around an open field, year round, but the sanitary facilities are open late spring-early fall only. During the summer the bathhouse facilities of Houghton's Pond are available 8 A.M.–8 P.M. Register at headquarters.

BREAKHEART RESERVATION (p. 188)   Stoneham area   Tel. 438–5690

Call for overnight camping and fireplace permits Monday-Friday 9–5. Running water and sanitary facilities (flush toilets) available late spring-early fall. Winter camping allowed.

CAMPING ON ISLANDS

Two islands now open to the public for primitive camping are: BUMPKIN and GRAPE ISLANDS. Caution: Until the control program is complete, there is a problem on both islands. Groups have first priority for the necessary camping permits that must be obtained at Wompatuck State Park, Hingham, Tel. 749–7161, at least 1 week in advance. Trail system on both places. Private transportation is the only way to get there. As Grape Island is 1,500 feet from lower neck in Weymouth, it is possible to reach it by rowboat. Grape is fairly small, can be hiked through in less than an hour, and offers shady areas. Swimming (not encouraged) on both islands off rocky beaches. More caution: plenty of poison ivy!
Note: See Ipswich, p. 216.

SOME MASSACHUSETTS CAMPING INFORMATION

Public and private campgrounds are listed in the brochure *Camping in Massachusetts.* For a copy, write to the Massachusetts Department of Natural Resources, Bureau of Recreation, 100 Cambridge Street, Boston, Massachusetts 02202.

STATE CAMPING AREAS

Season: May 1-October 15.

Fees: Campsites, $3; group campsites, $6; cabins, $6–$8 with electricity 50¢ per day.

Cabins available at Savoy Mt.-Florida State Forest, Savoy, Tel. 413–663–8469 (no electricity); Mohawk Trail State Forest, Charlemont, Tel. 413–339–5504; Willard Brook State Forest, Ashby, Tel. 617–597–8802.

All sites are available on a first-come, first-serve basis, and are often filled by Thursday for weekends. Between the last Saturday in June and Labor Day there is a 2-week maximum stay. Groups must make arrangements at least 1 week in advance.

For **winter camping** possibilities, check the regional offices for current conditions and arrangements:

> Southeastern Massachusetts Regional Supervisor
> Myles Standish State Forest
> P.O. Box 66
> South Carver, Massachusetts 02566 Tel. 295–2135

> Northeastern Massachusetts Regional Supervisor
> Lowell Skating Rink
> Douglas Road
> Lowell, Massachusetts Tel. 458–9673

> Worcester County Regional Supervisor
> P.O. Box 155
> Clinton, Massachusetts Tel. 365–5908

> Connecticut Valley Regional Supervisor
> P.O. Box 484
> Amherst, Massachusetts 01002 Tel. 413–549–1461

> Berkshires Regional Supervisor
> Pittsfield State Forest
> Cascade Street
> Pittsfield, Massachusetts 01201 Tel. 413–442–8992

Student groups: Overnight facilities available in the western part of the state. Contact Kenneth Dubuque, Connecticut Valley Regional Supervisor, P.O. Box 484, Amherst, Massachusetts 01002, Tel. 413–549–1461.

SOME NEARBY STATE AREAS
Rates: $3 per day.
All have flush toilets.

HORSENECK BEACH STATE RESERVATION   Westport   Tel. 636–8816
Rt. 6, 195, 24, 88. 100 campsites, ocean swimming and fishing.

MASSASOIT STATE PARK   Taunton   Tel. 824–0687
130 campsites. Charge for sewage connection is $4. Rest rooms equipped for handicapped. Cartop boating. New beach under construction.

R. C. NICKERSON STATE FOREST   Brewster   Tel. 896–3491
Winter tel. 896–3611. 400 campsites. Pond and ocean swimming, hiking, fishing.

HAROLD PARKER STATE PARK   Rt. 125   Andover   Tel. 686–3391
Tent and trailer sites, freshwater swimming. 120 campsites, hiking, fishing.

SALISBURY STATE RESERVATION   Salisbury   Tel. 462–4481

Rt. 495–95–110–1–1A. Essentially a camping (500 sites) and beach (5 miles) area. Tent and trailer sites. Rest rooms equipped for handicapped. Ocean boating, swimming, fishing. Weekend campers should arrive by Friday morning.

SHAWME-CROWELL STATE FOREST   Sandwich   Tel. 888–0351

Essentially a camping area. Beaches nearby. Rt. 3, 6A, and 130.

MYLES STANDISH STATE FOREST   Plymouth   Tel. 866–2526

Directions: p. 198.

Pond swimming, fishing, hiking, cycle paths, rest rooms equipped for handicapped. 240 campsites.

WOMPATUCK STATE RESERVATION   Union Street   Hingham   Tel. 749–7160

Rt. 3, 228, Nantasket exit. 400 campsites, 140 with electricity. Note p. 199. Nearest swimming: 15-minute drive.

SOME NEW ENGLAND CAMPING INFORMATION

(See also pp. 30 and 295.)

CONNECTICUT   Full camping site list available from Parks and Recreation Unit, Department of Environmental Protection, State Office Building, Hartford, Connecticut 06115. Rates: $2 per site/day for inland areas; $3 per site/day for shore areas. Season: April 15-September 30. 14-day limit. Reservations permitted in most areas. *Hammonasset Beach* in Madison and *Rocky Neck* in Niantic have saltwater bathing and are very popular. Day users swell the population.

MAINE   Sites for wilderness camping (some more developed than others) are in an annually revised publication, *Forest Campsites,* sent free upon request from: State of Maine, Department of Conservation, State Office Building, Augusta, Maine 04330. Complete list of state areas available from Maine Department of Conservation, Bureau of Parks and Recreation, Augusta, Maine 04330. Reservations accepted only at Baxter State Park.

NEW HAMPSHIRE   Annually revised brochure includes all details on privately operated and public campgrounds. Write: New Hampshire Vacations, P.O. Box 856, Concord, New Hampshire 03301.

VERMONT   List of state-operated areas available from Department of Forests and Parks, Montpelier, Vermont 05602. Reservations for 6 days or more can be made January 1-May 1 if you enclose full payment. After May 1 reservations made with office of each location. Rates: Tent site or trailer site, $3–$4.50 per night, depending on location and whether Vermont resident or not. Lean-tos where available: $1 more than tent or trailer sites. No cabins available.

Canoeing

(For rentals, see p. 215.)

Launching places along Charles River:

Riverside Recreation Area, Recreation Road, Newton area (Rt. 30, left at second traffic light after MDC police station near Marriott Hotel, go under railroad bridge, sharp left to Recreation Road.)

Red Wing, Needham (p. 217).

Kendrick Street, Neeham (on Newton Line)

Schaller Street off Washington Street (Rt. 16) on Wellesley-Dover-Natick Line.

Canoeing Guides:

A.M.C. New England Canoeing Guide, $7.75 postpaid, highly detailed and available from the Appalachian Mountain Club, 5 Joy Street, Boston 02108.

The Charles River Canoe Guide, $1.03, is published by the Charles River Watershed Association, 2391 Commonwealth Avenue, Auburndale 02116.

Clam Digging

Each coastal city and town has its own shellfish regulations. It is recommended that you check with town hall (e.g., Quincy) before digging—for license and contamination information. Nonresidents had best plan to make several trips before obtaining a season pass (only kind available) as the permit is frequently about $10 a person. The children could help and add excitement to the quest. Bring a strong back, digging fork, sneakers, and patience.

Farm Vacations

This kind of relatively inexpensive vacation is recommended for flexible families. Swimming may be on the property or a few miles down the road. Most offer little or no planned activity. Day trips are possible. Lunches may not be included. Home cooking is usually served. The "help" allowed with farm chores varies. Reservations strongly recommended. Suggested sources of farm information:

New Hampshire: Request information from Box 856, Concord, New Hampshire.

Vermont: Vermont Farm Vacation brochure compiled and published by Market Development Division, Vermont Department of Agriculture, Montpelier, Vermont 05602. Most places prefer families.

Publication: *Farm, Ranch and Countryside Guide*, 36 East 57th Street, New York, N.Y. 10022. It has details about old farmhouses, private cabins on farm properties, and places that are for children and teen-agers only. (And now it has added luxurious ranch resorts.) Current edition: $3.75 via book rate or $4.50 first-class mail. Published biennially; next edition January 1976, $4.25 book rate, $5 first class.

Fishing

Some basic information and a few suggestions:

SALTWATER FISHING

No licenses needed by individuals.

Deep-sea fishing excursions: See Index.

TWO MDC OCEAN PIERS:

CASTLE ISLAND—at the end of Day Boulevard, South Boston. A 250-foot public pier jutting out into the ocean. Less patient folk may watch fishermen and passing freighters from benches on the pier.

LYNN HARBOR—at the mouth of Saugus River, below General Edwards Bridge. A 435-foot bridge that projects from the Lynn shore.

FRESHWATER FISHING

Regulations: Licenses required age 15 and up. Available from city or town hall or directly from Division of Fisheries and Game, 100 Cambridge Street, Boston 02202, Tel. 727–3151.

Season: Late April-February.

Rates: Nonresidents, $14.25 for full season; $8.25 for 7-day license. Residents, $8.25; children 15–17, $6.25.

Publication: *Stocked Trout Waters in Massachusetts,* available free from Massachusetts Fish and Game Field Headquarters, Rt. 135, Westboro, Massachusetts 01581.

PONDS WITHIN A 10-MILE RADIUS OF BOSTON (stocked with trout): Horn Pond, Woburn; Upper Mystic Lake, Mystic Valley Parkway, Rt. 3, Winchester; Houghton's Pond in Blue Hills Reservation (p. 196); Whitman Pond in Weymouth. Jamaica Pond, Boston, has rowboats for rent (p. 216); call for license regulations.

QUABBIN RESERVOIR   Belchertown   413–323–6921

About 60 miles of tunnel connect Quabbin via Wachusett Reservoir to Boston.

Directions: Massachusetts Turnpike to Exit 8, north on Rt. 32 to intersection of Rt. 9 in town of Ware, turn left and go west on Rt. 9 toward town of Belchertown, about 4 miles to the MDC road on the right leading to the Administration Building.

Several mooring and fishing areas are designated on this huge beautiful reservoir. No rowboats under 12 feet allowed. No inboard motorboats, canoes, or collapsible boats allowed.

Season: April 15-October 15.

Fees: $1 per day for each person fishing from a private boat.

Rentals for Fishing: $4 per day or 60¢ per hour for outboard motor skiffs, $5 per day or 85¢ per hour for outboard motors (includes 3 gallons gasoline).

Parking: $1 per day per car when facilities used for shore fishing only.

DEEP-SEA FISHING

Boston Harbor Cruises   Long Wharf   Boston   Tel. 227–4320

Season: April-October. Leaves at 8 A.M.

Rates: Adults, $10; children under 12, $5, full charge on weekends. Family groups welcome. 1½ hours to fishing grounds. Bait supplied. Rods and reels for rent.

FISHING CAMP

It is not necessary to love the sport to be a guest at Woodrest, Box 85, Oakland, Maine 04963. But if you do, it is a good place to be. The Doucettes create a casual atmosphere, serve good home-cooked food, and provide cabins with Franklin stoves and a small dock with boats and swimming. Adults and entire families welcome. Three meals a day. Not too expensive. Reasonable children's rates. Tel. 207–465–7728.

Folk Dancing

Folk Dancing round Boston: Conny and Marianne Taylor, 62 Fottler Avenue, Lexington, Tel. 862–7144

Although there are several good leaders in the Boston area, the Taylors are considered by many as the deans of folk dancing in New England. They are the only local resource for the records they use; they issue a newsletter of all activities in the Greater Boston area ($1 for a year's subscription), and are available for a single program or a series. If you want information about ethnic groups or other leaders, they are a good clearinghouse.

They have regularly SCHEDULED PROGRAMS for beginners, inter-mediate, and advanced dancers. The Sunday afternoon FAMILY PROGRAM is for all ages—from the youngest, as long as they are walking, right up to the grandparents.

After 20 years in the same Cambridge location, the Taylors are about to make a change. Call for their current location and schedule.

Rates: Reasonable (usually under $2; student rates available).

Golf

(Check the Yellow Pages for full lists.)

MDC FACILITIES:

About a 2-hour wait on weekends.

SEASON: April 19-November 30, weekdays 7 A.M. until dark, weekends 6 A.M. until dark.

RATES: Weekdays, $3; Saturdays, Sundays, and holidays, $4. Rentals, $2 for golf clubs. Handcarts, $1. Gas carts—by the hour in Canton and by the course in Weston.

Lessons available by appointment. Memberships available.

Canton. Ponkapoag Golf Course on Rt. 138, near Rt. 128, Exit 64 north (if you have come from the expressway), south if you have come from the west. Tel. 828–0645. Pro Shop: 828–5828. Two 18-hole courses.

Weston. Leo J. Martin Memorial Golf Course on Park Road. Rt. 128, Rt. 30 exit, travel west on Rt. 30 to first left after traffic light onto Park Road. Tel. 894–4903. One 18-hole course.

CITY OF BOSTON FACILITIES:

Hyde Park. George Wright Golf Course   420 West Street   Tel. 361–0366

18-hole course open April-November.

RESIDENTS: Weekdays, $2.50; Saturdays, Sundays, holidays, $3; 5 o'clock, $2; nonresidents, double.

HOURS: Weekdays 8 A.M.–9 P.M.; weekends and holidays open at 6:30 A.M.

Dorchester. William J. Devine Golf Course   Franklin Park   Tel. 282–7524

9-hole course.

RATES: Monday-Friday: Residents, $2; nonresidents, $2.50; weekends and holidays: Residents, $2.50; nonresidents, $3.50; after 5 P.M., $1.50.

Hang Gliding

Because this is fairly new in the East—and due to the fascination of the sport—minimal information is included here. In no way is this intended as endorsement or encouragement! They say it is no more dangerous than downhill skiing, but it surely gives the appearance of being more hazardous.

A clearinghouse for information: New England Hang Gliding Association, P.O. Box 356, Stoughton, Massachusetts 02072. It will direct you to nearby dealers and/or flying schools in the area.

The association believes in proper training and practice. Flyers wear a harness attached to a motorless kitlike structure. They fly from a steep hill whose slope faces into the prevailing wind in order to obtain sufficient airspeed to become airborne. Costs vary from about $400–$600. Some schools have built a hang glider as a major interdisciplinary project.

Publication: *Sky Surfing Magazine* published by Man Flight Systems, P.O. Box 872, Worcester, Massachusetts 01613

Some slopes where you can usually see gliders: Nashoba Valley ski slopes, Littleton; Diamond Hill, Cumberland, Massachusetts; the dunes in Provincetown. They are in the air at the Jericho Hill Ski Area, Marlboro, every Saturday and Sunday.

Horses

HAY AND SLEIGH RIDES

North of Boston:

IPSWICH RIVER NATURE SANCTUARY   Perkins Row   Topsfield
Tel. 887–2241

Sleigh rides during January and February Saturdays and Sundays at 1, 2, and 3 P.M. Forty-five-minute ride. Reservations and prepayment required. $2 Audubon members, $3 nonmembers. Can hold 16 people.

PONDEROSA PINES RIDING CLUB   Pond Street, off Rt. 22   Essex Tel. 768–6669

Open year round. Sleigh and hay rides for 1–120 people. Up to 1½ hours. Down country roads, past fields, and along Chebacco Lake. $2 per person, $24 minimum. Picnic grove overlooks pond. Llamas and goats for children to see. Lodge with fireplace available to groups.

SILVER RANCH   Route 124   Jaffrey, New Hampshire (about 55 miles from Boston)   Tel. 1–603–532–7062

Sleigh rides, hayrides, and carriage drives. Can be given at night in winter. Usually able to accommodate transients. Rides given through the forest and fields of Silver Ranch.

Rates: Carriage drive: $10 for up to 3 persons; 20 minutes. Hay or sleigh rides in large groups: $2 per person. These are about an hour and can be followed by a country dance in their hall.

Eating: Drive-in restaurant on premises. Grounds to picnic on.

South of Boston:

APACHE RANCH   445 Old Fall River Road   North Dartmouth   Tel. 995–9866

Hayrides. One week's notice needed. Minimum: 20 people. Maximum: 40. Charge: $2.50 per person. A 2-hour ride on surrounding roads. Snack bar.

LAZY S STOCK FARM   300 Randolph Street   Canton   Tel. 828–1681

Hayrides. Maximum 30 to a wagon. Minimum $25 for wagon or $1 per person. Picnicking at nearby Houghton's Pond. Ride halfway around Ponkapoag Pond and back.

West of Boston:

ELLENDALE STABLES   Main Street   Sherborn   Tel. 653–0648

Sleigh and hay rides. Advance notice needed. Minimum: 20. Maximum: 70. One-hour ride. $2 each. Picnicking allowed. Hayrides on road; sleigh rides on trails. Hot chocolate arrangements in winter.

ELM BROOK FARM   Virginia Road   Concord   Tel. 369–7460

Sleigh and hay rides. One week's advance notice needed. Minimum $40. Maximum persons: 60. One-hour ride through woods and around farm.

HORSEBACK RIDING

Of those stables that offer sleigh and/or hay rides (see above), the following have horses for rent:

Apache Ranch, North Dartmouth. Horses $4 hour. Trails for riding.
Ellendale Stables, Sherborn. Horses $5.50 hour, $6.50 weekends and holidays. Indoor riding arena, outdoor pasture, and trails.

Elm Brook Farm, Concord. Horses for hire: $10 for lessons and trail riding.
Ponderosa Pines Riding Club, Essex. $4 hour. Wooded trails, old stagecoach
    roads that go around wilderness, lakes, and fields.
Silver Ranch, Jaffrey, New Hampshire. Horses $7 hour. Fifteen miles of trails.

For use in Blue Hills Reservation (p. 196):

Belliveau Riding Academy, Inc.   1244 Randolph Avenue   Milton
Tel. 698–9637
    Open 10–4 year round. Horses $5 hour.
Forest Hills Riding Stables   19 Lotus Street   Tel. 524–9739
    Open 9–8 year round. Horses and ponies $5 hour, $3 half hour.
The Paddock Stables   1010 Hillside Street   Tel. 698–1884
    Horses and ponies $6 hour. No charge for guide.

For use in Middlesex Fells Reservation (p. 189):

Medford Riding Academy   250 Woburn Street   Medford   Tel. 395–
9530
    Horses and ponies $5 hour. Open year round.

Pony Rides:

Lazy S Stock Farm   300 Randolph Street   Canton   Tel. 828–1681
    25¢ and 50¢.
The Paddock Stables   1010 Hillside Street   Milton   Tel. 698–1884

Hunter Safety School Program

Applications may be obtained from the Department of Natural Resources, Division of Law Enforcement, 100 Cambridge Street, Boston 02202, Tel. 727–3190. A series of 4–6 evening classes is held in the fall and spring for young men and women 15–18. There is no charge. Parent's consent needed. The location of classes varies, depending upon the concentration of applicants. In most cases students do not shoot a gun at all. Emphasis is placed on the handling of a gun and the right way to hunt.

Ice Skating

Note: It is popular! Check with a nearby rink for a quiet time for young children.

Local Suggestions: Ponds, flooded playgrounds, and tennis courts. "Special" in Boston: *Boston Public Garden* swan pond offers fairly hazardous conditions for a tradition. At this writing part of the *Boston Common Frog Pond* is being converted into an artificial ice-skating rink. With cooperative weather it may be open 4 months a year. Plans include a warming hut, floodlights, skating lessons, and Sunday morning curling clubs. Check with Boston Parks and Recreation, Tel. 722–4100.

Private Rinks: Check the Yellow Pages under "Skating Rinks—Ice."

. . . Almost all have lessons and public sessions.

. . . The schedules vary from season to season and year to year.

. . . Very few are limited to members.

. . . Most are open year round.

. . . The charges, particularly for children, are considerably more than MDC rinks.

. . . All are indoor rinks.

METROPOLITAN DISTRICT COMMISSION RINKS are used for school hockey at various times. The availability of skate rentals and lessons (individual and group) differ from rink to rink and year to year. Call for current information.

Season: Varies. Generally October-May for indoor rinks, November-March for others.

Hours: Call individual rinks for public sessions.

Rates: Adults, 50¢; children under 18, 10¢, except Sundays, evenings, and holidays, 25¢.

BRIGHTON-NEWTON: Nonantum Road, 527–1741

BRIGHTON-BROOKLINE: Cleveland Circle, 277–7822

CAMBRIDGE (indoor): Gore Street and 6th Street, 354–9523
    New Street near Fresh Pond Circle (under design)

CANTON (indoor): Blue Hills Reservation, Rt. 138 at Ponkapoag Golf Course, Tel. 828–9849

CHARLESTOWN: Rutherford Avenue, 242–9648

DORCHESTER: Garvey Playground, Morrissey Boulevard, 436–8755

EAST BOSTON (indoor): Constitution Beach, Orient Heights, 567–9571

EVERETT: Elm Street, near Glendale Square, 389–9401

HYDE PARK (indoor): Stony Brook Reservation, Turtle Pond Parkway, 364–9753

JAMAICA PLAIN: Jamaicaway at Brookline, 524–9700

LYNN (indoor): Shepard Street, 599–9474

MEDFORD (indoor): Veterans Memorial Parkway, 395–8433

MEDFORD-STONEHAM: Woodland Road, 395–9700

MILTON: Blue Hills Reservation, Unquity Road, 696–9869

NORTH END (under design): Commercial Street

QUINCY (indoor): Blue Hills Reservation, Willard Street, 472–9325

REVERE (indoor): Revere Beach Parkway, 284–9491

ROXBURY: Washington Street at Martin Luther King Jr. Boulevard, 445–9519

SAUGUS: Breakheart Reservation, Lynn Fells Parkway near Route 1, 233–9632

SOMERVILLE (indoor): Somerville Avenue, 623–9717

SOUTH BOSTON (indoor): Day Boulevard, 269–9401

WALTHAM (indoor): Totten Pond Road, 893–9409

WEST ROXBURY, Veterans of Foreign Wars Parkway, 323–9512

WEYMOUTH (indoor): Broad Street, 335–9454

ICE SKATING LESSONS

(They are offered for preschoolers through adults at most rinks.)

The following attract enrollment from a wide area:

METROPOLITAN FIGURE SKATING SCHOOL   21   Regent   Circle
Brookline

Weekly group lessons are held on weekends for boys and girls at 19 MDC rinks
in Greater Boston. The program is also offered at state rinks in Plymouth, Fall
River, Taunton, Franklin, and Marlboro. Enrollment is on a first-come, first-
served basis. Fee: $30. Held mid-November–February.

BOSTON SKATING CLUB GROUP FIGURE SKATING LESSONS   1240
Soldiers Field Road   Allston   Tel. 782–5900

All ages (toddlers to adults) are eligible for these lessons, under the direction
of Mrs. Marion Proctor. Groups are formed according to ability rather than age.
Preschoolers welcome on Saturdays only. Beginners should come on Saturday.

Season: Mid-October-April 1, Saturdays 2:30–4, Sundays 6–7:30.

Fees: $2 per lesson. This is a pay-as-you-go advance-as-you-go arrangement.
No membership necessary.

SPEED SKATING offered by Northeastern Skating Association. These lessons
are open to all interested boys and girls. Call the Charles Moores at 244–9332
for this year's schedule; they can also provide information about speed-skating
meets for registered amateurs as well as novices.

Season: Mid-December–mid-March at the Arlington MDC rink on Thursday
evenings.

Fees: $2 per lesson. Each session has instruction time and races.

Handicapped: Program usually conducted at the East Boston rink. Call 727–
5250 for information.

Mountain Climbing

A common sequence of preparation is to first try Blue Hill, p. 196, about an hour
or so round trip depending upon your route. Next time it is Mount Monadnock
in Jaffrey, New Hampshire (a four hour ride from Boston), and then it is an
overnight trip in the White Mountains.

Note: Mount Monadnock can be considered a full day's adventure (round trip).
It is the most climbed mountain in the United States and the largest in southern
New Hampshire. Hundreds of people enjoy the spectacular views on a nice
Saturday or Sunday, particularly in the spring or fall. Remember that coming
down can be much harder than going up; get an early start.

APPALACHIAN MOUNTAIN CLUB   5 Joy Street, Boston   Tel. 523–0636

The best source for information about guided trips, mountaineering school,
and annual mountain leadership workshop.

The Hut System: AMC has 9 hostelries located a day's hike apart in the White Mountains. The huts are manned by high school and college age staff who pack supplies on their backs to the huts, cook all the meals, and do the general caretaking. Hot meals served at 7 A.M. and 6 P.M. Memberships not necessary for use. Camp groups accepted along with other guests.

SEASON: Mid-June–early September, except Carter Notch and Mizpah Hut, which are open until mid-October. Reservations especially recommended for weekends.

RATES (include lodging, breakfast, and dinner): Adults, $12; children under 10, $6.50 per day. Paper sheets available for 25¢. Trail lunches, $1.25 per person.

RESERVATIONS: Should be made with Pinkham Notch Camp, Gorham, New Hanpshire, Tel. 603–466–3994.

Bunks, mattresses, pillows, and blankets provided in dormitories. Children old enough to make the trip and sleep through the night are welcome. Some huts have family rooms. Hikes range from 2–7 miles. Shortest ascent may take about 2 hours. All huts have plumbing. Gas lamps available for evening activities. Bring flashlights and warm clothing. Hiking boots or high sneakers suggested. Additional information available at Boston office.

Publications: *AMC White Mountain Guide, AMC Massachusetts-Rhode Island Guide, Mountain Flowers Guide of New England, AMC Maine Mountain Guide.* Available at the Boston office and many bookstores.

Orienteering

Contact: New England Orienteering Club. George Atkinson, 199 South Street, Hingham, Tel. 749–7652, or Hans Bengtsson, 102 Dutton Road, Sudbury, Tel. 443–8502.

Fees: 25¢–$1 at gatherings. Instruction is available to newcomers. Rental of compass fee: 25¢–50¢.

Minimum Age: Children under 10 should be with an adult.

Newsletter: Lists all meets. Free to organizations. $3 contribution requested from families and individuals.

Meets are very informal and instruction is always available. Families are particularly encouraged to try this recreational pastime that provides mental and physical activity.

Orienteering originated in Scandinavia. It combines map and running skills and can be competitive or done just for fun. A course could be set up in a local area by an organizer who places—in a wooded area—flags that designate points that everyone must pass. At each point there is a special stamp or punch to be used by the runner on his card. Runners are aware of the location (on a map) of these points. Aided by map and compass, individuals design their own course from marker to marker. The most direct route is not always the quickest. Competitors start at intervals, and the total time on the course is what counts. It is a sport that takes you into new terrain, provides a goal or destination, and gets you outdoors—and maybe into shape!

Parachuting

ORANGE PARACHUTING CENTER   Orange, Massachusetts   Tel. 544–6911

Directions: It is about 1½ hours from Boston within a mile of Rt. 2 or Rt. 202.

Open: Year round. Best times for observing: sunny weekends spring through fall.

Admission: Free for looking.

Visitors are welcome to observe experienced jumpers who free fall (first part of jump is with closed parachute) and students. If you want to have a closer look at the landing, 50¢ per person is charged for admission to that area. Rides in the jump aircraft ($5 per person for ½ hour) are available for those over 12. Fall considered a particularly colorful season for this activity. Minimum age for students: 16–18 (requires parental permission). Picnic tables provided.

Playgrounds

Check with City Hall or with MDC (p. 203) for the facilities in a particular area. If you are going on a company tour or planning a trip, this is one way to locate a picnic site or running place.

Two playgrounds that seem to attract families from many communities are:

BOSTON COMMON PLAYGROUND near the Frog Pond. Lots of climbing possibilities.

BRIGHTON: Charles J. Artesani Playground (across the road from WBZ at the prominent pedestrian bridge near Howard Johnson's), Soldiers Field Road, Tel. 782–2105

Equipment includes jungle gym tree, tunnels, as well as traditional slides and swings. Wading pool open when weather permits. Extensive picnic area with barbecue grills along the Charles River—with views of passing boats. Open space for kite flying. Very little shade in entire area. No admission charge. Playground is a fun place for the very young through 10 or 12. (Gate is locked late fall–mid-April.) Matrons are on duty 7 days a week June 1-Labor Day, 8 A.M.–8 P.M., and some days in spring and fall.

Roller Skating

For the few—but active—rinks in the Boston area, check the classified section of the telephone book. Most offer vacation schedules, lessons for children and adults, group rates, package rates for birthday parties, and mothers' weekday groups. The public sessions often vary from season to season. Here are some of the rinks that have shoe-skate rentals:

MEDFORD: BAL-A-ROUE   376 Mystic Avenue   Tel. 396–4589

Ⓣ**Stop:** West Medford bus from Sullivan Square.

Open: Year round. Public skating every night but Tuesdays and Thursdays starting at 7:30. Live music. Saturday sessions 1:30–4:30. Wednesday night is family night: $3 for whole family.

Admission: Mondays and Wednesdays, $2; weekends, $2.50; Saturday afternoons, $2.

NORTH DARTMOUTH: LINCOLN PARK (p. 206).

NORWOOD: ROLL-LAND SKATING RINK   Rt. 1   Tel. 762–6999

Open: September-May, Saturdays 10–12 A.M. for special children's session that includes skates and skating lessons for $1. Saturday and Sunday afternoon sessions September-May. Wednesday and Sunday evenings year round.
Admission: Afternoons, $1; evenings, $1.50. Skate rentals, 50¢. Group rates available.

QUINCY: DI MARZIO'S ROLLER RINK   1284 Sea Street   Tel. 472–9521

Open: September-June, Friday nights and Sunday afternoons (younger crowd).
Admission: $1 includes skates. Small rink. All sessions very well attended.

WALTHAM: WAL-LEX RECREATION CENTER   800 Lexington Street Tel. 894–1527

Open: Year round. Rates: Afternoons $1, evenings $1.50.
Rentals: 50¢. (A bowling alley and miniature golf course are in the complex. Some summer days there is a combination rate.)

WEYMOUTH: WEYMOUTH ROLLER SKATING RINK   979 Washington Street   Tel. 335–1590

Special feature is the well-attended Wednesday family night year round: Admission $3 for the whole family—up to 5 in number—includes skate rentals. Other public sessions: Wednesday-Sunday evenings. Admission: $1.25. Skate rentals 40¢. Weekend afternoons (September-June) $1. Skate rentals 50¢. Will open specially for groups on rainy days.

Sailing

Rentals (p. 216).   Harbor Cruises (p. 220).

Of particular note is this centrally located facility on the Charles River that offers everything to everyone at reasonable rates. (The junior program has to be the biggest bargain in town.)

COMMUNITY BOATING   21 Embankment Road   Tels. 523–1038, 523–8751, 523–9763

Ⓣ **Stop:** Charles, then a few minutes via pedestrian crossing over Storrow Drive.

Junior Sailing Programs: For youngsters age 11 (10 if there is an older sibling in the program)–17. Junior season: From the closing of the Boston schools until they open in the fall. Enrollment may take place anytime during the summer. A swimming certificate and parent's permission are required. Juniors have their own shore school, racing program, social program (outings and dances), and hours (Monday-Friday 9–3 and Saturdays 9–1). Only expense: $1 for season. Minimal fees for social program events.

Adult Membership Rates: Full season April 1-November 1, $55. Spring, $30; summer, $40; fall, $25; 30 days, $18.

SAILING INSTRUCTION

Many YACHT CLUBS, particularly those in Quincy Bay, have active junior programs for children as young as 8. If you are not a member, it may still be possible for your child to participate in the junior program. Call a club near you for its policy.

Through the METROPOLITAN DISTRICT COMMISSION two places offer instruction to youngsters only, ages 6–17, during the days and to adults in the early evening. It happens in the summer. There is no charge. The two locations:

Pleasure Bay, Day Boulevard, Castle Island, South Boston

Shore Drive, near Rt. 93, Mystic River, Somerville

No telephones. Just go and see what the present arrangement is. The season varies according to the funding.

COMMUNITY BOATING (see p. 235).

JAMAICA POND BOAT HOUSE   507 Jamaicaway   Jamaica Plain   Tel. 522–4944, has free sailing lessons for Boston residents 12–18 who can pass a swimming test. Register any time during the summer 9–5. Sailing takes place 9 A.M.–8 P.M. 7 days a week.

Skiing (Downhill)
ORGANIZATIONS

AMERICAN YOUTH HOSTELS   Greater Boston Council   251 Harvard Street, Brookline   Tel. 731–5430, has a full list of hostels used as ski lodges.

BLIZZARD SKI CLUB   22 Hillcrest Road   Weston 02193   Tel. 899–3451

The Boston area franchise of this national organization offers instruction, supervision, and transportation to members. Membership: $55 (less for additional siblings) plus $10–$12 for each Saturday trip, depending on where skiers ski. Trips: 10 Saturdays, weekends, and during vacation weeks. Ages: 8–12 junior program, 13–18 senior program. Beginner to expert.

MASSACHUSETTS JUNIOR SKI CLUB   1116 Great Plain Avenue Needham   Tel. 449–3074

Supervised ski trips, skiing instruction, and "just transportation" offered to members through this organization open to Greater Boston (Brockton to Burlington) youngsters aged 9–17. Racing team for those 13 and under. Transportation is by chartered bus from local areas. Enrollment takes place September-December. Locations vary according to interests and abilities. Lessons are not required. Finances: $45 membership fee. Trips are about $11 or $12 each (includes bus and lift ticket).

SOME NEARBY SKI AREAS

BLUE HILLS SKI AREA   14 miles from Boston   Canton   Tel. 828–5070

Directions: Southeast Expressway to 128 west to Exit 64, Rt. 138 north to ski area.

Facilities: Double chair lift, 2 J-bars, 2 rope tows, 3 trails, 2 slopes.

Rates: Weekdays, $4.75; weekends, $6.50; night skiing. Snow making.

BOSTON HILL   22 miles from Boston   North Andover   Tel. 683–2733

Directions: Rt. 1 north, Rt. 114W to area.

Facilities: 1 trail, 5 slopes, 1 double chair lift, and 3 rope tows. Snow making.

Rates: Weekdays: Adults, $5; children, $3.50; weekends: Adults, $6.50; children, $4.

NASHOBA VALLEY SKI AREA   between Rts. 2a and 110 on Power Road   Westford   Tel. 692–7025

Directions: 5 miles from Concord Circle on Rt. 2a.

Facilities: 7 slopes, 1 trail, 1 T-bar, 7 ropes.

Rates: Weekdays: Adults, $4; children 12 and under, $3; $1 more on weekends and holidays. Half day tickets available.

PROSPECT HILL SKI AREA   Rt. 128 Winter Street exit   Waltham   Tel. 893–4837

Facilities: 2 expert trails, beginners' slope, 1 T-bar.

Rates: Differ according to residency, hours (morning, afternoon, evening), and age. Call for this season's arrangements.

WARD HILL   Old Post Road   Shrewsbury   Tel. 842–6346

Facilities: 3 slopes, 2 trails, 2 T-bars, 2 ropes.

Rates: Weekdays: Adults, $4; children under 12, $3; $1 more on weekends; nights, $3.50.

SKIING INFORMATION

Note that 800 indicates a toll-free number.
Within a 2-hour drive there are many areas
to choose from. (Mount Sunapee and King
Ridge are about 90 minutes away.)

There are several Boston snow phones to call for areas throughout New England. The only personal service is the ELLIS SKI INFORMATION CENTER, Tel. 1–800–243–6600, offered 24 hours a day, 7 days a week November-April. The available information is changed twice daily and applies to those areas that subscribe to the service. Details are provided about an area (night skiing, arranged baby-sitting, established nurseries, ice skating, skidoos, tobogganing) as well as snow conditions.

New Hampshire Information:
New Hampshire Ski Report Phones:
    Attitash, 1–800–258–0316

Gunstock, 1–800–258–8902
King Ridge, 267–7474
Mount Sunapee, 338–6922
Pat's Peak, 1–800–243–6600
Tyrol, 1–800–243–6600
Wildcat, 267–4800
Wilderness at the Balsams, 227–8288

New Hampshire state area rates: Cannon and Sunapee: weekends and holidays: Adults, $9; children 14 and under, $6; weekdays: Adults, $7; children 14 and under, $5.

Vermont Information:

Killington, 1–800–451–4276
Lodging, 1–800–451–4205
Stowe, 1–800–451–3260

SKI CAMPS

Most ski camps bus Boston-area youngsters to a lodge on weekends or during school vacation weeks. Frontenac and Mount Pero have their own tows and facilities at the lodge; others use nearby ski areas for instruction. For the current age range (about 9–16), prices, and schedules, contact:

AGAWAM KEZAR, RFD, Lovell, Maine 04051
Contact: David W. Mason, Tel. 207–925–3883
FRONTENAC SKI CAMP, Plymouth, New Hampshire 03264
Tel. 603–536–1652. Local contact: George C. Greer,
30 Beachview Avenue, Malden 02148
MOUNT PERO SKI CAMP, Plymouth, New Hampshire 03264
OTIS RIDGE JUNIOR SKI CAMP, Otis Ridge, Otis, Massachusetts 01253
SNOWBIRD LODGE, Harrison, Maine 04040 (limited to girls 12–18).
Contact: Dorothy F. Mason, Fortunes Rocks, Biddeford, Maine 04005

INDOOR INSTRUCTION

BOB JOHNSON'S SKI CENTER   45 Hollis Street (Hollis Theater Building)
Framingham 01701   Tel. 875–4343

The largest indoor ski school in the country has a slide that is 7,000 square feet. Classes are held September-March. Minimum age: 7.

Lessons: 3 hours each. All equipment included in rates: Children, 7–15, $17.50 for 6 hours, $27 for 9 hours; adults, $35 for 9 hours.

Skiing (Cross-country)

WHERE TO GO

In the Boston Area: Almost anywhere. That is one of the many joys of the sport. Many of the open space areas (pp. 185–200) and golf courses (p. 227) are commonly used. No waiting lines.

Up North: Many ski resorts have rental facilities. At most areas rentals of skis, boots, poles, and bindings average $7 per day with lower rates for multiple day use. Many operations that maintain trails charge a moderate trail maintenance fee for those who are not renting equipment or participating in clinics. These fees, usually about $1 per person, help to offset the costs of repairing and maintaining trails.

LOCAL ARRANGEMENTS

You do not have to rent skis and carry them to a site. Possibilities exist for renting them locally where there is a track and/or trails.

LINCOLN GUIDE SERVICE has two locations.
Equipment rental: $3.50 for 3½ hours.
Group lessons (1 hour) $3.50.

Lincoln Center: Tel. 259–9204. Location uses nearby town conservation lands.

Leo J. Martin Golf Course: Tel. 894–4903, is in Weston on Park Road between Rts. 16 and 30 at Rt. 128. It is a short walk from the Riverside stop of Riverside (Green) Line of Ⓣ.
This is a new center where you can learn to ski on a maintained track (thanks to a snow-making machine and track equipment). On good snow days there is a system of trails throughout the golf course and marked trails on other MDC properties and public lands. Instruction and guiding are major parts of the program.
USE OF GROOMED TRAILS: $2.

PONKAPOAG GOLF CLUB   Blue Hills Reservation   Canton   Tel. 828–0645   (No charge if you just want to use the course.) Lessons offered. A good place for varied interests: You are at an MDC skating rink, p. 231, and a fantastic sledding and tobogganing area.

PONKAPOAG OUTDOOR CENTER (p. 245) has instruction-rental combinations by the half or full day.

RENTALS

A good way to try this invigorating sport is to rent equipment—at least for the first time. Rentals are available at many sports centers including Eastern Mountain Sports, 1041 Commonwealth Avenue, Brighton; Back Country Shop, 50 Boylston Street, Cambridge (Harvard Square); Wilderness House, 117 Brighton Avenue, Brighton. Many of these shops also have weekly winter clinics.

DAY TRIPS AND CLINICS

Often held by American Youth Hostels, p. 213, the Sierra Club, p. 204, the Appalachian Mountain Club, p. 200, the Lincoln Guide Service (above), and the Cambridge Sports Union, p. 245. (See also rentals, above.)

Snowmobiling

For areas where it is allowed, check with the Metropolitan District Commission (p. 203) and the Massachusetts Division of Marine and Recreational Vehicles, 64 Causeway Street, Boston 02114, Tel. 727–3900.

Spectator Sports (Professional)

Final major league results are available 24 hours a
day on a special *Boston Globe* telephone number: 338–6600.

Tickets for any of the games should be sent for several weeks in advance. No
telephone reservations are accepted.

BASEBALL
BOSTON RED SOX   Ticket Office: 24 Jersey Street   Boston 02215   Tel.
267–2525

Ⓣ **Stop:** Fenway on Green Line.

Season: April-October.

Tickets: $3.50-$4.50.

Specials: Several designated youth games for 10 children or more under age 15,
50¢ when chaperoned. Make advance arrangements.

BASKETBALL
BOSTON CELTICS   North Station   Boston   Tel. 523–6050
Games played in Boston Garden. Ⓣ **Stop:**   North   Station   on   Green   Line.

Season: October-March. Played evenings only until the first of the year, then
there are games Sunday afternoons.

Group Rates: Available for some games. Special promotional days with give-
aways for children under 14 are held a few times during the season.

Tickets: $3–$8.

FOOTBALL
NEW ENGLAND PATRIOTS   Schaefer Stadium (about 25 miles south of
Boston) Foxboro, Massachusetts 02035   Tel. 262–1776 (Boston number)

Season: Preseason in August Sunday evenings. Home games Sunday afternoons September–mid-December.

Tickets: $5–$8.

HOCKEY
BOSTON BRUINS   150 Causeway Street   Boston 02214   Tel 227–3206
National Hockey League team. Games played in Boston Garden.

Ⓣ **Stop:** North Station on Green Line.

Season: October-March with home games mostly Thursday and Sunday evenings.

Tickets: $5–$9. No season tickets. No group rates.

LACROSSE
BOSTON BOLTS   121 Newbury Street   Boston 02116   Tel. 262–1665

Season: Begins in April. Games played at Boston Garden.

Tickets: $3.50–$6.50.

SOCCER

BOSTON MINUTEMEN   1 Boston Place   Boston 02108   Tel. 227–8520

Games played at Boston College Alumni Stadium. Ⓣ **Stop:** Boston College on Green Line.

Preseason tournament held at Boston Garden in winter. Outdoor season: May–August.

Tickets: $1–$4. Special youth day with autographs. Group rates available.

BOSTON ASTROS   739 Boylston Street   Boston 02116   Tel. 262–2807
Season: May-September.

Games played at Boston University Nickerson Field. Ⓣ **Stop:** Armory on Boston College-Commonwealth Green Line.

Tickets: $1–$3. Group rates available.

TENNIS

BOSTON LOBSTERS   1300 Soldiers Field Road   Boston 02134   Tel. 783–2110

Season: May-August.

Games played at Boston University Walter Brown Arena. Ⓣ **Stop:** Babcock Street on Boston College-Commonwealth Car (Green Line).

Tickets: $2–$6. Special racquet and T-shirt nights for youngsters. Group rates available.

Square Dancing

Although most square dance groups are for adults, there are others offered through Ys and community centers. Kramer's Hayloft in South Weymouth regularly has western square dancing for children. Many of the adult groups are progressive and require a commitment. The clearinghouse for information is the monthly publication *New England Dance Caller Magazine*, P.O. Box NC, 80 Central Street, Norwell, Massachusetts 02061. Editor Charles Baldwin, Tel. 659–7722, would be happy to help with any questions. New England square dancing resources are available from the Taylors (p. 227).

Swimming

(Beach information is on p. 208.)

Lessons: Try the Ys, Girls and Boys Clubs, and community pools. During the summer many communities have lessons at local beaches or ponds.

Preschool Lessons: Water-Babies programs for those as young as 6 months are given at several Ys (e.g., Boston, Dorchester, Natick). Adjustment to the water rather than perfection is the goal.

Handicapped: Programs offered at several MDC pools. Call 727–5250 for information.

MDC SWIMMING AND WADING POOLS (all outdoors except Weymouth):

Admission: Adults, 25¢; children 18 and under, 10¢.

BRIGHTON: North Beacon Street, Tel. 254–2965

BRIGHTON-BROOKLINE: Cleveland Circle (no wading pool), Tel. 277–7822

CAMBRIDGE: Alewife Brook Parkway and Rindge Avenue, Tel. 354–9154
Memorial Drive at Magazine Beach, Tel. 354–9381

CHELSEA: Carter Street, near Chelsea Stadium (no wading pool), Tel. 884–9846

DORCHESTER: Blue Hill and Talbot avenues, Tel. 436–9080

EVERETT: Elm Street near Glendale Square, Tel. 389–9401

HYDE PARK: Stony Brook Reservation, Turtle Pond Parkway, Tel. 364–9683

MALDEN: Mountain Avenue, Tel. 324–9350

MELROSE: Tremont Street, Tel. 662–5229

ROXBURY: Washington Street at Martin Luther King Jr. Boulevard (no wading pool), Tel. 445–9519

SOMERVILLE: Alewife Brook Parkway, Tel. 623–9141
Foss Park, McGrath Highway at Broadway, Tel. 623–9174

STONEHAM: Rt. 28 at North Border Road, Tel. 438–9888

WALTHAM: River and Newton streets, Tel. 899–0106

WATERTOWN: Pleasant Street, Tel. 923–0073

WEST ROXBURY: VFW Parkway, Tel. 323–9512

WEYMOUTH: Broad Street, Tel. 335–9454 (open year round, enclosed)

Tennis

COURTS

MDC courts are available on a first-come, first-served basis. The only exception is Charlesbank in the West End; permits for that facility have to be picked up at 20 Somerset Street.

Locations:

BELMONT: Beaver Brook Reservation
DEDHAM: Riverdale Park, Bridge Street, Ryan Playground
EVERETT: Recreation Center, Elm Street
HYDE PARK: Martini Music Shell, Truman Highway
MATTAPAN: River Street
MILTON: Houghton's Pond, Blue Hills Reservation
NAHANT: Nahant Beach
READVILLE: Meigs Playground, Stanbro Street
SOMERVILLE: Dilboy Field, Alewife Brook Parkway
WEST END: Charlesbank Park

The **City of Boston** maintains 64 tennis courts. Call the Recreation Department, 722–4100, ext. 145, for information about arrangements and free lessons given throughout the city year round.

Check with local recreation department for arrangements in other communities.

The Boston Common courts (2) are available April-December (weather permitting) 8 A.M.–10:30 or 11 P.M. Summer permits for 1 hour are issued at the courts. Spring and fall it is first come, first served.

Indoor Courts: Check with local recreation department. In the Yellow Pages of the telephone book ("Tennis Courts—Public") you will find places that rent court time to other than season members. Many also offer lessons to several age groups.

ORGANIZATIONS

SPORTSMEN'S TENNIS CLUB   950 Blue Hill Avenue   Dorchester
Tel. 288–9092

This is a private, nonprofit organization that gives free tennis instruction to Boston youngsters ages 7–17. Its facility, the Franklin Field Tennis Center, has 14 indoor courts, 8 outdoor courts, and 2 double-sided bangboards. The young people's summer program runs from June-September 9–5, October-May 3–6 P.M.

YOUTH TENNIS FOUNDATION OF NEW ENGLAND   Mrs. R. M. Patrick, Secretary   94 Arlington Street   Winchester, Massachusetts 01890

This, the fund-raising, tax-deductible arm of the New England Lawn Tennis Association, helps to promote the growth of amateur tennis by working with and counseling groups. It is always available with help on programs and, in rare instances, can give financial support. Please write if you wish to inquire about assistance.

Tobogganing and Sledding

Boston and its surrounding areas have many slopes used for tobogganing, and some communities have their own toboggan run.

If your immediate area does not have steep enough, traffic-free areas, there are slopes on golf courses in Hyde Park, Franklin Park, Larz Anderson Park in Brookline, The Sheepfold in Stoneham, Ponkapoag Golf Course in Canton, and more. (Check Open Space, p. 183.)

Organizations

(Resources, Activities, Facilities)

INFORMATION

HANDICAPPED   Many communities offer programs for children with special needs.

LOCAL RECREATION DEPARTMENTS   Lists of all local recreational facilities may be available from the Recreation Department of your community or from a local guide and telephone directory. The Boston Recreation Department can be reached at 722–4100.

METROPOLITAN DISTRICT COMMISSION   20 Somerset Street   Boston 02108   Tel. 727–5250, publishes a brochure with all recreation facilities. No charge.

THE LEAGUE OF WOMEN VOTERS OF MASSACHUSETTS   120 Boylston Street   Boston   Tel. 357–8380, has a list of communities that have made a local recreation study; reports are often obtained for the price of postage.

ORGANIZATIONS

Recreational and cultural activities take place in many community centers, Ys, and clubs. In addition to opportunities for individuals, there are family fun sessions, bowling, swimming, and games.

An example of programs that may be duplicated elsewhere:
THE YMCA   316 Huntington Avenue   Boston, Tel. 536–7800, has a youth program for ages 8–17 and provides special interest clubs, 5 gymnasiums, swimming, bowling, special trips, and a summer program at the Y.

AMERICAN YOUTH HOSTELS, INC. (p. 213).

APPALACHIAN MOUNTAIN CLUB   5 Joy Street   Boston   Tel. 523–0636

Activities include snowshoeing, skiing, smooth and white-water canoeing, and rock climbing. Programs of instruction in all these sports are offered for beginners and leaders. The club conducts a great variety of outings, excursions, and charters. (See p. 200 for general information.)

AMC FACILITIES OPEN TO ANYONE

Huts (p. 233).

Cardigan Lodge   Alexandria, New Hampshire (lakes region, 10 miles from Bristol). Open in summer and on fall weekends. Has semiprivate, private, and bunk rooms, 2-person platform tents in nearby woods, and some camp sites available. Five miles of careful driving off main road. Weekly rate: $81. Some camp sites available at $3–$4 per night plus charge per child over 3; campers have optional meal arrangement—be served or cook your own. Special rates for camps, school groups, and other organized groups.

Pinkham Notch at Mount Washington, open year round, provides lodging and meals (half price for children under 10 accompanied by parents). Adults: About $12 per night includes 2 meals. Rates vary according to arrangements.

CONTACT THE BOSTON AMC OFFICE FOR RATES (REASONABLE) ON:

Cold River Camp: North Chatham, New Hampshire. Family double and single cabins, canoe rental, tennis courts, square dancing. Hiking and lodging from June–September.

Echo Lake Camp: Mt. Desert Island, Maine. Eight-week season. Tents with beds, furnishings, and linen provided. Meals served. Rare combination of good mountains and pounding surf. Organized program (boat trips, mountain climbing, lobster cookouts) offered. Minimum age: 3.

Ponkapoag Camp: Located in the Blue Hills Reservation, Canton. Cabins for rent by the day, week, and month from Memorial Day-early September. Meals served in The Lodge weekends in May-late June and daily thereafter until Labor Day. Toddlers' pool, swimmers' floats, and fireplaces and tables for cookouts.

Three Mile Island Camp: Lake Winnipesaukee, New Hampshire. Nine-week season. Screened cabins. Some tents. Water activities galore. No telephone. No organized trips or programs. Served meals. Minimum age for children: 4.

Wonalancet Cabin: Tamworth, New Hampshire. A do-it-yourself site used as a base camp for nearby areas. No employees or staff.

BOSTON YWCA VACATION FACILITIES

The Boston YWCA   140 Clarendon Street   Boston   Tel. 536–7940, has two facilities that are open to the public. The Rockport Barn in Rockport, Massachusetts, can accommodate up to 12 and is open May-October. Camp Blazing Trail in Denmark, Maine, has heated cabins that are generally available September-May. Reasonable rates. Booked early.

CAMBRIDGE SPORTS UNION   23 Fayette Street   Cambridge   Tel. 868–7416

This sports club focuses mainly on competitive activities, although some participants are not competitively oriented. The principal interests at the moment are cross-country skiing, running, and orienteering. Participants find that—through exposure—they may be more likely to try more than the one sport they originally had an interest in.

Ages: No minimum (or maximum) for participation.

Membership: (Not necessary for most activities. Competitions and clinics usually open to anyone.) Adults, $5; children 18 and under, $3.50. Family, $7. Monthly newsletter distributed.

PONKAPOAG OUTDOOR CENTER   Blue Hills Reservation   Canton   Tel. 696–4520

Office Hours: Monday-Friday, 8–4:30.

This is a year-round, multipurpose facility operated by the Greater Boston YMCA. It is located just 12 miles from downtown Boston. Facilities include heated family and dormitory units, dining lodge, nature craft center, stable, pool, sugar shack, and miles of trails for hiking, riding and cross-country skiing.

It offers programs—in just about every conceivable combination—for people to get away from it all. WEEKEND RECREATION is offered year round to families, groups, and individuals. Instruction, lodging, and meals provided. Programs vary according to season. A special weekend camp is held for children only.

School Vacation Camps: For 8–13-year-olds; held fall, winter, and spring.

Outdoor Education Programs: Conducted with school groups.

Summer Programs: Include day and overnight camps. Various possibilities for ages 7–16. Some family backpacking trips.

Membership: Not necessary for registration in any of the many programs open to the public. Members are offered special programs, demonstrations, clinics (from bicycle repair to orienteering), and use of pool and other facilities.

SIERRA CLUB (p. 204).

TOURS AND VISITS

. . . Extensive research has resulted in this exclusive list. Please observe the restrictions and provide more than enough supervision.

. . . All suggestions are a public-relations service. There is no charge.

. . . Many of the listings do not offer a formal tour service, but are happy to show you their activity.

. . . If the day is just right for an inside visit, and plans have not been prearranged, call to see if your family may join some expected organized group. But please note the minimum age; it may denote interest level.

. . . Group leaders find that the benefits are always greater with orientation and follow-up projects.

. . . If parents supervise a group, it may be best if they do not bring younger siblings.

. . . Often the guide makes a difference. If you do not happen to have someone who gives an adequate explanation, try to ask questions and explain details to the children. This is particularly important for those "at the end of the line."

. . . Some tours (visits) are geared for those with a particular interest. If you are looking for "something to do," please shy away from those.

. . . If you suggested a place and find it among the missing, it is likely that they have occasional arrangements and preferred to have their name unpublished.

. . . If you have a specific interest, check the Yellow Pages of the telephone book, call and speak to the public-relations department. If they have not been deluged with recent requests, they may take on a vocationally oriented group.

. . . Check tour information in other chapters: Animals, Day Trips, Historic Sites and Exhibits, Museums.

Local Suggestions

. . . For almost any age, but particularly for those who would like suggestions for young children. (Please check safety regulations and double-check on maximum number allowed.)

. . . Make an appointment.

ARCHITECT'S OFFICE. An awareness of space and how to use it.

BAKERY. Make your own before you visit. *Note:* They start early in the day.

BUS RIDE (for young children). Let child pull the cord to signify stop.

CANDY HOUSE. One-man, small, local, and delicious smelling.

CAR WASH. Some may let children sit in car surrounded outside by suds.

CLEANING PLANT AND LAUNDRY (particularly one that has a shirt presser).

CONSTRUCTION PROJECT (hard-hat industry).

CRAFTS PEOPLE (with a home studio).

DAIRY. Find out when they milk the cows.

DOUGHNUT SHOP. Watch the hole, too.

FARM. If you can find a pick-your-own roadside stand, the children may be able to join in.

FAST-FOOD PLACES. They often include samples.

FIRE STATION. Sleeping quarters, communications system, the engines and their necessary gadgets, explanation of gear—some nursery school groups have found this exciting; others have reported that an alarm has made it a frightening experience.

GREENHOUSE. Buy a plant or bring home seeds.

HOSPITAL. Particularly recommended for a youngster about to enter. Will they show an X-ray reading?

KENNEL. Will they show you a dog having a bath or being clipped?

LIBRARY. Do they have special programs for children?

LOCAL NEWSPAPER. Do they go to press weekly?

LUMBERYARD. Maybe take home some odd piece from the scrap barrel.

PET SHOP. Difficult to plan just a visit and not a shopping trip.

PHOTOGRAPHY WORKSHOP OR STUDIO. Shows the various processes involved.

POLICE DEPARTMENT. The main station and its responsibilities. Do they have a dog officer?

POST OFFICE. Activity may be greatest in the morning, but personnel may not be available then.

PRINTING PLANT. When do the presses roll?

RADIO STATION. Where does the voice come from?

SAVINGS BANK. What happens to deposited money . . . How is it recorded . . . A coin counter demonstration . . .

THEATRE. Backstage is the most revealing.

Places

ASHWAY FARM   Thornton Street (about 1 mile from Southwick Animal Farm, p. 45)   Mendon (west of Boston, via Rt. 16)   Tel. 473–6812

Tours: By arrangement only. May-November, 11–5.

Take a field tour and see the cattle, calves, and barns. If you are there about 4 in the afternoon, you can see milking time on the farm.

BOSTON CITY HALL   One City Hall Plaza   Government Center   Boston 02201   Tel. 722–4100

Ⓣ **Stop:** Government Center on Green Line.

Tours: Year round, Monday-Friday 10–4.

The guides give you a feeling of enjoying their work as they talk about the historical significance of the architecture (ramps represent lanes, concrete and brick represent the mixture of the old and new). On the fifth floor is the mayor's office facing Faneuil Hall, the council chambers with public galleries, and the main art gallery. Vistas of old and new Boston are available from the many windows throughout the building. The architecturally controversial structure has offices surrounding a huge inner court.

Perhaps an explanation of what makes a city government work—licensing, registry of births, deaths and marriages, the retirement board, treasurer, assessor, and many more—would be more meaningful if children saw and possibly met the "real people."

It is an interesting ½-hour tour that can be appreciated by all ages. Many natives are unaware of this free service, as well as the information and perspective shared by the guides. Go!

BOSTON EDISON COMPANY   Mystic Station Power Plant   Everett   Tel. 424–2460

Contact: Joseph G. Lannan.

Tours: Offered year round, Monday-Friday, by appointment made at least 10 days in advance.

Minimum Age: 13

Minimum Number: 10–15.

Length: 1 hour.

Visitors see the production of electricity from fuel to finished "product." You tour the boiler facilities, turbines, environmental control equipment and facilities, main control room, and the electrical operation control room.
Note: Boston Edison has films and speakers for various age groups.

BOSTON GLOBE   135 Wm. T. Morrissey Blvd.   Dorchester 02107   Tel. 929–2653

Ⓣ **Stop:** Columbia Station (10-minute walk) on Red Line.

Directions: Exit 17 on Southeast Expressway.

Tours: Monday-Friday, year round, by arrangement only.

Minimum Age: At least junior high school.

Length of Tour: 45 minutes.

See the editorial staff at work, reporters coming, going, and writing, the news machines clicking with items of the moment, the composing room where the type is set, the photoengravings made from the negatives, and the mats and plates being made. Then the plates are put onto the presses. The presses are usually running during the day; hours vary. It may be possible to see the printing of a section that is in the edition on the newsstands when the children arrive home.

BOSTON PUBLIC LIBRARY   Copley Square   Boston 02117   Tel. 536–5400

ⓉStop: Copley (you are there) on Green Line.

Tours: 1 hour. Offered year round, Monday-Friday 9–12 and 2–5, by arrangement only. Two weeks' notice required. Written requests, please.

Minimum Age: For children in the 8th grade or below, requests for tours and special events should be directed to Mrs. Cullinane, children's librarian.

Open one of the bronze doors sculptured by Daniel Chester French and enter the main vestibule with its marble inlaid floor and marble mosaic ceiling bearing the names of famous Bostonians. Before you is the magnificent main staircase made of marble mottled with fossil shells. Built in 1895, this is now a National Historic Site for its architecture and art objects. You see murals, statues, paintings, prints, and dioramas as you walk from hall to hall. If a group is interested in a particular area of literature or fine arts, a tour can be planned to show how the facilities of different rooms are used. The microtext room would be included. (Please see p. 272 for regular hours, borrowing privileges, and other suggestions.)

The pamphlet *A Casual Tour* gives a preview of the art and architectural details. Request copies when you make an appointment.

BOSTON STOCK EXCHANGE   Exchange Building   53 State Street (corner Congress)   Boston 02109   Tel. 723–9500

Contact: Gay Spiegel.

ⓉStop: Government Center (Green and Blue Lines) or State (Blue and Orange Lines).

Guided Tours: Year round, Monday-Friday 10–2, by arrangement only, at least a week in advance.

Minimum Age: Juniors in high school.

You are welcome to stop in to see the bustling activity on the small exchange trading floor where securities are bought and sold. Some companies are listed exclusively here, others are dually listed in Boston and New York. If arrangements have been made for groups, a guide will explain seats on the Exchange, how the price is determined, who is doing what (with phones and tape reading), and the role of the Boston Stock Exchange.

BRATTLE BOOK SHOP   5 West Street (between Tremont and Washington, ½ block from Boston Common)   Tel. 542–0210

Contact: George Gloss.

Ⓣ **Stop:** Washington, Essex, Boylston, Park.

Minimum Age: 1–100.

Minimum Number Required: 1.

Length of Tour: "At least half an hour—or a lifetime."

Visits with Comments Offered: Monday-Saturday 9–12, 1:45–5:45. Groups should avoid the noonday rush. Those in groups may make purchases at 10 percent discount.

Although you may locate several used bookstores that are grand for browsing, only this one, the oldest continuous antiquarian book shop in America, has George Gloss as proprietor. He describes what you will see: "Five floors of beautiful books, prints, music, magazines, records, postcards, autographs, pamphlets, newspapers, 350,000 books, underground tunnels—many curiosities, especially GG!"

Groups are given an idea of what is where—and then you are on your own. Go when you are not on a schedule. It is all right if your child sits on the floor and becomes engrossed in some publication. And perhaps an inexpensive treasure will be found. Leaflets about the bookshop are given freely to visitors.

BRIGHAM'S CANDY PLANT   4 Alger Street   South Boston   Tel. 269–8195

Ⓣ **Stop:** Andrew (5-minute walk) on Red Line.

Tours: September-June, Monday-Friday 10:30–11:30, 12:30–1:30 by appointment only.

Minimum Age: 6.

Minimum Number: 4.

Maximum Number: 25.

Don a junior candy-maker hat and you are off for one of the tastiest tours in town. See and smell the ingredients as they are mixed in enormous kettles. "Center" ingredients are deposited into preformed starch molds for overnight hardening and then removed for chocolate covering. Fudge is poured into pans and hard candy centers go from the kitchen on a cooling conveyor to the packing area. The taffy puller has many twisting arms. It is a delicious experience.

BRIGHAM'S ICE CREAM   30 Mill Street   Arlington   Tel. 648–9000

Ⓣ **Stop:** Central Street on Arlington Heights bus line from Harvard Square.

Directions: Rt. 2 to Rt. 60. Left on Massachusetts Avenue. Right at first set of lights, second left into parking lot.

Tours: Year round by appointment only, Tuesdays, Wednesdays, and Thursdays at 10 A.M. One month's advance notice requested.

Minimum Age: 6.

Minimum Number: 10.

Length of Tour: 45 minutes.

Start at the receiving docks, then see the pipes and equipment that prepare the mix before it goes into a holding tank. (There is no way to see inside.) The mix gets some flavor before it experiences the fruit and nut feeder (you hear that!). You see the filling of 5-gallon containers, which are put into a hardening room (−20°). Visitors are offered the treat of tasting fresh ice cream that has not been hardened.

CHRISTIAN SCIENCE CENTER   Boston   Tel. 262–2300

Ⓣ **Stop:** Symphony or Prudential.

Mapparium and reflecting pool, p. 265.
Christian Science Publishing Society   One Norway Street

Contact: Hostess, ext. 2426.

Tours: Year round, Monday-Friday, except holidays. Offered several times daily starting at 9:30 A.M. Contact hostess for other tour times.

Groups: Requested to make an appointment, preferably a week in advance. *Maximum Number:* 25, but several groups can follow each other through.

Length of Tour: 30 minutes.

Minimum Age for Groups: 12. Young children in family groups are welcome. (Although the presses will fascinate younger members of the family, the tour is not really geared to them.)

Guides explain the procedures involved in publishing the *Christian Science Monitor,* as well as periodicals of the First Church of Christ Scientist. Among the departments you are taken through are the newsroom, pressroom, composing and advertising rooms. The Mapparium (p. 265) is part of the tour.

THE MOTHER CHURCH OF THE FIRST CHURCH OF CHRIST SCIENTIST

Tours: Monday-Friday 10–5, Saturdays and Sundays 12–5. None given on Christmas and holidays.

It is a ½-hour tour with the focus on the architecture of this Romanesque edifice, which has carved stone walls, stained glass windows, and a mosaic floor. The domed extension is without any supporting columns to obstruct one's view. The organ with 13,389 pipes is one of the largest in the Western Hemisphere. A new stone-carved portico has been added to provide a magnificent entrance from Massachusetts Avenue.

JOHN DONNELLY & SONS   3134 Washington Street   Boston   Tel. 522–8800

Contact: Community Relations Department.

Ⓣ **Stop:** Egleston Square on Orange Line, 1-block walk.

Tours: Monday-Friday 10–2 by arrangement only.

Minimum Age: 12.

Maximum Number Allowed: 10.

Length of Tour: 2 hours.

Orientation is with a ½-hour film or slide presentation, which gives the background of outdoor advertising. You then see how a poster is created in the art department and follow it to the bill room to watch the pieces (eventually mounted outside in puzzle fashion) being collated for proper placement. Each piece is glued and folded into an airtight bag.

Transportation is provided to the paint shop 3 miles away to see the process of scaled artwork: From an opaque projector the image is aimed at a white papered wall to give an idea of the finished look. After the projected image is drawn onto the paper, it is put onto a table for diamond wheel cutting. Holes are punched around the lines, a template is put onto the face; it is chalk-powdered before the template is removed. The dots are connected, and the paper is painted.

FISHER JUNIOR COLLEGE   118 Beacon Street   Boston   Tel. 262–3240

Tours: For groups Monday-Friday. Please make advance arrangements. Individuals may stop in.

Length of Tour: 10–45 minutes, depending upon interest of visitors.

Here is an opportunity to see one of Back Bay's most elegant town houses. Number 118 was built in 1903; Fisher has been at this address since 1939.

From the moment you step through the door you see magnificence: A reception hall that extends upward through the second story is covered by a decorative opaque glass dome, the hanging stairway of marble has a metal balustrade covered with 24-karate gold plate, and the rugs are woven with the Greek design of the walls and balustrade. The dining room is now the president's office: It is paneled in Circassian walnut and has a European marble fireplace. The circular pattern in the ceiling is duplicated in the rug, which was custom made in Burma. The library on the second floor is entered through carved rosewood doors that have handwrought sterling silver doorknobs. On the third floor there is a balcony overlooking the river. Some of the upper floors are now used as classrooms.

There is a snack bar in the mall that connects the town houses (and one former apartment building), which are now the buildings of this secretarial and liberal arts school.

GENERAL MOTORS ASSEMBLY DIVISION   Western Avenue   Framingham 01701   Tel. 873–7421, ext. 213

Tours: October 15-July 30, Monday-Friday at 1 P.M. Tours may be arranged with advance notice for 9:30 A.M. and 1 P.M.

Minimum Age: 10.

Length of Tour: 1 hour.

Automobiles are completely assembled in this plant and the tour includes the entire process. Be prepared for a long walk, and for safety reasons covered feet (no sandals, please) and covered legs (no shorts or miniskirts allowed) are requested.

H. E. HARRIS & CO.   645 Summer Street   South Boston   Tel. 269–5200

ⓉStop: City Point bus from South Station.

Tours: Monday-Friday 9–3. Groups should make advance arrangements. Available to accompanied youngsters or adults.

It is a surprise to find this enormous facility, which is the home of the world's largest stamp dealer. (It has about 300 employees, and its own advertising department.) During your guided visit (not a formal tour), you see how stamps are stored, the assembly of albums, packaging for over-the-counter retail sales, preparation for wholesalers and retailers, and the filling of mail orders.

HARVARD UNIVERSITY   Cambridge   Tel. 495–1000   Tour Tel. 495–1573

Tours: From the Information Center located in the Holyoke Center, 1353 Massachusetts Avenue, June-August, Monday-Friday at 11 A.M. and 2 P.M.; October-May, Monday-Saturday at 11, 1, and 2.

Taped Tours: Cassettes ($2) may be rented at the Holyoke Information Center. Professor Mason Hammond's narration concerns "Revolutionary Harvard Today."

Information Center Hours: Monday-Saturday 9–5.

Length of Tour: 45 minutes to an hour.

Special Tours (e.g., for children or handicapped): Can be arranged with advance notice.

A student guide will offer a history of the first college in the country, take you through the Yard, and by the main academic buildings, museums, and graduate area. The only interior visited is Memorial Church.
 Maps of the Harvard University area are available in English, French, German, Japanese, Portuguese, and Spanish.

LOGAN INTERNATIONAL AIRPORT   East Boston   Tel. 482–2930

Ⓣ**Stop:** Airport bus from Ⓣ Airport Station (Blue Line) stops at tour meeting place.

Tours: Year round Monday-Saturday at 10 A.M. and 1 P.M. Three weeks' notice required. March, April, and May are heavily booked. Groups should be well supervised. (Families and individuals may visit the observation areas and terminals anytime, p. 137.)
 Arrangements for tours should be made through MASSPORT, Tour Coordinator, Logan International Airport, Tower Building, East Boston 02108. Appointments should be made with applications, which will be mailed on request.

Minimum Age: 3rd grade. Younger groups allowed in summer.

Length of Tour: 1–3 hours, depending on age level.

What is seen on this guided tour depends upon the size of the group, the age level, the day, and the weather. If you have a particular interest, requests can be made for a tour of customs, the interior of an airplane and (possibly) the cockpit, the weather reporting bureau, observation deck, fire control unit, a hangar, or the flight kitchen. Visitors are taken in a bus onto the inner apron of the airfield for a close-up view of activity. Group feedback: "It is an exciting field trip."

LOWELL CANAL TOURS   Lowell, Massachusetts (about 30 miles north of Boston)

Contact: Human Services, 144 Merrimack Street, Lowell 01852, Tel. 1–454–0460

Tours: Year round, Monday-Friday, by appointment only. Written requests preferred. Please request orientation material when making an appointment. One week's notice required. Please provide 1 adult for every 8 children.

Length: 2 hours.

Minimum Age: 4th grade.

Maximum Number: 30.

Lowell is the scene of much activity these days: There is considerable interest in the Lowell Urban Park, an enormous revitalization project that, if adequately funded, would refurbish the canals, open space areas, mills, and historic sites.

The canals, still used for power, dot the city, and are the focus of the stops on the tour that takes visitors through historic sections of the city. The tour, which has particular relevance for students interested in the industrial revolution, begins on the main street of Lowell at the Merrimack Canal, built by Irish immigrants. The locks have since been removed; the gatehouse, which was manually run, now has gates that are left open. You drive by historic houses that represent the positions of those involved in the mill. Included are row houses, an agent's house (made of stone), and the Ayer mansion. About 1 hour is spent in vehicles. Visitors are taken into an 1847 gatehouse, which now operates by motors and remote control. As the original equipment is still there, you can see how it functioned with a water turbine and a three-story belt that connected to a drive shaft that lowers and raises gates. The importance of parkways is evident during a ¼-mile stroll along the Northern Canal walkway.

MASSACHUSETTS INSTITUTE OF TECHNOLOGY   77 Massachusetts Avenue   Tel. 253–4795

Tours: Monday-Friday at 10 A.M. and 2 P.M. year round except holidays. Not really intended for anyone under junior high school age. Meet at the Information Center, Building 7–111. Length: 1½ hours.

The student-guided tour includes the libraries, laboratories, Kresge Auditorium, the chapel, Hart Nautical Museum, and the Computation Center. It is an energetic tour with lots of walking.

MASSACHUSETTS INSTITUTE OF TECHNOLOGY BOATHOUSE   409 Memorial Drive   Cambridge 02139   Tel. 253–6245

Contact: Boathouse manager.

Visits: Informal. By arrangement only Monday-Friday; written requests preferred. Not usually with a guide. Please give a week's notice. Offered 8–8 except November 15-March 1: 3:30–6 P.M. and some evenings. Shells are on the river during fall, spring, and some summers.

Maximum Number: About 20.

Minimum Age: Groups under 18 must be well supervised.

Length of Visit: 30 or more minutes, depending upon interest of group.

If you have never seen a close-up view of these huge, beautiful rowing boats, this is a very exciting visit. Visitors have the opportunity to learn about the sport—the role of the coxswain, the length of a race, the size of the crew, and the effect of water conditions. You may see a crew on the Charles River or in training with the rowing simulator, an indoor eight-oared device with moving water that simulates outdoor conditions. Other facilities in the Pierce boathouse include an exercise room with weights and chinning equipment, the area where 40 to 50 racing boats (several kinds) are stored and repaired, and the dock for launching.

With enough advance notice, it may be possible for visitors to go out in the launches to observe practice sessions on the river.

MORGAN MEMORIAL GOODWILL INDUSTRIES   95 Berkeley Street   Tel. 357–9710

Contact: Stuart D. Chase.

Ⓣ **Stop:** Arlington on Green Line.

Tours: Year round Monday-Friday 9–3, preferably with at least a day's notice.

Maximum Number: 30.

Minimum Age: 13.

Length of Tour: 1 hour.

As you visit this rehabilitation workshop, you will see handicapped adults training in dry cleaning, sewing, pressing, furniture repairing, refinishing and reupholstering, shoe repairing (where a small collection of foreign and antique shoes is on display), and radio and television repair.

OCEAN LINERS   Commonwealth Pier   Northern Avenue (off Summer Street next to Fish Pier, p. 153)   Boston

Ⓣ **Stop:** Fish Pier (bus from South Station).

Most of the liners that sail from Boston are in port for a very short time. Often weather conditions may influence schedules. A few of the ships allow visitors on board when they are in port. Check with the Maritime Division of the Massachusetts Port Authority, 470 Atlantic Avenue, Boston, Tel. 482–2930.

OLD SCHWAMB MILL (p. 123).

PAIRPOINT GLASS WORKS   851 Sandwich Road   Sagamore   Tel. 888–2344   It is on the Cape side of the canal under the Sagamore Bridge. Factory store open every day 9–5:30.

Blowing Room Open to Visitors: Monday-Friday 10–4:30.

Average Length of Visit: ½ hour.

Admission to Blowing Room: Adults, 50¢; children under 12, 25¢.

This is a superb excuse for spending some time around the canal and a real Cape town—Sandwich (p. 102).

Stand on the balcony overlooking the blowing room and stay as long as you like to watch the skilled craftsmen as they put a rod into the furnace, gather molten glass on the end of the rod, and then shape it into a vase, bowl, candlestick, or paperweight. Whether it is the formation of a handle, a spout, or a foot, the reheating of the molten glass to allow for additional shaping, or the removal of the object of beauty from the rod, this is an art that holds fascination for all ages.

No guide is present, but the attendant in the factory store is very helpful with questions. (The store sells seconds as well as perfect products.)

PARKER BROTHERS   190 Bridge Street   Salem 01970   Tel. 745–6600

Tours: By arrangement only, for groups only, year round at 10 A.M. and 2:45 P.M. Booked months in advance.

Minimum Number: 6.

Maximum Number: 15.

What goes into the manufacture of a Monopoly game? Or some other game that you may be familiar with? The printing process, the puzzle machines, the cutting of game money, the making of boxes, and the assembly of all the pieces into the box are among the fascinating processes you see during this colorful tour.

PHILLIPS CANDY HOUSE   818 Morrissey Boulevard   Dorchester 02122
Tel. 282–2090

Ⓣ **Stop:** Fields Corner on Red Line.

Tours: Year round except week before Easter and Christmas, Monday-Friday 9–5. By arrangement only. At least 4 days' notice requested.

Minimum Age: 4.

Minimum Number: 6.

Maximum Number: 25.

It is just the way you would imagine a candy kitchen to be—with experienced hands at work in this business that a single family has operated for 50 years. All candy is made in small batches (5–50 pounds). You see the cooking of cream and cherry candies, fudge, mints, jellies, and hard candies. Chocolates are hand-dipped the old-fashioned way, as well as dipped by modern machinery. You may also see the making of novelty candies. The last step to be observed is the packing process.

PRISCILLA OF BOSTON   40 Cambridge Street   Charlestown 02129
Tel. 242–2677

Ⓣ **Stop:** Sullivan Square on Orange Line (2-block walk).

Tours: By arrangement only, year round, Tuesday-Thursday 10–12:30, 2–3 weeks' advance notice required.

Minimum Age: 15.

Minimum Number: 10.

Maximum Number: 25.

Length of Tour: 1 hour.

This renowned house of bridal attire shows you the complete process of constructing a dress—from the cutting of the fabric to the machine stitching and handwork. You see the beading frames that are worked under ultraviolet light, how those long rows of buttons are sewn on, and the method for applying the lace appliqués to layers of skirts.

PUTNAM PANTRY CANDIES   Rt. 1   Danvers 01923   Tel. 774–2383

Tours: Year round except 3 weeks before Easter and Christmas, Tuesday-Friday 9–12:30 and 1–4. Make arrangements at least a day in advance. One adult with 10 children.

Groups are given a 20-minute guided tour. Individuals and families may visit on their own (at the same designated hours) to see the entire process of candy-making (hand-dipped chocolates are among the products), packing, and shipping. The shop features an ice-cream smorgasbord with make-your-own junior sundaes for 70¢.

QUABBIN RESERVOIR   Winsor Dam   Belchertown, Massachusetts 01007   Tel. 413–323–6921   (Note description on p. 195.)

Tours: Offered to groups Monday-Friday 8–4:30. One week's notice requested.

Minimum Age: None, but there is quite a bit of stair climbing.

Maximum Number: More than 50 becomes awkward.

Length of Tour: Variable, possibly 2–2½ hours.

See the daily operation of the reservoir, which is Metropolitan Boston's water supply source. The construction of Quabbin, completed in 1939 and filled to capacity in 1846, required relocating boundaries of six towns. (About 2,500 people living in 650 houses had to find new homes.) There are about 60 miles of tunnel, which connect Quabbin via Wachusett Reservoir to Boston.

The tour includes the water quality laboratory, repair shops, and airplane hangar. Groups drive from one site to another via whatever vehicles they have arrived in. At Winsor Dam the guide compares the existing land to the pre-reservoir valley. At Winsor Dam Power Station there is a short tour through the small hydroelectric generating station. Then onto Rt. 9 to Quabbin Park Cemetery, which was established for the reinterment of the thirty-four displaced cemeteries. There is a stop at the fire observation tower for a magnificent view of islands and three states.

Second graders hear Indian lore; high schoolers are given more technical data.

Picnic tables throughout the area. No fires allowed.

SHERBURNE LUMBER CO.   Coburn Road   Tyngsboro   Tel. 649–7413

Directions: Exit 34 off Rt. 3, continue to single arch bridge on Merrimack River. Follow signs after crossing bridge.

Tours: During reasonably warm months, weekdays 9–12, 1–4.

Maximum Number: 12.

Length: 1 hour.

This is a small sawmill that is not able to provide tours, but if a well-supervised small group would like to see areas where trees are cut and logs are loaded, how the logs are sawed into boards, and then the planing of these boards, call Mr. Sherburne to inquire about a convenient time. Weekdays are preferable.

The use of a century-old waterwheel (not the kind used in a gristmill) during a heavy rain period in the spring or fall emphasizes the importance of the pond location.

STAR MARKET CO.   625 Mount Auburn Street   Cambridge   Tel. 491–3000

Store Tours: By appointment only. Contact store manager 2 weeks in advance. Written requests preferred.

Minimum Age: 5.

Maximum Group Size: 18.

Offered: Any month. Summer may be best in some stores. Tuesday and Wednesday mornings and early afternoons.

A complete tour of a modern supermarket including back room operations, cutting of meat and packaging produce, bread baking (from frozen dough) in the deli department, the receiving area, stocking arrangements, baling of cardboard boxes, and recyling. Each tour is designed to highlight the interests of the age group. Refreshments usually served.

Warehouse Tours: University Avenue   Norwood (via Rt. 128)   491–3000, ext. 272   contact: Nat Silverman

Tours: Offered year round Tuesdays, Wednesdays, Thursdays 9–4. Two weeks' advance notice. Written requests preferred.

Minimum Age: 10.

Maximum Number: 25.

The presentation depends upon the age of visitors, but generally a sense of economics and the background of supermarket merchandising is given as visitors see volumes of groceries and perishable products. Trailers are loaded and unloaded, trucks are washed inside and out, there are dairy and flower operations, and orders from individual stores are filled. Refreshments possibly served.

STOP & SHOP, INC.   393 D Street   Boston 02210   Tel. 463–7425

Tours: Through one of their supermarkets offered for organized groups only, by appointment only, year round, in the morning, preferably Monday or Tuesday. Contact individual store manager or the public-relations department of Stop & Shop at the above number.

Minimum Number: 10.

Maximum Number: 30.

Minimum Age: 4.

Length of Tour: About 45 minutes.

The visitor sees what goes on "backstage." Follow the operation of a supermarket as you see receiving points, frozen-food storage, produce packaging, and display. Older youngsters are given the economic background of marketing.

TRINITY CHURCH   Copley Square   Boston   Tel. 536–0944

Tours: Sundays following the 11 A.M. morning service. Exception: No tours the first Sunday of the month.

Henry Hobson Richardson was the architect for what is considered to be one of the most magnificent churches in this country. John La Farge designed the interior, which has rich black walnut pews, stained glass windows, a brass lectern, and marble font.

Exterior details of interest include the stone walls of Dedham and Westerly granite and the English carved stone window in the cloister facing the garth.

You may enter the church daily 9–5. During the ½-hour guided tour you learn about the architect, architectural details, history of the parish (Phillips Brooks was rector from 1869 to 1891), interior decorations, the organ, and stained glass.

Handicapped: Ramp on Stuart Street side, 2 steps.

U.S. POSTAL SERVICE—SOUTH POSTAL ANNEX   Dorchester Avenue (behind South Station)   Boston   Tel. 223–2457

Contact: Irving Shear.

Tours: Year round except December. One week's advance notice needed.

Minimum Age: 12. (Local post offices will receive younger children.)

Minimum Number: 10.

Maximum Number: 25.

Length of Tour: 45 minutes.

You can see what happens to a letter from the time it comes to the South Postal Annex until it is put on a train, plane, ship, or truck. The delivery mail from 25 cities and towns around Boston is handled here, plus bulk mails for the New England states. Conveyors, canceling machines, the handling of parcel post, and waiting trains (but mostly hundreds of trucks) are involved in the operation of this mechanized post office. An optical character reader sorts letters at the rate of 42,000 per hour.

WILSON FARMS, INC.   10 Pleasant Street   Lexington   Tel. 862–3900

Contact: Mary.

Directions: Rt. 2 to Rts. 4 and 225 (about ¾ mile off Rt. 2).

Tours: Family groups are welcome to browse Tuesday-Sunday 9–5. Organized groups should make an appointment at least 2 days in advance for a visit Mondays, Wednesday-Friday 9–5. The farm is able to accommodate handicapped youngsters.

Minimum Age: 4–5.

Minimum Number: 4.

Maximum Number: 20.

Poultry Area: As soon as eggs are laid they are automatically collected and wait in a tray until they are taken to a grader. (Yes, you see and hear the chickens!) Although the grading machine is operated at varying hours and requires four men, it may be possible to turn it on for visiting groups.

Flower Greenhouse: Open November-June.

Vegetable Farm: Open May-October. If personnel is available, a guide is provided through these areas.

WLVI-TV (Channel 56)   75 Morrissey Boulevard (next door to the *Boston Globe*)   Tel. 288–3200

Ⓣ **Stop:** Columbia Station on Red Line.

Tours: By arrangement only September-June, Monday-Friday 9–4. Ten days' notice required. Written requests preferred.

Minimum Age: 6. Can accommodate 10–25 people.

Length of Tour: 30 minutes.

A guide is provided through studios, control rooms, and the art and printing departments. What you see may depend upon the hour of the visit.

WNAC-TV   RKO   General   Building   Government   Center   Boston   Tel. 742–9000

Ⓣ **Stop:** Government Center on Green Line.

Tours: Tuesdays and Thursdays 1:30 and 3, by arrangement only. Two weeks' notice required.

Handicapped Youngsters: Special arrangements will be made.

Minimum Age: 10. Can handle 5–30 people.

Length of Tour: About 1 hour.

A guide is provided through three television studios, the control room, videotape room, announcer's booth, the television news department, film department, and the WRKO and WROR radio facilities. If you have a particular interest, inquire about programming when making an appointment.

Have you ever been curious about THE BOSTON ATHE-NAEUM at 10½ Beacon Street? It is a private research library that, in addition to important book collections, has 5 stories filled with significant art and sculpture. Tours (not child-oriented) are offered at specific times to those who call in advance. Tel. 227–0270.

THE WORLD AROUND US
PLACES AND RESOURCES

Viewing Sites

BABSON WORLD GLOBE   Babson Institute   Babson Park   Wellesley
Tel. 235–1200

> If you drive to Washington Street from Babson, turn left for
> a few minutes to arrive at Wellesley Town Hall—on your
> right—where there are many geese and ducks fenced in a
> very pretty setting. Feeding allowed.

Directions: Travel west on Rt. 16 to Wellesley Hill Square. Turn left, just beyond the post offfice, onto Abbot Road to end. Turn left onto Forest Street
to motor entrance of campus.

Open: April 1-October 31 10–5 daily; November 1-March 31 2–5 daily. Closed
Thanksgiving and Christmas. Other hours by appointment. Special tours
arranged for school groups.

Parking: Free.

Average Visit: 30–45 minutes.

The change from day to night as well as the progression of the four seasons is
simulated as the 25-ton globe, mounted out of doors, revolves on its 6-ton hollow shaft. The countries, their capitals, mountain ranges, rivers, islands, and
oceans are portrayed as if you were 5,000 miles above the earth. A topside view
of the Globe is possible through the windows of the balcony of the nearby
Coleman Map Building. (Inside the building is the Giant Relief Map, the largest
relief model of the United States, 65 feet long and 45 feet wide.)

BOSTON UNIVERSITY OBSERVATORY   725 Commonwealth Avenue (5th
floor)   Tel. 353–2625

Its two (7-inch and 12-inch) telescopes are available to the public free of charge
every week throughout the year, including the summer months. For the exact
times and days, call the Astronomy Department at the above telephone number.

At least one major event is planned annually for children and high-school
students with astronomical movies, talks with slides, displays, use of the telescopes, use of computer terminals, and refreshments. No charge. Call in early
October to find out the fall date.

HARVARD COLLEGE OBSERVATORY   60 Garden Street   Cambridge
Tel. 495–3967

"Open Nights" are given in October and May on Friday evenings at 7 and 8:15
with special 45-minute talks for two age groups: 6–12 and 12–16. Depending
on weather conditions, children may be allowed to look through a telescope. It
is a very special evening, but between arriving early, a possible tour of the observatory, and waiting for a turn at the telescope, it is a long visit for young
children.

To obtain tickets it is necessary to be on the mailing list for series announcements. Send a self-addressed stamped envelope at any time between
programs, and a schedule will be sent about a month before presentations.
From this schedule you make your selection. Three tickets allowed for each
request. Because seating is limited, tickets should be for one night per season
per person.

MAPPARIUM   The Christian Science Publishing Society   One Norway Street   Tel. 262–2300

. . . Within walking distance of the Prudential Center, p. 137.

. . . Regularly scheduled tours of the Christian Science Publishing Society, p. 253, and the First Church of Christ Scientist, p. 253.

Ⓣ**Stop:** Symphony or Auditorium.

Open: Monday-Friday 8–4:45, Saturdays 8:15–4, Sundays 12–3. No admission charge. Average visit: 15 minutes.

As you walk on a glass bridge through a glass globe (30 feet in diameter), pretend you are at the center of the earth and notice the time zones and various depths of the ocean as indicated by blue shading. You gain an impression of the relationships of land and water surfaces of the world from the 608 individual sections, each ¼ inch thick. The globe, which shows the political divisions of 1932, has brilliant colors that are heightened by 300 electric lights outside the glass sphere. As the hard surface of the glass does not absorb the sound, the spoken word assumes enormity.

In the lobby of the building some youngsters notice the barometer and other instruments that indicate wind velocity and direction.

The reflecting pool with fountain (on the Huntington Street side of the Christian Science Center) is just for looking. It serves a functional as well as aesthetic purpose. The water is part of the air-conditioning system of the Church Colonnade and is recirculated every 10 hours.

People

BOSTON COUNCIL FOR INTERNATIONAL VISITORS   55 Mount Vernon Street   Tel. 742–0460

This nonprofit organization acts as a reception center, clearinghouse, and liaison between foreign visitors, usually government-sponsored, and the Boston community. Membership is $10. Members can help with sight-seeing or be hosts in their own homes for meals or for overnight or brief stays.

ENGLISH SPEAKING UNION   939 Boylston Street   Tel. 536–4740

Among its activities are weekly open house gatherings for young people of all nationalities; more Americans would be welcome. They very often have travelers and students (age 18 and up) who would appreciate home hospitality. Applications are kept on file and you will be called when the need arises.

INTERNATIONAL FRIENDSHIP LEAGUE, INC.   40 Mount Vernon Street   Tel. 523–4272

Fee (Contribution) for Service: $2.

The organization matches names, for the purpose of correspondence, using lists from 140 free countries and territories around the world. Anyone who can write a letter is eligible, but children under 13 must have pen pals from English-speaking countries.

Teen-age Volunteers Accepted: Minimum age—16.

INTERNATIONAL INSTITUTE OF BOSTON, INC.   287 Commonwealth Avenue   Tel. 536–1081

The International Institute is a nonpolitical, nonsectarian social service agency that helps meet the needs of newcomers to the United States and is a meeting place for people from many nationalities. It offers interpreting service, group activities, and informal education. Volunteers (minimum age: 18) are always welcome.

This is the local center for the "Americans-at-Home" program, administered by the U.S. Department of Commerce and the U.S. Travel Service. Independent foreign travelers who would like to meet Americans give 24–48 hours' notice to the institute. Most of the requests come during late summer. Prospective hosts should call for a registration card.

PAN AMERICAN SOCIETY   75A Newbury Street   Tel. 266–2248

Students—upper elementary through college age—may use the extensive collection of newspaper clippings, magazine articles, and pamphlets concerning Latin America. Exhibitions and lectures are scheduled periodically. Spanish conversation groups are held biweekly; there is no charge, anyone may attend, and people group according to ability. Assistance and hospitality are given on request to visitors to and from Latin America; call about host possibilities.

UNICEF   261 Washington Street   Newton 02158   Tel. 965–3365

Together with matching funds of the less developed countries receiving aid, UNICEF helps to meet the physical, intellectual, vocational, and emotional needs of children. This office of the United Nations Children's Fund serves Boston and its surrounding suburbs. Projects include "Trick or Treat," greeting cards, notepaper, books, and games for children.

UNICEF has extensive educational programs for schools: study guides for teachers, a library of films, records, sheet music, plays for children, and slide sets. A wide variety of materials are available through the Information Center on Children's Cultures, a service of the U.S. Committee for UNICEF, 331 East 38th Street, New York City 10016.

U.S. SERVAS, INC.   International Institute   287 Commonwealth Avenue   Tel. 536–1081

This nonprofit, nonpolitical, interracial, interfaith, and volunteer-staffed organization promotes understanding through an international system of travelers and hosts. The basic intent is an exchange of ideas with hospitality. No fees are exchanged between host and visitor. The list of countries grows as the idea grows. All visits are arranged ahead of time.

Hosts: Anyone may register as a host or host family, but the greatest need is for those who are located in areas that are easily accessible to Boston. Visits are usually a day or two.

Travelers (individuals or families): Apply with letter about yourself, your plans, and supply two letters of reference. All traveler applicants are interviewed. There is a small contribution to cover expenses for postage and supplies. You plan your own trips using lists of hosts whose activities may be of particular interest. Expect to share in the everyday life of the home, rather than be entertained.

Speakers: Both foreigners and Americans who have lived with Servas hosts in the United States, Europe, and Asia will share their experiences and color slides with youth and adult groups.

Volunteers: New helpers (minimum age: high school) would be welcome at meetings, which are held the second Monday of every month.

OTHER LOCAL HOST POSSIBILITIES

Colleges   Several Boston-area colleges have host family programs. Others are in the process of establishing programs. The greatest need for hosts is usually in early fall; you receive the incoming individual or family, assist with settling, and often establish a rewarding experience for your entire family with ongoing contact throughout the year.

Two well-established international programs that provide travel and host possibilities:

American Field Service, 313 East 43rd Street, New York, New York 10017

The Experiment in International Living, Putney, Vermont 05346

Many Boston-area students (mostly high school) have participated in these programs. It may not be necessary to have a high schooler in your family to host a foreign student. If there is a representative in your local community, the national offices can direct you to him.

For Children with Special Needs

CHILD ADVOCACY PROJECT OF THE EASTER SEAL SOCIETY   14 Somerset Street   Boston 02108   Tel. 227–9608

This project develops programs for the identification of and solutions to the special needs of physically handicapped children and their families. It has information on parents' advocacy groups and compiles and distributes such publications as the *Rights Handbook for Physically Handicapped Children*, 69 pages filled with useful information.

The Easter Seal Society offers swim and recreational activities, programs and services for physically handicapped persons, and has two comprehensive publications that list accessible buildings: *Wheeling through Boston* and *Access to Cambridge*. Sent free upon request. Similar booklets are being prepared on the North Shore and Cape Cod.

W. E. FERNALD STATE SCHOOL   Media Resources Center   200 Trapelo Road   Waltham   Tel. 891–7178

Mailing Address: School House, Waverley

Open: Monday-Friday 9–5.

The focus is on developmentally disabled children. A resource library includes audio-visual and written materials and is open to parents and professionals.

MEDFORD PUBLIC LIBRARY INSTRUCTIONAL MATERIALS CENTER 111 High Street   Medford   Tel. 396–0789

Open: September-June, Monday-Thursday 3–5, 6–8:30, Tuesday-Friday 3–5, Wednesdays 6–8:30.

As a center for parents of children with special needs, it provides books and materials for parents to take home and use with their children. The only professionals that are allowed to borrow materials from the center are Medford special education teachers.

NATIONAL BRAILLE PRESS   88 St. Stephen Street   Boston 02115
Tel. 266–6160

This nonprofit communication center serves the blind and visually handicapped with several services including: tape and recording Braille transcribing for all levels of educational materials from elementary through graduate studies; Braille publications including *Weekly News*; a library of tapes and Braille volumes; large print reproduction, primarily for low vision children in the Massachusetts school system; and a ⊤ System Tactile Route Map.

Publication:
THE EXCEPTIONAL PARENT   262 Beacon Street   Boston
Subscription Address: P.O. Box 964, Manchester, New Hampshire 03105.
Rates: $10 year, $18 2 years, $24 3 years.

This magazine is published 6 times a year and provides practical guidance for parents and professionals concerned with the care of children with disabilities—physical disabilities, emotional problems, mental retardation, learning disabilities, perceptual disabilities, deafness, blindness, and chronic illness.

Volunteering

Volunteer work is an excellent method of exploring career possibilities, yet opportunities are not limited to those with a particular interest in a field. If you plan to inquire in person, it is best to make an appointment. If you inquire in writing, provide a résumé of your education, experience, interests, and skills.

Often those who enroll because they wish to "give" find that they grow as persons.

As credited release time has become a part of many school systems, there are times when the number of young people seeking volunteer experience seems to exceed the possibilities. The match of interests—and personalities— is delicate and important for a worthwhile experience. Guidance is essential. Exposure to the real world is not enough. As a result, many institutions and businesses find that they are not geared to provide the supervision and support that young people are looking for and need. Because continuity is important to both parties, it helps to be committed for a concentrated period of time.

As the concept grows, more local organizations are receptive to working with youngsters. Some communities have their own clearinghouses, and/or have drawn up a list of nursing homes, craftsmen, cross-age tutoring possibilities, businesses, institutions, adopt-a-grandparent programs, and apprenticeships. Check with City Hall or your local paper. Museum junior curator program information is included in the individual museum listings (p. 157).

Most Boston HOSPITALS are within a block or two of a ⊤ stop. The Voluntary Action Center (see below) has comprehensive information on hospital volunteer opportunities. If you wish to make direct inquiries, most hospitals have their own volunteer office. Volunteering during the school year usually requires a minimum of 3 hours once a week. Some hospitals suggest early application for summer programs. The minimum age for specific responsibilities differs from hospital to hospital, but the opportunities for young people under 16 need to be carefully searched out.

Two Helpful Organizations:

CIVIC CENTER AND CLEARING HOUSE, INC.   14 Beacon Street   Tel. 227–1762

This private nonprofit organization offers opportunities beyond the traditional type of volunteer service. After careful personal screening, the interviewer makes suggestions and referrals. Emphasis is on adults but they do interview applicants from age 16 up. Appointment needed for an interview. Office hours: 10–4. A donation is requested to help defray overhead expenses of this all-volunteer service.

The staff is responsible for the "Opportunities for Volunteers" column that appears every Wednesday in the *Boston Globe*. The Career and Vocational Advisory Service has resources on possible career choice and training possibilities. $10, consultation fee.

VOLUNTARY ACTION CENTER OF METROPOLITAN BOSTON   14 Somerset Street   Tel. 742–2000

The center, part of the United Community Planning Corporation (formerly United Community Services of Metropolitan Boston), acts as a clearinghouse for more than 250 organizations in the Greater Boston area. They do have some openings for 12-year-olds, but most start at age 14.

Call for information about volunteer clearinghouses in telephone toll-charge surrounding communities.

Environment

(See also New England Wildflower Society, p. 192, and Open Space organizations, p. 200.)

COUNTY EXTENSION OFFICES:

Concord: Middlesex County Extension Service, 105 Everett Street, Tels. 369–4845 (Concord), 862–2380 (Lexington)

Hawthorne: Essex Agricultural and Technical Institute, 526 Maple Street, Tel. 774–0050

Walpole: Norfolk County Agricultural High School, 460 Main Street, Tel. 668–0268

These offices offer services similar to the Suburban Experiment Station in Waltham (p. 271). In addition, they have home economics and 4–H Club departments.

ENVIRONMENTAL PROTECTION AGENCY LIBRARY   John F. Kennedy Federal Building, 2211–B   Boston   Tel. 223–5791, is used primarily by the EPA, but is open to the public. The specialized collection of materials is rather technical and is used by some high school and college students. The librarian may suggest that you try the Museum of Science (p. 172) or the Massachusetts Audubon Society (p. 202) libraries.

MARGARET C. FERGUSON GREENHOUSES   Wellesley College Wellesley   Tel. 235–0320, ext. 637

Open: 8:30–4:30 daily.

It is a treat to walk through the 14 individually heated greenhouses. The Palm Houses has bird of paradise, coffee trees, cocoa trees, pineapples, mangoes, and bananas. The collection in the Cryptogram House includes mosses and ferns. You stand on a small rustic bridge and are sure that some youngster (yours?) has touched something when you realize that an automatic mist is sprayed every few minutes. It is a beautiful setting. The Desert Garden has many varieties of cactus. There is an Orchid House and a warm temperature house with orange, lemon, and tea plants, and passion flowers. You will see leaves that are big enough to hide under and blossoms that invite exclamation.

Wellesley has a spacious campus, which has acres of grass and trees. The Jewett Arts Center is open when the college is in session (closed vacations including summer). As you walk around Lake Waban, you see the shaped evergreens (topiary) on the Honeywell estate.

HABITAT INSTITUTE FOR THE ENVIRONMENT   10 Juniper Road Belmont   Tel. 489–3850

Directions: Rt. 2 to Rt. 60—Arlington-Belmont exit, at end of ramp turn left onto Pleasant Street (Rt. 60). At Clifton Street light turn right, left onto Fletcher Road, left onto Juniper.

Open: 9–5 daily.

Here is a 26-acre environmental education wildlife sanctuary where interns in environmental problems are trained. There is a beautiful seasonal self-guided nature trail (about a 40-minute walk). The extensive wild flower garden is best in May and June. This area is adjacent to the Highland Farms Sanctuary (Massachusetts Audubon Society), which has unmarked footpaths.

Summer: Environmental day camps and afterschool programs offered for ages 6–10. Many short- and long-term courses are offered that are cross-age in appeal and enrollment.

Groups: Nature walks, wild flower and greenhouse tours by arrangement only. Fees: 50¢–$2 per person.

Library: It is extensive and focuses on environment; open to teachers.

MASSACHUSETTS DEPARTMENT OF AGRICULTURE Division of Markets 100 Cambridge Street Boston 02202 Tel. 727–3018, distributes booklets for garden tips (growing vegetables in home gardens and minigardens) and recipes (rhubarb, dandelions, chicken), as well as current lists for pick-your-own vegetables. Send self-addressed stamped envelope with request.

MASSACHUSETTS HORTICULTURAL SOCIETY 300 Massachusetts Avenue Tel. 536–9280

The excellent library and Garden Information Center are open to the public Monday-Friday 9–5, but borrowing is limited to members. Memberships (June-June) include magazine subscription: Individual, $15; family, $20.

Several flower shows are held throughout the year at Horticultural Hall. When admission is charged, student rates are available. (Spring flower show, p. 283.)

MASSACHUSETTS JUNIOR CONSERVATION CAMP Thompson's Pond Spencer

For boys 14–17. Held for 2 weeks in July. Tuition: $100. Usually filled by previous January. Focus: Conserving natural resources and outdoor skills—fishing, boating, shooting sports, and swimming. For information write: Information and Education Section, Division of Fisheries and Game Headquarters, Westboro, Massachusetts.

UNIVERSITY OF MASSACHUSETTS SUBURBAN EXPERIMENT STATION 240 Beaver Street Waltham Tel. 891–0650

Services: If you bring in (Monday-Friday) or mail soil samples, take one-cup samples from different parts of the plot, tell where each came from, what you want to do with it, and how large the space is. Put the soil in a plastic bag and enclose it in a box. You are limited to three samples per time. Recommendations are usually made within 3 weeks. No charge for this or for home horticultural information about vegetables and flower gardens, insect pests, and diseases of trees and shrubs. Experts on hand provide information. Leaflets are available.

What to See: You are welcome to visit and see the different stages of several labeled varieties of flowers, the magnificent formal gardens, and some vegetables in greenhouses.

Hours: The grounds are open all the time. Buildings and greenhouses 9–12 and 1–6 Monday-Friday.

URBAN AWARENESS AND ENVIRONMENTAL UNDERSTANDING PROGRAM 23 Main Street Watertown 02172 Tel. 492–3475

This program is a collaborative venture between the Boston Society of Architects and the Cambridge Public Schools. Through a carefully planned sequence of activities between architects, planners, children, and teachers, it is hoped that greater awareness and appreciation of the urban environment will develop with the involved fourth-grade students. Volunteer architects and planners conduct classroom sessions, walking tours, and field trips, and mapping and model-building sessions.

Although this program is limited to one community, it is an interesting experiment. Contact the office for more information.

Libraries

BOSTON PUBLIC LIBRARY   Copley Square   Tel. 536–5400

Open: October-May, Monday-Friday 9–9, Saturdays 9–6, Sundays 2–6; June-September, Monday-Friday 9–7, Saturdays 9–6, closed Sundays.

This is the oldest free municipal library supported by taxes in any city of the world. The Dartmouth Street entrance leads to the Research Library (the "older building"), which has much architectural interest, including the main entrance hall with the names of famous Bostonians in its mosaic ceiling and the impressive marble central stairway. A collection of art works by Daniel Chester French, Puvis de Chavannes, and Saint-Gaudens is in the library.

All materials in the Research Library must be used on the premises.

The street level Boylston Street entrance leads to the General Library Building in which the borrowing collections are housed. (This building is widely acclaimed for its architectural achievement as an addition that blends with the old. However, on the inside it is fairly sterile, but funds for plants or artwork may relieve that feeling. Nevertheless, it offers accessibility to an extensive collection of materials.) Both buildings are connected on the first floor.

Tour Information: p. 251.

Borrowing Privileges: Free to all residents of the Commonwealth of Massachusetts. Cards may be obtained at the central library or at any branch library or bookmobile. Books may be returned to those branches that have agreed to accept them. Check in advance with your nearby library. Loan period: 14–20 days, depending upon borrowing date.

Audio-Visual Department: Recordings may be borrowed by card holders. Listening booths available for recordings. Film loans, p. 56.

Children's Room: This very inviting room has large collections of books and comfortable furnishings that are sized to the height of its users. Its collection includes foreign language books. A variety of special programs are held during the week.

Microtext Room: On the first floor in the research building (in the former Children's Room). Open whenever the library is open. Heavily used for research during the academic year. It is easier to get in during the summer. If there is space, children can see a Boston newspaper published on their birth date or the news from another century (in newspaper form—back to 1704) on the screen. Or you can request a copy of the first street directory of New York City with its short population list, which includes the name of Peter Stuyvesant.

Newspaper Room: Current editions from every state in the Union.

Magazines: Obtained on the second floor of both buildings. Check the General Library second-floor periodical area—most popular or more recent issues are housed here—before searching the Research Library. No periodical may be taken out for home use.

Courtyard: A secluded pleasant place to relax and read in the summer. Complete with bubbling fountain and shade trees. (All seats are taken at lunch hour.)

Programs: During the school year there are many programs—story hours, creative crafts, film showings—for children. Some branches have extensive youth-oriented programs. Lectures and audio-visual programs are offered for adults.

Exhibits: In many areas throughout the building. Through December 1976 the focus will be on the Bicentennial. The exhibits include puppets, dolls, paintings, models of railroads and ships, and commemorative and historical exhibitions by individuals and organizations.

Calendar of Events: Monthly publication. Subscriptions available without charge.

KIRSTEIN BUSINESS BRANCH of the Boston Public Library   20 City Hall Avenue   Boston   Tel. 523–0860

Open: Monday-Friday 9–5.

Tucked in a walkway between School and Court streets on the side of Old City Hall is this business information center. In addition to general books on business subjects and a full collection of trade periodicals, it offers a telephone reference service (not to be used for bibliographies on school projects!) through which you may locate professionals, retailers, manufacturers—or just an address.

FRENCH LIBRARY   53 Marlborough Street   Boston   Tel. 266–4351

Open: September-July, Tuesdays, Thursdays, Fridays 1–4, Wednesdays 10–7, Saturdays 10–2.

Membership: $10 per year.

Use on Premises: Free to public.

Approximately 20,000 volumes in French are housed here. There are books for adults and children, a small collection of newspapers and magazines, some records, and multimedia materials. Loan materials are restricted to members. The children's area is charming.

GOETHE INSTITUTE   170 Beacon Street   Boston   Tel. 262–6050

As the German Cultural Center for New England, it offers German language courses at all levels for persons over 17 and a lively cultural program for every age group. Children's afternoons, concerts, exhibitions, lectures, and films are scheduled periodically.

Library: No charge for borrowing. Eighty percent of materials are in German. Children's books are almost all in German.

Reading Room: Includes German newspapers and periodicals. Open weekdays 8:30–5 and until 8:30 P.M. Tuesdays, Wednesdays, and Thursdays.

Children's Classes at the German-Language Saturday School: Contact Karl Ludwig, German Overseas Service, 453 Lexington Street, Auburndale, Massachusetts 02166, Tel. 542–2373.

JOHN F. KENNEDY LIBRARY   380 Trapelo Road   Waltham   Tel. 223–7250

Plans are to have the library—with its teaching exhibits in government and politics—located in Cambridge near the Charles River. Meanwhile the library has much of interest to groups and scholars. Millions of documents and thousands of objects and memorabilia have been acquired.

There is an oral history program with more than 500 interviews available in transcript form, an audiovisual collection with film and videotape, still pictures, thousands of sound recordings, and newspapers on microfilm. The staff now prepares special exhibits, has internships for high-school and college students, and conducts teacher workshops. Educational packets—with participatory elements—are units on press conferences, political cartoons, economists, ambassadors, language arts (e.g., speech preparation), and one entitled "The Seven Roles of the President."

Organizations and Agencies

BOSTON ASSOCIATION FOR THE EDUCATION OF YOUNG CHILDREN

This organization is open to anyone interested in the education and welfare of young children; most members are in the education field.

Information Bureau: Membership not necessary for this service. If you want to know about nursery schools in the Greater Boston area, call 899–7585 between 9 A.M. and 1 P.M. Tuesdays or Thursdays. Written requests should be addressed to 23 Pinecroft Road, Weston, Massachusetts 02193.

Publications: "Choosing a Nursery School for Your Child" (single copies available without charge) is a helpful leaflet, particularly for those who may be on their first search. Job opportunities list is free to members and $1 for nonmembers.

CHILD CARE RESOURCE CENTER   123 Mt. Auburn Street   Cambridge 02138   Tel. 547–9861

Open: Monday-Friday 9–5.

As a clearinghouse of existing child-care programs in Greater Boston, it can offer information about ongoing child-care arrangements or help those who wish to initiate child-care programs. (It is not a baby-sitter information service.)

Other Child-care Suggestions:

. . . Check the Yellow Pages under "Baby Sitters" and "Day Nurseries."

. . . Licensed nursery schools in any one community may be located through the local health department.

. . . The Office for Children (p. 276) is charged with coordinating statewide day-care development by other state departments.

. . . Call a nearby high school or college. Some may post your needs; others may have a registry.

THE CHILD STUDY ASSOCIATION OF MASSACHUSETTS, INC.   145 Yarmouth Road   Chestnut Hill 02167   Tel. 232–7416

This is a voluntary nonprofit organization for parents and professional people concerned with the well-being of children. Members will help to organize a child study group within a neighborhood or existing organization. Discussion groups are organized for parents of preschool children, school-age children, and adolescents. Those sessions that are conducted simultaneously with library story hours are free. Groups are formed in any area for a nominal charge. In addition to practical sessions, there is a speakers' bureau for lectures on such subjects as cultural and ethnic differences in rearing children, as well as the changing structure of the family. A month's notice is appreciated.

CHILDREN IN HOSPITALS, INC.   1 Merrill Street   Belmont

This is a nonprofit organization of parents and health-care professionals that seeks to educate all those concerned about the needs of children and parents for continued and ample contact when either is hospitalized. Through personal counseling, a newsletter, information sheets, and meetings, it supports parents who are strongly motivated to keep in close touch with their children during a hospital experience. It encourages hospitals to adopt flexible visiting policies and to provide living-in accommodations whenever possible.

Membership: $2, includes newsletter and hospital policy information. For 50¢ you can obtain a copy of the survey of Boston-area hospital policies.

EXPLORERS COUNCILS

Although the programs are under the auspices of the Boy Scouts of America, scouting membership is not required. All programs, open to boys and girls 14–21, are packaged according to interests, e.g., automotive, skin diving, architecture, medicine, marine biology, insurance, hotel management, and kayaking. Costs: Minimal. Vary with interest. Meetings held twice a month. Some groups meet year round. For a group in your area, contact your local council.

Nearby Offices:
  891 Centre Street, Jamaica Plain, Tel. 522–4000
  411 Unquity Road, Milton, Tel. 361–3015
  140 Mt. Auburn Street, Cambridge, Tel. 547–2760
  245 North Street, Stoughton, Tel. 438–9500
  2044 Beacon Street, Newton, Tel. 332–2220

LA LECHE LEAGUE OF MASSACHUSETTS

This is an organization for those women who are interested in—or are—breast-feeding their babies. For current address and telephone number, please see the Boston telephone book. Different members act as secretary each year.

La Leche is a source for printed information on breast-feeding, portable baby food grinders (nonelectrical), and baby carriers (for infants up to 30 pounds).

MASSACHUSETTS ADOPTION RESOURCE EXCHANGE   600 Washington Street   Boston   Tel. 727–6180

M.A.R.E. serves as a clearinghouse for adoption information. It does not place children directly but makes referrals to bring parents and children together.

MASSACHUSETTS CHILDREN'S LOBBY   100 Franklin Street   Boston Tel. 426–5088

This is a nonpartisan organization of citizens who share a concern for the well-being of children and families. The lobby reviews legislation and appropriations pertaining to children under 18 and provides timely information and evaluation of this legislation to the public. It lobbies for legislation for children that embodies sound principles and valid standards. In this, its second year, it intends to enlarge its involvement in the legislative process and to monitor ongoing programs and agencies that deal with children.

MIT HIGH SCHOOL STUDIES PROGRAM   77 Massachusetts Avenue
Cambridge   Tel. 253–4882

College students, mostly from MIT, conduct 10-week sessions in about 60 courses: photography, computers, mathematics, social sciences, crafts, foreign languages, etc. Spring and fall classes are held on Saturdays; summer sessions are on weekday evenings. Up to three different subjects may be taken during any one semester for a total registration fee of $4. Those who enroll have access to MIT libraries. Several festivals are held during the year.

Registration: Early October, late February, late June. Cost: $4.

Age Requirements: 13–18.

MASSACHUSETTS MOTHERS OF TWINS CLUBS   Founding Chapter: P.O. Box 24, Arlington Heights 02175 (covers Boston and surrounding communities)

For addresses of chapters in other areas, write: Mrs. Norman Zankel, Executive Secretary, 20 Appleton Road, Natick.

Members give each other support, assist in medical research, and have programs that benefit parents of twins. There is an exchange room, and they are allowed discounts at certain stores.

OFFICE FOR CHILDREN   120 Boylston Street   Boston 02116   Tel. 727–8997

This is a state agency mandated to coordinate all children's services by state and private agencies and to advocate for children. It includes:
COUNCILS FOR CHILDREN, community-based citizens' advocacy groups, and HELP FOR CHILDREN, a statewide system of information, referral, and advocacy program. There are many regions including: Boston 727–8898, Cambridge 492–1572, Everett 389–5075, Lynn 581–7677, Quincy 472–4224, Wakefield 245–4339, West Newton 965–5770, Westwood 329–0045. Telephone service is designed to help parents "get through the system of service delivery." In addition to providing information, the program staff facilitates service by intervening actively with other agencies, and where appropriate requests funds for programs for the child whose needs cannot otherwise be met.

STUDENT SERVICE CENTER   182 Tremont Street   Boston   Tel. 727–7040

Open: Monday-Friday 9–5 year round.

A federally funded project within the Department of Education organized, staffed, and run by students from schools in Massachusetts. Anyone may partake of services, but it primarily serves secondary school students. It offers a speakers' bureau, referral services, an alternative education information file, and a friendly shoulder for frustrated students to cry on. Student staff members are involved in a variety of research projects—from legal aspects of involving students in major policy-making decisions to legislation on students' rights.

VOCATIONS FOR SOCIAL CHANGE   353 Broadway (between Inman and Antrim streets)   Cambridge 02139   Tel. 661–1570

Open: Mondays and Wednesdays 1–7, Fridays 1–5, Saturdays 11–3.

"Although we work with high-school-age people and some junior high, most of those who come here are through with school. We keep a good supply of toys on hand for people who come in with small children."

The VSC storefront office is an information clearinghouse on groups working for change in such fields as health, law, education, and peace. It has a library of periodicals and literature; there is detailed information on groups working in many areas, including work options. The People Card File helps find others wishing to become involved in similar activities.

People's Yellow Pages is a valuable directory of Boston-area groups and individuals involved in the process of social change. $1 at VOC, $1.25 in stores, $1.50 postpaid.

Getting Together a People's Yellow Pages: An Overground Underground toward Social Change—a 65¢ booklet that tells you how to do it.

Do-It-Yourself

ADVISORY FOR OPEN EDUCATION   90 Sherman Street   Cambridge
Tel. 661–9310

The facilities are open to everyone. There is a teachers' center for getting ideas (what to do with collectibles), a scrounge room, a publications sales area (p. 59), and a completely outfitted woodworking shop.

Shop Equipment: Open for use Monday-Saturday 9–9. *Charges:* $2 per person for a day or $6 per month allows use anytime during the month. Good idea to sign up in advance.
Minimum Age: Children may come with parents or supervising adults. A one-to-one situation must be provided.

For Sale: Drywall. The AOE also has those usable tubes that are "waste" from the International Paper Company in Framingham. You may try to stand in line in Framingham for a free one, but it is of interest that AOE has a supply twice a month, which it sells for 50¢ each. AOE also has a special tube cutter.

There are three marvelous places in an old
nineteenth-century spinning mill on the Charles River:

JIM BOTTOMLEY   5 Bridge Street   Watertown   Tel. 969–1674

He is always finding new things to do with paper—dollhouses, jewelry, wall hangings, mobiles. Workshops given to people of all ages.

NEW ENGLAND CRAFTSMANSHIP CENTER   5 Bridge Street   Watertown   Tel. 923–1130

Here you can learn how to use tools, design furniture, and have access to tools for a major project. $60 for 12 lessons. Minimum age for participation: 9. Most instruction is on projects, but structured courses can be arranged. Visitors welcome, but call ahead please.

WORKSHOP FOR LEARNING THINGS, INC.   5 Bridge Street   Watertown   Tel. 926–1160

"We work with teachers on the development of new materials for classroom use . . . hold workshops . . . design and manufacture classroom materials."

Note: The Saturday workshops, 9 A.M.–noon, deal with some idea (e.g., making simple books, numerical activities, classroom photography, cardboard carpentry) that you can come to grips with in a morning. Each session costs $5 (plus materials in some cases), requires no advance registration, and is open to teachers and parents. Children old enough to join comfortably in the work are welcome, too.

Call for a place on the mailing list for seasonal brochures.

MORE WORKSHOPS for adults who work with children exist in various categories (e.g., museums, pp. 157–181, and environment, p. 269). A variety of offerings are also given by the Boston Center for Adult Education, 5 Commonwealth Avenue, Boston, Tel. 267–4430, and the Cambridge Center for Adult Education, 42 Brattle Street, Cambridge, Tel. 547–6789. The Greater Boston Teachers Center, 131 Mount Auburn Street, Cambridge, Tel. 876–2760, has workshops in various locations in the Boston area.

THE BIG PICTURE   134 Mt. Auburn Street   Cambridge   Tel. 547–9754 (2 blocks from Harvard Square)

Open: Monday-Saturday 10–6, Thursdays until 9.

Poster-sized enlargements made on nonglossy paper stock from negatives, snapshots, slides, or anything really. Black and white 18 by 24 maximum. Instruction offered to do-it-yourselfers. Simple photographic processes are carried out in normal light.

"Children about 7 or 8 may be able to participate in washing and fixing pictures, 11- and 12-year-olds are able to dry mount."

FRAMEWORKS   7 Upland Road   Cambridge   Tel. 354–9867

Ⓣ **Stop:** North Cambridge bus from Harvard Square. Traffic light after Sears is Upland.

Open: Tuesdays, Wednesdays, Thursdays 10–9, Fridays and Saturdays 10–6.

Anyone who is capable of handling hammer and hand drill and glass (if desired in work) can use the equipment. No appointment necessary. By doing it yourself, saving is about ⅓ of usual custom framing costs. *Note:* They are concerned with safety.

MUDFLAT   196 Broadway   Cambridge   Tel. 354–9626

A private nonprofit educational organization devoted exclusively to the development of craft skills in ceramics. Equipment includes 20 potters' wheels, gas and electric kilns, space for hand building, and glaze file. Open to public. Facilities and classes for age 14 and up. Special spring classes for high-school students.

Scrounge

WHERE?

Advisory for Open Education (p. 59).
Children's Museum Recycle (p. 163).
Lists of places that welcome scavengers go out of date quickly. Think about local businesses, factories, and shops that may be discarding useful things. Then ask! They are usually happy to recycle waste.

WHAT?

Lots of beautiful junk: Computer printout sheets for artwork, old punch cards, string from manufacturing companies, burlap (cheap) for a reconditioned burlap place, scrap wood and sawdust from a furniture manufacturing plant or wood-carving place, wallpaper and oilcloth samples, ends of newspaper rolls, ends from printers' shops.

CARDBOARD TUBES used as room dividers, as storage, for furniture and toys are available from International Paper Company, 125 Pennsylvania Avenue, Framingham (Tel. 1–875–6135), at certain times. Call for the schedule— and arrive early. (They are regular stock at the Advisory for Open Education, p. 59.)

HOW TO USE

Places that can help you think of ways to recycle waste materials include the Advisory for Open Education (p. 59), Children's Museum Recycle (p. 163), and Educational Development Center (55 Chapel Street, Newton, Tel. 969–7100), as well as many neighborhood art centers.

CALENDAR

January

MUSEUM GOERS MONTH   You can visit one museum and receive a free ticket good for admission to any of the other museums during weekday afternoons. Cooperating institutions vary from year to year. The last January before press time included Children's Museum, Drumlin Farm, Institute of Contemporary Art, Museum of Afro American History, Blue Hills Trailside Museum, Museum of American China Trade, Museum of Fine Arts, Museum of Science, Museum of Transportation, and the New England Aquarium.

ICE FISHING with proper equipment. If there has been a cold spell, maybe the local pond or lake is a source. Fishermen come complete with barbecues and make a day of it. Pickerel and perch are sought during this season at Whitehall Reservoir in Hopkinton (p. 215).

FOOTPRINTS IN THE SNOW—maybe at Arnold Arboretum or other Open Space (p. 183) areas. Bring bread to feed the birds.

DUCK FEEDING   They ARE hungry and do not have too many visitors this time of year. If you go to Norumbega (p. 40), you are near cross-country skiing (p. 239), or see Brandeis University and the Rose Art Museum (p. 174).

WALKING ALONG THE BEACH   If we have the usual January thaw, this could be an unusual experience for many.

February

WINTER SCHOOL VACATION WEEK   Call recorded information (p. 22) and museums (pp. 157–181) for special plans. Also note Ponkapoag Outdoor Center (p. 245).

DOG SLED RACES held in New Hampshire. (It is cold—and fairly passive—for observers.) Note newspaper sports pages for schedule.

LOGAN AIRPORT   Where not to go the Friday that school vacation starts. Also stay away from there on the Sunday that vacation concludes. If you must use the Expressway, change your plans! You will spend all your time in a massive backup.

OLD STURBRIDGE VILLAGE (p. 90) has sleigh rides, weather permitting on weekends and during Washington's Birthday week. For other sleigh rides, see p. 228.

ICE FOLLIES   This fully staged ice show comes to the Boston Garden for about 2 weeks. Group rates available. Tel. 227–3200.

CHINESE NEW YEAR is ushered in with a dragon dance (driving the devil out to let good luck come in) and firecrackers on the corner of Tyler and Beach streets. It is held on a Sunday afternoon from 2 to 4. For the exact date call the Chinese Christian Church of New England, 338–8789.

As part of the New Year celebration, the church sponsors a special Friday night program designed to share their culture with others. The same menu is served in several designated restaurants in Chinatown at 6:30 P.M. Provide your own transportation to John Hancock Hall for a 2-hour performance, beginning at 8 P.M., that includes Chinese melodies, folk songs, a Chinese play (in English), a talk on Chinese New Year customs, fashion show, dragon dance, and folk and classical dance. Tickets are available through the church office, 60 Harvard Street, Boston.

SCHOLASTIC ART EXHIBITION at State Office Building Gallery, Government Center, sponsored by the *Boston Globe*. Held for 1 week. Entries of students in Grades 7–12 are screened by a regional advisory committee of high-school art educators. Includes painting and drawing, graphics and design, three-dimensional art, and photography. The exhibition gallery faces the plaza with its bubbling fountains. For information: 929–2649.

JUNIOR ACHIEVEMENT TRADE FAIR (headquarters at 256 Huntington Avenue, Boston, Tel. 262–7272)   Each student company has a display booth with the product it is manufacturing and marketing—everything from jewelry to small furniture. Members are high-school juniors and seniors. Call for location(s) of trade fairs in the city and suburban areas.

March

NEW ENGLAND SPRING GARDEN AND FLOWER SHOW   Held for 9 days at Commonwealth Armory (near Boston University). Northeast residents are starved for outdoor greenery by this time of winter. Lines form first thing in the morning for the magnificent displays and ideas. The space is relatively small and the show is not really child-oriented. Call 536–9280 for this year's schedule. Admission: Adults $3, children under 12 accompanied by adults free.

MIT's annual rocket convention takes place on a weekend. Usually more than 100 rocket enthusiasts attend.

ST. PATRICK'S DAY PARADE, March 17, South Boston, in the afternoon. Floats, bands, politicians, and drill teams galore in this gay 1½-hour procession. (The date has reason for double celebration in Boston as it was on March 17, 1776, that the British left Boston. This first major success in the Revolution is noted by a monument at Dorchester Heights, South Boston.)

COMMUNITY BOAT HOUSE (p. 235) open house. Held last weekend of the month. Movies, refreshments, and possible sailboat rides. No charge.

March and April

TIME TO WALK THE BEACH, weather permitting, and possibly collect driftwood.

SUGARING OFF   The season depends on the weather. Ideal "running days" are cold nights followed by warm (40 degrees) weather. There are about 400 sugarhouses within a 3-hour ride from Boston, and they vary in methods and facilities. Progress means that not all farmers go from tree to tree. They may have plastic lines that connect the trees from the top to the bottom of the hill. Visitors are usually welcome at the sugarhouses anytime, but it is a good idea to check the situation before leaving from home. Dress for the hike in the orchard with warm clothing and boots. In all places you will see the collection of the sap and the boiling that results in maple syrup. It takes 40 pints of sap to make 1 pint of syrup. There is no charge for observation, but tastes may have a price. Sugar-on-snow—the chewy product after boiled-down maple syrup is poured on snow—is often served for about $1 per person.

IN MASSACHUSETTS (could be combined with a stop to see the bison in Southboro, p. 46, on the way home): Thomas E. Southwick, 132 Marshall Street, **Leicester** (near Worcester), Tel. 617–791–5258, collects the sap in buckets and empties it into trucks with tanks. The evaporator has a wood fire. He would like to have arrangements for tasting sap and syrup, but it is not always possible. The Southwicks have a Christmas-tree farm and visitors are welcome to take a walk through the area. In **Orange** (1½ hours from Boston) Philip Johnson, Tel. 617–544–3614, has a small operation that is fine for families, but not really big enough to handle large groups. Tastes of syrup given; it is boiled in a sugarhouse with a wood fire. From Rt. 2A take a right by the Waltz Club onto Wheeler Avenue and drive for about 2 miles to the sugarhouse that is right beside the road. Beyond Amherst is Montague and Williams on Rt. 47 in **Sunderland,** Tels. 413–665–3127, 413–773–8301. It is about a 2-hour drive to the operation of two families who enjoy the fun and hard work of farm life. Homemade doughnuts and sugar-on-snow are served in the sugarhouse; the evaporators are right above the eating area. Oil is used for boiling the sap. In this location they may get a head start, and they try to operate from March 1 until early April, but as always the weather dictates the season. They are open 7 days a week once they start. Maple products sold. Visitors allowed to walk into the sugar bush. Still a little farther is Lesure Farm (135 miles from Boston) in **Ashfield,** Tel. 413–628–3956 (Rt. 5, north to Rt. 9, west to 112, north on 122 to sign), where there is a museum of old and new equipment. It may be possible to see the actual tapping of a tree if you give advance notice of group arrival. No sugar-on-snow arrangements. Visitors can see the sap being collected and the sugarhouse where oil is used for boiling sap. Waffles, muffins, and sausages served for about $1.

IN VERMONT: 2½ hours away in **Putney** is a large operation at Harlow's Sugar House, Tel. 802–387–5852 (Rt. 2 to Greenfield, north on Interstate 91 to Putney turnoff, Rt. 5 to sugarhouse). If groups call ahead, they can have a guided tour, sugar-on-snow, doughnuts, pickles and coffee. No charge to come into the sugarhouse to see the boiling; there are both wood and oil fires. Maple sugaring movie shown; no charge. A team of horses takes you into sugar bush (50¢); sugar-on-snow 50¢. Nearby is another sugar producer, George Ranney, Rt. 2, **Putney,** Tel. 802–254–2635. He is 5 miles north of Brattleboro, 2 miles south of Putney. Casual visitors are welcome, but if you let him know that you are coming, he will plan to give a tour through his dairy operation (or crops in season). Milking time: 3:30–5:30.

IN NEW HAMPSHIRE: Holt's Sugar Bush, just out of Wilton in **Lyndeboro Center** on Rt. 31, Tel. 603–654–9090, uses plastic tubing—and gravity—to get the syrup from the trees on the hill. Wood fire in the sugarhouse. Fried dough served outside; charge for food. At Ednew Farm on Rt. 202 in **Bennington** (Rt.

3 to 31 to 202, 75 miles, 1½ hours, from Boston), Gladys Newhall will welcome families (too small to accommodate groups) on weekends. This is a small operation that has been state champion. Tel. 603–588–6661. She uses a wood fire, and collects the syrup with pails in a truck. Tastes cheerfully given. Trees are right alongside road. She also makes her own maple sugar shapes, but it is unlikely that you will see the process because the syrup has to set at least a month before sugar is made. Raymond Parker in **Mason** (60 miles from Boston), Tel. 603–878–2308, uses a tractor and pickup trucks to collect from his orchards in 6 towns. Visitors see the tapped trees, the sugarhouse with its 5- by 16-foot evaporator—and get a chance to have sugar-on-snow (and pickles) outdoors for 50¢. In operation on weekends during the season. Take Rt. 128 to Rt. 3 to Nashua, Rt. 130 to Brookline, and follow the signs to Mason for about 3 miles and you will see signs to the Parkers'. The restaurant, decorated with antique sugaring items, serves pancakes and syrup during sugaring-off season, and then it uses its own syrup for pancakes on weekends right up to Thanksgiving. Open 8–6 Saturdays and Sundays during sugaring off; restaurant serves home-cooked food Friday nights, Saturdays, and Sundays through the fall.

BIRD WALKS   Take your own in one of the open space areas (pp. 183–200) or contact the Massachusetts Audubon Society (p. 202) for the schedule of walks that leave from various locations at 8 or 9 A.M. Beginners—and children —are welcome in many groups. Keep in mind that "quiet" is necessary on walks. During this season birds are more visible before foliage appears.

April

BOSTON TEA PARTY SHIP (p. 160). Annual bending (putting on the sails and unfurling them) of the sails to celebrate the beginning of the spring/ summer season. Date changes from year to year.

SHEEP-SHEARING DEMONSTRATIONS at Merrimack Valley Textile Museum (p. 168) grounds. No charge. Call for schedule.

SCHOOL VACATION WEEK   Call recorded information (p. 22) and museums (pp. 157–181) for special programs.

M.I.T. OPEN HOUSE   Held on a Saturday afternoon biennially in odd-numbered years. No admission charge. Every department plans special programs with demonstrations and exhibits in engineering, science, architecture, the humanities, and industrial management. You may possibly see computers at work, the world's most powerful magnet, processes for dating rock specimens, a model of a space capsule, optical illusions with a strobe light, a "magic show" in the chemistry department, and a computer and plotter in the civil engineering department that may draw, at request, the shortest route between any two buildings on the M.I.T. campus. More than 200 exhibits. Hours: 12–5 P.M.

NATIONAL LIBRARY WEEK   Watch for special programs.

SPRING VACATION   Book sale at Horticultural Hall held Thursday through Tuesday. For a mailing reminder, call the Women's Committee of the

Children's Hospital Medical Center, 734–6000. This huge marvelous sale has an entire section for children, complete with tables and chairs—hardly expected at a used book sale.

HERRING RUN SEASON—late in the month. To check on a nearby ladder or to inquire if the season is on, call the Division of Marine Fisheries, Tel. 727–3193, Frank Grice.

This is the time that the fish spawn in lakes and ponds. Many do not survive because of the difficulty or length of the journey. Those that do survive come back year after year. (Survivors go back to the ocean eventually; the young ones swim down in late summer or fall.) Watching the fish, by the thousands, accept the challenge of the ladder is a memorable sight.

The observation area nearest to Boston is the revitalized ladder near WATERTOWN SQUARE at California Street. Follow Storrow Drive to Watertown Square. About ½ mile before the square there on the south side of the Charles River by MDC parkland is the ladder used by fish that have come from Boston Harbor. More ladders are scheduled to go over several other dams on the Charles so that the herring may go as far as South Natick.

Some other locations: EAST WEYMOUTH. Take Southeast Expressway to Rt. 18, first left at first light onto Middle Street into East Weymouth. The herring come in from the ocean to the fresh water of Whitman's Pond to spawn. The herring swim against the flow to get to this point, so you may notice them resting or see them actually jump up a concrete stepladder through the falls. No fishing allowed.

BOURNEDALE along Cape Cod Canal. A very large run. (Take Rt. 3 to Rt. 6 at Sagamore Bridge, travel less than a mile to the parking lot, near a comfort station.) The herring come from the canal up the steps, go under the road on their way to a herring pond. They later retrace their swim. Enjoy the canal activity, bicycle along, fish in the canal (equipment rental information, p. 103), or combine with other places (p. 103) in the area.

PATRIOTS' DAY   Although the date of celebration has been moved to the third Monday of the month, Concord still celebrates on April 19.

REENACTMENT AND CELEBRATIONS—some at dawn—in many towns. Sunrise activities in Littleton and Sudbury. Carlisle has ceremonies and a march; Jamaica Plain has a morning parade; there is a pilgrimage from Acton to Concord; the Minutemen mobilize in Concord and reenact the battle at the Old North Bridge. Exact schedules are published in newspapers.

THE FAMOUS RIDE   William Dawes leaves from John Eliot Square in Roxbury and Paul Revere starts from Hanover Street in the North End of Boston for a ride "through every Middlesex village and farm"; a uniformed horseman arrives near the Minuteman statue about 1 P.M. and a long wonderful parade— often held in freezing rain—starts at 2. While searching for a parking place (even in non-Bicentennial years), keep in mind that it takes about an hour for the parade to reach the Green from the official starting point.

MARATHON RACE   Many nations are represented in the 26-mile race (first held in 1892). It starts in Hopkinton at noon and finishes 2–2:30 on the Boylston Street side of the Prudential Center. Much of the route includes Commonwealth Avenue; many spectators turn out to cheer the runners.

NEW ENGLAND FOLK FESTIVAL   Experience not necessary to enjoy this. Held on a weekend (Friday evenings 6:30–11:30 P.M., Saturdays 10–noon, 12–5 (performances begin at 2, audience participation follows), and 5:30–11. Sunday sessions also held. Ethnic groups give folk dancing demonstrations, with Saturday planned especially for youngsters. The wide variety of marvelous homemade international foods (snack or meal), to be found nowhere else (and at reasonable prices), is served by the chefs themselves in native dress. Sometimes New England craftsmen demonstrate weaving, woodworking, batik, and whittling. Admission charged per session or combination ticket may be available. Reasonable. Group rates available with advance reservations for children. Call or write for location and schedule: New England Folk Festival Association, 57 Roseland Street, Somerville, Tel. 354–2455.

STATE DRAMA FESTIVAL held in John Hancock Hall, 180 Berkeley Street, Boston, the first weekend in April. The "angel" for this is the *Boston Globe*. Tickets available at the door. One ticket may admit you to all performances. All casts (16 finalists from regional competitions) must have students from their own school only, no musicals are permitted, essentially no props are allowed, and costumes must be simple. The acting ability of the students is considered the most important feature. Scripts must be cut as each presentation is limited to 40 minutes. Two plays are sent to the New England Festival and an all-state cast is selected. For information: 929–2649.

April and May

REGATTAS ON CHARLES RIVER   Crew races are held Saturday afternoons during April and through mid-May. The crews of Boston University, Harvard, and Northeastern race courses of varying lengths, the longest being 1¾ miles, all between Longfellow Bridge and the M.I.T. Boat House. Depending on the number of races scheduled for the day, they start at 2 or 3 and end at 6 or 7.

May

CIRCUS   The Ringling Bros. Circus arrives in the Boston Garden for 8 days. Children 12 years and under are usually half price at all performances except weekend afternoons. Box office: Tel. 227–3200.

   CIRCUS PARADE: Unloading of the 30-car circus train at Southampton Street begins at 11 A.M. followed by the traditional animal walk across town to the North Station arena. It includes about 20 elephants, 50 thoroughbred horses, camels, ponies, and zebras, together with members of Clown Alley that march to Andrews Square, up Dorchester Avenue, across the Broadway Bridge to Herald Street, up Washington, Stuart, and Elliot streets to Park Square, down Charles Street to Leverett Circle and along Nashua, Causeway, and Beverly streets into the Boston Garden.

OLD STURBRIDGE VILLAGE (p. 90) has sheep-shearing demonstrations.

ART FESTIVALS, ART SHOWS, AND FAIRS   Everywhere! Some are free. Some are for fund-raising. Many are outdoors. Watch the newspapers.

LILAC SUNDAY   Arnold Arboretum. More than 400 kinds of lilacs in the collection, which is classified in seven color groupings, with single- and double-flowering forms within each. Transportation through the Arboretum may be offered on this one day.

DRUMFEST   Groups from miles around gather for the Drum and Bugle Corps competition. For information: Tel. 646–5472.

DRUMLIN FARM (p. 191). It is likely to be sheep-shearing and hayride time. Check the plans.

ASHUMET HOLLY RESERVATION (p. 196) open house. Third weekend usually. Guided walks along trails lined with holly, heather, herb gardens, and flowering trees.

APPLE BLOSSOM TIME   Late in the month. Drive in Stow and Harvard (around Rt. 117, Rt. 62) or around Littleton and Groton. If you bring bicycles, you will find the countryside a little hilly for young children or inexperienced adults.

NEW ENGLAND FIDDLERS' CONVENTION in Granville, Massachusetts, last Saturday. Goes on all day until last fiddler has been judged. Baked bean supper served at 5.

SCIENCE FAIR   M.I.T. Rockwell Cage, Vassar Street and Massachusetts Avenue. Sponsored by the *Boston Globe*. Held during one weekend, Fridays 6–9, Saturdays 1–6, and Sundays 2–4. Free. Accessible by Ⓣ. High-school students demonstrate their scientific know-how for teams of judges from faculties of colleges and secondary schools and from local industrial firms. Each project has a central theme and answers a definite scientific question. Almost any aspect of science may be included. Students remain with their exhibits during the fair and are delighted to answer questions. Tel. 929–2649.

APPLE BLOSSOM FESTIVAL, Harvard, Massachusetts, on third Sunday (with plans to coincide with actual blossoming). There are churches at the top and bottom of the sloping land that constitutes the Harvard Common, the site of the festival. The annual fund-raising event has arts and crafts exhibits, cotton candy, game booths, and rides. Bus tours through orchards and historic sites along the way may be offered. The day is over by 5 P.M.

KITE FESTIVAL in Franklin Park at golf course. Sponsored by the Better Use of Air and the city of Boston Parks and Recreation Department. Kite clinics held at various locations around the city on the 3 Saturdays before the contest. Hundreds of kites of various sizes, shapes, and designs are in the air in the afternoon. It is possible that supplies for making simple ones may be available. Bring picnic lunch. Great day.

CASE ESTATES (p. 191) open house. Held early in the month on a Sunday. Members of staff on hand.

HARVARD SQUARE MAY ARTS FESTIVAL   Second weekend. Many events planned for children. Most performances are free.

SPRING REVELS   A grand celebration of the season in Sanders Theatre, Cambridge. Good fun with folk groups and individuals performing. Recommended for all ages. Admission charged.

BOSTON PARKS AND RECREATION GREENHOUSE open house: On a Sunday, mid-May. Location: Corner of Morton Street and American Legion Highway in Jamaica Plain. Horticultural experts on hand to answer questions. Tropical plants, annuals, and bedding plants. Guided tours. No charge.

Memorial Day:
PARADES. Many short processions in several areas of Boston.

DEDHAM HORSE SHOW at Dedham Country and Polo Club, Westfield Street (about a mile off Rt. 109), Dedham. Admission charged. Stadium jumping usually starts about 1 P.M. Children and adults participate in two rings, which are both scheduled continuously through the day.

May and June

BOSTON POPS   Programs are made up about a week in advance for this traditional 9-week series during which tables and chairs replace the regular first-floor audience seats. A mixture of the classics, popular favorites, hit parade numbers, and novelties are conducted by Arthur Fiedler. Refreshments sold. The first floor is the most expensive and most social. Audio is better upstairs. Held Monday-Saturday at 8:30. No concerts on Sundays. All seats reserved. All but second balcony may be reserved by phone, Tel. 266–1492. Second balcony tickets seldom available the night of the concert.

ESPLANADE CONCERTS—free—by the Boston Pops Orchestra at Hatch Shell on the Charles River, Boston. Everyone is welcome to sit under the open skies at the 8 P.M. performances. Schedule available in newspapers or from Symphony Hall, Tel. 266–1492. Attendance is heavy. Take public transportation. Check for possible additional locations.

June

DAIRY OPEN HOUSES   On a designated Sunday some dairy farms welcome visitors to see the cows, barns, and pastures. Some farmers are receptive to observers at the early morning milking, but most schedule the hours in the afternoon. The list of this year's locations is usually published in the newspapers. Or check with the Massachusetts Farm Bureau Federation, 85 Central Street, Waltham, Tel. 893–2600.

(Sunny Rock Farm, 654 North Street, Walpole, Tel. 668–3448, usually participates. It is a working family farm where they do not always have time to give guided tours, but people are always welcome to look around and stay as long as they wish. There are 5 teen-agers who may be available to show people around. There are 40–50 dairy animals and 4,000 laying hens, 150 acres of woods, fields, pasture—and a farm store.)

BUSCH-REISINGER MUSEUM's (p. 161) garden is at its prettiest with roses, lilies, and hollyhocks. Small; not a place for youngsters to run around. Okay to bring lunch and sit at outside tables.

JUNE ART IN THE PARK   Likely to be second weekend. On Boston Common. More than 400 area artists, painters, sculptors, and craftsmen exhibit. No charge.

MIDDLEBORO FAIR and BROCKTON FAIR   Major fairs (p. 296) held at Raynham Park in Raynham. Admission charged.

WESTON DRAMA WORKSHOP   Box 441   Weston 02193. This community drama group offers a 6-week summer program for youngsters 12–21. There is no residency requirement. Tryouts take place on Saturdays in June. Nominal fee charged. About 250 do everything including lighting, costumes, and sound.

BLUE HILLS TRAILSIDE MUSEUM (p. 159). Special "Let's Discover" courses for grades 2–6.

MOUNTAIN CLIMBERS   Black flies come to life in May, are at their worst in June, and supposedly taper off in July. They flourish in 72–94° temperature. Long-sleeved heavy shirts and slacks, wool socks, and hat are all necessary. Bill Riviere of the *Boston Globe* says: "Modern fly dopes are moderately useful if you spray or apply liberally, walk fast, smoke excessively, don't take a bath, don't wear perfume, and don't inhale carelessly."

SUMMER PREVIEW ISSUE   A special section worth looking for. Published about the third week of the month in both the *Boston Phoenix* and the *Real Paper* (p. 23).

BOSTON COMMON DAIRY FESTIVAL   Held for one week early in the month, Saturday-Saturday 9–7. Free. Arrangements for guided tours may be possible. Call in March: The New England Dairy and Food Council, 1034 Commonwealth Avenue, Tel. 734–6750.

There is an old law still on the books that states that cattle are supposed to appear annually on the Common. There are about 100 penned cattle, together with some calves, gathered for the event. Personnel will answer questions and possibly allow onlookers to try milking; it happens about 5 P.M.

MILITIA DAY, first Monday. Visiting delegations from the eastern seaboard join the Ancient and Honorable Artillery Company for a full dress parade on the route from Faneuil Hall (starting at 1) to the Boston Common. After stopping for a memorial service in a church, ceremonies on the Boston Common take place from about 3 to 4:30. The spectacle, which seems to attract mostly passersby, includes the drumhead election. (A hollow square is formed so that all may see what is going on, and each ballot is cast upon a huge centuries-old drum.) A booming cannon announces that the governor has commissioned the new officers. A parade on the Common follows.

BUNKER HILL DAY, June 17. A 1½-hour parade, starting at 2 P.M., is part of the remembrance of the fortification of Breed's Hill, although Bunker Hill was the original site selected by the colonists. In the morning children hold their own parade of decorated carriages and bicycles on the streets near Bunker Hill Monument on Breed's Hill in Charlestown.

U.S. PROFESSIONAL GRASS COURT TENNIS TOURNAMENTS held during the day at Longwood Cricket Club, 564 Hammond Street, Brookline (near Chestnut Hill Ⓣ Stop), Tel. 731–2900. Admission charged.

KITE FLYING TIME. Note that beaches (p. 208) provide a good open space—without the summer crowds.

June-September

MASSACHUSETTS AGRICULTURAL FAIRS   If you have never been, you should experience at least one in your life. There are horse pulls, handcraft exhibits, garden prizes, duck-calling contests, entertainment, ecology exhibits, industrial exhibits, animal shows, championship oxen pulls, beef cattle judging, sheep day . . . variations on a theme. It is usually crowded and the nights can be close to carnival atmosphere. Massachusetts has: MAJOR FAIRS that run several days, with extensive exhibits, a large midway that you are either attracted to or try to avoid, and unique contests. Admission charged. COMMUNITY FAIRS—sponsored on a local level; YOUTH FAIRS are run for and by young people, usually 4–H or Future Farmers of America; GRANGE FAIRS are local fairs, most often featuring home economics and crafts. For the current list of all fairs, check with the Division of Fairs, Massachusetts Department of Agriculture, 100 Cambridge Street, Boston 02202, Tel. 727–3037.

June, July, and August
"Pick-your-own"

The list of places is not constant; plans change from year to year. It is always a good idea to CALL BEFORE GOING; variables (including weather and supply) influence the decision of the farm. You may find that there is not much of a saving, but it is fun and the produce is fresh.

STRAWBERRIES are usually available late June and sometimes into July. Try Colonial Orchards or Verrill Farm (see below). Or maybe Learoyd Farms, Rt. 1A, Rowley (north of Boston), Tel. 984–3859.

BLUEBERRIES may be picked mid-July–mid-August. There are cultivated and "natural" blueberries. Those who pick the wild variety are hesitant to divulge their hideouts; a sure giveaway is the lineup of cars along the road. Some suggestions may be the Rt. 128-Trapelo Road interchange area in Waltham, Prospect Hill (p. 237) in Waltham, the Milton side of Blue Hills Reservation

(p. 196), and Quabbin Reservoir (p. 195). It may be a good idea to have supplies in the car so that you are ready for action: buckets for berries, repellent for you.

Cultivated berries may be available at Antonio Balboni, 416 Central Street, East Bridgewater, Tel. 378–3996 (containers not provided), and at the Alger Farm in West Bridgewater, Tel. 586–6769.

PLACES THAT OFFER A VARIETY during the season are likely to include Edward Benischeck, 118 Central Street, Rowley, Tel. 948–3912 (could combine with a visit to Plum Island, p. 190). Colonial Orchards, Rt. 122A, Millbury, Tel. 865–6707, may have strawberries, peas, and some blueberries. Verrill Farm on Wheeler Road (off Sudbury Road) in Concord, Tel. 369–5952, has strawberries, and after a lull in early July there is usually something to pick until September 1: raspberries, beans, tomatoes, peppers, corn, squash, cabbage, eggplant, carrots, beets, lettuce, chards, and/or brussels sprouts.

For a current list of places that have pick-your-own opportunities, check with the Massachusetts Department of Agriculture, 100 Cambridge Street, Boston 02202, Tel. 727–2018. A self-addressed stamped envelope is required.

July

JULY 4   Fireworks and celebrations. Many towns and cities sponsor displays starting at 9 or 10 P.M. Boston newspapers usually publish the events for all surrounding communities in the July 3 edition.

MARBLEHEAD RACE WEEK   Saturday-Saturday last week of month. The races, starting every afternoon after 1:30, have approximately 30 classes participating. Pleasure craft—large and small—come for a waterside view of the full-blown sails. Some old legend says that you can cross the populated harbor by stepping from boat to boat from the town to Marblehead Neck. If you tote the children for the worthwhile shore view, warning: Traffic to, from, and in the town is extremely slow moving this week.

SUBURBAN EXPERIMENT STATION (p. 271) open house and horticulture show. No charge. Staff on hand to answer questions.

July and August

SUMMERTHING   Boston's neighborhoods have their own workshops in painting, sculpture, ceramics, music, photography, drama, dance, and other subjects. Neighborhood events (block parties, square dances, etc.) are periodically scheduled. Local performing groups travel to the various neighborhoods. Funding is an annual problem, so activities may vary. Call 261–1660 for full listing of entertainment and participatory events.

GOVERNMENT CENTER is likely to have noonday concerts. Some dangle their feet in the fountain while listening. There may be Wednesday evening performances in the outdoor amphitheatre. No charge.

FILMS   Scheduled at the Boston Public Library and its branches. No charge.

BOSTON CHILDREN'S THEATRE (p. 49), Tel. 536–3324, gives plays in eastern Massachusetts from a stagemobile. No charge when at MDC playgrounds or when sponsored by local recreation departments. There is usually a nominal admission fee when presented by a local organization. Call for the date of appearance in your area.

FOLK DANCING   It may be on some plaza, held weekly—free. The Taylors (p. 227) are probably conducting outdoor sessions somewhere. They have a special talent for getting large crowds involved. All ages attend—and find that it is really fun. (It is time to make reservations for the Taylor's fall Stowe Folk Festival. Check for details with Folk Dancing 'Round Boston, 62 Fottler Avenue, Lexington 02173, Tel. 862–7144. Relatively inexpensive—depending upon accommodations you arrange.)

OUTDOOR CONCERTS   Wednesday evenings—bands, barbershop quartets at 7 P.M. at the Prudential Center. No admission fee. Pink lemonade served.

AUCTIONS are held year round in the Boston area. Children may be very uncomfortable in a small overheated hall in December, but check the advertisements in the Sunday papers for those old-fashioned country auctions held outdoors. (They are getting scarce.) Bring lunch, folding chairs (or a blanket). Choose one with a potpourri of listings rather than the exquisite variety. Some auctioneers have a good sense of entertainment—and education —while enumerating the use and age of some relic.

MAGIC CIRCLE THEATER at Tufts University, Medford. Two plays presented by children (ages 10–15) enrolled in summer theatre program. One-hour productions are given in this small intimate, air-conditioned arena theatre on Thursday and Friday mornings (and some afternoons) during July and part of August. Admission: $1. Group rates available. Reservations suggested. Tel. 623–3880. Audience appeal: Age 4 and older.

ICE SKATING at several indoor rinks, including Boston Skating Club (p. 232), Charles River in Newton, Lynn, Melrose, and Cohasset.

WALKS IN THE CITY   Plenty to see. Fairly quiet—and manageable on a Sunday. People seem to cluster at the North End festivals, the Flea Market, and along the banks of the Charles River.

BEACHBUGGY WILDLIFE TOURS at Wellfleet Bay Sanctuary, South Wellfleet (at Cape Cod National Seashore area). Daily 2-hour tours scheduled during summer shorebird migration. A Massachusetts Audubon Society guide accompanies no more than 12 people to remote salt marshes, sand dunes, and the tide-scoured shore. Suggested minimum age: 6. $4 per person. Reservations strongly recommended. Write in advance or call 349–2615.

MYSTIC MARINER TRAINING PROGRAMS   The Conrad Program, instruction in elementary sailing and seamanship, is offered to youngsters between 13 and 18. It is a popular program that often fills by Christmas. For information write to Mystic Seaport (p. 84).

MUSEUMS   Many offer special onetime programs or a short series for children of a specified age group. (Blue Hills Trailside Museum, p. 159, has Bee Days scheduled; honey is extracted from the hives and the public can sample the results.)

PEACE   Have you been to the Garden Court of the Museum of Fine Arts or read in the Boston Public Library courtyard?

ELMA LEWIS PLAYHOUSE-IN-THE-PARK, Franklin Park, Dorchester. Local, national, and international performers included in the presentations that are given nightly; free.

SUMMER THEATRE PERFORMANCES   Many are appropriate for youngsters. Matinees usually planned at least once a week.

BOSTON FLEA MARKET   Held 1–6 P.M. on Sundays May-October near Faneuil Hall, outside of Quincy Market. Parking somewhat easier then weekdays. A little of everything including food and entertainment. (Office is at 29 Newbury Street, Tel. 536–0300.) Admission: $1, under 12, 25¢.

HARVARD COLLEGE OBSERVATORY roof, 60 Garden Street, Cambridge, open every Friday night (weather permitting) from dusk until 11 P.M. Admission: Free. Telescopic observations of stars, planets, and the moon under the trained eye of an observatory staff member.

WESTON DRAMA WORKSHOP (p. 290). Performances given the last 2 weeks in July and early August. Children's play Tuesday-Saturday at the Country School on Alphabet Lane, off School Street in Weston. Tickets: $1. Group rates available. A musical and straight drama given outdoors Monday-Saturday evenings. Adults, $2.50; students, $1.50. Dial 411 for this season's telephone number or write Box 411, Weston 02193.

DECORDOVA MUSEUM (p. 164). Every Sunday afternoon a professional concert is held in an outdoor amphitheatre that features music or dance, ranging in style from classical to contemporary folk, and there is a sidewalk sale of arts and crafts where DeCordova Museum School students and teachers display their work. Refreshments are available. There is no charge beyond the regular admission fee to the grounds. Come early to see facilities and beautiful surroundings, which close about the time the concert is over. Inexpensive. Delightful.
[A special summer program is held outdoors for 6 weeks during the summer. It focuses on a specific theme in creative arts for ages 6–8 and 9–12. Programs also offered for teens.]

TANGLEWOOD   Berkshire Music Festival, Lenox, 140 miles from Boston. Massachusetts Turnpike to Lenox (2½-hour drive). Ticket sales and information from Symphony Hall, Boston, Tel. 266–1492.
This 200-acre estate, where Nathaniel Hawthorne lived and wrote, is the summer home of the Boston Symphony Orchestra. The administration requests that infants and children not yet ready to enjoy the concerts be discouraged from attending. There are no reduced prices for children. Those who bring children who are not serious musicians will be happiest with the lawn space outside the Music Shed.
In addition to the scheduled evening performances, open rehearsals are held the 8 Saturday mornings of the festival at 10:30. There is one break during the 2½-hour nearly finished concert, and the informal atmosphere allows families to come and go if they wish. There are plenty of seats available and many choose to sit on the grass outside the Shed.
Direct buses provided for Sunday concerts by Peter Pan Bus Company, Tel. 482–6620 (Boston), Natick (653–5660), and Worcester (754–2611).

MDC TRAVELING ZOO   Exhibits from the Franklin Park Zoo are transported to local playgrounds and other sites in the area. For the schedule call 442–2002.

FESTIVALS IN THE NORTH END   Carrying out customs that date back hundreds of years, several societies have weekend celebrations related to the Patron Saint of the Italian town from which the participants or their ancestors came. On Sunday a procession weaves slowly through the streets from about 2–6; donations collected are applied to expenses and any profit is given to charity. Some of the streets in the relatively small area have lighted arches. Band concerts add to the festive atmosphere on Sunday evenings, usually from 8 to 11. Stands, most active from dusk on, sell stuffed quahogs, Italian sausages, fried dough, hot corn on the cob, slush, and pizza. As a visitor you feel that you are at a neighborhood party—where you are welcome.

You can spend an hour—or many—at a festival. One could be combined with a walk along the waterfront (from North and Fleet streets you are a block from Lewis Wharf), or if it is a *Sunday,* you could browse at the *Flea Market* (p. 294).

The festival schedule is usually close to this:

July—2nd weekend, Saturday and Sunday; last weekend, at least Saturday and Sunday.

August—1st weekend, Saturday and Sunday. Procession, lasting until 8 P.M., includes 20 men who carry a statue on a solid oak framework that weighs a ton and a half. The next three weekends in August have larger processions with 5 or 6 bands, drill teams, and floats (some years).

The second weekend in August has a Friday-Saturday festival. The third weekend is Thursday-Sunday; this is Madonna del Soccorso (Our Lady of Perpetual Help), the Fisherman's Feast with the highlight taking place on Sunday when young girls are dressed as angels on the balconies of North Street. One girl is lowered via a pulley into the street, she gives a speech (about 5:30) in Italian, pigeons are released from a decorated cage, and then the air (and street) are filled with confetti. Arrive before 5 so you will be on time.

SOME SUMMER CAMP INFORMATION SOURCES

CAMPFINDER   14 Somerset Street   Tel. 742–2000
Published by United Community Planning Corporation, revised biennially in even numbered years. Price to individuals: $2.

The almost 300 camps included in this booklet are conducted by social agencies and other organizations serving children, youth, and adults of Greater Boston.

NEW ENGLAND CAMPING ASSOCIATION,   29 Commonwealth Avenue,   Tel. 536–0225, publishes a directory ($3) of day and resident camps in New England accredited by the American Camping Association. The counselor placement service is limited to those who are at least 18 (for day camps) or 19 (for overnight camps).

August

DUSTERS' MEET   First Sunday in August. Held at Larz Anderson Park in Brookline on the grounds of the Museum of Transportation (p. 173). Many owners—and their families—arrive costumed, in working antique autos. Picnic and visit in the park (p. 187).

FEAST OF THE BLESSED SACRAMENT   Held first weekend in New Bedford at Madeira Field, Hathaway Street. Feast continues until midnight every day with decorations, bands, Portuguese singers and dancers, and a huge midway. The specialty of the feast, *carne de spito*, is barbecued at a 50-foot fireplace. A parade with drill teams and floats starts at 2:30 P.M. Sunday from Brooklawn Park (Rt. 140 takes you there).

FOCUS OUTDOORS   Usually the first weekend. A natural history and environmental conference with talks, walks, and seminars. Families welcome. Not really child-oriented. Fascinating and exciting for interested junior and senior high school students. For information, contact the Massachusetts Audubon Society, p. 202.

MARSHFIELD FAIR in Marshfield and **REHOBOTH FAIR** in Dighton are considered major fairs (p. 291).

BROCKTON SUMMERFEST at the Brockton Community School, the sprawling high school that is one of the biggest in the country—performances (bands, theatre, and dance troupes), games, parades, athletic demonstrations, a large flea market, crafts, puppet shows, movies. It is enormous and goes continuously for 3 days. Most events are either free or about $1.

MOON FESTIVAL in Chinatown. It is the Chinese Thanksgiving with songs and dances, a parade, and traditional chicken dishes and moon cakes. It comes at the time of the full moon, the fifteenth of the month according to the Chinese calendar; watch the newspapers for the specific date and scheduled events.

September

Reminder: Write to Harvard Open Nights program (p. 264) for tickets. Requests accepted for Boston University's Observatory Open Nights (p. 264).

CHILDREN'S MUSEUM   Closed for the month.

FIREMEN'S MUSTER   Last Saturday of the month. On Boston Common with a parade from the Prudential Center starting at 11 and pumping contests on the Common starting at 12:30. About 22 companies arrive from all over New England with their restored machines that were built between 1828 and 1895. North America's oldest organized formal sport is demonstrated as they fill the tubs and hand-pump away to see which water drops go the farthest along a long paper.

MAJOR FAIRS (p. 291) have hundreds of agricultural exhibitors in large barns (often missed!). At times the numerous carnival booths and amusements seem to take over. Fairs scheduled this month are in Foxboro, Weymouth, and Springfield (one of the ten largest in the country—at 1305 Memorial Avenue, West Springfield).

SUFFOLK COUNTY 4–H FAIR held at Franklin Park Zoo on a weekend, Saturdays and Sundays 10–6. Bring a picnic lunch and spend the day seeing exhibits, baby chicks in the eggmobile, horse show, demonstrations, and contests galore—pie eating, ice cream, hula hoop, and milk drinking. For exact dates check with the Roxbury-Dorchester Beautification Program, Inc., 612 Blue Hill Avenue, Roxbury, Tel. 288–3313.

1747 FARM—a huge horse show with a small show atmosphere. Held the weekend after Labor Day on the grounds of Regis College, Wellesley Street, Weston. Well over 100 classes. A great variety of horses. Two rings and an outside hunt course. Saturday 9 A.M. until about 10 P.M., Sunday noon until about 8. Admission charged.

September-October

APPLE COUNTRY VISITING TIME

FRUIT STANDS   There are many that are colorful, sell cider, and have a display of pumpkins. Try Bolton Orchards, Jct. Rts. 110 and 117W, Tel. 779–2733 (could be combined with Fruitlands, p. 165, through September), or C. A. Dowse & Son, 98 North Main Street, Sherborn, Tel. 653–2639, not far from Broadmoor Sanctuary (p. 190); they have their own cider press as does Lawson's on Rt. 2 in Lincoln.

PICK-YOUR-OWN arrangements may be possible at several orchards from Labor Day through early October; if they don't have those plans, it is likely that they will sell apples by the bushel. If the weather has been unkind, "drops" may be for sale. Even when the newspapers publish a list, it is possible that the diminishing supply means the practice is discontinued for a while. ALWAYS CALL TO CHECK ON PICKING DATES. There are several variables that influence the decision to have pick-your-own arrangements. Within the last few years the policies have gone almost full circle. Untrained pickers often cause some unintentional damage to trees; for that and other reasons it isn't necessarily a money-saving activity for visitors. However, it is fun for all ages to spend some time in an orchard—on or off a ladder. For the current list of places, contact the Massachusetts Department of Agriculture, Division of Markets, 100 Cambridge Street, Boston 02202, Tel. 727–3018. Enclose a self-addressed stamped envelope.

Some orchards worth checking for current arrangements:

Arnold's Orchards, off Rt. 135, 1 mile south of Westboro, Tel. 366–2845. Go over turnpike bridge to top of hill where there is a sign.

Brookfield Orchards, Inc., Orchard Road, off Rt. 9, North Brookfield, Tel. 867–6858.

Deershorn Apple Farm, Chase Hill Road, off Rt. 62, Lancaster, Tel. 365–3691. Picnicking allowed; refreshment stand.

Honey Pot Hill Orchard, Sudbury and Boon roads, off Rt. 62, Stow, Tel. 562–5225.

Meadowbrook Orchards, Chase Hill Road, off Rt. 62, Sterling Junction, Tel. 365–7617

Shelburne Farm, West Acton Road, Stow, Tel. 897–9287.

October

CHILDREN'S MUSEUM HAUNTED HOUSE   Quake through 14 frightening rooms in an old brick house. You may see the creature world, the Crypt, Sherlock Holmes on a new case. 50¢ per person. This is so well done that it is particularly recommended for older children and suggested with reservation for younger (under 5?) ones who may be somewhat frightened.

DRUMLIN FARM (p. 191) **HARVEST DAYS.** Two Saturdays. Country crafts, farm exhibits, demonstrations, live animal interviews, and colorful contests 10–4. Demonstrations such as making bread, butter, and jelly, blacksmith working at his forge, cider pressing, wool dyeing using native plants. Admission: Adults, $1; children, 50¢.

IPSWICH RIVER WILDLIFE SANCTUARY (p. 188). Probably third weekend of the month. Admission: Adults, $1.50; children, 50¢. Hay jump, outdoor games, scarecrow contest, pony rides, a blacksmith, cider pressing, dyeing with native plants, a wood carver, weaving and spinning, canoe jousting, an annual fundraising day. Additional charge for some events.

COLUMBUS DAY PARADE, BOSTON   October 12. An hour and a half of marching units in the afternoon. Route published in newspapers the day before.

BOSTON CAT CLUB   Annual cat show held for 2 days in Horticultural Hall, Massachusetts Avenue, sponsored by the Cat Fanciers' Association.

LA SEMANA HISPANOAMERICANA   Annual Spanish week at the Science Museum. Science demonstrations and programs in Spanish. Exhibits and programs on the Spanish cultural heritage.

CANADIAN GEESE MIGRATING TIME   Drive to Plum Island (p. 190) to see the hundreds of geese. It almost appears that they can read the sign that reserves places for them. Dozens of photographers there on weekends.

November

THE WHOLE WORLD CELEBRATION held at Hynes Auditorium (Prudential Center) by the International Institute of Boston (p. 266). A festival of crafts, dancing, and food from around the world. Many booths selling wares. The performances, scheduled periodically, and the food are the highlights. Admission charged. Call 536–1081 for information.

THANKSGIVING DAY, PLYMOUTH   Demonstrations of cooking in 1627 style at Plantation. *Mayflower II* open; special open houses and programs held. Dinner in town hall is an experience (reportedly "just fair"!).

THANKSGIVING AT STURBRIDGE VILLAGE (p. 90). Dinner reservations have been filled for many months, but while the Village is open 9:30–4:30 a dinner is prepared at the Pliny Freeman Farmhouse at the fireplace as it would have been in 1800; from 10 to 1 there is a demonstration of antique flintlock firearms, and at 3:45 there is a nonsectarian worship service in the Village meetinghouse.

DAY AFTER THANKSGIVING   Just a note of warning: This is a banner day for the stores. Plan to do half of what you would like to do. Everything is crowded. Do not drive into the city. Only those with unusual stamina should plan to visit Toyland.

VETERANS' DAY PARADE, November 11, Boston. The route for the 90-minute afternoon procession is published in newspapers the day before.

November and December

ASHUMET HOLLY RESERVATION, Route 151. East Falmouth is at its best with scarlet, orange, and yellow berries on the holly trees. Woodland trails wind through more than a thousand trees, some as high as 20 feet. Guided tours may be available. Parking: $1.

EDAVILLE RAILROAD   Just before Thanksgiving through first week in January. Open rain or shine. Closed Christmas Day. Weekdays 4–9, Sundays 2–9. Ride heated trains on the 5½-mile ride through forests, by ponds and cranberry bogs. Lighted tableaux are placed along the "countryside." Museum (p. 75) open. Adults, $2; children under 12, $1. Combination ticket to museums: Adults, $2.40; children, $1.20. Discount coupons may be printed in newspapers.

STORE WINDOWS   "Special" windows are usually in Filene's (along Summer Street) and Jordan Marsh (along Washington Street) in downtown Boston. The animated displays may be dismantled the day after Christmas.

CHOP OR SAW YOUR OWN FIREWOOD arrangements in state forests vary from year to year. Check with the Massachusetts Department of Natural Resources, Division of Forests and Parks, Tel. 727–3180.

December

CHRISTMAS PARADE   First Sunday of the month. Held in Quincy. Starts at 1 from Wollaston Beach and proceeds to Rose parking area in Quincy Square. About 70 marching units and bands along with competing floats (for a cash prize) participate in this big one.

OLD STURBRIDGE VILLAGE (p. 90). Christmas week tours. During the holiday week Village visitors are invited to participate in special 1-hour guided tours. Several tour topics are offered.

ICE CAPADES   This fully staged ice show comes to the Boston Garden for about 2 weeks. Group rates available, Tel. 227–3200.

MUSEUM OF SCIENCE (p. 172). Planetarium Christmas show may have special 5 o'clock presentations on some Fridays. If so, the usual age restriction is waived, and the regular admission fee (50¢) is charged. Check with the museum, Tel. 723–2500.

CHRISTMAS VACATION WEEK   Many museums have special weekday programs for children. Check to see if tickets or reservations are needed before you leave home.

LIVING TREES   The Massachusetts Audubon Society and the Sierra Club have lists of garden centers that sell living Christmas trees.

CHRISTMAS TREES   If you would like to select and cut down your own tree, there are several Christmas tree farmers who allow this. Current lists are often printed in the newspapers and are also available from the Massachusetts Department of Natural Resources, 100 Cambridge Street, Boston 02202, Tel. 727–3184.

It is a good idea to check before setting forth. Some years some farms sell out. In some cases you are required to bring your own ax or saw. Wear heavy shoes or boots. Bring rope to tie the tree in or on car. A tarpaulin will help to prevent scratches or dropped pitch from marring the finish of the car.

The Nottingham Tree Farm, Wood Avenue, East Rindge, New Hampshire, Tel. 603–899–6646, writes: "We expect to have lots of trees in years to come. We are 45 miles from Rt. 128."

RECYCLING CHRISTMAS TREES   Check with the Massachusetts Audubon Society (p. 202) for locations. May be received at some places for use as deer shelters and wood chips.

THE NUTCRACKER presented by the Boston Ballet Company (p. 49). Two performances each weekend day. Tickets: $3–$7. Given in the enormous Music Hall, 268 Tremont Street. Order tickets early.

AMAHL AND THE NIGHT VISITORS presented as a family Christmas special by the Associate Artists Opera Company (p. 49). Adults, $5; children under 12, $2.50. Group rates available.

TEA PARTY REENACTMENT at Boston Tea Party Ship (p. 160). Admission charged to those on outside decks of museum or in museum. Reservations for groups on that day should be made in advance. First come, first served. Standing on Congress Street Bridge allowed—no charge. It is cold and possibly rainy—and maybe a little disappointing, but you can say you were there!

EASTERN DOG SHOW   Held on a Saturday at the War Memorial Auditorium, Prudential Center, Boston. More than 1,000 dogs are "benched" by breeds, and you may see them before or after they are shown. There are specific handling classes for children as well as adults. Obedience tests often included. Dogs and owners are fun to watch. For schedule call 262–8000. Adults, $3; children and senior citizens, $1.50.

CHRISTMAS ANTIQUES AND CRAFTS SHOW   Held early in the month at Hynes Auditorium, Prudential Center, by the Boston Flea Market, Tel. 523–2062. Considered one of the better shows of many held this time of year. It is enormous. Lots of people attend. Admission: $2; children, free.

CONCERTS   Prudential Center, Boston Common, Boston City Hall—among other places. No charge. Watch newspapers. Plenty of special performances given in churches, schools, institutions, and conservatories.

CHRISTMAS REVELS—in celebration of the winter solstice. Held in Harvard's Sanders Theater on the weekend before Christmas. A matinee may be included in the schedule. Adults, $3.50; children, $2. It is a recently established, glorious tradition. The audience sings along in this marvelous setting and watches the colorful performances of Highland pipers, a brass ensemble, country dancers, mummers, St. George and the Dragon with song, slapstick, and invective, and much more.

SKI CLINICS given by Bob Dunn and his staff from Boston Hill (p. 237) at various locations in the area. No charge. A complete program for the would-be skier, an explanation of ski instructions, a movie, and information about equipment. Locations published by the sponsoring *Boston Globe*.

SPECIAL PLANETARIUM PROGRAM   Brockton high-school complex. Two shows nightly for several evenings in December. Tel. 588–7800, ext. 619. Adults, 50¢; children, 25¢.

BLACK NATIVITY presented by the Elma Lewis School of Fine Arts (p. 62), 122 Elm Hill Avenue, Roxbury, and at several locations in the Boston area. Call 442–8820 for this year's schedule for the performances of the Christmas story written by Langston Hughes and given in Gospel style by the Black Persuasion, the Children of the Black Persuasion, the Primitive Dance Company, and the National Center of Afro-American Artists Theater Company.

Index